UNDERSTANDING
UNDERGRADUATE EDUCATION

Sponsored by

THE SCHOOL OF EDUCATION

of

THE UNIVERSITY OF SOUTH DAKOTA

Financial Support Provided by a Grant from the University Bush Foundation and by the School of Education of The University of South Dakota.

UNDERSTANDING UNDERGRADUATE EDUCATION

Edited by

Robert L. Emans

University of South Dakota Press
Vermillion, South Dakota

Distributed by arrangement with
University Publishing Associates, Inc.

4720 Boston Way
Lanham, MD 20706

3 Henrietta Street
London WC2E 8LU England

Library of Congress Cataloging–in–Publication Data

Understanding undergraduate education / edited by Robert L. Emans.
p.   cm.
"Sponsored by the School of Education of the University of
South Dakota"—P. ii.
Includes bibliographical references and index.
1. Education, Higher—United States—Aims and objectives.
I. Emans, Robert L.   II. University of South
Dakota. School of Education.
LA228.U46   1989   378.73—dc20   89–35544 CIP

ISBN 0–929925–04–1

The paper used in this publication meets the minimum requirements of American
National Standard for Information Sciences—Permanence of Paper for Printed Library
Materials, ANSI Z39.48–1984.   ∞

Contents

INTRODUCTION ix

THE CHALLENGE OF UNDERGRADUATE
EDUCATION, *Robert L. Emans* 1

Part I: Mission

INTRODUCTION 13

THE PURPOSE OF UNDERGRADUATE EDUCATION: A
PHILOSOPHIC PERSPECTIVE, *Bruce G. Milne* 15

THE AESTHETIC SIDE OF A COLLEGE EDUCATION,
John A. Day 31

INTERNATIONALIZING THE UNDERGRADUATE
CURRICULUM: "YOU'VE GOT TO KNOW THE
TERRITORY!", *Gale K. Crouse and Robert W. Wood* ... 47

LEARNING TO LIVE AND EARNING A LIVING: AN
INTERACTIVE BLEND IN UNDERGRADUATE
EDUCATION, *Joan T. England and Quentin Oleson* 61

THE UNDERGRADUATE EXPERIENCE AND
COMMUNITY SERVICE: EDUCATION AS
TRANSFORMATION, *Michael P. Roche* 69

Part II: Curriculum

INTRODUCTION 77

CRITICAL THINKING AND THE HISTORICAL
    PROCESS, *Stephen R. Ward*   79

WHAT SCIENCE SHOULD BE TAUGHT, *Paul B. Otto* ...   91

COPING WITH MATH ANXIETY, *Cleland V. Cook* 107

SOME POSITIVE VALUES OF SPORT IN AMERICAN
    UNIVERSITIES, *Mary S. Mock* 121

Part III: Means

INTRODUCTION 133

EFFECTIVE COLLEGE TEACHING, *Michael R. Hoadley*
    and Philip A. Vik 135

THE VENERABLE LECTURE: ALTERNATIVES AND
    IMPROVEMENTS, *H. Virginia Monroe and Charles E.*
    Eicher 143

HELPING THE STUDENT WITH LEARNING
    PROBLEMS, *John W. Woodley and Joe N. Crank* 155

Part IV: Environment

INTRODUCTION 169

THE BROADER COLLEGE COMMUNITY, *Loren M.*
    Carlson and Jack A. Sumner 171

COCURRICULAR ACTIVITIES, *William C. Edwards* 185

HELPING TO MAKE THE TRANSITION FROM HIGH
    SCHOOL TO COLLEGE, *John F. Bryde and Corinne M.*
    Milburn 203

FRONT LOADING THE FRESHMAN EXPERIENCE,
    William R. Donohue 215

ACADEMIC ADVISING, *Don Monroe and Gale Wiedow* ... 227

COUNSELING THE COLLEGE STUDENT:
    DEVELOPMENTAL FACTORS AND COUNSELING
    NEEDS OF TRADITIONAL AND NONTRADITIONAL
    UNDERGRADUATE COLLEGE STUDENTS, *Orla J.*
    Christensen and Alvin D. Albertus 241

Part V: Students

INTRODUCTION 257

MOTIVATING THE COLLEGE STUDENT, *Joseph D. Huber and Loraine Webster* 259

BOREDOM: WHAT'S IT ALL ABOUT? *Frank O. Main and E. Gordon Poling* 269

NATIVE AMERICANS IN HIGHER EDUCATION, *Dauna B. Browne and Wayne H. Evans* 279

SOURCES OF STRESS AND SUPPORT FOR THE NONTRADITIONAL UNDERGRADUATE STUDENT, *Barbara A. Yutrzenka and Lois B. Oberlander* 289

MEETING THE PROBLEMS OF THE HANDICAPPED, *Donald R. Potter* 307

Part VI: Evaluation

INTRODUCTION 319

ASSESSMENT OF STUDENT ACHIEVEMENT, *Marilyn Hadley and Patrick Vitale* 321

A CLOSER LOOK AT VALUE ADDED, *William R. Donohue and David L. Struckman-Johnson* 331

FACULTY EVALUATION IN HIGHER EDUCATION: IS IT TAKING US IN THE DIRECTION WE WANT TO GO? *Arlen R. Gullickson* 345

Part VII: The Future of Undergraduate Education

INTRODUCTION 361

THE FUTURE OF UNDERGRADUATE EDUCATION: REALITIES, *William E. Gardner, Dean, College of Education, The University of Minnesota* 363

THE FUTURE OF UNDERGRADUATE EDUCATION: DREAMS, *Virgil S. Lagomarcino, Dean, College of Education, Iowa State University* 379

INDEX 393

Introduction

No fewer than a score of major studies on the educational systems of this country have been reported in the last few years. Up to now the focus of the studies has been on elementary and high schools. The spotlight is changing. Colleges and universities are under scrutiny, especially their undergraduate programs. One recently published report on higher education, *Involvement in Learning: Realizing the Potential of American Higher Education* states:

> Our nation will require citizens who have learned how to learn—who can identify, organize, and use all of the learning resources at their disposal. It will depend on creative people who can synthesize and reshape information and who can analyze problems from many different perspectives. And it will require people who will share their knowledge and intellectual abilities in family, community, and national life (p. 2).

The purpose of most of the reports is not to dictate what colleges and universities should do, but to encourage them to examine their policies and practices. There is, however, a need extending beyond that of merely responding to the charges of a recent report. Institutions must be vigilant in maintaining standards. Faculties, students, and administrators need to review the quality of their programs in order to effect positive changes. The interrelated areas that need examination can be organized into the following six categories.

1. *Mission*: The goals, objectives, and purposes of colleges and universities as related to undergraduate education.
2. *Curriculum*: The subject-matter to be learned and related issues.
3. *Means*: The teaching strategies, methods, and technology used to accomplish the undergraduate mission of colleges and universities.

4. *Environment*: The climate most productive for accomplishing the undergraduate mission of colleges and universities.

5. *Students*: The nature and characteristics of undergraduate students in colleges and universities that must be considered; how students learn.

6. *Evaluation*: What is to be evaluated; how the evaluation takes or should take place; who does or should do the evaluating.

The volume begins with a chapter, "The Challenge of Undergraduate Education," by Robert L. Emans. The five areas of "Mission," "Means," "Environment," "Students," and "Evaluation" are then addressed. The concluding chapters on "Realities" and "Dreams" are written by William E. Gardner, Dean of the College of Education at the University of Minnesota and Virgil S. Lagomarcino, Dean of the College of Education at Iowa State University.

The Challenge of Undergraduate Education

Robert L. Emans

Upon assuming the post at a prestigious university, a newly appointed president was advised by a faculty member and friend to discontinue the undergraduate program. The faculty member's reasoning was that professors are best prepared to teach graduate students and conduct research. Professors had little expertise or desire, the colleague argued, to be involved in undergraduate education and did so only grudgingly and poorly (Bok, 1986). Likewise, Combs (1965) wrote,

> Overwhelmed with students and charged with the responsibility for "weeding them out," harassed instructors often cover the subjects as best they can and escape as quickly as possible to teaching the majors. As a consequence, general education programs are often badly taught and deadly dull (p. 43).

Universities have been variously described as being holding pens for keeping young people out of the labor market; places providing teaching jobs for graduate assistants and employment for scholars; instruments for preserving the class system; and a group of special interest groups loosely held together by a parking problem (Astin, 1985, p. 14).

Yet, most former students hold with fondness memories of college life—their undergraduate experience—more so than their graduate or professional education. The undergraduate years seem to be the ones that shape the individual the most. Auchincloss (1974) has stated:

Never again does one receive impressions with quite the same kind of emotional intensity that one does between the ages of seventeen and twenty-one. It is so brief a time, so very brief, yet one can build a lifetime on the exploitation of it (p. 7).

Furthermore, "above all, baccalaureate education makes a vital contribution to the health of American democracy" (Association of American Colleges, 1985, p. i). Boyer and Hechinger (1981) conclude that "[A]lmost all young people will, at some time in their lives, need some form of post-secondary school education if they are to remain economically productive and socially functional" (p. 29).

A recent national survey shows that most college students take their schooling seriously, are satisfied with the instruction they receive and the colleges they attend, and trust their professors (Carnegie Council, 1979, pp. 1, 3). Nevertheless, another opinion poll shows that, although students believe a college education is more important than ever, colleges do not give "good value for the dollar" (Most Think Colleges Aren't a Good Value, 1987).

In the past few years, there has been a flurry of reports and authors complaining about higher education:

Higher education in America is suffering from a loss of overall direction, a nagging feeling that it is no longer at the vital center of the nation's work (Boyer & Hechinger, 1981, p. 3).

[There is] a general loss of self-confidence and of a sense of mutual trust . . . (Ducharme, 1987, p. 3).

Evidence of decline and devaluation is everywhere (Association of American Colleges, 1985, p. 1).

The nation's colleges and universities now face unprecedented challenges that derive from an overall mismatch between the educational needs of the nation and current practice in undergraduate education (Education Commission of the States, 1986, p. 11).

[G]eneral education is now a disaster area (Carnegie Council, 1978, p. 11).

[A]ll is not well in American higher education (Study Group, 1984, p. 29).

On too many campuses, the curriculum has become a self-service cafeteria through which students pass without being nourished (Bennett, 1984, p. 29).

Numerous explanations have been cited for the increased loss of confidence in higher education (Association of American Colleges,

1985; Bok, 1986; Conrad & Wyer, 1980; Education Commission of the States, 1986; Newman, 1985). Among the factors cited are: the expansion of knowledge, a need for specialization, declining job markets, a more diverse student body, changes in economic developments, foreign competition, increased social problems, students' increased desire for financial success, greater emphasis on vocational and professional preparation, and budgetary constraints. Boyer and Hechinger (1981) summarize the concerns as, "[We] are underscoring the fact that the workplace is changing dramatically, that traditional notions about prework preparation are becoming obsolete, and that more education will be required to meet the nation's diverse social and economic needs" (pp. 29–30). As stated in the Association of American Colleges' (1985) report, *Integrity in the College Curriculum*, "Scientific and technological developments have so outpaced the understanding of science provided by most college programs that we have become a people unable to comprehend the technology that we invent . . ." (p. 2). In short, "[U]ndergraduate education must once again respond to changing demands" (Education Commission of the States, 1986, p. 8).

The problems confronting higher education are manifested in a number of ways. In *Involvement in Learning* (1984), a report sponsored by the National Institute of Education, the problems confronting colleges and universities are characterized by: only half of the students starting college finish, excessive emphasis placed on vocational preparation, a fragmented curriculum, a lack of integration of the knowledge presented, and an unwillingness on the part of students to be involved in their own learning. Colleges and universities seem to be more interested in maintaining enrollments than in the quality of student learning (Astin, 1985, p. 16). Others have lamented an increase in financial aid abuse, easy awarding of credits, elective courses, academic dishonesty, off-campus programs, and grade inflation (Carnegie Council, 1979; Education Commission of the States, 1986, pp. 27–28). Fewer students are majoring in the traditional arts and sciences disciplines (Conrad & Wyer, 1980, p. 51). "[T]he humanities and cultural ideals have given way to the sciences and technical innovations" (Conrad & Wyer, 1980, p. 54). "[S]pecialization . . . has made the undergraduate experience little more than vocational preparation" (Education Commission of the States, 1986, p. 11). The situation is so bad that "For over a decade, it has been argued that the liberal arts no longer liberate . . ." (Conrad & Wyer, 1980, p. 1).

At the same time, there is a need for students to develop strong critical thinking and interpersonal skills (Education Commission of the States, 1986, p. 11), to be educated as citizens (Boyer & Hechinger, 1981, p. 47), and to be able to solve multi-faceted problems. "The replacement of democratic government by a technocracy or the control of policy by special-interest groups is not tolerable" (Boyer & Hechinger, 1981, p. 47).

A Historical Perspective

Criticism of higher education is not new. Its roots in the United States go back to European traditions. During the time of the Greeks and Romans, education was viewed as culture itself, not merely about culture. It involved basic verbal and quantitative literacy, artistic creations, physical fitness, personal and moral inquiry, freedom of the individual combined with responsible citizenship for the Good of the State, and the commitment to take personal risks. The Middle Ages saw an emphasis on the *trivium*—grammar, rhetoric, and logic; and the *quadrivium*—arithmetic, geometry, astronomy, and music. During the Renaissance, the purpose of education was the development of the virtuous and noble man. Throughout these periods, there was a blending of theory and practice. The concept of education as taking place in an "ivory tower" is only a recent phenomenon (Murchland, 1979, p. 47).

As was true in respect to the development of education in Europe, education in the United States has changed continuously. Colonial higher education was a transplantation from England and Scotland with classical and theological focuses. Eventually, religion gave way to scientific practice and more general learning. The study of Latin and Greek was discontinued and replaced by studies of history, politics, commerce, physics, and zoology. The study of grammar was substituted for rhetoric and literary criticism.

With the rise of merchants, tradesmen, skilled artisans, and science-minded farmers, the newer colleges concluded that their mission should be to serve these emerging groups. In this spirit, Thomas Jefferson founded the University of Virginia as a forward looking institution. Throughout this period, as there has nearly always been, there was a tension between the ideals of transmitting the culture of the past and addressing contemporary needs and interests. The German University, with its emphasis on research and specialization, also had its influence felt. The Morrill (Land Grant) Act of 1862 was passed.

It was enacted, not so much to reform higher education, but to increase support in the north for the Civil War. Nevertheless, probably more than any other single event, the act is considered to have helped to create the modern university with its emphasis on technical, utilitarian, and vocational careers. With its emphasis on social service, advanced research, and specialization, the emphasis on personal growth, general studies, and ethical concerns diminished. Conrad and Wyer (1980) have summarized the consequences of this transformation of higher education:

> The inclusions of graduate research and study and undergraduate education within the same institution dealt a severe blow to liberal studies. . . . [A] separate graduate faculty was rarely established at the universities . . . [T]he institutional framework often rewarded research and disciplinary specialization, not . . . undergraduate instruction. . . . [T]he undergraduate schools . . . became preparation schools for the professions and the graduate departments (p. 14).

The changes have not come about without resistance. As long ago as 1828, the Yale Report attempted to reject professional and vocational education as part of the undergraduate experience. In 1909, A. Lawrence Lowell, then President of Harvard University, reacted against electives in courses of study and academic specialization. Colleges, he wrote, "ought to produce, not defective specialists, but men [today he hopefully would have included women] intellectually well-rounded, of wide sympathies and unfiltered judgements" (Conrad & Wyer, 1980, p. 15).

Conflict confronting higher education continues today. The student unrest on the campuses of the 1960s was replaced by curricular turmoil and experimentation in the 1970s. The concern for the acquisition of knowledge gave way to an emphasis on relevancy and values. As jobs became scarce, students turned increasingly toward vocationally oriented studies (Bok, 1986, p. 39). Students' interests helped shape what was taught and how it was taught (Association of American Colleges, 1985, p. 4). Now, in the 1980s, higher education is experiencing a reaction, perhaps equivalent to the "back-to-the-basics" movement in the elementary and high schools (Ducharme, 1987, p. 256). Much is being questioned, including what should be the purpose of an undergraduate education.

Purposes of Undergraduate Education

Terms such as undergraduate education, general education, liberal education, and the liberal arts are often used interchangeably, although not everyone believes they should be. Usually what is being referred to is education at the baccalaureate level outside the area of vocational or academic specialization. Even then, definition is extremely difficult (Conrad & Wyer, 1980, p. 4). "There is rarely agreement on what is meant by a 'liberal education' " (Education Commission of the States, 1986, p. 251). It often reflects personal philosophy and usually means what the individual wants it to mean (Conrad & Wyer, 1980). Some define general education as what the more prestigious colleges and universities include in their course of study; and seldom are claims for it modest (Ducharme, 1987). As Conant (1963) writes:

> Let me caution the reader against the terms "liberal arts college" and "liberal education." Their meaning has become so varied as to render them almost useless . . ." (p. 90).

And Hirst (1965):

> The phrase "liberal education" has become today something of a slogan which usually takes on different meanings. . . . It usually labels a form of education which the author approves . . . (p. 113).

The purpose of general, undergraduate, or liberal education is sometimes considered to be the acquisition of the cultural heritage, e.g., literature, history, a foreign language, some science, mathematics, government, and physical education (Ducharme, 1987). An educated person should "understand and know the critical persons, events, philosophical, social, and political movements, and the major texts that dramatically affected the world they live in . . ." (Ducharme, 1987, p. 263).

Often general education is viewed as more than the learning of knowledge and skills, and goes beyond such purposes to include learning how to think. Kagan (1980) believes, "[W]e need adults who love the use of the mind and are good at it . . . who have faith in the power of thought" (p. 123). Sarason, Davidson and Blatt (1962) state, "The value of the liberal arts and sciences lies not only in the knowledge which they contain and produce, but in the spirit of inquiry which is their hallmark" (p. 32).

Others add concerns related to questions pertaining to society and the individual, but, include more than the preparation for a vocation. Boyer and Hechinger (1981) have written:

> The aim is not *only* to prepare the young for productive careers, but to enable them to live lives of dignity and purpose; not *only* to generate new

knowledge, but to channel that knowledge to humane ends; not merely to increase participation at the polls, but to help shape a citizenry that can weigh decisions wisely and more effectively promote the public good (p. 60).

In recent years, there has been a movement to identify the *outcomes* of undergraduate education, independent of specific content. Dressel (1979) lists:

1. They know how to acquire knowledge and how to use it.
2. They possess a high level of mastery of the skills of communication.
3. They are aware of personal values and value commitments and realize that often persons and other cultures hold contrasting values which must be understood and respected in interaction with them.
4. They cooperate and collaborate with others in studying, analyzing, and formulating solutions to problems and in taking actions on them.
5. They are aware of, concerned about, and accept some responsibility for contemporary events and their implications.
6. They continually seek coherence and unity in accumulating knowledge and experience and use the insights they achieved to further their development and to fulfill their obligations as responsible citizens in a democratic society (p. 319).

Likewise, Boyer (1981) has identified the following outcomes:

1. All students should come to understand the shared use of symbols.
2. All students should understand their shared membership in groups and institutions.
3. Students should understand that everyone produces and consumes and that, through this process, we are dependent on each other.
4. All life forms on the planet earth are inextricably interlocked, and no education is complete without an understanding of the ordered, interdependent nature of the universe.
5. All students should understand our shared sense of time.
6. All students should explore our shared values and beliefs (pp. 11–16).

A discussion of the purposes of undergraduate education would be incomplete without including the auxiliary benefits. In addition to intellectual skills and knowledge, benefits often cited involve: learning to live independently from home, discovery of a mate, developing social poise and personal relations, forming peer contacts, and participating in extracurricular and recreational activities. Some people consider such outcomes to be as important as academic learning.

The Challenges

In spite of many advocates of general education proclaiming its virtues, little objective evidence has been gathered to support the claims that general education achieves its purposes. Most of the purposes of general education are idealistic statements. They are rarely grounded in any systematic research efforts to establish their impact on the learning of students. Part of the problem has been that "Universities have no adequate way of measuring the effects of undergraduate education or assessing the methods of instruction they employ" (Bok, 1986, p. 66). As Lawler (1983) has stated, "It is difficult to show the utility of a liberal education . . ." (p. 301). On the other hand, as Winter, McClelland and Stewart (1981) have written:

> The "guardians" of the liberal education tradition are not accustomed to thinking this kind of support [research] is necessary. From the classical tradition, they have apparently inherited both an emphasis on the power of rhetoric and form and a distrust of the empirical method . . . (p. 13).

In addition, research on the teaching and classroom effectiveness is often threatening to professors (Bok, 1986, p. 67). Professors, like everyone else, are reluctant to have what they do evaluated.

Demonstrating its effectiveness is just one of the challenges facing general education at this time. There are many others.

Faculty have devoted much time and effort to *what* should be learned, but little to *how* learning can take place more effectively. The issues have remained much the same since the 1900s (Carnegie Council, 1979). What should be the core of every student's education? What should be left up to the student's choice? How can breadth of learning be achieved? How can the integration of what is learned be attained?

In an effort to solve the problems associated with these questions, colleges use a number of themes for organizing their curricula. These themes of organization can be categorized into five types. Most colleges use one type or another, or a combination.

1. *Required Core*: Students are required to take certain specified courses, e.g., Freshman Composition and History of Western Civilization.

2. *Distributive Requirements*: Students are required to select a number of courses from a variety of disciplines, e.g., the humanities, fine arts, physical science, and mathematics.

3. *Great Books*: Students are required to study certain books identified as being of particular importance and having significance to a number of areas of study.

4. *Integrative Approach*: A theme is identified and stressed in various courses and serves to tie the courses together, e.g., the environment, human responsibility, and ideas of progress.

5. *Competency Expectations*: Certain skills (e.g., related to reading and writing) and modes of thinking (e.g., analysis, synthesis, comparison) are identified and stressed across the curriculum.

Within these five themes of organization are a number of issues currently receiving attention. Many are not new, but have been of concern to higher education since the turn of the century, if not before:

• defining general education as process rather than content—reasoning, critical thinking, problem solving, development of skills.

• developing the whole person—personal growth, self-awareness appreciation, physical dexterity, moral development, ethics, relating facts to values, concern for solving social, national, and international problems.

• relating and integrating general education to career and vocational development—the professions, academic specialization, technology.

• involving students in their own learning process—planning and monitoring their own education, participating in campus and extracurricular activities, committing themselves to learning.

• providing educational opportunities for students of diverse backgrounds—members of ethnic and racial groups currently underrepresented in higher education, older students, part-time students, off-campus programs, independent learning.

• evaluating techniques—testing of problem solving and reasoning, assessment of values awareness.

The challenges confronting higher education today are not going to be met merely by adding more courses and more programs or rearranging old offerings. There will be no easy answers or definitive solutions. Curricular debates will always be inconclusive. Yet, the close examination of undergraduate education by colleges and universities will reap its own rewards. The challenge of attempting to balance students' needs for learning to earn a living and learning to live will always be present. Perhaps Whitehead (1929) stated the challenge best: "There can be no adequate technical education which is not liberal and no liberal education which is not technical" (p. 48).

References

Association of American Colleges. (1985). *Integrity in the college curriculum.* Washington, DC: Association of American Colleges.

Astin, A. W. (1985). *Achieving educational excellence.* San Francisco: Jossey-Bass.

Auchincloss, L. (1974). *Yale Alumni Magazine*, pp. 7, 9.

Bennett, W. J. (1984). *To reclaim a legacy: A report on the humanities in higher education.* Washington, DC: National Endowment for the Humanities.

Bok, B. (1986). *Higher learning.* Cambridge: Harvard University Press.

Boyer, E. L. (1981). The quest for common learning. In *Common learning.* Washington, DC: Carnegie Foundation for the Advancement of Teaching.

Boyer, E. L. & Hechinger, F. M. (1981). *Higher learning in the nation's service.* Washington, DC: The Carnegie Foundation for the Advancement of Teaching.

Carnegie Council on Policy Studies in Higher Education. (1979). *Fair practices in higher education.* San Francisco: Jossey-Bass.

Combs, A. W. (1965). *The professional education of teachers.* Boston: Allyn & Bacon.

Conant, J. B. (1963). *The education of American teachers.* New York: McGraw-Hill.

Conrad, C. F. & Wyer, J. C. (1980). *Liberal education in transition.* Washington, DC: American Association for Higher Education.

Dressel, P. (1979). Liberal education: Developing the characteristics of a liberally educated profession. *Liberal Education*, 65(3), 313–332.

Ducharme, E. R. (1987). Liberal education and teacher education: Two forces in search of fusion. In M. Huberman & J. M. Backus (Eds.), *Advances in teacher education: Volume 3.* Norwood, NJ: Ablex.

Education Commission of the States. (1986). *Transforming the state role in undergraduate education.* Denver: Education Commission of the States.

Hirst, P. (1965). Liberal education and the nature of knowledge. In R. Archambault (Ed.)., *Philosophical analysis and education*. New York: Humanities Press.

Kagan, T. (1980). Core competencies. In M. Kaplan (Ed.), *What is an educated person?* New York: Praeger Publishers.

Lawler, P. A. (1983). Tocqueville on the place of liberal education in a democracy. *Liberal Education, 69*(4), 301–306.

Most think colleges aren't a good value, poll shows. (1987, September 1). *Argus Leader*, 9.

Murchland, B. (1979). Reviving the connected view. *Commonwealth, 106*, 42–48.

Newman, F. (1985). *Higher education and the American resurgence*. Princeton: The Carnegie Foundation for the Advancement of Teaching.

Sarason, S., Davidson, K. S., & Blatt, B. (1962). *The preparation of teachers*. New York: Wiley.

Study Group on the Conditions of Excellence in American Higher Education. (1984). *Involvement in learning: Realizing the potential of American higher education*. Washington, DC: National Institute of Education.

Whitehead, A. N. (1929). *The aims of education*. New York: Macmillan.

Winter, D. G., McClelland, D. G., & Stewart, A. J. (1981). *A new case for the liberal arts*. San Francisco: Jossey-Bass.

Part I: Mission

The purpose of undergraduate education has probably been debated for as long as colleges and universities have existed. What should a college educated person know? How should undergraduate education be related to earning a living? What do students have a right to expect from college? What does society have a right to expect? These are some of the central questions for which answers are sought in this section. The goals and objectives of undergraduate education must be considered by all concerned with higher education.

In "The Purpose of Undergraduate Education: A Philosophic Perspective," Bruce G. Milne asks and answers five questions: (1) Who should be taught? (2) Who should teach? (3) What should be taught? (4) How should the curriculum be taught? (5) Why? In addition, he makes seven recommendations for improving undergraduate education. Stating that colleges and universities have been given an undergraduate mission by society and culture, he challenges higher education to use its time and resources for fulfilling that mission rather than spending its time merely in an attempt to define its mission.

Aesthetic education provides unique experiences related to what it means to be human. The arts, the primary vehicle for aesthetic education, use a non-discussive, yet highly sophisticated, system of symbols. John A. Day describes the challenges facing undergraduate education in the arts. He argues that the arts have an integral part in the philosophical and practical mission of colleges and universities. There should be a commitment to assuring that aesthetic education runs through the entire educational system. Its mission is the acquisition of wholeness, imagination, and freedom.

Many Americans are shamefully ignorant about the world in which they live. Gale K. Crouse and Robert W. Wood define international education, describe its needs, assumptions and goals, and how institutions of higher education can go about strengthening their international education programs. The key, they believe, to the "internationalization" of a university is in the desire and commitment of the faculty and administration. As international education is better understood, it will become stronger and more successful. Knowing about the world and its people has never been more important than it is today.

Although some educators may believe general education and education for a profession are incompatible, J. T. England and Quentin Oleson believe that learning to live and earning a living are not discrete goals. Liberal education, they contend, is the foundation for all undergraduate education. It should be extended into education for the professions, and involves the participation of students in the learning process. It should lead students to critical awareness, help students use what they learn in everyday life, and increase a sense of power. Education should not become a mechanical routine result of technology, but should add to the development of the personality.

Michael P. Roche explores community service as part of the undergraduate experience. He argues that undergraduate education focuses too much on individual efforts and not enough on the spirit of community.

The Purpose of Undergraduate Education:
A Philosophic Perspective

Bruce G. Milne

Education in any society among any people at any time is, among other things, a social process. Any society attempts to perpetuate its own ideas and hopes and dreams, its own knowledges and skills, its own arts and sciences, its own values by teaching these to the young in such a manner that they will accept them as desirable and will in turn apply them to the management of their own lives, add something of value to them, and in turn pass them on to the generation that follows in the part of this culture (Nakosteen, 1966).

As a social process, the educational system reflects the society in which it serves. Historically, conservative forces look to the educational system as the agent of preservation and perpetuation of the knowledges, skills and cultural mores. Liberal forces at the same time look to the system of education as society's critic and change agent to be critical of its knowledges, skills and mores, and, if need be, to set forth theory and practice to cause the society to correct its ills and initiate progress (Bigge, 1982).

Regardless of which ideological base is in control, the educational system in any society is seen as the agent of transmission of the cultural way, knowledges, skills, and understandings (Hutchins, 1936). The purpose of any educational program must be defined in this context. As society changes, the contents of its knowledges, skills and understandings may change. Yet, the purpose of education does not change—the transmission of the culture.

Undergraduate education, without undue semantic argument, refers to the post-secondary four years of education in a baccalaureate program in a liberal arts or science college or university. Academic and legislative leaders have diligently tried to protect this designation by keeping it separate from other post-secondary education programs, for example junior colleges (sometimes called grades 13 and 14), trade schools, normal schools, polytechnical institutes, land-grant colleges, community/business and vocational/technical colleges.

Historically, the baccalaureate degree culminates a four-year program of studies in higher education, and so "degreed," a student then is prepared for entry into professional training fields and/or advanced or graduate study. Until recent times, the baccalaureate degree has not been seen as a terminal degree with the student prepared to enter the world with career training and job ready. A bachelor's degree, traditionally, is simply a preparatory step toward advanced education or training (Brubacker, 1969).

The concept behind undergraduate level school is to establish a common level of basics or educational foundations upon which to build upper level and advanced education. Paramount among those foundations are assured competency in basic communication and accounting skills. Public and parochial elementary and secondary programs generally arise and gain support from the local communities, towns and cities. Such schools in earlier times, and still today, served the youth of that locale utilizing the vernacular of the people to perpetuate its ways, and which leads to a lack of uniform basics (Butts, 1947).

Thus, one of the first purposes of undergraduate education becomes that of enculturation of students from different and distant communities, states, and nations. By giving them a common educational foundation in the larger enculturation context, the philosophic concept of preparation for advanced study becomes possible. In the context of curricular exposure in the liberal arts, sciences and humanities, the undergraduate student becomes educated in the knowledges, skills and understandings contained in the student's cultural heritage. Dependent upon political, social and academic censorship, faculty expertise, and the extension of academic freedom, a university rises in prestige for its openness, dynamics and universal nature or is perceived as closed, static, staid, provincial and parochial. "Education locked into a rigid pattern with few alternatives is a blueprint for disaster" (Pulliam, 1982).

Philosophic Questions of Education

Philosophy asks five basic questions of education: (1) Who should be taught? (student), (2) Who should teach? (teacher), (3) What should be taught? (curriculum), (4) How should the curriculum be taught? (methodology), and (5) Why? (purpose). Although this paper is specific in seeking perspectives relative to the fifth question, purpose, it is necessary to look at each of the other questions as they dictate purpose (Bigge, 1982).

As to the question of *who should be taught*, without exception all cultures have designated their higher education for a "privileged few." From whatever base, political, social, economic, ethnic, sexual, or competency level, all societies within cultures have established a hierarchy or social strata from which a designated group was given the privileges of advanced or higher educational opportunities. With very few exceptions, the access to higher education, and with that under-graduate preparation, began from the hierarchical strata level of the privileged class. Societies created their own elite—aristocratic "blue blood" lines of nobility, citizens not slaves, landowners not serfs, American not Indian—and provided that the privileged few would be perpetuated through birth and heredity. In rare societies the records speak of selection of the most capable as having access privileges— Spartan physical abilities, monastic selection of the youth with the most potential, Hitler's screening for the Master Race—the selection invariably being based in a cultural value such as intellect, physical ability, academic record, technological potential and leadership abilities.

Higher education presumes the education of the masses is separate and complete, and even though it "feeds" the universities, higher education is above and beyond mass education in scope, breadth and depth. In theory and practice, only a select few are capable of compet-ing and completing the baccalaureate program, and from that number, only a small segment are destined to go on to advanced or graduate study. Yet, it is from that baccalaureate degree that the screening for most professions makes its selection for the training of its kind—legal, medical, technological, education, business, engineering, etc.

Mass education at public expense is the product of American plural-ism and democratic thought; however, the roots of educating all of the citizens is the product of Renaissance thinking of men like John Amos Comenius in 1657:

The education that I propose includes all that is proper for a man and is one in which all men who are born into this world should share. . . . Our first wish is that all men be educated fully to full humanity, not any one individual, not a few, not even many, but all men together and singly, young and old, rich and poor, of high and lowly birth, men and women— in a word all whose fate it is to be born human beings, so that at last the whole of the human race become educated, men of all ages, all conditions, both sexes, and all nations (Adler, 1983).

Higher education has never been seen as a component of mass education. Today, in America, equal opportunity legislation guarantees the right of each individual to seek admission to institutions of higher education and to compete in undergraduate education if selected without discrimination or limited by consideration of race, color, sex or national origin. In keeping with this, student loans, scholarships and financial assistance benefits open the door of opportunity to those unable to finance their education.

Equality is one of opportunity, not one of ability. Higher education is justified in selecting only those "privileged few" who have completed their public education and can meet the admission standards of the institution of higher learning of their choice. Society and the institutions of higher learning can rightfully demand more rigorous and rigid post-secondary entrance requirements. Once admitted, however, the individual student need only be limited in his/her academic field by his/her own abilities, aspirations, and self-determined needs in the pursuit of excellence.

The change in philosophic positions form a hierarchy based in an inherited, innate "blue blooded" aristocracy to one of allowing the most capable, or those showing the greatest potential for academic success, had only begun to appear in higher education. Post-"Sputnik Craze" selection of math and science students indicated to the world that Americans will provide public support for what it values (Gallagher, 1985). The space race crisis passed for the time being and support for such high ability students has largely been withdrawn.

In concluding the section on "who should be taught?" it is well to note that many of the discriminating barriers which surrounded unlimited education's access to all humans have been attacked and fairly well destroyed in America. Behavioralist thinking still prevails in most institutions of higher education, causing the educators to look to societal needs rather than the needs of the individual as the focus of teaching. Newer cognitive-field theories and the resultant practices are making an impact on educational thought and learning is being perceived more as an individual enterprise.

The epistemological base for educational thought taking us into the 21st century will be in all probability more subjective and individualistic. This is the result of influencing thought from this century's existential thinking following through on the pragmatic thought that it is the individual who learns through experience. Cognitive-field, holistic thinking adds that learning occurs within each individual's life-space—into the student's force field—cognitive, affective, and psychomotor. In selecting its students, undergraduate education should look beyond academic records as its sole criteria for admission. Who then should be taught? The most capable of learning—total learning.

The question of *who should teach?* directly relates to the ideological structure of the society or stratum within that society in which higher education resides. Historically, the most prevalent system was idealistically based in authority. (An authority figure represents the patriarchal wizardry which comes from age, experience, wisdom and the blessing of the established political, religious, philosophic, military, social, scientific or technical agency funding the academic institution.) In the liberal arts and humanities the authority figure is perceived as the one who rises through scholarly pursuits, art work or published works. Science and technological fields call for investigative accomplishment that manifests itself in a theoretical or practical end product.

With the rise in course work relevant to the industrial and business world, the demand came for teachers with practical experience in their respective fields. Although this is more applicable to the applied and professional training fields, there is merit given to the artist, musician, writer, and other humanists who have experienced and successfully competed in the public arena as well as the academic community.

Perceptions of who should teach has not changed much. Still perceived in the idealistic light, the teacher is the molder of minds and characters. His mission, as it was perceived by ancient mentor and tutor, is to teach by precept and example. Careful preparation is imperative, a strong personal academic record is mandatory, evidence of personal scholarly accomplishment, and unquestionable moral and ethical character. Above all, superior teachers exhibit a genuine interest in their students and a sense of awe with the content and process of instruction.

The more prestigious institutions of higher education demand much more than highly idealistic character of their faculty. High priorities are given to those who can exhibit scholarly achievement in the national and international arena of their respective discipline. Travel, conference attendance, foreign study, academic leadership and technical competencies are on a par with research, publication and service in the traditional sense. Today's superior university faculty member is all that the idealistic and romantic realist projected in the Renaissance man, plus the prototype of the international scholarly diplomat—educated, traveled, well respected and self-competent (Power, 1982).

A third perspective of purpose centers largely around the *curricular offerings* related to the types of education or modes of learning. Mortimer Adler speaks to three modes: (1) the acquisition of organized knowledge in the fields; (a) language, literature, and the fine arts, (b) mathematics and natural sciences, and (c) history, geography, and the study of social institutions; (2) the development of intellectual skills, all of which are skills of learning and thinking; and (3) the enhancement of the understanding of basic ideas and values (Adler, 1983). This means teaching knowledge, skills and understanding (cultural enrichment).

From ancient times the liberal arts have been defined, modified or adjusted and incorporated into advances in the arts, mathematics and sciences. Somewhat parallel to the development of communication systems, values on oratory gave way to written works, thesis to book, book to encyclopedic works, written to audio-visual media, and massive library collections to small microfilm or chip. Generally, the perspective of the Renaissance humanist and that of the undergraduate curriculum has been to look to the past rather than to the present or to the future for its content. The charge of "lack of relevance" to the immediate needs of society has plagued undergraduate education since it began.

Two forces working to bring "relevance" in undergraduate education can be seen: American pragmatism and the advances in industrial developments. The first calls for utilitarian outlets for an education and the other demands an educated person with skills suitable for application in the business, economic and industrial communities of society. A society which also sees itself supporting higher educational pursuits through taxes or direct endowments believes it can make such demands. Students eager to gain employment and subsequent economic independence began to choose undergraduate programs which would give both the educational merits of liberal arts and direct career preparation—another force working for more "relevance."

Another force opposing the traditional undergraduate offerings is occurring in more recent times. Those two-year colleges, normal schools, trade/industrial/technical schools, business and vocational institutions which were located on a more regional basis—close to population centers or sources of employment and ancillary training— developed generic liberal arts, science and humanities programs as part of their offerings. Under the guise of giving the student a well-rounded and balanced program, such schools flourished in America following World War II and many eventually applied for and gained full status as baccalaureate granting institutions and even expanded into graduate course offerings.

The two combined forces which have caused the erosion of maintaining the traditional undergraduate educational endeavors at the university level are: (1) the pragmatic demands for applied and career related skills on the part of those being graduated, and (2) the attempts of the colleges and other training institutions to meet educational demands of their students (liberal arts in nature) beyond the professional and career preparation programs.

The net result has been a confusion of roles, lowering of academic quality, and the forming of an indistinguishable grayness where a clear-cut black and white demarcation was intended. There is no clear-cut distinguishable difference between most university/college programs and those career preparation institutions. Economic burdens of state and private support for a dozen or more quasi-academic/career preparation programs emulating universities, plus the university systems too, are causing much scrutiny over duplicated services, questionable standards, fluctuating enrollments and maintaining tenured, senior professionals. What is a well-documented perception is that academic standards and course offerings have been lowered in order to attract, hold, and exit students. And, in answer to the demand that career training be given, most taxpayers see such training being accomplished in the shorter, more intensive vocational preparation program and question the need for such preparation being accompanied by a degree.

Ultimately, whereas training programs have flourished under the demands for technologically trained persons, undergraduate educational programs have lost much of their prestige, lost much of their breadth and depth in scholarliness, and are virtually open to anyone who has the financial ability to pay for such an education. As a result, the typical student graduated from the university or college goes forth reasonably well trained, but in the tradition of higher education, poorly educated. Therein lies the challenge to examine the foundations of undergraduate education.

Much of the current dilemma over deterioration in undergraduate education can be attributed to the breakdown of a clear-cut distinction between that which is education and that which is training. The balance between and among curricular offerings based around "knowledge and understanding" centered in the liberal arts, sciences and humanities has been eroded and disproportionately been replaced by "skill development" which is career oriented instead of academically rooted in intellectual, learning, and thinking skill development.

Another curricular eroding factor in undergraduate education is perceived as its inability to expand its treatment of the liberal arts and humanities much beyond the European/Greco-Roman/Judaic-Christian roots. Failure to recognize oriental as well as occidental background in social and philosophic thought and virtually ignoring the Native American, African, Hispanic and Asiatic contributions to human existence justifies the charges that undergraduate education is provincial and parochial—whether through censorship by design, oversight or ignorance. One would do well to recall Wendell Willkie's statement during World War II:

Today, because of military and other censorships, America is like a beleaguered city that lives within high walls through which there passes only an occasional courier to tell us what is happening outside. I have been outside those walls. And I have found that nothing outside is exactly what it seems to those within (Willkie, 1943).

From the perspective of the American pluralistic ideology, higher education should reflect the world-wide knowledges and aesthetics in its undergraduate offerings. So should the other arts and humanities look to the world which feeds its pluralistic society and economy. Regardless of how well our baccalaureate graduates achieve within the "ivy covered walls" of institutions of higher education, they leave with a limited perspective of the world—European/Greco-Roman/American biased—and enter a culturally diverse world of humans who are not so educated and also who occupy more than three-fourths of the world's land mass and represent 70% of the world's population. As American businessmen, the military, and athletes already know, they must compete or lose in the action arenas of the world. So must our scholars measure up, not just in science and technology, but also in the intellectual and academic arenas of the liberal arts and humanities.

American institutions of higher education historically have accepted the thesis of John Jay, "Education is the soul of the republic" (Ellis, Cogan & Howey, 1981). Although seldom listed as a specific course in undergraduate education, civic responsibility has been included in the cultural understandings that are to be transmitted in the liberal arts, sciences and humanities. "Colleges are abdicating their mandate to teach students civic responsibility," is the text of a recent Carnegie paper. Frank Newman, president of the Educational Commission of the States, calls upon colleges "to rededicate themselves to making sure their institutions graduate civic-minded students" (Newman, 1985). Broad recommendations are made for programs of work and community service attached to undergraduate training.

Curricular offerings at the undergraduate level must be viewed in more holistic terms and not only as enculturation—adapting to the language, the customs, the culture and the transmission of the arts, skills, and sciences. The curriculum must also respond to pragmatic pressures of insuring that the baccalaureate opens pathways to a career (Ellis et al., 1981). Ultimately, we must realize that the major goal of education is still that of opening channels for the student to become more educated (Marler, 1975).

Methodology or the answer to "how should the student be taught?" is directly related to the ideological base which reflects an epistemological search for truth and meaning—educational philosophy also searches for how one learns. Simply, if one learns from authority, then one is expected to listen, study and absorb that which the authoritarian system provides. Truths thus gained are accepted on faith, faith in the authority of the teacher, text, or doctrine. When this type of learning is extended to a more realistic and empirically based realm, faith is replaced by reason and verification through the testing of theories, hypotheses, and theorems. Regardless, the learning is passive in that the truths existed prior to learning them. The teaching may be an active input process, but the learning is merely that of assimilation.

Active teaching and passive learning occur in a manner which can be analogous to the strewing of cut, polished, and processed diamonds into the sands of the dry and arid desert created by the teacher. It is the student's responsibility to seek, find, and accumulate those gems hidden from open view. Through diligent, perseverant, and systematic ways the student searches, uncovers and recovers an appropriate collection of the hidden gems. To that student who recovers and amasses the greatest quantity, the highest merits are given. To the one who finds the least or none at all, failure is labeled. In between the two extreme measures of success and failure, the remainder of the students are appropriately given individual ratings, percentile ranks, and allocated standard deviation slots—not from success or from failure but from the performance of the average seeker, finder, and accumulator. In such normative ways, each is rewarded by the teacher relative to the number of cut, polished and processed gems he or she retrieves and returns. In all of this, however, no new gems were found, no new ones were cut, polished, or processed. For the value of active teaching and passive learning is not placed upon seeking and searching for diamonds in the rough which are new, uncut, and unprocessed. The value is only on those gems already found, cut, polished, and processed—simply a diamond version of trivial pursuit.

In the history of educational thought, the rise in experience-based learning can be tracked back to the writings of Roger Bacon in the mid–1500s. Under his aphorism "knowledge is power," Bacon challenged and condemned the great body of learning then extant as non-knowledge, as "pseudo-and-pretentious-knowledge." For such knowledge does not give power. It is otiose, not operative—it neglects the conditions and methods which such knowledges alone can obtain. By declaring things as not-knowable, it deliberately leads the earnest scholar astray, causing him to challenge authority and leads him into a search or discovery through his own experience (Dewey, 1920). In any case, learning was subsequently redefined by Locke, James and Dewey to be that of discovery through individual experience—the oft misquoted axiom, "learn by doing" (Brameld, 1955).

Methodology throughout history has reflected not only the changes in media but also technological advances in other areas; building design, laboratory equipment, and more recently electronic devices and computers. In many of the advancements affecting higher education, that of the computer is the most profound, or has the potential to be profound. Computerized retrieval of library and research data has taken the drudgery out of information processing. Programmed learning potentials in the liberal arts are unlimited through the use of audio-visual and computerized techniques, yet, are largely untapped in those fields. It would be well for academic instructors and administrators to look to those areas for compacting much of the routine knowledge assimilation which consumes much class time, and which could be better spent on the development of critical thinking, creative thinking, and problem solving skills (de Bono, 1971).

Much is known about the advancements in educational thought relative to methods of instruction. That which is known, however, calls for an individualized form of instruction and smaller faculty-student ratios. The information is there, and there are sufficient valid and reliable experiences to support the use of such methodology, but it challenges large lecture hall presentations and the "sage on the stage is reluctant to become the guide on the side" (Webb, 1982). Modern tech and high-tech sophistication could do much to increase teaching and learning effectiveness.

Methodological considerations are of prime importance in fulfilling the purpose of undergraduate education. Basic cultural exposure, knowledge input, and skill development can be enhanced by better instruction. Oral tradition limited instruction to a single medium, writing and printing advances opened both curricular and instructional doors, and modern technology opens the universe of information and learning to the student. The ideas are here; "the great difficulty in education is to get experience out of ideas" (Santayana, 1955).

From the philosophic perspective examined through the classic questions asked of education, it is possible to then define the purpose of undergraduate education. Realistically, the definition has never changed—that of transmission of the arts, skills, knowledges, under-standings and cultural ways to the privileged few. What has changed is the definition of the privileged few, arts, skills, knowledges, and cultural ways.

The privileged few in America today are, or at least should be, those who are the most capable of competing in higher education and those who have the potential for unlimited education through the baccalau-reate and advanced study or training. Federal legislation, uniform accreditation practices and compliance by educational institutions have removed many of the barriers to higher education imposed by discriminatory practices of the past. Financial assistance, too, is available for most of the capable students who show success potential. Whether the American public extends its support to mass education through the baccalaureate degree or not, there will always be a demand to open the doors of higher education for those most capable. From this position it is possible to conclude that one of the purposes of undergraduate level education is to take the most capable students, in the most holistic terms, and provide them with the potential for unlimited education.

The second question examined was that of who should teach. Educators at the undergraduate level of instruction fall victim to the classic image of the person who can teach by both precept and example—the scholar who not only lives a scholarly life, but exempli-fies that scholarliness in life and living. The change in perception is little less than viewing the educator in the context of the modern international world of technology.

The purpose of higher education from the standpoint of administration of undergraduate programs is to cause the capable student to come in contact with the best and most capable faculty who can bring both the wisdom of learning from antiquity to the present. Additionally, such a teaching program should give relevance to the world we live in and project an entry into the 21st century.

Curricular offerings at the undergraduate level must be a blend of knowledges gleaned from the pluralistic roots of American culture and the skill development needed in the realistic international and intercultural world of the present and the year 2000 and beyond. Cultural enrichment must include the accepted ways of life and living as an individual and member of the international community as well as in this nation.

History records countless tales of failure in societies which did not maintain a balance between the preservation of its cultural heritage and skill development commensurate with the growth and development of the world around them. To progress and lose hold of one's cultural heritage is equally disastrous as that of holding onto the past ways and failing to keep up with the present and anticipated future. There is a perceived danger in an over-emphasis on career preparation at the undergraduate level at the expense of weakening the educational foundations in the liberal arts, sciences and humanities.

Also recorded in history is the lesson that when the privileged few became the educated elite and failed to assume civic responsibility, both the elite and the society itself perished. Curricular offerings isolated within the institutions of higher education and which do not reflect the mainstream goals of American culture are destined to be viewed by taxpayers as alien to the goals of life and living in the democracy.

Lastly, the philosophic question of "how should the curriculum be taught?" is viewed as the most critical in defining the purpose of undergraduate education. Sufficient data gained from sociological, psychological and educational research declares that learning is an individual process. Education is a social process, as stated at the outset in this paper. Yet, education must be separated from learning— the actual process generally accepted as an individual experience. Therefore, the desirable method of instruction, in current American epistemological thought is to individualize that instruction to meet the ability, needs, and aspirations of the individual student.

To accomplish this, undergraduate educational purposes must be defined in terms of providing students with information and skills necessary to learn for themselves, at their own ability level and rate of learning. It has been suggested that by utilization of modern technology, programmed learning may well be the best method for teaching many of the knowledges and understandings related to cultural enrichment. Time made available through curricular compacting through programmed learning, may be better spent on individual and group problem-solving and skill development necessary to learn more effectively as an individual (O'Neill, 1981).

What are some options to consider?

1. Seek greater *public support* of undergraduate education for individuals with success records in academic, leadership, and civic responsibility, and who have met rigorous and rigid competency level expectations in the wide range of public, secondary offerings and who show potential for continued high performance regardless of age, sex, race, color or national origin.

2. Place greater academic demands on undergraduate students to perform at *higher achievement levels* in the liberal arts, sciences, and humanities.

3. *Suspend training* in the professional schools, applied programs, and practical/career oriented programs until students have fulfilled the prescribed basic liberal arts, sciences, and humanities courses at a better than minimal level of competency—suggested 75th percentile on a scholastic achievement test.

4. Require all students to complete a minimum number of course hour equivalents of experience in *public or civic service* at the national, state, county or municipal level—suggested 30 hours or two full semesters—to be completed before the baccalaureate degree is conferred.

5. Provide greater access to undergraduate students to *use advanced technology* for the transmission of knowledge, information processing and production, and academic acceleration of content.

6. Place greater emphasis and appropriate *incentives for faculty members* to work with undergraduate level instruction in individualized educational programming, lesser teacher-pupil ratios, more conference, advisory time and with attention to different ability and need levels—incentives to include not only salary adjustments, but support for advanced/world oriented study, travel and improved use of technological equipment and services.

Summary

The purpose of education has been set forth in all societies at all times as a means of perpetuating the cultural knowledges, skills and understandings by transmitting them to the young and unlearned.

In each society a select or privileged few were provided access to higher education. Idealistically, in America today, those privileged few are they who can qualify for undergraduate instruction under rigid and rigorous standards for admission.

Thus, the purpose of undergraduate education is to bring together students from separate and diverse backgrounds and expose them to a wide range of knowledges, skills and understandings which are representative of their collective cultural heritage.

Undergraduate education, by the very nature of its title, presumes that an advanced education or professional training will be open to those who can successfully complete the baccalaureate program. Such undergraduate education, therefore, should not be viewed as complete within itself, but a means for further education.

All that is of value is not from antiquity. In America, the pluralistic and pragmatic ideological foundations dictate that education reflect the total of its culture and that the public demand for career preparation be considered as part of the mission of undergraduate education. Yet, a carefully defined balance must be maintained between education and training, even though undergraduate educational programs must be extended in time and credits.

Finally, the purpose of undergraduate education is to open doors of learning to unlimited levels of excellence for those most capable of being educated. Society and the institutions of higher education can impose the most rigid and rigorous entrance and progress requirements. Yet, for that person who is admitted and can compete, education becomes that—unlimited—or limited only by his or her own intellect, abilities, aspirations, and self-determined needs in his or her pursuit of excellence.

Each institution of higher education has been charged with an undergraduate mission by our society and culture. We, in higher education, must choose whether to spend our days defining that mission or to use our time and resources fulfilling that mission.

References

Adler, M. J. (1983). *Paideia problems and possibilities*. New York: The Macmillan Publishing Company.

Bigge, M. L. (1982). *Educational philosophy for teachers*. Columbus, OH: Charles E. Merrill Publishing Company.

Brameld, T. (1955). *Philosophies of education in cultural perspective*. New York: The Dryden Press, Inc.

Brubacker, J. S. (1969). *Modern philosophies of education*. New York: McGraw-Hill Book Company.

Butts, R. F. (1947). *A cultural history of education*. New York: McGraw-Hill Book Company.

de Bono, E. (1968). *New think*. New York: Avon Books.

Dewey, J. (1920). *Reconstruction in philosophy*. New York: Holt, Rinehart and Winston, Inc.

Ellis, A. K., Cogan, J. J., & Howey, K. R. (1981). *Introduction to the foundation of education*. Englewood Cliffs, NJ: Prentice-Hall, Inc.

Gallagher, J. J. (1985). *Teaching the gifted child* (3rd edition). Newton, MA: Allyn and Bacon, Inc.

Hutchins, R. M. (1936). *The higher learning in America*. New York: Simon & Schuster, Inc.

Marler, C. D. (1975). *Philosophy and schooling*. Boston: Allyn and Bacon, Inc.

Newman, F. (1985, October 1). Carnegie paper report: Community service. *Sioux City Journal*.

O'Neill, W. F. (1981). *Educational ideologies: Contemporary expressions of educational philosophy*. Santa Monica, CA: Goodyear Publishing Company, Inc.

Power, E. J. (1982). *Philosophy of education*. Englewood Cliffs, NJ: Prentice-Hall, Inc.

Pulliam, J. D. (1982). *History of American education* (3rd Edition). Columbus, OH: Charles E. Merrill Publishing Company.

Santayana, G. (1955). *Skepticism and animal faith*. New York: Dover Publications, Inc.

Webb, J. T. (1982). *Guiding the gifted child*. Columbus, OH: Ohio Psychology Publishing Co.

Willkie, W. L. (1943). *One world*. New York: Simon & Schuster, Inc.

The Aesthetic Side of a College Education

John A. Day

Introduction: Definition of Aesthetic Education

Aesthetic Education teaches unique and distinctive ways of experiencing, understanding, and expressing what it is to be human through intuitive and holistic modes. The primary vehicle for this branch of education is the arts which, by definition, operate through a non-discursive yet highly sophisticated system of symbols.

In the past, the term "Aesthetic Education" would have implied a vague acknowledgement of the affective dimension of learning and a nebulous endorsement of the value of an individual's ability to respond to beauty. Undoubtedly, it would have carried with it a suggestion that the arts were subjective, impractical, and lacking in discipline—attitudes which justified relegating them to the fringes of the educational community.

After emerging in the 1940s and gaining significant credibility during the past two decades, Aesthetic Education is coming into its own as a field of academic investigation. It is founded upon the conviction that the aesthetic side of human nature is fundamental and essential to learning. It focuses upon the systematic investigation of the nature, content, and processes of aesthetic learning and it utilizes the full range of educational research to this end. Based in the arts, it strives to understand and to formalize appropriate and effective means of teaching aesthetic literacy.

As Aesthetic Education enters its majority, dramatic changes and

31

new levels of sophistication are on the horizon. In identifying its goals, advocates will argue the relative merits of the traditional subjective justifications for the arts against those of the more objective modes which are current today. In this debate, higher education will assume the decisive leadership role refining the definition and directing the future of Aesthetic Education towards a reasonable balance between the two points of view.

This paper is dedicated to placing the arts into the context of the challenges currently facing America's colleges and universities in terms of the new dynamics of Aesthetic Education. That Aesthetic Education is in a transitional period relative to the future of higher education as a whole is attested to by Jack Burnham when he says,

> As a culture producer, man has traditionally claimed the title, *Homo Faber: Man the Maker* (of tools and images). With continued advances in the industrial revolution, he assumes a new and more critical function. As *Homo Arbiter Formae* his prime role becomes that of *Man the Maker of Aesthetic Decisions*. These decisions—whether they are made concertedly or not—control the quality of all future life on the Earth. Moreover these are value judgments dictating the direction of technical endeavor (Burnham, 1968, p. 1).

The Arts and the Current Debate in American Education

To cite the current debate over the condition and future of American Education as a context for this paper has considerable risk. For the past several years, endless numbers of reports, position papers, and manifestos about our nation's schools have commanded public attention to the point of saturation.

With the publication of "A Nation at Risk: The Imperative for Educational Reform," problems became crises and issues became news under the harsh light of political and media scrutiny. The report catalyzed an educational world already agonizing over how to "modernize" in a time of declining resources and assertive retrenchment. As a result, all aspects of education sought to enter the arena to justify, criticize, proclaim, advise, proselytize, or contribute to the renewal.

Some chose to ignore that such debates are cyclical in education— waxing and waning like the moon, which despite its predictability continues to surprise and inspire. This viewpoint brings an anxiety and intransigence to the forum which aggravates rather than resolves.

Others, recognizing times of intense public interest as welcome opportunities to analyze, evaluate, and redirect education, chose to dream and plan. It is with the latter perspective and objectives this author offers the following thoughts about the mission of the arts in undergraduate education.

To begin with, it is instructive to review the landmarks of our current educational debate for points of reference on the arts and related issues and prospects. Despite their specific focus, the majority of the recent commentaries on American education stress a return to a basic, discipline-based education which emphasizes multi-faceted literacy. The key appears to be the determination to revitalize our society through the rebirth of the individual. This citizen of the future is seen as equipped educationally to participate in a world dependent upon the exchange of information and the dynamics of high technology.

Such a view would appear to have significant promise for Aesthetic Education since few dispute the power of the arts to foster creativity or to celebrate the uniqueness of the individual. Strangely enough, the literature presents a confusing and contradictory view of the importance of the arts in education. A considerable number of reports essentially ignore the arts while others politely suggest that they are nonessential frills. In balance, there is an equal amount of material which advocates for the arts as basic but, even here, questions about past productivity and future directions are common. Some would have the arts emulate more discursive disciplines to stress the objective dimensions of history and theory, while others emphasize the unique ability the arts possess to foster self-expression and creativity. Apparently, considerable work must be done to develop a consensus on the proper place of the arts in our schools as well as a clarification of their mission, goals, objectives, and means of evaluation.

Two key documents have direct bearing upon the issue of this paper concerning the aesthetic side of a college education. The first, "Academic Preparation for College: What Students Need to Know and Be Able to Do," a 1983 report of the College Entrance Examination Board, was compiled in an attempt to strengthen the academic quality of secondary education by defining skills students need in order to succeed in higher education. It is philosophically significant that this comprehensive report identifies the arts as one of six educational basics and characterizes them as "valuable to college entrants whatever their intended field of study" (College Entrance Examination Board, 1983). By extension then, it is a premise of this paper that Arts Education should be an element in the preparation of undergraduates on a par with the other disciplines traditionally recognized as an essential part of general education.

The second study which serves as an important reference for this article is the report issued by the National Institute of Education in 1984, entitled, "Involvement In Learning: Realizing the Potential of American Higher Education." While the report does not specifically touch on the arts, its directives promise to have a broad-ranging impact upon undergraduate education in all disciplines over the next several years. Consequently, it must serve as a resource when incorporating Aesthetic Education into the new agenda for American education.

At the beginning of "Involvement In Learning," the authors present a mission for undergraduate education which has considerable implications for the arts when they say,

> The United States must become a nation of educated people. Its citizens should be knowledgeable, creative and open to ideas. Above all, they should learn how to learn so they can pursue knowledge throughout their lives and assist their children in the same quest. To attain this goal, higher learning in America should be broadened and deepened so as to provide increased opportunities for intellectual, cultural, and personal growth for our citizens (National Institute of Education, 1984, p. 1).

This report also ascribes a primary leadership role to institutions of higher learning relative to the future of American education as a whole. As the segment of education which establishes the overall character of all levels of education and the values of students and teachers, the pressing questions of Aesthetic Education must be addressed most fundamentally and comprehensively in America's colleges and universities.

As the arts seek increased and more substantive participation in setting new goals for education, it is important to recognize that many proposals will find precedents, or at least harbingers, in the past history of American art education. While it would be folly to deny a significant degree of dependence upon European educational theory, American education has claimed its own character and imperatives almost from the beginning.

The American perspective has produced a unique approach to Aesthetic Education by incorporating it into all levels of schooling. The implications of this decision for undergraduate education are clearly stated by the Working Group on the Arts in Higher Education in their position paper, "The Arts, Liberal Education, and the Undergraduate Curriculum." Here, they state,

American higher education has developed a unique approach to the arts disciplines. In Europe, the sciences and humanities, including historical studies in the arts, are taught at the universities while instruction in the practice of art is conducted in separate institutions. The American approach is to remove this distinction for both comprehensive colleges and universities and single-purpose institutions devoted to the arts—this so that the undergraduate education of the practicing artist can readily include studies in the sciences and humanities. This approach has made creation, presentation, education, and scholarship in the arts disciplines integral to American higher education.

Clearly, this concept creates improved conditions for developing the intellectual capabilities of professional artists. Equally important, however, is its provision of unparalleled opportunities in the arts for all undergraduate students (Working Group on the Arts in Higher Education, 1984, p. 5).

The arts community has been extremely vocal of late in proclaiming aesthetic training as one of the basics in education . . . a virtual fourth "R"—as essential as reading, writing, and mathematics. A publication of the National Endowment for the Arts entitled, "Arts in Education, Education in Arts: Entering the Dialogue of the 80's," offers excellent examples of the impassioned philosophical arguments, the impressive range of statistical studies, and the staggering list of endorsements which have been marshaled in defense of the importance of Aesthetic Education (Fowler, 1984).

At the bottom of all of this rhetoric is a statement about the mission of Aesthetic Education in general and, by extension, its application to undergraduate education in particular. One of the best and most concise statements about the values of the arts in education is contained in a position paper entitled, "The Arts: An Essential Ingredient in Education," produced for the California Council of Fine Arts Deans. Its authors summarize the justification for the arts as basic by citing that they "motivate learning, develop imagination and aesthetic understanding, add meaning to other areas of study, promote teamwork and self-discipline, provide historical record, develop problem-solving skills, enrich our lives, add to economic development and bolster the basics." (Milley, 1984, p. 1).

These claims, and others, find ample support in educational literature and contribute to a formulation of a multidimensional mission statement for Aesthetic Education. Consequently, they deserve to be expanded upon and translated into applications for undergraduate curricula of the future.

The Mission of Aesthetic Education

The answer to why the arts should be an integral part of the mission of general education has a philosophical and a practical side. Philosophically, the arts are seen as essential to a meaningful life and, as a consequence, are demanded to a degree never before seen in this nation. Today, an impressive chorus of voices across the nation echoes John Dewey (1934) in his statement that, "Aesthetic experience is a manifestation, a record and celebration of the life of a civilization, a means of promoting its development, and is also the ultimate judgment upon the quality of a civilization" (p. 326).

On a more immediate level, J. Kent Clark offers a poignant testimonial to the desire for Aesthetic Education in an article entitled, "The Creative Arts and Twentieth Century Education,"

> It is a profound human waste for people to go through life half-hearing, half-seeing, and only dimly aware of the range of their own perceptions and capabilities. In this connection, it is both encouraging and sad to see the swarms of middle-aged people enrolling in adult classes in drama, dance, music and visual arts. It is encouraging because it demonstrates the hunger for self-expression and the demand for creative activity; it is sad because it often reflects years of frustration and cultural poverty (Clark, 1979, November, pp. 7, 9, 10).

Literacy is a highly popular term in today's discussions about education, and rightly so. In its simplest form, it signifies a competency in a specific language or system of communication and it is communication that is our most fundamental social function.

Thus, literacy or competency in the language of the arts is the primary goal of Aesthetic Education. The language and the content of the arts are unique and inaccessible via any other means. This is such a truism among artists that it is a virtual critical dictum to insist that if the essence of a work of art can be expressed in words, then that work has failed. John Dewey (1934) testifies to this when he states that, "There are values and meanings that can be expressed only by immediately visible and audible qualities, and to ask what they mean in the sense of something that can be put into words is to deny their existence" (p. 74).

Accepting this perspective as a traditional truth has tremendous implications for the present and the future, considering the revolution society is experiencing in communications technology at a time which has been christened the "Age of Information." Report after report attests to the fact that human communication is increasingly dominated by electronic media and that this runaway trend will continue for the foreseeable future. Therefore, it seems imperative that a society so dominated and so conditioned by powerful aesthetic media such as television, film, and computers should embrace the arts as a system for teaching a new and appropriate literacy.

The second major goal of Aesthetic Education is to foster creativity and to stimulate imagination, both of which are central to learning. While creativity and imagination are not the unique provenance of the arts, they are especially facilitated by, and honored in, the arts, and this is one of the strongest justifications for including the arts in formal education.

Most would agree that the ability to bring into being an idea, solution, or invention which has not existed before is the ultimate goal of education. Some even maintain that it is through such creativity and imagination that our society will survive.

The sad truth is that these capacities are not sufficiently fostered within our schools despite claims to the contrary. In point of fact, studies show that creativity declines dramatically in the majority of people as they progress through our educational system with the result that the average person is only two percent as creative at age forty as at age five. The responsibility for this sorry situation must be shared by all in education. However, the point is not blame, but an affirmation that both imagination and creativity can and should be taught in our schools. Neither capacity is the special preserve of the "talented" nor the "inspired," but the birthright of every human being!

Here again, this goal of Aesthetic Education takes on special significance in light of the future. One must recognize that contemporary society is so dynamic it is only possible to educate students to be creative, flexible, and imaginative enough to adapt to rapid and inevitable change.

The next important goal of Aesthetic Education is a paradigm of the "double-edged sword" in that while it has produced eloquent testimonials for the arts, it has also been employed to dismiss them as expendable frills. Nonetheless, it is necessary to reconfirm the role played by the arts in the quality of life. The arts clarify, interpret, and intensify life. It is through the development of an aesthetic understanding and a capacity for aesthetic judgment that an individual is able to claim the elusive human territory which transcends function, job, and social position. The arts expand an individual's choices about environment, lifestyle, and leisure pursuit.

This quality of life issue in Aesthetic Education, while based upon a concern for the individual, has significant implications for our culture as a whole. America has a legion of critics who attack our collective disregard for environmental aesthetics and more who fault our culture as superficial and faddish. Despite questionable motives on the part of some of these commentators, there is sufficient evidence that it is time for our nation to come to terms with its aesthetic manifestations and to become generally more discriminating and critically demanding. This can be accomplished only through serious arts education which is equally accessible to everyone.

Another major goal for Aesthetic Education is to provide a perspective on human history. Our academic heritage is richly illustrated with masterpieces of art which are acknowledged as offering a significant and distinct perspective on human history. This tradition celebrates the ability of the arts to contribute insights into the human condition not available through verbal analysis.

As J. Carter Brown (1983), Director of the National Gallery of Art, indicates,

> The texts of man's achievements are not written exclusively in words. They are written, as well, in architecture, paintings, sculpture, drawing, photography and in urban, graphic, landscape, and industrial design. They are recorded in the dialects of marble, steel, clay, glass, paper and ink, not to mention oils, pastels, and acrylics (p. 11).

This certification of the power of the visual arts as a record of human intent should be expanded to all components of the world of aesthetic endeavor.

In much the same context, it should be acknowledged that Aesthetic Education has a special role in multi-cultural education. Utilizing the same qualities that equip the arts so well as transmitters of historical perspective, the arts serve as powerful interpreters of other cultures and viewpoints. In an age when active awareness of the interdependence of the human community is paramount, the arts offer one of the most accessible bridges across philosophical chasms which historically divide elements of that community.

As a final element of the mission of Aesthetic Education, it should be noted that the arts function as a powerful communicator of societal beliefs, values, and goals. As Edmund B. Feldman (1983) states, "The desire to preserve civilization, to renew the best of the past, and to build a better future, needs to be firmly established in every generation. And that is the real job of Art Education'' (p. 9).

In addition to its primary goals, Aesthetic Education has a number of secondary goals of considerable significance to the mission of education as a whole. One of the most important contributions the arts offer other areas of education is its ability to foster or motivate learning in general. Work by Nobel Laureate Roger W. Sperry (1983), in identifying functions of the right and left hemispheres of the brain, has led to a new appreciation for the complexity of human intellect and has done much to establish the academic credibility of traditional aesthetic functions of learning. He suggests that development of the aesthetic functions associated with the right hemisphere of the brain can result in an acceleration of the pace of learning, reduction in learning-related stress, improvement in memory and comprehension, and enhancement of the motivation to learn.

This material reinforces theories many educators have known and practiced for a long time. In point of fact, the arts have been traditionally acknowledged and promoted as teaching tools across the curriculum and have proven particularly useful in the areas of history, language, and social science. Unfortunately, they have been employed largely as illustrations and much remains to be done to fully realize the interdisciplinary potential of the arts in education. The arts themselves will have to take the lead in moving forward on this front, and in convincing others that they have legitimate cognitive dimensions which offer significant opportunity for articulation with their more "academic" counterparts.

Much more provocative is the assertion that the arts can actually bolster learning in the traditional basics of reading, writing, and mathematics. To maintain that the arts contribute to the richness of imagery and experience which fuel these disciplines is probably acceptable. One can hardly disagree with Oscar G. Brockett.(1985) when he says,

> We should not forget that the "basics" are tools and that how they are used is as significant as their acquisition. Without intellectual, attitudinal, and psychological motivation and learning, basic tools will probably remain unused or will be used minimally (p. 2).

However, it is another matter to accept that performance in the basics actually improves when the arts are an integrated part of the curriculum as is suggested by several recent studies.

It should also be noted that inherent qualities in the arts contribute to general educational outcomes in a unique way. In these areas, the arts accomplish far more than serving as yet another facilitator of desirable attitudes and skills—they are primary tools providing an active mode of teaching which require the student to take greater responsibility for learning. Through the arts, self-discipline and self-confidence are developed as a result of the need to master intricate processes and techniques, the emphasis upon feedback, and the well-defined system of recognition of accomplishment.

The arts also have a special capacity to promote problem-solving skills. The identification and definition of the basic problem is an initial step in many arts activities. This leads to analysis of potential solutions followed by planning and implementation of an individually-selected solution. Here, the very ambiguity of the arts serves the student well since the process helps to develop the reflection and judgment so necessary in life and so rarely confronted in other areas of the curriculum.

Certain of the arts are commonly recognized for an ability to promote teamwork and to aid with the general process of socialization of the individual. This capacity for teaching teamwork is obvious in musical ensembles and in theatre productions. However, the student in the arts also learns to work with others in a meaningful and personal way through the mentoring relationship between the instructor and the student and the intense camaraderie generated between students who share artistic challenges.

The final result of successful Aesthetic Education is an individual who is literate in the language of the arts, whose imagination is alive, who is creative enough to respond to change in a positive way, and who continues to struggle with the quest to understand the nature and purpose of humanity. This person's life will be celebrated for its sensitivity, responsiveness, capacity to guess wholes from parts, and ability to recall the tangible from the intangible. This is the true test of the power of the arts and the record of human history is rich with testimonials from such people—these are the real proofs of the value of Aesthetic Education.

Applications in Undergraduate Arts Education

There are three distinct, but interrelated, areas of responsibility to the practical side of undergraduate Aesthetic Education. Most broadly is the area of general education which requires the arts to develop the greatest possible degree of aesthetic literacy in students majoring in non-arts disciplines. The second area of responsibility is the development of teachers in the arts. The third, the education and training of students who plan careers as professional artists.

The role of the arts in general education is perhaps the most difficult to approach with tangible commentary. The issue has been debated within higher education since the introduction of the arts into the college curriculum in the nineteenth century and has produced adversarial relationships in the most unlikely places. Traditionally isolated in the university community, the arts have been forced to operate as separate and independent entities emphasizing professional training and offering service courses with only superficial connection to other academic programs. In point of fact, this is exactly opposite to the mission of the arts in general education . . . the arts should not be separate, but integrated into the curriculum in order to accomplish the goals set forth earlier in this paper.

The Working Group on the Arts in Higher Education correctly notes the inherent diversity of approaches to general education in the nation's colleges and universities. Accepting this as an inevitable and perhaps desirable condition, it is important to recognize that each institution must develop its own formula for ensuring that students receive a broad educational foundation irrespective of major. Each institution must understand that if it ignores arts education, other forces will formulate the aesthetic values of America. The Working Group suggests that educational institutions "give serious thought to the meaning of this situation for the quality of their own futures. For example, how do the aesthetics and commercial values of television, rock videos, newspapers, movies, etc., relate to the values of liberal education in American post-secondary institutions?" (Working Group on the Arts in Higher Education, 1984, p. 9).

The significance of this question is underscored when one realizes that Aesthetic Education is essentially postponed until the undergraduate years. The extent to which this is true is commented upon by Laura H. Chapman (1982) who states,

> Eighty percent of our nation's youth graduate from high school with little or no instruction in the arts. Most youngsters spend twelve years in school, and during that time receive about twelve thousand hours of instruction, but less than one percent of this time is likely to be spent in studying the arts (except literature) with a qualified teacher. The typical high school graduate has a token education in the arts (p. 1).

Consequently, higher education has a primary role to play in the improvement of general Aesthetic Education of America, not only in filling a fundamental gap but in doing so creditably. While America's colleges and universities are fairly well-equipped to meet this challenge given the considerable arts resources built up over the past thirty years, forces exist which militate against success. Primary among these is the dominance of introductory arts courses in the curriculum vulnerable to dismissal as simplistic, diversionary, and nonacademic. This major obstacle is reinforced by the current emphasis upon specialization and professional training and a resistance to significant interdisciplinary cooperation.

To respond sincerely to the recognition of the importance of the arts in general education, institutions of higher learning must go further than the quotas established in cores or general graduation requirements since such a solution is limited and highly vulnerable to the whims and forces of politics and personal perspective. Undergraduate programs need to come to grips with the central issue of how to truly integrate the arts into the broader curriculum in order to take advantage of their unique capacity to reinforce the goals of general education. Undoubtedly as many means will emerge for meeting this objective as there are colleges and universities, but success will be measured by the commonality of purpose and the degree of effort marshaled to the cause of making the arts an essential part of a contemporary undergraduate education.

From this united front will come a definite and emphatic national acknowledgment of the importance of Aesthetic Education for undergraduate students. This commitment will spread throughout all levels of America's diverse system of education. For higher education, it will mean changes in admission standards which recognize aesthetic talent, the incorporation of aesthetic skills and attitudes in the goals and projected outcomes for a general education, increased opportunities for students to elect a significant sequence of course work in a specific art form, and a greater integration of the arts into other academic areas through interdisciplinary offerings.

Turning to professional and pre-professional arts education at the undergraduate level, whether it be the preparation of teachers or the education of students who aspire to careers as artists, one must return to the role of general education. In both cases, the general education components of the student's curriculum must be broad enough to ensure a firm grasp of the other educational basics, to provide a foundation which allows for integration of the arts with other disciplines, and to develop life-enriching skills and attitudes beyond those taught in the major.

While this position may seem obvious given earlier comments about the role of the arts in general education, undergraduate programs in the arts have come under increasing scrutiny and criticism for their requirements relative to other disciplines. This issue must be confronted directly since it is the only way potential discrepancies between professional and general curricula can be understood and put into perspective.

Aesthetic Education takes on an entirely different dimension when discussion shifts from general education to the preparation of students who enter undergraduate programs with the intention of making a profession of the arts. This group can be subdivided into those who wish to become teachers of the arts and those who wish to become professional artists.

As different as these career goals may seem, there is more correlation between them than has been traditionally acknowledged. In both cases, the undergraduate curriculum must ensure breadth as well as depth. The breadth comes from a solid general education compatible with that expected in other disciplines. The depth is provided through a specific sequence of professionally-oriented courses prescribed by national norms. Ultimately, both the prospective arts teacher and the "would-be" professional artist must have a common ground in the production or execution of the arts which welds them together through mutual respect and a sense of shared cultural goals.

The preparation of arts educators at the undergraduate level is the joint responsibility of the college/university as a whole, the schools or departments of education, and the various fine arts programs. This partnership requires a unique balance and integration between often warring elements in undergraduate studies. A whole new level of communication and cooperation must be developed within colleges and universities relative to the preparation of teachers in the arts.

The education of arts teachers today is an especially challenging and significant task. It has been long recognized that arts educators are essential to the development of an appreciative audience for the arts and the fostering of artistic talent required to produce the artists of the future.

To these traditional tasks is added a new awareness of the arts educators' responsibility to advocate for the aesthetic side of life. While arts educators have traditionally championed the importance of the arts, they must be especially well-equipped today to do battle across this nation against those who would reduce the importance of the arts in favor of more putatively practical subjects. In order to meet this challenge, arts educators must be completely grounded in the history, aesthetics, and techniques of the arts they advocate, and equally capable of presenting this perspective to students, parents, school officials, and the general public. Undergraduate education must recognize this as one of the primary challenges its arts education graduates will face and address this need with determination and confidence.

The preparation of those who aspire to a career as a professional artist is probably the most demanding aspect of undergraduate Aesthetic Education. Despite reports which might suggest the contrary, many young people continue to enter institutes, colleges, and universities hoping to become practicing artists. That these prospects come to higher education from a pre-college system which does not favor development of artistic talent gives one pause to consider the integrity and commitment a student must sustain in order to persevere in this ambition until entering higher education in hopes of finding a receptive aesthetic educational environment.

With this in mind, higher education must accept the responsibility to nurture students who have survived with their aesthetic interests intact and consider them as a national cultural resource. Such an attitude has a variety of implications, but the most significant is a new commitment to recruiting aesthetically talented people into America's colleges and universities on a par with students who have been evaluated as having potential for success in other specialized disciplines.

In summary then, Aesthetic Education, while relatively new as a systematic study, runs through the whole of the educational system and is as essential to that whole as oxygen to the bloodstream. The arts have brought energy to the teaching of people since before written language and will continue to do so in an information age again characterized by non-discursive communication. The mission of Aesthetic Education, at whatever level, is the acquisition of wholeness, of imagination, and of freedom.

References

Brockett, O. G., & Davis, J. H. (Ed.). (1985). Drama, a way of knowing. *Theatre education: Mandate for tomorrow*. Anchorage Press, Inc. and Children's Theatre Foundation.

Brown, J. C. (1983). Excellence and the problem of visual literacy. *Design for Arts Education, 85.* (2).

Burnham, J. (1968, September). Systems aesthetics. *Art Forum VII* (l).

Chapman, L. H. (1982). *Instant art, instant culture: The unspoken policy for American schools.* New York: Teacher's College Press.

Clark, J. K. (1979, November). The creative arts and twentieth century education. *NASSP Bulletin, 63* (430).

College Entrance Examination Board. (1983). *Academic preparation for college: What students need to know and be able to do.* New York: College Board Publications.

Dewey, J. (1934). *Art vs. experience.* New York: Minton, Balch & Co.

Feldman, E. B. (1983). Art in the mainstream: Ideology and hope. *Art Educator, 36.* (4).

Fowler, C. B. (Ed.). (1984). *Arts in education/education in arts.* Washington, DC: National Endowment for the Arts.

Milley, J., Buchen, I., Okerlund, A., & Montarotti, J. (1984). *The arts: An essential ingredient in education.* California Council of Fine Arts Deans.

National Institute of Education. (1984). *Involvement in learning: Realizing the potential of America.* Report of the Study Group on the Conditions of Excellence in American Higher Education.

Sperry, R. W. (1983). *Science and moral priority: Merging mind, brain and human values.* New York: Columbia University Press.

Working Group on the Arts in Higher Education. (1984). *The arts, liberal education, and the undergraduate curriculum.*

Internationalizing the Undergraduate Curriculum: "You've Got to Know the Territory!"

Gale K. Crouse and Robert W. Wood

Americans in the World Community

According to a recent news article, when over 1,800 college students in North Carolina were asked to locate the Seine River, only a third of them knew it was in France. Of freshmen tested at St. Mary-of-the-Woods College in Indiana, ninety-five percent could not locate Vietnam on a map. In north Dallas, one out of five twelve-year-olds mistook Brazil for the United States on a map of the world (Solorzano, 1985). These findings are not unlike those of a study done in 1982 by the Association of American Geographers which was given to 3,000 students at 185 colleges and universities. In this survey of basic geographical knowledge, college seniors missed half the questions. The final report of this study, "Geography and International Knowledge," concluded that Americans' knowledge of basic geography is "appallingly low" (Shabad, 1982).

There is an ever-increasing belief in the United States that this lack of knowledge of other lands and other peoples has reached a critical stage. In a world that grows smaller every day through satellite communications, supersonic jet travel and economic interdependence, there is more than ever a need for mutual understanding and appreciation among all peoples.

It may not be crucial that an individual does not know the river

47

Seine is in France (unless, of course, that person is our partner in a game of Trivial Pursuit). But may we not draw a corollary to suppose that this individual probably does not know much about France and her people either (not to mention the developing countries in Asia, Africa, and South America)? Ignorance of basic geography points toward an insouciance regarding world affairs in general. And therein lies the problem.

Most Americans seem content to know little about the rest of the world. Consider, for example, the case of the Soviet Union, the superpower whose technology rivals our own, whose influence in world affairs is of a magnitude which cannot be ignored, and whose direction and intention, according to many observers, is nothing short of world domination. We fear the Soviets, and we hear our President call Russia an "evil empire," but how well do we really know and understand the Union of Soviet Socialist Republics and the Soviet peoples? Not very well at all, apparently, if the study of the Russian language is any indicator. In an article published in 1983, the Soviet newspaper *Izvestiya* charged that there were more American nuclear warheads aimed at the Soviet Union than there were American students studying the Russian language. (In 1983 there were approximately 24,000 students of Russian in American colleges, universities, and secondary schools). The same article pointed out that there are more students of English in the city of Leningrad alone than there are students of Russian in the entire United States (ACTFL). Furthermore, the Soviet Union has more teachers of English than we have students of Russian (Simon, 1980).

The Soviets cannot be blamed for knowing and understanding us better than we know them; in large measure, it is our own fault. As an editorial in the *New York Times* stated,

> In few fields do so many rely so much on the brains of so few as in Soviet studies. You could fit around a card table all the Americans who are bilingual experts on Soviet policy in Africa. Or China. Or anywhere . . . Americans who complain that the Soviet Union is a closed society need to acknowledge that we have done pitifully little to open our own eyes (ACTFL, 1983, January, p. 5).

Senator Paul Simon (1980) of Illinois, a strong advocate for international understanding, has pointed out that during the last decade the United States spent more on 3/4 mile of interstate highways than on all exchanges with countries of the Soviet bloc. Furthermore, since 1965, government and institutional funding for study of Soviet and Eastern European affairs has declined by 70 percent. Between 1975 and 1979, fifty-two colleges and universities in this country dropped Russian language offerings. Our technological knowledge and understanding may have increased dramatically in the last twenty years, but our humanistic knowledge and understanding has actually diminished. We did successfully meet the technological challenge of the first Sputnik, but we have neglected to keep pace in our knowledge of the people who made the challenge. U. S. Ambassador in Moscow, Arthur A. Hartman, summed up the problem when he stated that "the tremendous gap in historical knowledge and lack of continuity in theory in attitudes toward the Soviet Union is one of the serious defects in American foreign policy" (ACTFL, 1983, November, p. 7).

There are signs that Americans' attitudes toward their position in the world community are changing, however. There is today a general movement to correct what is perceived as a lack of global perspective in our society. Educational reforms increasingly call for more study of geography, more attention to the ultimate benefits of foreign languages, and more international content throughout the curriculum. Knowing our international neighbors is becoming a priority item to many Americans. As an example, to return to the specific area of U. S.-Soviet studies, it is interesting to note that Harvard University has launched a five million dollar fund-raising drive to upgrade its Russian Research Center and to train academic and non-academic specialists on the Soviet Union. Citing its "concern over the disturbing decline in Soviet studies, particularly in the area of political science and economics," the Rockefeller Foundation in 1984 gave grants of one million dollars each to Columbia University and to the University of California—Berkeley to "encourage research and study of the foreign policies of the Soviet Union" (ACTFL, 1984, January, p. 5).

It should be evident to everyone concerned that a better understanding of the Soviet Union is in our own best interests. How can we compete effectively, though, if we don't know the competitor? As Charlie Cowell put it in *The Music Man*, "You've got to know the territory." Across the United States, not only at Harvard and Berkeley, but also at other universities, efforts are being made to expand students' experience in global awareness, to encourage students and faculty alike to become more involved in knowledge of world affairs—to "internationalize the curriculum."

What is International Education?

An exact definition of international education that is agreeable to all is difficult at best. To some educators, it means the study of foreign languages. To others it is synonymous with a more rigorous study of the social sciences—history, political science, and economics in particular. To still others it means sending U. S. students abroad to study and inviting foreign students and faculty to the local campus. A number of individuals insist that disciplines such as mathematics, physics, and chemistry are also international in character and should be included within the parameters of any definition. Our own belief is that internationalization should take place across the curriculum, reaching beyond traditional limitations of the disciplines and addressing all the broad issues confronting humankind.

It is useful to call attention to a definition of international education adopted by the National Council on Foreign Language and International Studies:

> International education is a term which encompasses diverse educational goals and strategies at different levels of the school system, colleges, and universities. Based on differing goals, there are different definitions of international education, with six broadly recognized subdivisions:
>
> - Area studies and foreign language
> - Multicultural and intercultural education
> - International development studies
> - Global issues education
> - Education with a global perspective (Rosengren, Wiley, & Wiley, 1983, p. 3).

The Need for International Education

The need for international understanding has never been greater. The world today is in a state of flux. The changing nature of world society is perhaps the strongest single argument for an internationalized curriculum for college and university students. The world population of 4.7 billion will be doubled in 35–40 years; tensions are heightened in the Middle East, in South Africa, in Central America, in Chad, in New Caledonia, and in dozens of other places most of us might have difficulty locating on a map. International relations are more complex than ever before in history; as Henry Kissinger has stated,"The national interest can no longer be devised or attained in isolation from the global interest. We are wired together so tightly that a short circuit could fry us all'' (Leinwand, 1983, p. 6). International understanding is imperative if the world community is to deal with and to resolve many of the problems now facing humankind.

The commercial practicality of international interdependence is another major reason to provide university students with international knowledge and skills. A number of economic realities make it essential that university graduates entering the labor force not only possess the required skills to complete their work but also have an understanding of the various peoples competing in the international marketplace. We have only to consider facts such as the following:

> By the year 2000, the U. S. will be primarily dependent upon imports for its supply of twelve out of thirteen minerals required by a modern industrial society (Rosengren et al., 1983, p. vii).
>
> At least one in eight American jobs depends on exports (Hansen, 1982).
>
> One out of every three acres now producing in this country is devoted solely to export. Seventy-seven percent of wheat is exported. Forty-eight percent of soybeans is exported. Forty percent of corn is exported (U. S. Department of Commerce, 1983).
>
> In 1980, ten developing countries accounted for fifty-eight percent of $51 billion of all U. S. exports. These were, in order of sales, Mexico, Saudi Arabia, Korea, Venezuela, Brazil, Taiwan, China, Singapore, Hong Kong, and Argentina (Hansen, 1982).

It is clear that international trade is responsible for jobs and income in the United States. With the world becoming more and more interdependent, it is imperative that our universities prepare students to meet the challenges of an accelerating international trade.

Graduates of U. S. universities can no longer afford to respond to world conditions and events with ethnocentric biases, inadequate information, and a general lack of interest. We truly are, as Archibald MacLeish has named us, "riders on the earth together." Our educational programs at the university level must develop students' competencies in international affairs so that we can all work together to solve the problems of the present while we plan for nothing less than the future of the planet itself. A truly international perspective consists of knowledge, skills, and attitudes that will enable us to understand better and to appreciate more our roles and responsibilities in our increasingly complex global community.

Assumptions

International education should be an integral part of the total university curriculum. The assumptions behind the internationalization of the curriculum are reflected in the following statements of belief:

1. Students and professors are interested in other people.
2. Education makes a difference in the way people think and behave.
3. Students and faculty need to be better prepared for living in a global community.
4. Students and faculty generally have not been prepared for global interdependency.
5. Better understanding and awareness of the world can occur as a result of integrating international education into the total curriculum.
6. International education is involved with laying groundwork for world peace and global survival.

Goals

The main goal in internationalizing the curriculum is to help students and faculty develop the ability to make intelligent decisions regarding the international system. Sound decisions are not made in a vacuum; they are based on knowledge. Decisions cannot be better than the knowledge from which they are derived. Because each of the various academic disciplines within a university deals with a specialized body of knowledge and has unique ways to view the international system, the decision makers should be able to see human events from the perspective of the several academic disciplines.

The multidisciplinary goals established for the internationalization of the curriculum include:

1. Understanding and valuing cultural diversity.
2. Recognizing the world as an interdependent system.
3. Being aware of prevailing world conditions, emerging trends, and the processes of change.
4. Developing effective skills to respond creatively to local, national, and international events.

Internationalization of a university's curriculum is, then, an attempt to produce a globally-literate citizen. We believe that this "world" citizen is an individual:

1. who acknowledges the symbiosis of the world community;
2. who wants to learn about other cultures and their beliefs;
3. who has the ability to accept the similarities and differences of other cultures;
4. who has the open mind necessary to live in a pluralistic world; and
5. who considers international situations objectively.

"Can the United States afford to have a population ignorant of global history, economics, and politics, not to mention language and cultural differences among nations, when so much of American life is tied to people and places abroad?" (Klassen & Leavitt, 1983, p.v). The answer to this question is obvious. We must recognize that our students are citizens of the world. Geographic and demographic isolation are no longer (if they ever were) valid reasons for a parochial attitude. Our graduates need an international perspective to understand how rural America is influenced by international issues, especially trade of agricultural products, and they need to develop a respect for cultural diversity. Graduates who leave their home state with an international consciousness will find it easier to adapt to the issues of cultural diversity and global concerns which they will inevitably find in their respective new communities.

Structuring and Developing International Programs

Every institution of higher education should be engaged in an examination of all the experiences it is offering to its students and faculty alike. In the process of internationalizing the undergraduate curriculum it is essential that, before the process goes very far, a number of policy questions be decided. President Walter Waetjen of Cleveland State University, speaking in Washington, D.C., at a workshop dealing with internationalizing the curriculum and the campus, raised the question of establishing policies for international education. The policies that should be tailored to an institution's needs are:

1. Preliminary Policy Planning. The first element in making policy is to agree to have one.
2. Curriculum Considerations. Some decision should be made, in advance, as to what proportion of the curriculum should be devoted to international education.

3. Library Holdings. Policy decisions should be made with regard to the number of books in the library that ought to relate specifically to global concerns.

4. Student Issues. Policy decisions should be made with regard to the number of foreign students the campus can effectively educate at any one time and how rapidly additional foreign students should be encouraged to attend.

5. Faculty Exchange Policies. Decisions need to be made with regard to the number of professors who should be encouraged to go abroad during any one year.

6. The Nature of Exchange Agreements. Much of what takes place under the umbrella of international studies is developed on an informal, *ad hoc* basis. How much is such informality desirable?

7. Institutional Expectations. It should be a part of policy to set forth the expectations that the institution hopes to achieve by internationalizing the campus and the curriculum.

8. Internal Organization. Policy decisions should be made with regard to the internal organization of international education, its funding, the kind of planning that is to take place, and who shall do the planning.

9. Resources. In internationalizing the campus and the curriculum, resources in kind are often made available for international programs. These should be identified (Leinwand, 1983, pp. 17–20).

Such policy statements should not be set in stone, but they should be available for review and modification while being utilized to give direction to the process of internationalizing the undergraduate curriculum.

A Model Program

The philosophy behind the internationalization of the undergraduate-curriculum at The University of South Dakota (U.S.D.) has been to make important international content available to all students, not just to those specializing in international studies. The need exists, as was pointed out in a 1982 random sample of 168 graduating seniors. Of these, only 25 percent had taken a non-language course with significant "international" or "foreign" content, and a mere 2 percent had taken a course whose focus was non-Western. In the three years since that sampling was taken, there has been an effort to expand students' horizons through a number of general education courses as well as through a wide variety of international events such as foreign films, speakers on international topics, and symposia that are geared to the undergraduate population in general.

As we have already stated, to be most effective, international education must infuse the entire undergraduate curriculum. At U.S.D., international or global perspectives are growing and are being made available to all undergraduates. During the past two years, for example, eighteen undergraduate courses have been significantly modified to include international content. Nearly all of these courses can be taken by any undergraduate student, regardless of his or her major. Twenty new courses involving international education have been developed and added to the University's curriculum.

As might be expected, the area of greatest growth for international-courses is the College of Arts and Sciences, where most general education courses are taught. In addition, however, the University has three undergraduate professional schools: the School of Education, the School of Business, and the College of Fine Arts. All have international dimensions built into their programs of study. The undergraduate experience at The University of South Dakota has been enriched by professors from the professional schools who have participated in university-wide international activities. Students in other schools and colleges across the campus share in the benefits and in the opportunities that stem from such participation.

The School of Education has integrated international components into a number of key courses required of all students majoring in elementary and secondary education. The international studies model currently being followed in the School of Education was developed during the 1972–74 academic years when a grant was received from the U. S. Department of Education to initiate "An Undergraduate Program in International Studies in Teacher Education."

The School of Business has a number of international studies courses which are open to all business majors. During the past two years, two new business courses have been developed and four courses have been modified to include international components. The School of Business is also in the process of affiliating with The International Association of Students in Economics and Business Management which will provide business majors the opportunity to work abroad as interns with an international company. Furthermore, each year the School of Business offers a study trip to Europe to investigate the various enterprises and business institutions in several European countries.

The College of Fine Arts offers a number of courses that emphasize important international contributions in the areas of art, music, and theatre. The Mass Communications area has a specialization in international communication. During the past two years the faculty in the Art History area have concentrated on building the slide collection of Third World art.

A university-wide development program to improve faculty attitudes and increase their international understanding is essential to the goal of internationalizing the undergraduate curriculum. Numerous developmental activities are now available to all faculty members. Frequent noon luncheons with speakers presenting programs on international topics are open to all faculty members and students. A slide program dealing with countries of the world is presented monthly by faculty members for the entire university community. An annual Scholar in Residence program brings to campus an individual with an international expertise which is not available locally. This scholar presents public lectures, conducts seminars, and is available to visit classes.

Faculty development is centered around helping the professor gain more international experience, background, insight, and concern. The effectiveness of any institution depends largely upon the calibre of its faculty. Consequently, every institution which is trying to develop its international dimensions needs as many persons on its staff as possible who have lived or traveled abroad. University of South Dakota faculty members annually have the opportunity to travel to Europe on the Business School trip or to Germany with a group sponsored by the Modern Languages Department. Faculty exchange programs offer the opportunity to teach abroad. One program with the University of Oldenburg in Germany is already in operation, and another with the University of Orleans in France is in the planning stage. A third faculty exchange program is presently being sought with Sukhothai Thammathirat Open University in Bangkok, Thailand. A special Fulbright-Hays Faculty Development Project is being developed which will take a group of eleven faculty to spend the summer studying and traveling in Egypt. It is planned to include professors who have had a limited amount of international travel experience.

The University must also do whatever possible to encourage and assist students to study, work, or travel abroad sometime during their undergraduate years. This is important today, but it will be imperative tomorrow. If students are to deal effectively and realistically with problems of the international community they should have some first-hand experience in other countries, living in and interacting with cultures different from their own. If the student experience abroad is to be successful, then the program should also be clearly relevant to the objectives of the University. It should be designed to provide educational experiences integrally related to the institution's undergraduate curriculum, to include extensive preliminary orientation for intended participants, and to include clearly defined criteria and policies for judging the success of such a program.

Two student exchange programs have been initiated already to give U.S.D. students the opportunity to live and study in a foreign environment. The University of Oldenburg and the University of Orleans have both entered into a partnership with the University of South Dakota to exchange students on an annual basis.

It should be recognized that the presence of foreign students on the local campus will provide a more heterogeneous environment for the University's students and thereby provide unique enrichment opportunities for them. It is essential to achieve integration of foreign students in a way which will enable them to contribute to the enhancement of campus and community life. The University can use a foreign student to embellish the undergraduate curriculum in a number of ways. Foreign students should be invited to talk to classes, to serve as guest lecturers or resource persons whenever appropriate, to serve as tutors for language students, to present programs in their home countries, and to become members of an international studies organization. Foreign students will talk with students about their country, expanding the campus knowledge of the "global village." The University must do whatever it can to make each foreign student's experience a good one. In a small way, the foreign student is already an ambassador of his or her native land, and important bonds of international friendship are already being formed.

Once a university has developed a number of its international activities, it then becomes appropriate to seek additional funds from grants, contracts, or even state money. The University of South Dakota received a two-year grant from the Department of Education to "Enrich International Studies Undergraduate Instruction." Many of the activities mentioned throughout this paper have been fostered by this grant. There are stories in higher education about programs built around grant monies, programs which collapse after funding ends. It goes without saying that in building an international undergraduate curriculum project on grant monies, the institutions should be willing to move the program to some more permanent status at the end of the grant period.

Conclusion

As a nation, we require a cadre of people who know about other peoples' cultures. If we are to survive and prosper in this interdependent world we certainly need teachers, professionals in business and government, lawyers, farmers, ranchers, scientists, and technicians who can respond intelligently to the global challenges and opportunities we will most definitely face in the years ahead. We need a general citizenry which is conscious of the world in which we live and one which expresses global concerns at the ballot box as well as in everyday life.

The key to internationalization of the university is the desire and the commitment of faculty and administration. Where talent exists, it should be encouraged and nourished. Where expertise is lacking, it should be sought out and acquired. The first and perhaps greatest steps will be made by dedicated faculty who introduce international components into existing courses, who initiate enrichment activities, or who create totally new courses. Enthusiasm is contagious. As the importance of the task becomes more evident and more relevant to more individuals, a synergy will develop which can only lead to the improvement of the total educational program.

We learn parochialism and even xenophobia at a very early age. In a *Child's Garden of Verses*, Robert Louis Stevenson (1885) wrote:

> Little Indian, Sioux or Crow,
> Little frosty Eskimo,
> Little Turk or Japanee
> Oh! Don't you wish that you were me?
>
> You have curious things to eat,
> I am fed on proper meat,
> You must dwell beyond the foam,
> But I am safe and live at home.

Foreigners are curious individuals, indeed. But no longer can we feel safe and snug in our far-away home. Today we must meet the foreigner, we must talk with him or her, we must transact business together, and we must assure each other that we are not out to destroy each other.

We Americans must learn to see ourselves in a proper perspective—which will likely be different and may even be difficult for us—and we must be prepared to draw new conclusions about ourselves. Consider for example:

- Most of the people in the world today live in Asia. Of the seven largest countries, in terms of population, five are completely in Asia and one is partly in Asia.
- Most of the people of the world are non-white.
- Most of the people of the world are ill-fed, ill-housed, ill-clad, and ill.
- Most of the people of the world are non-Christians.
- Most people of the world live under different forms of government and economy than ours.
- Most of the people of the world do not speak English. More people speak Chinese than any other language (Kenworthy, 1970, pp. 1–2).

The importance of knowing more about the world and the peoples who inhabit it has never been greater than it is today. Internationalization of the curriculum is not a luxury, it is a necessity. Edwin Reischauer, former U. S. Ambassador to Japan, has summed up the problem eloquently and succinctly:

> We need a profound reshaping of education if mankind is to survive in the sort of world that is fast evolving. . . . Before long humanity will face grave difficulties that can only be solved on a global scale. Education . . . is not moving rapidly enough to provide the knowledge about the outside world and the attitudes toward other people that may be essential for human survival within a generation or two (Rosengren et al., 1983, p. xiii).

References

ACTFL Staff. (1983, January). Russian studies championed. *ACTFL Public Awareness Network Newsletter*, p. 5.

ACTFL Staff. (1983, November). International studies in the news. ACTFL *Public Awareness Network Newsletter*, p. 7.

ACTFL Staff. (1984, January). International studies in the news. ACTFL *Public Awareness Network Newsletter*, p. 5.

Hansen, R. D. (1981). *U. S. foreign policy and the third world: Agenda 1982.* New York: Praeger Publishers.

Kenworthy, L. S. (1970). *The international dimension of education.* Washington, DC: Association of Supervision and Curriculum Development, NEA.

Klassen, F. H. & Leavitt, H. B. (1982). *Teacher education and global perspectives.* Washington, DC: American Association of Colleges for Teacher Education. (ERIC Clearinghouse on Teacher Education No. SP 019 496)

Leinwood, G. (1983). *Without a nickel: The challenge of internationalizing the curriculum and the campus*. Washington, DC: American Association of State Colleges and Universities.

Rosengren, I. H., Wiley, M. C. & Wiley, D. S. (1983). *Internationalizing your school: A handbook and resource guide for teachers, administrators, parents, and school board members*. New York: National Council on Foreign Language and International Studies.

Shabad, T. (1982, May 27). Americans get a failing grade in geography. *The New York Times*, p. A7.

Simon, P. (1980). *The tongue-tied American*. New York: Continuum Publishing Corporation.

Solorzano, L. (1985, March 25). Why Johnny can't read maps, either. *U. S. News and World Report*, p. 50.

U. S. Department of Commerce. (1983). *U. S. commodity exports and imports as related to output 1981 and 1980*. Washington, DC: author.

Learning to Live and Earning a Living: An Interactive Blend in Undergraduate Education

Joan T. England and Quentin Oleson

Learning to live and earning a living are not discrete entities but an interactive blend in the undergraduate educational process. The purpose of this chapter is to describe this phenomena further in terms of the social, psychological, and economic forces extant in undergraduate education which influence the student's attitude toward self, education, and the work place in a mutually refractory sense.

At one time an undergraduate education was for the self-improvement of the elite and career preparation for service, government, and clergy. In later years, college graduates were actively recruited as workers because it was believed that having survived the rigors of academic learning, they were capable of any undertaking. Frank Koe (1985) commented that in the past, merely gaining admission to a college or university was seen as an intellectual feat. Society has had changing expectations of the kinds of work roles appropriate for college graduates. Today's employers are seeking college graduates who have highly specialized training to deal with the complexity of the latter twentieth century. College graduates are coupling career choice with personal and family happiness. Higher education in the '80s has found it necessary to adjust their programs and services to meet the multifaceted needs of students and society.

61

The Purposes of Education: As Viewed by Educators and Students

Educators, and traditional (18–24 years of age) and nontraditional (over 24 years of age) students are voicing shared beliefs that learning to live and earning a living are compatible and not discrete goals. Elebash and Critchen (1983) said that liberal education transcends discipline boundaries: It is not the exclusive province of colleges of arts and sciences. In indicating the values for vocational preparation, they present three points for consideration: (1) Liberal education is still the foundation for all education; (2) Liberal education can and should be extended into the professional schools and colleges; and (3) The essence of liberal education is the creative participation of the student in the learning process. As a part of a project funded by the U.S. Department of Education and initiated by the Fund for the Improvement of Post-Secondary Education (1979) the Commission National Project IV discussed the need for education to be liberating. This concept means active participation of teachers and students in the process of learning. Riesman (1980) has pointed out the danger of allowing students to view themselves as passive consumers rather than active producers of their own education. The Commission (1979) elaborated three specific aspects of a "liberating" education: (1) It leads students to a broad critical awareness; (2) It helps students apply what they learn to everyday life; and (3) It increases a student's sense of power.

Education is defined to embrace not only the formal academic curricula, classes, and laboratories but also those influences upon students stemming from association with peers and faculty members and from the many and varied experiences of campus life. Colleges and universities are seen as environments exerting influence in many ways and not merely as formal academic programs having only intellectual goals. College education has come to be known as the key to success, and consequently the goal of every average or above average high school student and his/her family.

According to Bowen (1977), education should be directed toward three principles: the growth of the whole person, uniqueness of individuals, and accessibility to persons of a broad range of abilities, circumstances, and ages. Students should be helped to develop as a person through three types of learning: cognitive learning to expand their knowledge and intellectual powers, affective learning to enhance their moral, religious, and emotional interests and sensibilities, and practical competence by improving their performance in citizenship, work, family life, health, and other practical affairs (Organization for Economic Cooperation and Development, 1973; Bailey, 1976). An earlier study by Meyerson (1974) indicated a fusion of liberal learning and professional education could be achieved by restoring the ideas of vocation and service to their central place in the hierarchy of educational values. Liberal learning, he observed, ought not exist in isolation, divorced from "the instruments, the utilitarian, the professional" (p. 174). Nor should professional education be concerned primarily with preparation for a career in a narrow sense. They rather need to be synthesized, cross-fertilized, and animated by the notion of service. This requires, first of all, "interaction," the cultivation of "creative tension between the concrete and the theoretical, the rationalistic and the empirical" (p. 175). Bowen (1977) also observed that through college education people contribute new ideas for improvement of technology and organizational design applicable to business, government, and other institutions and the education of professional persons directly improves social conditions. Koe (1985) reported that many higher education institutions have developed special programs to meet current employment needs. These programs frequently include internship and field experiences. Providing students with relevant classroom and field experiences plus the knowledge of how to market these experiences effectively can help some graduates successfully locate employment. Happily employed graduates can, in a multitude of ways, directly and indirectly improve the quality of a college or university.

The Impact of Baccalaureate Degrees

Astin (1977) and Ochsner (1979) found self-satisfaction, personal growth prevailing themes in the lives of the traditional-aged graduates. There was widespread job satisfaction and little underemployment. The many job-related benefits reaffirmed the value of a college education in the world of work. Before the Mishler Study, the study of adults had been limited to adults who had graduated from special (nontraditional) B.A. programs for adults. The largest of these studies was by Sosdian and Sharp (1978) who studied the external degree as a credential. In 1983, Mishler conducted a follow-up study of adult graduates (age 25 or more at entry level) and the perceived effects of baccalaureate degrees in their lives three to five years after graduation. Mishler's research yielded prioritized themes in the lives of the graduates. The "comments" section of the questionnaire spoke to gains in the areas of life and learning as a result of the college experience. One hundred fifty people out of a total of two hundred fifty-four used the "Comments" section to express their responses. The enjoyment of learning was described as the ability to appreciate the fine arts, to think analytically, write and speak effectively, and to develop tools to better understand self and life. These tools were described as leading to achievement and self-satisfaction. The enjoyment of life was further enhanced by a sense of identity, satisfaction, achievement, and accomplishment realized through full-time employment, financial independence, increased responsibility, security, and status following graduation. In general the outcomes experienced by adults who got their degree did not seem much different from their younger counterparts' experience.

The following quote captures the students' perceptions of the value of education:

> You become more active, more aware of people. You can change. You become sensitive and objective. You can take a stand. You become positive about life. If something goes wrong, you don't blame yourself (Gamson, Zelda & Associates, 1984, p. XI).

Earning a Living: Past and Current Perspectives

Work means different things to different people: social recognition, self-respect, sense of worth, social opportunity, social participation, service to mankind or community, enjoyment of a particular activity, security of a certain kind of lifestyle, creative self-expression, and so forth. Moreover, personality characteristics such as the needs for achievement, security and autonomy, and conformity, which are formulated in childhood affect the meaning of work (Okun, 1984).

Before the late 1960s, American society assumed that college graduates would look for occupational niches that gave meaning and importance to their lives. Adults had the option to choose which part of the country to settle in, which particular job (of many) to take, and which kind of lifestyle to seek. A myriad of options appeared as new fields opened up, and new opportunities seemed endless. Adults considered work as the most important aspect of life, and deemed family and individual sacrifices necessary in the pursuit of work. This meaning of work changed radically during the counter-cultural revolution of the 1960s as values were reassessed and reformulated. The emphasis was on the "socially useful" aspect of work, the aspect of doing something that contributed simultaneously to one's self-worth and to society (Okun, 1984).

The 1970s saw a proliferation of human service type occupations. In addition, a growing number of young people adopted trades and artistic endeavors, they were interested in creative self-expression more than in making money. They scorned upward mobility. For many, work became a lower priority, a means to an end, a way of supporting a particular lifestyle or avocation. People no longer felt the push to translate their interests into a career. This new attitude was reflected in more frequent job changes and more persistent demands by workers for modifications in working conditions and job opportunities. These latitudes and freedoms exist only in an expanding economy (Okun, 1984).

With the 1980s some changes began. The effects of a reduced birthrate began to show up in reduced enrollments. Whereas college graduates used to have their choice of jobs, they were now fortunate simply to find a job even remotely related to their major field of study. Those high school graduates who went to college began to demand that their training have relevance to career development. While today's young adults have more choices than their counterparts of a generation ago, many options have disappeared. As colleges and universities began to compete for a rapidly dwindling student body and as inflation began to spread, attitudes and demands regarding education and training changed.

As more and more women enter the work force in an effort to earn a living and to help support the family, they have changed the previous goals of the college coed. They no longer are interested in a stepping-stone job or a preparation to fall back on as a hedge for the future. Today's women have raised their sights to management or professional careers as a major goal and have expanded out of the "traditional" female roles (Okun, 1984).

We have considered the outcomes of higher education as changes in students during the college years and later. We have shown that college students, as individuals, are changed in knowledge, emotional and moral development and practical competence. The influence of higher education is not confined to its life-long impact on its students as individuals. It also has direct and indirect consequences for society at large.

Through the influence of college educated people, various elements of the academic ethos may be transmitted to the general public. Human values may become more pervasive, the concept of social responsibility may gain influence, prejudice and discrimination among persons may be lessened, concern for conservation of natural resources and the preservation of the environment may be increased (Ashby, 1976).

Society cannot delay in providing the education for the worker and student of tomorrow. A dynamic education needs to be developed to prepare the individual for living. Efforts expended in education and in earning should bring growth and happiness. Neither should become a mechanical routine result of technology. Both endeavors should add to—not detract from—the development of the personality. As Alexander Heard (1973) has remarked:

> Our largest common goal in higher education is to create and stimulate the kind of learning that breeds strength and humor and hope within a person, and that helps build a society outside self that stirs pride and commands affection. (p. 16)

References

Ashby, E. (1976, June 23). A case for more mass education. *London Times, Higher Education Supplement*, p. 4–5.

Astin, A. W. (1977). *Four critical years: Effects of college on beliefs, attitudes and knowledge*. San Francisco: Jossey-Bass Publishers.

Bailey, S. K. (1976). *The purposes of education*. Bloomington, IN: Foundation Monograph Series, Phi Delta Kappa.

Bowen, H. R. (1977). *Investment in learning—The individual and social value of American higher education*. San Francisco: Jossey-Bass Publishers, 33–39.

Elebash, C. C. & Critchen, B. W. (1983). Liberal education and business education: Are they mutually exclusive? *Journal of Business Education*, *58*(4), 151–153.

Gamson, Zelda F. & Associates (1984). *Liberating education*. San Francisco: Jossey-Bass Publishers, xi-xv.

Heard, A. (1974, Spring). The consequences of knowing. *Educational Record*, 16–17.

Koe, F. T. (1985, Winter). The marketability of graduates: Why colleges should care. *Journal of College Placement*, 15–16.

Meyerson, M. (1974, Fall). Civilizing education: Uniting liberal and professional learning. *Daedalus*, 173–179.

Mishler, C. J. (1983). Adults' perceptions of the benefits of a college degree.

Research in Higher Education, Agathon Press, Inc., Vol. 19, No. 2, 213–220.

Ochsner, N. L. & Solomon, L. C. (1979). *College education and employment: The recent graduates*. Bethlehem, PA: CPC Foundation.

Okun, B. F. (1984). *Working with adults: Individual, family, and career development*. Monterey, CA: Brooks/Cole Publishing Company, 120–126.

Organization for Economic Cooperation and Development (OECD). (1972). *Alternative educational futures in the United States and in Europe*. Paris: OECD.

Riesman, David (1980). *On higher education*. San Francisco: Jossey-Bass Publishers.

Sosdian, C. B. & Sharp, L. M. (1978). *The external degree as a credential: Graduates' experiences in employment and further study*. Washington, DC: National Institute of Education.

The Undergraduate Experience and Community Service: Education as Transformation

Michael P. Roche

The Problem

One of the most important issues facing contemporary American society is the role of higher education as a force for public responsibility. According to Frank Newman (1986), president of the Education Commission of the States and founder of Campus Compact: The Project for Public and Community Service, two questions arise when confronting this issue:

> Are universities effective in accomplishing their original purpose—namely, the preparation of young people for civic responsibility? And where within the university does responsibility lie for addressing this key issue? (p. 5)

In Newman's view, the answer to the first question is "no" and to the second question, "the responsibility lies with all of us" (p. 5).

Ernest Boyer begins one of the later chapters in his recent book, *Colleges: The Undergraduate Experience in America* (1987), by recounting an interview conducted as part of his Carnegie Foundation study. A professor in his early forties was asked about the difference between his generation and the present one. He responded:

I'm blue jeans and they're suits and ties. We joke that many of the students dress better than the professors. I ask them why they're in college and they say, "to get a job." All they think about is money, money, money. They don't have any social responsibility. That bothers me. There's all this emphasis on having careers (p. 213).

It appears to many that students today are far more interested in themselves than in their civic responsibilities. Richard Lyman, president of the Rockefeller Foundation and former president of Stanford University, recently declared that there is a great challenge awaiting American universities: how to convert "egocentric, pleasure-seeking, and upwardly mobile students into models of Jeffersonian civic-mindedness" (Newman, 1986, p. 5). Each of these commentators overstates the "me generation" accusation so often leveled against the students of today—but there is a problem. "Students are torn by ambiguous feelings—idealism on the one hand, and, on the other, the temptation to pursue narrow career interests that would leave them politically and socially disengaged. They are struggling to establish themselves, reaching for identity and meaning" (Boyer, 1987, p. 213). The remainder of this paper will explore how the academy might better serve its students in their quest for identity and meaning while at the same time encouraging them to place their lives in the larger context of community.

Urging Students to Serve

Hidden just beneath the surface of the self-preoccupation from which many undergraduates appear to be suffering lies an irrepressible need to serve. They are seeking outside confirmation of the desire for unity and community that is hidden within their inner selves. Boyer (1987) and others agree that students today "may be uncertain about where to apply their good intentions, but many want—and have begun—to escape a preoccupation with self" (p. 213). The academy needs to offer undergraduates more opportunities to apply their good intentions.

If education is to be the most certain and the most legitimate engine of government, then students must be given opportunities to develop skills, beliefs, and confidence that will enable them to be the committed compassionate citizens upon which this world depends. They need experiences that reinforce this ability to work together. The academic world is too focused on individual effort (Newman, 1986, p. 5).

Citizenship, like other attributes, can be habit-forming, and habits formed during one's higher education can be enduring. A recent college graduate put it well: "Compassion, like any other virtue or vice, grows with regular exercise. And in a country where most of the people live in comfort—and a world where we are, by all comparison, rich—compassion counts. At the least, people will *think,* and thinking is the great enemy of smugness and self-satisfaction" (Newman, 1986, p. 5). Frank Newman (1986) and other respected commentators recommend that, in addition to coursework that emphasizes civic responsibility, every student must participate in community service.

> One cannot learn to be responsible by listening to a lecture about responsibility. One cannot learn to be creative by listening to a lecture about someone who was creative before us. The only way to fully understand the complexity of our world and each person's role in it is to practice involvement in the process of solving larger issues (p. 5).

It is worth noting that there are several major national coalitions that have recently been formed to encourage and coordinate service opportunities for undergraduates. Boyer (1987) has identified the Campus Outreach Opportunity League, the Overseas Development Network, and the Project for Public and Community Service (p. 214). Frank Newman is the founder of the Project for Public and Community Service. Outside of these nationally organized programs, evidence of the spirit of service can be found in a recent report by the Carnegie Foundation for the Advancement of Teaching. A national survey of undergraduates revealed that nearly one-half of those questioned participated in some kind of service activity during their college years, ranging from work with the elderly, homeless, incarcerated, ill or disabled to election campaigns, environmental projects, fund raising drives, and the like (Boyer, 1987, p. 214). Colleges presently do too little to acknowledge and encourage this spirit.

Intercultural Experience and the Spirit of Community

Thus far it has been argued that one of the great deficiencies of the undergraduate experience today is that it focuses much too exclusively on individual effort and not enough on the spirit of community. Works of service have been suggested as one means of helping students place their lives in the broad context of community. Another possibility with very great potential involves some sort of intercultural experience for undergraduates. Encounters with peoples and perspectives from other lands and cultures can foster the development of a more comprehensive identity—an identity not of interests but of being. David Burrell (1986) justifies and describes the powerful nature of such experiences as follows:

> The need for some form of displacement, for faculty as well as for students, is to allow them a vantage point from which to put their world in its place; to recognize, in short, the context in which one truly lives, and of which one can remain quite unconscious. This is all the more true because we normally presume ourselves to be at the center of a universe and hence naturally relegate everyone and everything else to the periphery. The presumption, moreover, leaves us little imagination for alternatives, and hence without a coherent context ourselves. One has only to compare the proportion of global to local news in an ordinary American newspaper with dailies anywhere else in the world, or to consider the average English-speaking person's linguistic ineptitude in order to realize how *deprived* an upbringing in a dominant society can be. As shocking as it is when put that way, the shock can be a salutary one if it manages to fix attention on what members of the dominant society are missing (p. 28).

In 1983, fewer than 1 percent of the 5.7 million students enrolled in undergraduate programs in the United States participated in college sponsored overseas study (Boyer, 1987, pp. 228–229). These figures reveal something about the extent to which we are overlooking opportunities to help students see beyond themselves and better appreciate the interdependent nature of our world. More must be done. "It may be that out of our relationship with peoples who belong to other cultures, we may yet find a way to survive" (Norton, 1984, p. 104).

Service as a Curriculum of Unity

Service activities and intercultural programs have at least one very important characteristic in common—they are both grounded in experience. Students cannot read or study communal values into positions of prominence in their lives. Neither can teachers preach such values into positions of significance. In order for a value to be internalized, it must be established in a person's life. Values are established in life through living them—through action. A recent report of the Potomac Institute (1979) concludes: "To make a healthy transition to adulthood, to work out an identity that includes a sense of citizenship, and to affirm positive social values, young people need to become actively involved in the lives of others and in the needs of society" (Boyer, 1986, p. 217). Formal education itself cannot adequately address this need and, although intercultural experiences can be very influential, they are presently available only to a relatively few students. The academy can do better, but due to the practical difficulties involved in the organization and funding of intercultural programs, most undergraduates will not be fortunate enough to participate in such an experience. Opportunities for service, on the other hand, can be made available to everyone.

Formal education is consumed with the task of providing students with new skills and information. Students also need help in growing into the fullness of their lives. Hearts as well as heads must be "educated" and works of service may offer the most effective curriculum available. Students consistently report that service activities have operated as unique and sometimes transformative paths to greater self-awareness and an appreciation that each self is connected to all others. In a recent Georgetown University report (1985), a student characterized his service experience as follows:

> When you begin doing service, you're doing it in a sort of subject-object relationship . . . you're still a Georgetown student and they're only people in the city. But after you stop to reflect on it, you find that there's not that significant a difference between you and that person, and you share more as human beings than you don't share. When you realize that, I think that's where the real learning begins. When you feel that he or she is a human being, you realize that you share something more important than your differences (p. 18).

Another student commented that service work can be "the first step in deciding how to live your life" (Georgetown University, 1985, p. 11). In his report, Boyer (1987) quotes a student who, when asked about his volunteer work with a Special Olympics Program, said: "I need this kind of extracurricular activity to balance my life. It's a way for me to give back a little of what I've been blessed with. I think there's a new trend in my generation—it's a loving generation" (p. 216). Finally, after participating in a course with a heavy service component, a University of South Dakota student reflected as follows:

> At times before, I'd been so angry with this world's injustices and distractions that I began to grow cold. Though I was confident in my

worldview, there was something missing. Within the last semester, I've rediscovered that "something"—the compassion I'd lost somewhere along the way. I've come to realize that love, above all else, is what this world needs. I knew that once, but I think I lost it for awhile. Maybe I had to go through that time. I guess it was the way it should be. Awareness itself is such a fine edge to rest your soul upon. You must *be* love (Henderson, 1987).

Perhaps the essence of these student commentaries shines through in the following excerpt from a recent book of readings on service.

When we see that service is not a one-way street, we find that those we are helping give us a continuous stream of clues to help us escape the prison of our self-image. More than simply letting us know what might be working or not, they help us when they question our very models of ourselves. . . .

The struggles of those we are helping confront us with life at its purest. Their suffering strips away guile and leaves what is real and essential. The deepest human qualities come forth: openness, yearning, patience, courage, forbearance, faith, humor, living truth, living spirit. Moved and touched by these qualities, we've no choice but to acknowledge and reaffirm our humanity (Dass, 1985, p. 142).

At this point, it is important to mention that it is not students alone who have an obligation to serve. It is hypocritical and perhaps even counterproductive for teachers to profess the positive value of community if they do not live it themselves. If teachers seldom practice involvement, is it so surprising that students follow suit? Students must be exposed to mentors who learn, not so they can accumulate knowledge as another prized possession, but so that they may devote their learning to the service of the world. Douglas Amy (1983) suggests that perhaps we only truly "teach" in those rare moments when we are able to embody our espoused values through the examples of our lives. "Only then do we make that crucial transition from simply transferring bits of abstract knowledge to actually touching the lives of our students" (p. 6). Erich Fromm (1956) probably offered the best description of this process and its ramifications in his classic, *The Art of Loving*:

While we teach knowledge, we are losing that teaching which is the most important one for human development: the teaching which can only be given by the simple presence of a mature, loving person. In previous epochs of our own culture, or in China or India, the man most highly valued was the person with outstanding spiritual qualities. Even the teacher was not only, or even primarily, a source of information, but his function was to convey certain human attitudes. In contemporary capitalist society—and the same holds true for Russian Communism—the men suggested for admiration and emulation are everything but bearers of significant spiritual qualities. . . . If the coming generations will not see these traits anymore, a five-thousand-year-old culture will break down, even if its knowledge is transmitted and further developed (pp. 98–99).

Conclusion

In the Epilogue to his report, Ernest Boyer contends that a good college is one that affirms that service to others is a central part of education. In order to assist each institution in assessing the character and depth of its commitment, Boyer (1987) poses the following questions:

Are students encouraged to participate in voluntary service? Does the college offer the option of deferring admission to students who devote a year to service before coming to campus? Are the service prospects drawn into the larger educational purposes, helping students to see that they are not only autonomous individuals but also members of an international community? And does the faculty set an example and give leadership to service? (p. 294)

If each of these questions can be answered affirmatively, then the academy is offering profound service to itself and its students as we all grapple with a much more ancient inquiry: "Who is thy neighbor?"

References

Amy, D. (1983, Winter). Teaching the moral analysis of policy issues. *News for Teachers of Political Science*, pp. 1, 4–6.

Boyer, E. (1987). *College: The undergraduate experience in America*. New York: Harper and Row.

Burrell, D. (1986). Philosophy. In D. Johnson (Ed.), *Justice and peace education*. Maryknoll, NY: Orbis.

Dass, R. & Gorman, P. (1985). *How can I help? Stories and reflections on service*. New York: Alfred A. Knopf.

Educating the heart. (1985). *Georgetown University Annual Report*, pp. 11–18.

Fromm, E. (1956). *The art of loving*. New York: Harper and Row.

Henderson, D. (1987, Spring). Campus compact: Urging students to serve. *The Wingspread Journal*, p. 5.

Norton, J. (1984). *South Asia*. Guilford, CT: Dushkin.

The Potomac Institute. (1979, January). *Youth and the needs of the nation*. (Report of the Committee for the Study of National Service.) Washington, DC: Author.

Part II: Curriculum

Closely related to the *Mission* of undergraduate education is the *Curriculum*. The curriculum involves the subject-matter, or knowledge, to be learned by the student and is often organized by academic discipline. This section addresses issues related to four important disciplines: history, science, mathematics, and sport. What content is to be included within the subject-matter area and some of the problems in learning that subject-matter are explored.

Stephen R. Ward summarizes various views on critical thinking and its relationship to undergraduate education. He describes how the historical process may be used to foster critical thinking on the part of students. Ways of including critical thinking in the curriculum should utilize history as history offers students unique opportunities for the evaluation of information. Teachers need to become more knowledgeable about the basic disciplines they teach in order to teach their students to think critically.

Paul B. Otto raises various hypotheses for examining the science undergraduate curriculum. Otto believes introspection as to the purpose of science in colleges and universities is needed. He raises the question, "Should we continue to concentrate on the elite . . . or consider scientific literacy for all citizens?" Although not advocating that integrated science courses replace single disciplinary courses, he suggests, among other recommendations, that integrated science courses may meet the needs of certain groups of students. He believes that consideration should be given, not only to a study of what should be taught in undergraduate science, but to how science should be taught. Such efforts would require the cooperation and efforts of many departments, schools, and colleges.

The learning of mathematics is important to the personal growth and careers of undergraduate students. Nevertheless, many students avoid taking mathematics courses because of their concerns that they will not do well. Cleland V. Cook's paper deals with the topic of "coping with math anxiety." He starts out his paper with a summary of anxiety in general and mathematics anxiety in particular. Then he reviews research and procedures for reducing mathematics anxiety. Finally, he addresses what universities can do. Preventive measures and suggestions for teaching mathematics are among the measures that he advocates.

In spite of negative publicity, each year sees a renewed interest in sports in American colleges and universities. Mary S. Mock focuses on the positive nature of sport and emphasizes the value of sport in collegiate communities. She discusses three major objectives of sport as related to morality, beauty, and the common good. In so doing, she reveals a number of intangible values associated with university athletic programs that promote learning throughout life.

Critical Thinking and the Historical Process

Stephen R. Ward

A developing debate has emerged in American education in the 1980s on the issue of critical thinking and whether or not it is being effectively taught in classrooms at every level. Concern is expressed as we have moved further into a highly technical culture of portable calculators, information banks easily accessible through computers, and other paraphernalia that produce quick answers. Our students, and indeed their instructors, have become less critical about how information is produced. Worse still, they rarely question its authenticity or reliability. As with so many fears that grip our society (Sputnik, Johnny can't read, et al.), we turn to the educational system for salvation, and simultaneously we criticize it for a deficiency probably not entirely of its own making.

This essay will present a brief summary of views on critical thinking and its place in education. It will also suggest how the discipline of history, or rather the historical process, may be used to instruct students in critical thinking. Proposals to revitalize critical thinking in the curriculum should include history; for it is a subject that offers students unique opportunities to evaluate information.

Although one may discover several definitions of critical thinking and how it might be taught in secondary and collegiate education, one explanation proposes that,

Instruction in critical thinking be designed to achieve understanding of the relationship of language to logic, leading to the ability to analyze, criticize, and advocate ideas, to reason inductively and deductively, and to reach factual or judgmental conclusions based on sound inferences drawn from unambiguous statements of knowledge and belief (Benderson, 1984, p. 4).

Therefore, critical thinking is the act of being insightful, philosophical, analytical; and it requires some specialized knowledge of a subject. In his work, *Critical Thinking and Education*, John McPeck defines it as "reflective scepticism," or the act of questioning and evaluating arguments from a position of intelligent inquiry (McPeck, 1981, p. 7). His brief and workable definition will be referred to throughout this essay.

Teachers of every discipline should know how critical thinking can be employed in their classrooms. Most secondary and collegiate instructors would claim that they teach it continually. Almost by definition, teaching is the process of evaluating information and questioning its authenticity. Nevertheless, this assertion has been challenged by those who claim that the back-to-basics movement of the past decade has brought about the decline of critical thinking (Benderson, 1984, p. 2). Critics complain that when the disciplines reasserted themselves in the 1970s, this forced students back into rote memory activities that curtailed their capacities to analyze. Some reports concluded that

> While data indicate that basic reading, writing, math and science skills have improved during the past decade, consistent declines have been measured in students' abilities to interpret reading passages, classify and solve math problems, marshal arguments in support of theses, and evaluate scientific data (Benderson, 1984, p. 2).

But is the back-to-basics movement to blame? If the allegation that critical thinking has declined among current school-aged children is correct, then the blame would seem to rest with the faddish educational practices of the 1960s and 1970s. For, if the pre-1960s students were reasonably good critical thinkers (a premise that needs to be accepted in order to be pre-disposed to accept the notion that a crisis now exists), then a return to similar forms of education, or back-to-basics, will probably reverse the trend.

Perhaps those who study such patterns should investigate more carefully the growth of vocational education and pre-professional programs at the high school and collegiate levels. At the college level, newer disciplines, particularly those directed at preparing students for particular occupations, are often more fact-oriented than older disciplines. These vocational disciplines have been required to meet accreditation standards, which mean an accumulation of restricted credit hours and an emphasis upon an exit examination in order to be certified. More established disciplines have not experienced the compulsion to train students, but rather to educate them. As vocationally-oriented students have entered employment, however, there has been a complaint from the private and public sectors that students cannot think and do independent work. Even graduate schools are making different choices: medical schools looking for humanities majors and law schools searching for good minds, regardless of major. Business is crying out for independent and creative thinkers; and the communication industry is seeking educable, trainable graduates with backgrounds in literature, history, economics, and politics. One may speculate that a source of consternation about the lack of critical thinking may come from the consumers, rather than from the producers.

If there is a common thread in this discussion, it is that critical thinking needs to be taught in every subject, in old and new disciplines, and at every level. Perhaps now that secondary education is returning to fuller requirements in science, mathematics, languages, grammar, literature, and disciplinary social sciences (rather than social studies), we will witness a marked improvement in scores on national tests and performance on the job.

Regardless of where the fault lies, there remains the matter of doing a better job of teaching critical thinking. How can it be accomplished best and by whom? Are certain disciplines more applicable to teaching critical thinking than others? Some authorities believe that it belongs only in higher education and should be taught by philosophy and psychology instructors. Others encourage teaching critical thinking to elementary students and that its success may only be limited by the teaching and thinking ability of individual instructors.

McPeck maintains that every discipline ought to be responsible for teaching critical thinking because one cannot think critically without first knowing something about a subject (1981, p. 13). Some do not trust disciplinary teachers with this important task, however. They assert that these discipline-oriented specialists are so content-directed that they compromise process in their classrooms.

This writer agrees with McPeck that students should be taught critical thinking in every discipline. It also can be taught early on in our educational system as such programs as National Science Fair, Future Problem-Solving, Olympics of the Mind, and National History

Day are proving. Sophistication in a field cannot be expected from younger students, but most certainly the process of thinking through problems in many disciplines, regardless of the level, can be a useful exercise. Teachers and students can develop critical thinking skills in a particular subject if they first learn the process of thinking it through. The remainder of this essay will be devoted to discovering the elements that make up one of the traditional disciplines, history, and how important critical thinking is to the historical process.

History offers students many opportunities to develop their critical thinking skills. First, it is the study of human society from several points of view, or interpretation. It is sometimes erroneously spoken of in terms "history tells us," but in fact, it is what historians have written. There is no Buddha-like figure intoning history in a cave somewhere. Therefore, all of history is subject to reflective skepticism. Interpretations develop from the discovery of new sources or often from differing attitudes that reflect contemporary society. The student of history therefore develops a relativistic approach; and again, if critical thinking is defined as being reflectively skeptical, then an appreciation of alternative viewpoints is an important asset. Historians do not advocate nihilism as much as they insist upon a questioning posture. Second, history is the study of all society—politics, economics, culture, etc. This feature will be explored further, but no other discipline views humankind as broadly or insists that its students take a universalist approach when searching for answers. Third, it emphasizes causation or understanding and explaining why and how things happen. Who, what, and when are also important, but only as weigh stations on the trek to why and how. Finally, it is a plain-speaking subject relatively unencumbered by jargon, symbolism, and other language impediments. Because of its clarity, students are not obliged to memorize a glossary of disciplinary terminology that often becomes a barrier to learning a subject.

Sometimes these advantages are overlooked by teachers of history themselves. They do not use the subject as a vehicle to convey ideas, concepts, controversies, and interpretative debate—all essential ingredients for critical thinking. One reason is that not all college history majors and future teachers take a solid historiography course that explores aspects of the discipline's critical thinking in such works as Allen Nevins' *Gateway to History*, Herbert Butterfield's *The Whig Interpretation of History*, Louis Gottschalk's *Generalization in the Writing of History*, and David Hackett Fischer's *Historians' Fallacies, Toward a Logic of Historical Thought*. Often secondary history teachers do not major in the field and thereby avoid such courses as historiography, a history of historical inquiry, and/or the philosophy of history that help to explain the complexities of analysis and encourage students to teach history more thoughtfully and provocatively. Perhaps their exposure to history has been a pedestrian stroll from one event to another, interspersed with a humorous anecdote or an interesting sidelight. Some teachers never learn to be insightful and critical about their own subject. Consequently, students may come to enjoy history for its own sake, but may not realize or appreciate how useful and important it can be in their total education. A recent poll of high school student leaders revealed that history ranked third among the most popular subjects (behind English and Math), but a very distant fourth in terms of educational importance (behind English, Math, and Science) (Ordovensky, 1985). Perhaps if they were shown how practical and analytical history can be, their level of appreciation for it would rise.

In order for students to develop an approach to critical thinking they must first understand its component parts. Below is a taxonomy that can be taught to students in a beginning Western Civilization or European history course.

Topical Areas	**Civilizations**
Political	Egyptian
Social	Mesopotamian
Economic	Hebrew
Philosophical	Persian
Religious	Greek
Military	Macedonian
Artistic	Roman
Legal	etc.
Scientific	
Intellectual/Cultural	

The column on the left represents virtually all of the topics covered, to a greater or lesser extent, in a typical course. The course outline would generally follow civilization by civilization, as depicted in the right column, in which any discussion of each would touch on some or all of the categories on the left. History instructors think in terms of topical analysis and often organize their notes in this manner. Politics, economics, society, and the rest are terms mentioned repeatedly in texts and monographs. Nevertheless, in twenty years of college teaching, this writer is amazed how uninformed students are about the composition of history. Therefore, we cannot expect to introduce critical thinking without informing our students how to think history. They may be full of information of what, who, when, and how, but they cannot analyze information without understanding the taxonomy.

Critical thinking requires a starting point—a question posed to begin a process. The instructor not only wants to find out what the students know, but also how well they can mobilize information to respond to a proposition or premise. There are three general categories of historical questions: Cause/Effect, Comparison, and Development. All historical questions ask for probabilities in one form or another, but these three categories are typical and ask the students to produce plausible answers. If one takes a beginning Western Civilization course, for example, the following questions might be asked:

1. What caused the growth of the city-state system in Greece? (Cause/Effect)
2. Compare the growth of city-states in Egypt and Greece. (Comparison or Compare/Contrast)
3. Trace the rise and fall of the Greek city-states. (Development)

All of the above questions are purposely simplistic to illustrate that, although there are different categories of questions, the themes are similar as is the information to be supplied in answering all three. For too many entering college freshmen, the above examples represent a dramatic departure from previous educational experiences and they are often terrified. But here they are asked to carry out a task defined earlier in critical thinking, that is, "to reach factual and judgmental conclusions based on sound inferences drawn from unambiguous statements of knowledge and belief."

It is here that the instructor needs to show students how information can be mobilized and how critical thinking can be used. One can certainly suggest reviewing notes and reading until the information is etched in their brains—and that works for many. Or they can restructure their notes and reading in order to recall usable information in an organized fashion as follows:

! Pol. ! Econ. ! Soc. ! Phil. ! Rel. ! Mil. ! Art. ! Legal ! Scien. ! Int/Cul. !
 !   !   !   !   !   !   !   !   !   !   !

Using these categories, the student would review each civilization separately, annotating briefly events, people, issues, ideas, and other pertinent information as it appears. He might take economics and list every economic matter that is mentioned. Not only is the student re-writing his notes and reading in this format, but he is also engaged in two other important functions—actively studying through writing things out and searching out the components that make up history. Perhaps of greatest benefit, the student is provided with a check-off list for organizing and answering any question posed. Regardless of how the essay is presented, the same type of information will be needed—political causes, economic causes, and so on. And thus we have "factual and judgmental conclusions drawn from unambiguous statements of knowledge and belief." Further, the student has the opportunity to develop his own answer not based upon opinion but rather with support provided through examples and illustrations gleaned from the notes and reading.

Some instructors believe that the students should receive the precise information and then be asked the question that properly fits the answer. Causes and effects will be outlined, discussed, and evaluated so that students may memorize them in preparation for an examination. This method certainly teaches causation and interpretation, but it does not produce critical thinking or problem-solving techniques that can be learned in history. Rather, it would seem to be more valuable to impose upon the student the responsibility for learning how histori-cal information is used—critically and creatively.

There are several examples of how information might be annotated in the above categories, but perhaps one will suffice. Consider the issue of irrigation in ancient Egypt. One may first decide that it belongs in the economic category, reasoning that irrigation is associated with farming, the production of goods, and hence, an economic matter. Further reflection, however, would suggest that it also belongs under politics because the government controlled irrigation, water rights, and land usage. So in preparation for an examination, the student would annotate irrigation in both places and be ready to use it if the appropri-ate question arises.

In a later period of European history, the same topics, with sub-division modifications, can be used. Modern countries will replace ancient civilizations.

Topical Areas	Countries
Political	France
(national, diplomatic, imperial)	Britain
Economic	Prussia (Germany)
Social	Russia (USSR)

Philosophical   Austria (Austria/Hungary)
Religious   Italy
Military   Spain
Legal   Greece
Scientific   etc.
Intellectual/Cultural

The categories of questions remain the same. Here, using the pre-First World War alliance system as a point of departure, one might ask the following questions:

1. The creation of Germany in 1871 brought about the alliance system. Why? (Cause/Effect)
2. Compare the alliance system that developed following the Congress of Vienna, 1815, with alliance system prior to the outbreak of the First World War. (Comparison)
3. How did the alliance system develop after the Franco-Prussian War of 1870–71? (Development)

The taxonomy can be easily modified. A national history (United States, France, et al.) would require only one entry in the right column and a topical history course (American Social, European Intellectual) might limit entries in both columns.

Once the techniques and processes by which history is thought out are understood, the next step is to apply critical thinking even beyond essays. An exercise might explore historical dilemmas, comparing viewpoints that differ in time and geography, or exploring influences of events and people in different cultures, but during the same time period. The prospects are endless. When students learn to mobilize information, apply that which is appropriate and excise that which is not, they are learning to think critically. Maturity of thought, organization of ideas, defense of judgments, and an awareness of the complexities of issues, all come into play. Further, the reasoning process must be developed in order to produce a defensible answer.

Historical writing also offers opportunities to explore critical thinking. Since Herodotus and Thucydides gave us their interpretations of the Greek wars, there has been constant disagreement from trivial events to sweeping generalizations. As one historian has noted, the middle class in history "has been found rising most remarkably in every period from the twelfth century to the twentieth . . ." (Fischer, 1970). Even an apparently straightforward matter such as the discovery of the new world offers an opportunity for questioning as Louis Gottschalk points out. In his essay on historiographical generalization, he wrote that,

A simple sentence like "Columbus discovered America on October 12, 1492" is loaded with comparative and general terms (of chronology, philology, exploration, geography, biography, etc.); only some of the difficulties are avoided by a less simple wording such as "On a day conveniently labeled 'October 12, 1492' a group of sailors captained by a man known in English as 'Christopher Columbus' landed on an island which was apparently the one now called 'Watling Island' " (Gottschalk, 1963, p. 116).

Even apparently uncomplicated issues and statements of fact may be reflected upon skeptically, as this illustration suggests. The lesson learned, among others, is not to accept all information as truth—or at least be prepared to test it.

Historical writing has also been manipulated throughout time, thus making it an interesting target for evaluating truth and fact. The further one explores it, the more one learns to be reflectively skeptical. For example, history has often been used as a patriotic device and thus documents the views people held at the time it was written. Historian Henry Steele Commager recounts a story about an offending passage contained in an American history text written by Andrew C. McLaughlin. Criticized by the Hearst newspapers and political elements in Chicago for a pro-British bias on the Battle of Bunker Hill, McLaughlin finally offered to change the sentence, "Three times the British returned courageously to the attack," to read "Three times the cowardly British returned to the attack" (Fitzgerald, 1979, p. 35). One difficulty in teaching American history at the elementary and secondary levels is that textbooks must come under the scrutiny of school boards, concerned citizen organizations, minority groups, religious sects, and other self-appointed watchdogs who demand truth in history—or rather history as they interpret it. If critical thinking is introduced with any kind of rigor at the elementary and secondary levels, then tolerance and good sense must prevail on both sides of the classroom door.

There are other impediments to teaching critical thinking beyond social and political pressures. The size of classes, for instance, often determines the amount and intensity of discussion. Larger classes prompt instructors to give more objective exams that can be graded by computer. Perhaps no format can accurately measure a student's ability to think critically, but most certainly the objective examination is least effective. Essays in which the student develops his position in a creative fashion and at some length are preferable. But essays take more time to read and evaluate, and an instuctor has less protection from the charge of subjectivity. Objective questions have right and wrong answers, and debate seldom arises from a test of fifty questions worth two points each. If a student misses seven, he receives an eighty-six. An essay examination of one hundred points might have two questions equally weighted. If the student received a forty and forty-six for a total of eighty-six points, the instructor is placed in a defensive position because he might need to justify why he awarded points in this manner or why he gave the grade equivalent of an A and B- on the two essays. The old argument that objective and essay examinations can be used interchangeably because there is a correlation in scores is not applicable here. Objective examinations cannot adequately measure analytical ability, organization of ideas, and comprehension of the inter-relationships of information.

Developing this point further, it is noteworthy that the perceived decline in critical thinking actually coincides with increased student activism, grade inflation, and a greater emphasis upon teacher accountability. The pressure to measure knowledge quantitatively rather than qualitatively is evident. Essay examinations, term papers, and other unpopular exercises that have been the staple of educational evaluation for centuries, received short shrift. It is more than coincidental that the back-to-basics movement and critical thinking discussion have emerged after the phase of student activism subsided in the late 1970s and early 1980s.

History's emphasis upon causation, its reliance on the use of several sources to produce a point of view that holds up under scrutiny, its systematic questioning through inductive and deductive reasoning, make it an excellent platform to teach students critical thinking. It has none of the jargon of its sister disciplines in the social sciences, and yet is an excellent training ground for mounting arguments, formulating ideas, and even waxing cynical on occasion. More than that, the process of dissecting history is more transferable than McPeck suggests. Its methodology can be used in other disciplines and, perhaps more important, it is an excellent device for using problem-solving techniques in all types of occupations. Learning to order things meaningfully either in temporal or topical fashion has many applications.

Understanding multiple causation is essential in all types of work, along with appreciating the notion that facts are debatable.

There is one more advantage to studying history and applying critical thinking to it. Its study will reveal that even the best plans, buttressed by the best verifiable information, circumscribed by the most cautious of conclusions, may still lead one to the wrong choice in any situation. At the moment of failure, the student of history is left to reflect on the subject's greatest legacy—perspective. Others, too, have failed and survived.

Those who have decried the diminution of critical thinking should look more carefully at what the basic disciplines such as history can offer. The back-to-basics movement and the return of core curriculum are not the cause for the decline of critical thinking but rather, as has been suggested here, these movements may well provide the best solutions. Basic disciplines can be reworked to do a better job of teaching critical thinking, but teachers need to become more astute about the disciplines they teach and how individual taxonomies can be used to achieve those goals. On this issue, as with so many other things we face, it is the old things that work rather better than expected—and so it is with history.

References

Benderson, A. (1984). *Critical thinking* (Focus 15). Princeton, NJ: Educational Testing Service.

Fischer, D. H. (1970). *Historians' fallacies, toward a logic of historical thought*. New York: Harper.

Fitzgerald, F. (1979). *America revised*. Boston: Little, Brown.

Gottschalk, L. (1963). Categories of historical generalization. In Louis Gottschalk (Ed.), *Generalization in writing history* (pp. 113–129). Chicago and London: University of Chicago Press.

McPeck, J. (1981). *Critical thinking and education*. New York: St. Martins.

Ordovensky, P. (1985, September 7). Students give schools B-, teachers a C. *Argus Leader*, Sioux Falls, S.D.

What Science Should Be Taught

Paul B. Otto

It would seem a bit presumptuous to provide a catalogue of what science should be taught to undergraduate post-secondary school students. Perhaps a more plausible stance is to encourage examination. There is a danger perhaps in one being too specific. We live in a world of constant change where perhaps the only certainty is uncertainty. New discoveries and explorations become everyday occurrences in the media. The effects of these developments in science and technology now have implications for the very sanctums of our traditions, mores and religious convictions. Such decisions as who should live, who should die, who should be born and what quality of life should be maintained all can be controlled to considerable degree by science and technology. Therefore, the professional training in the science/technology professions as well as that of the nonscience majors should reflect the best interests of society.

Higher education during colonial times had a commonality of conviction, purpose and curriculum. The principal purpose was to educate citizens in the professions, specifically law and the clergy. Science was, typically, part of the curriculum in the form of natural philosophy (physical science). The emphasis was significantly on "education" rather than "training" (Fischer, 1975).

In contrast, the modern colleges and universities have a variety of purposes. Prior to the industrial revolution, technology tended to develop outside of the university. Theories followed technological development. Today institutions of higher education are involved heavily in original research. The colleges and universities have had considerable influence upon society, specifically in the area of science and technology. Society and its changes conversely have had considerable influence on higher education and the types of research conducted. Vocational emphasis is a large component of the present-day college and university curriculum. Institutions of higher learning are the principal training institutions for the science and engineering professions. Attesting to the success of the colleges and universities in producing quality scientists and engineers is the fact that since World War II, 51 percent of the Nobel Prizes outside of economics and peace prizes have been won by American scientists and engineers (NSF & DOE, 1980).

The primary goal of science departments during the growth period following World War II was to prepare people for graduate school. In spite of this, more students graduated with bachelors degrees in science and mathematics than entered graduate study or the professions. This trend continues even though present enrollments are declining (NSF & DOE, 1980).

Eighty-five percent of the students in United States colleges and universities graduated in 1981 with bachelors degrees outside of biology, physical science and engineering (Grant & Snyder, 1983). It is not uncommon for these "nonscience" majors to seek a background in science. Some recognize the value of a science background in dealing with the everyday activities in the nonscience professions such as law or business. Others are aware that employers value a diverse background in their employees. Still others may seek a broad liberal background to better function as an educated member of society. Whatever the reasons, these people are not interested in a rigorous science course designed for research scientists and often lack the prerequisite mathematical background.

Paul DeHart Hurd (1984) urges a reconceptualization of the very meaning of an education in the sciences by bringing it into synchronization with how science and technology relate to human affairs, social progress and the culture as a whole. He argues that concerns about science education are really not school-related, but are the result of "changes in the social framework in which the sciences and technology are imbedded, changes in the relation of science and technology to each other, and the desire of people for a higher quality of life" (p. 3). Hurd concludes that science teaching today does not meet the "intellectual and knowledge demands of a science/technology oriented society."

In a recent report, the National Science Board of the National Science Foundation recognized science and technology as interrelated endeavors which have had a strong influence on our society and will continue to do so. Complex social issues resulting from employing science to solve practical problems must be "intelligently" addressed by all citizens (NSF, 1983).

The National Science Teachers Association position statement in respect to science, technology, and society advocates the necessity of persons having a good background in science and technology in relation to the problems we face today (NSTA, 1982). Declaring a crisis in science education, five science-technology-society problem areas were identified which require immediate attention:

- understanding of science and technology are central to our personal and national welfare, yet public appreciation of science education has declined;
- increasing number of individual and societal problems which have an impact on the quality of life are related to science-generated technology;
- as the impact of science and technology on society has increased, the support for science education has decreased;
- compared to its recent past, the United States has fallen behind in the production of technological goods and services; and
- women, minorities, and handicapped persons are under-represented in nearly all professional and technical roles in science and technology.

There is a growing awareness that merely more science and engineering is not the solution to solving our problems. The widely held view that a more profound understanding of the scientific discipline will lead to more intelligent decisions on social issues is in error (Aikenhead, 1985a; McCurdy, 1980; Shamos, 1983–84; Hardin, 1968; Landrie're, 1977). The confidence of the American public in respect to the ability of the scientific endeavor to yield public benefit has been eroded (Handler, 1980). Aikenhead (1985) argues that scientists and engineers do not appear to make more intelligent decisions in their personal lives than the general public. In fact there is no evidence that scientists and engineers espouse more similar values and ideologies among themselves than does the lay public. Manenschijn (1985) recognizes that science and technology have solved many problems which, in turn, have resulted in new problems. He identifies as a second problem, the

deception of increased scientific knowledge and human desires, as Plato made clear. It is socially and practically impossible to adapt the satisfaction of your desires to the possibility of technology, you must adapt the possibility of technology to the satisfaction of basic human needs of all people all over the world (p. 39).

Wiesner and York (1964) emphasize the futility of solving the nuclear arms race, which is a science-society-technology problem, through solely technical means:

> Both sides in the arms race are thus confronted by the dilemma of steadily increasing military power and steadily decreasing national security. It is our considered professional judgement that this dilemma has no technical solution. If the great powers continue to look for solutions in the area of science and technology only, the result will be to worsen the situation. The clearly predictable course of the arms race is a steady open spiral downward into oblivion (p. 35).

Hardin (1959) holds a pessimistic view of solving the overpopulation problem through interstellar migration. He sees such a proposal as favored only by men with "more faith in gadgetry than they do in rationality" (p. 70). Giving scientists full moral responsibility for the social implications of science is viewed as unthinkable by Arthur Kantowitz (1975).

The science community has been viewed as being value-free and efforts have been made to insure it so. The National Science Foundation stipulated that funding for the Biological Science Curriculum Study Program developed in the early 1960s depended on strictly omitting value issues (Barnum, Reesch, & Cooney, 1981). David Edge (1985) is concerned that social values, although "endemic", are often "coded and disguised" in science teaching. Charles Birch (1985) maintains there are two major defects in the teaching of science:

> One is its failure to lead to any adequate philosophic model of the world around us and within us. The other is the failure of science to invest its facts with values, with the consequence that it appears to be ethically and morally detached (p. 20).

Scientists and engineers are human and, therefore, are influenced by job allegiance, personal enhancement and professional advancement. Epstein (1978) cites numerous examples of research being distorted, data manipulated and misinterpreted by scientists employed by various industries or research companies conducting research for industries. Techniques such as the healthy worker effect, too-small cohort size and short time period duration have been used to distort epidemiology studies. The scientific community appears unable to police its ranks in the face of political and financial pressures. For example, Rosalie Bertell experienced pressures from colleagues in respect to her low-level radiation research which had serious implications for the nuclear power industry, to the point of having her tires blown out in heavy traffic. Stanley Adams' evidence against the Hoffmann-LaRoche pharmaceutical company led to a jail sentence in Switzerland. In Canada, the research on the possible negative effects of Hoffman-LaRoche's product Valium, conducted by David Horrobin, has been restricted (Aikenhead, 1985).

There are those that view the totality of science and technology in our society with alarm. Ferry (1972) states that high technology rules with efficiency its universal watchword. He emphasizes that "all decisions are made rationally, with the rationality of machines" (p. 279). People, especially the economically depressed, are objects rather than subjects, always to be "watched and manipulated, directed and fitted in." Jacques Ellul (1964) paints a bleak picture where everything is distilled into terms of maximum efficiency which he labels "the technique." Every value is weighed on the basis of its efficiency. People will only be useful in the technological society

> as members of a technical group, on the basis of the current criteria of utility—individuals who conform to the structure and needs of the technical group. The intelligentsia will no longer be a model, a conscience, or an animating intellectual spirit for the group, even in the sense of performing a critical function. They will be the servants, the most conformist imaginable of instruments of technique (p. 349).

Science began to assume its position of preeminence early in the nineteenth century from which it began to influence tremendous changes in society. As science became more successful it aspired to greater autonomy and less social regulation (Mendelsohn, 1976). Today there is concern that "Big Science" has invaded the university to the detriment of undergraduate education. Overindulgence in big science, warns Hart (1972), necessitates a professor to simultaneously become a journalist, publisher and an administrator with the resultant detriment to his students and intellectual eminence and proficiency. Charles Birch (1985) makes the most interesting observation of the compartmentalization of education in our universities by separating science into disciplines. Disciplines, in turn, lead to departments:

The function of a department is to produce experts in that discipline. Sometimes experts cross boundaries. Mostly they don't—scientists do not cross boundaries. They don't cross disciplines. There is a difference between an expert and a thinker. The thinker crosses boundaries. The expert sees knowledge as a jigsaw puzzle. You work on your bit and I work on mine. Then we put the pieces together to get the picture of truth. The general idea has been that if society has well-trained experts in all disciplines the experts would guide us in the truth and to right action. It hasn't worked out that way (p. 22).

Bowden, Goldberg, Gaudry and Margenau (1967) claim every country in the world spends large amounts of money funding projects just to keep science scholars in their universities. They offer a most intriguing hypothesis for the future if the matter continues:

Will the time ever come when Europe will deliberately export extravagant scholars to the United States in hope that they will bankrupt the American economy, and leave less enterprising countries to survive in peace? (p. 29)

Mendelsohn (1976) decries the scientific enterprise as being arrogant, out of harmony with nature, lacking of ethics and inaccessible to the general public. The National Science Foundation report (1983) states that science and mathematics have for too long been considered the exclusive domain of the elite and a preserve for only the gifted with the resultant widening of the gap between the science and the public they serve.

Clearly, introspection as to the purpose of science in the universities and colleges is needed. Should we continue to concentrate on the elite or consider scientific literacy for all citizens?

The Educational Policies Commission (1966) defined *the spirit of science* as "the spirit of rational inquiry driven by a belief in its efficacy and by restless curiosity" which encompasses many forms of education besides science itself. Interrelating science and technology, the commission characterizes seven values upon which the scientific endeavor is based and which should be taught to develop rational, thinking persons:

1. Longing to know and understand.
2. Questioning of all things.
3. Search for data and their meaning.
4. Demand for verification.
5. Respect for logic.

6. Consideration of premises.
7. Consideration of consequences (p. 15).

The final statement of the report recommended that one of the principal goals of education should be to communicate the spirit of science and utilization of its values—in short, to promote value-based scientific literacy.

One of the most important goals in science education today is the promotion of scientific literacy (Champagne & Klopfer, 1982; Collette & Chiappetta, 1984; Hurd, 1982; NSF, 1981 and Yager & Penick, 1985). The National Science Teachers Association (1982) identified the goal of science as producing scientifically literate citizens who understand the interrelationship of science and technology and who have enough knowledge of the concepts and nature of science to be able to effectively apply that knowledge in everyday decision-making. Scientifically literate citizens can think logically, continue to learn and appreciate the values and limitations of science. Glenn T. Seaborg (1966) recognized the importance of understanding the relationships between science, society and technology in respect to the problems confronting humanity. His classic statement:

> While citizens of a democracy are born free, they are not born wise. The only man who is truly free to choose is the man who knows the choices— makes it imperative that our schools produce both public-spirited scientists and scientifically educated citizens (p. 3).

The importance of producing scientifically literate citizens is emphasized by the fact that the National Science Foundation funds projects promoting scientific literacy. The NSF (1983) stated, "There is no excuse for citizens in our technological society to say 'I don't really know anything about science' " (p. x)!

Presently, schools, colleges and universities have not done a good job of producing scientifically literate citizens. Up to 90 percent of adults in the United States may be scientifically illiterate according to recent estimates (Yager, 1981). Few citizens, but more apropos to undergraduate education, few leaders can demonstrate competence in analyzing the technological or scientific facets of science and in making intelligent decisions. Present day decisions need to be made on the basis of scientific and technical concepts with which few leaders with nonscience backgrounds are familiar (Waks, 1985).

Unfortunately, integrated science programs designed to prepare undergraduate students in decision-making processes relating science technology-society problems are limited. Birch (1985) describes the science which is presently taught as the:

> science expounded in textbooks and in formal lectures. It is the information you need to build bridges and nuclear power plants or cure diseases. It is the science behind the technological society—science education is carried out as if the history, philosophy, sociology and aspects of life are unworthy of attention by a serious teacher and dutiful pupils. We need to develop structures to support and reward builders of departmental bridges (p. 29).

Rhodes (1985) views narrow departmentalization of the modern university as a serious weakness. The structure of disciplines discourages the coherency which is sought by students. The specialization of disciplines, although important for identity and professional growth of faculty and students becomes an impediment to learning and leads to isolationism of the disciplines.

Integrated science courses in undergraduate programs are usually viewed by the pure scientists in science departments as diminishing the position of their own courses. Integration of science courses are viewed as a dilution of "good" science. Thus it is feared that such courses may not carry out the desired preliminary screening and selection of the straight academic courses. Even the "service courses" departments, which supply students to the research and pure science departments, view interdisciplinary courses as a threat (Fensham, 1979). The power of the departments is based, in part at least, on the numbers of students enrolled. Thus, the student FTE, the bane of quality in higher education, has a powerful influence on the development of science courses integrated with technical-societal considerations.

What is not being suggested here is that integrated science courses replace the single disciplinary courses which are the mechanism for training specialists such as pure physicists, geologists, botanists, engineers, etc. The efficacy of these programs is demonstrated in the success of producing quality scientists and engineers which are the backbone of Western scientific eminence. It is true that there is concern that even the engineer needs to be aware of the societal implications of actions taken and the medical doctor needs to be well versed in areas of psychosomatics, nutrition, etc. A concern should be for the undergraduate student who is the nonscience major or the science major who has no designs on becoming a professional scientist or engineer. Fensham (1979) has identified groups of students who could use integrated science courses to their advantage:

1. Students of applied science and technology.
2. Vocational students such as home economics, arts and crafts, and technical trades.
3. Students in higher education not majoring in a scientific field.
4. Students in interdisciplinary fields such as environmental courses.
5. Students preparing for primary teaching.
6. Students preparing for secondary teaching (pp. 78–81).

The NSF (1983) report stressed that business will place greater emphasis on hiring people who are knowledgeable about science and technology.

Science courses which incorporate scientific and technological literacy have the common goal of developing intelligent decision-makers. Waks (1985) suggests two common components in almost every definition of scientific and technical literacy:

> The first is the *improvement of the scientific and technological thinking processes and problem solving skills of all learners* (the emphasis here is on all learners).
> The second is *understanding for use in life* and has personal, economic and political dimensions (p. 3).

245401

Included in the personal dimensions component is the utilization of scientific concepts, facts and generalizations for solving personal problems encountered in everyday life. The economic component encompasses career awareness and career choices, especially in respect to the products and processes involved in careers in which science and technology impinge heavily. The political component augurs for acquiring and conceptualizing knowledge skills and attitudes in science which equip individuals for effective decision making of public policy.

Students in interdisciplinary science courses which incorporate science-technology-society are led to realize that there is not always a *right* answer to problems but rather a *best* answer. Typically methods of instruction involve problem-solving, simulations, case studies, and values analysis. Emphasis is shifted from total factual knowledge consideration to the processes of decision making. Values are not inculcated, but are examined as to the least and most acceptable for the general welfare, often leading to trade-offs.

The professor in interdisciplinary science courses becomes more of a facilitator of learning rather than a purveyor of knowledge. Certainly such courses can be used for development of important concepts, principles and generalizations in science. Science courses which emphasize societal implications and seek scientific literacy should in no way be treated as "watered down courses" to accommodate the lazy or inept. Rather, the teaching methodology should be an examination of key objectives, discarding insignificant objectives and implementing a variety of teaching activities. For example, laboratory exercises should involve the student with activities in problem solving, hypotheses function and inferential procedures rather than the replication activities so replete in laboratory exercises.

Although claims exist to the contrary, the teaching of science should not be, or perhaps has never been, value-free. What is inferred in discussing science teaching as value-free is freedom from societal values. Glen Aikenhead (1985b) makes the cogent point that science is not value-free, but has been predominantly imbalanced in favor of constitutive values at the expense of contextual values. Constitutive values are those that guide the infrastructure of science, in determining which is the best theory, for example. Contextual values are those influenced by the ethics, ideology and cultural values of science.

Undergraduate science courses typically are didactic and taught at a high level of abstractions. Talley and Solomon (cited in Talley, 1973) found that over 75 percent of college instruction involves rote knowledge and almost 74 percent of the procedures used by college instructors is at the abstract level. Laboratory procedures in undergraduate science courses are principally of the verification type and rarely, if at all, reflect the scientific enterprise or involve thinking above the knowledge level. William Romey (1968) states if the instructor only stresses recall, what is taught is the history of science.

Piagetian developmental psychology classifies human development from birth through a series of stages to the final stage, the formal operational stage. All must proceed through these stages sequentially. During the pre-formal or concrete operational stage of development the student requires manipulation of objects and concrete experience during thinking processes. The formal thinker no longer requires physical manipulatives and quantities of objects but can deal in abstractions through reasoning with only verbal elements.

Observations indicate a low proportion of freshman undergraduate students can function at the formal operational level of thinking. A study done at the University of Oklahoma revealed that almost 75 percent of the freshman class was not completely functioning at the formal operational level and that 50 percent were operating entirely at the concrete operational level. The average ACT scores for these same students was well above the national average (McKinnon & Renner, 1971). Almost 60 percent of the college freshmen tested did not realize that volume is conserved when a clay ball is rolled into a cylinder (Towen & Wheatly, cited in Herron, 1975; Elkind, 1962). Concrete thinkers cannot function at the formal operational level. Not all students who can function at the formal level can function at that level in all disciplines. It is not uncommon for formal thinkers to revert to concrete functions when encountering unfamiliar areas (Herron, 1975). Students at the concrete or concrete/formal level of thinking encounter frustration, feelings of inadequacy and failure to see relevance when encountering the type of instruction typically used in undergraduate science courses.

One can argue that lack of intellectual development is the fault of the high school education. McKinnon and Renner make the excellent case that the elementary and secondary school teachers have been educated in the colleges and universities. Here they have been subjected to four years of being "lectured to, told to verify, given answers and told how to teach." Lest too much credit is given to departments, schools or colleges of education, one has only to realize that all of the content courses, which far outnumber the education courses taken by teachers *are taken in other colleges and departments*. The kinds of teaching employed by teachers in the precollege schools is that modeled in the colleges and universities. Social transmission is one Piagetian criterion for intellectual development. McKinnon and Renner (1971) hypothesize that "possibly more intellectual development goes on in dorms, fraternities, sororities and student hangouts than in the classroom" because little social transmission occurs in the classroom (p. 1051)!

Providing concrete experiences in undergraduate science courses can improve student learning and attitude and facilitate thinking at the formal level. In a study using visualization of chemical models in a freshman college chemistry course, Talley (1973) reported (1) greater student achievement and (2) higher scores on application, analysis and evaluation subtests, demonstrating higher cognitive thinking levels and ability to exercise critical thinking compared to the control group. Lawson and Renner (1975) reported research, spanning elementary school level students to freshman and sophomore level college students, demonstrating an elevation in thought levels through activities in exploration, invention and discovery (inquiry processes). The course content and degree requirements for the undergraduate major appears to be increasing in some sort of attempt to parallel the current knowledge explosion in science. Is there a critical mass for the undergraduate major? Would it be better to teach basic concepts well rather than attempt to "cover" so much? In a secondary school science teaching methods course taught by this writer, the students were assigned a consumer science activity with various pieces of bar soap. It was observed that none of the students who were seniors, about to do their student teaching in three weeks, placed the unknown mass on the appropriate pan of a simple IPS balance. Two biology majors and one physical science major in the class had no idea how to determine the volume of an irregularly shaped piece of soap.

There seems to be a need to sort out the important objectives from that which is trivia in science courses. Since science courses so religiously follow the textbook, it is the publishing companies which determine the content. Linus Pauling (1983) is critical of the size and content of modern day elementary college chemistry textbooks. He reflects fondly on his first college chemistry course, almost entirely descriptive, which developed in him a "keen interest in descriptive chemistry." Contrasting the 1947 introductory chemistry course with present day texts reveals descriptive chemistry beginning on page 57 vs. page 350 in the most popular freshman chemistry text today. The modern day textbook contains one and one half times as many pages, over twice the number of words and has double the mass. Dr. Pauling concludes that more students will become fascinated with chemistry and will want to learn more about it if the size, mass and cost of the textbook are reduced by a factor of one half.

A perusal of the literature indicates a need to seriously study not only what should be taught in undergraduate science programs, but how it should be taught. Several major concepts seem to consistently appear. One overarching concept is that of being relevant, with relevant meaning science programs should:

1. Meet the needs of the science majors pursuing a professional career in science and those not choosing to do so;

2. Meet the needs of nonscience majors;

3. Contain a component which relates science and technology to social implications for the culture and the personal needs of the student;

4. Develop scientifically literate citizens and intelligent, independent thinkers;

5. Be tailored to the intellectual development of the student; and

6. Develop career awareness.

The development and implementation of such a science program requires a tremendous amount of cooperation between departments, schools and colleges. To do so will require not only Herculean amounts of energy, but the burial of sacred cows in placing the welfare of the undergraduate student at the forefront.

References

Aikenhead, G. S. (1985a). Collective social decision-making: Implications for teaching science. In D. Gosling & B. Musschenga (Eds.), *Science education and ethical values* (p. 66). Washington, DC: Georgetown University Press.

Aikenhead, G. S. (1985b). Collective decision making in the social context of science. *Science Education*, 69(4), 466.

Barnum, C. R., Rusch, J. J., & Cooney, T. M. (1981). *Science and societal issues a guide for science researchers*. Ames, Iowa: Iowa State University Press.

Birch, C. (1985). Values and responsibilities and commitments in the teaching of science. In D. Gosling & B. Musschenga (Eds.), *Science education and ethical values* (p. 20). Washington, DC: Georgetown University Press.

Bowden, L., Goldberg, L., Gaudry, R. & Margenau, H. (1967). *Science and the university, the Frank Gernstein lectures*. Toronto: Macmillan of Canada, in association with York University.

Champagne, A. B. & Klopfer, L. E. (1982). Actions in a time of crisis. *Science Education*, 66(4), 503–504.

Collette, A. T. & Chiappetta, E. L. (1984). *Science instruction in the middle and secondary schools*. St. Louis: Times Mirror/Mosby.

Educational Policies Commission (1966). *Education and the spirit of science*. Washington, DC: NEA, p. 15.

Elkind, D. (1962). Quantity conceptions in college students. *Journal of Social Psychology, 57,* 459–465.

Ellul, J. (1964). *The technological society*. New York: Random House.

England, A. W. (1980). Technology and the integrated view. *The Science Teacher*, 47(6), 23–24.

Epstein, S. S. (1978). *The politics of cancer*. San Francisco: Sierra Club Books.

Fensham, P. (1979). Strategies and implementation of integrated science education at the post-secondary level. *New trends in integrated science teaching*. Paris, France: UNESCO, p. 77.

Ferry, W. (1972). Must we rewrite the Constitution to control technology? In F. H. Knelman (Ed.) *1984 and all that*, (p. 279). Belmont, CA: Wadsworth Publishing Co., Inc.

Fischer, R. B. (1975). *Science, man and society*, Philadelphia: W. B. Saunders Company.

Grant, W. V. & Snyder, T. D. (1983). *Digest of education statistics 1983–84*. (Report No. NC ES 83–407). Washington, DC: Specialist in Education Statistics, U. S. Department of Education, p. 120.

Handler, P. (1980). Public doubts about science. *Science, 208* (4448), 1093.

Hardin, G. (1959). Interstellar migration and the population problem. *Journal of Heredity*, 50 (2), 70.

Hardin, G. (1968). The tragedy of the commons. *Science, 162,* 1243–1248.

Hart, H. (1972). The hypothesis of cultural lag: A present day view. In F. H. Knolman (Ed.) *1984 and all that*, (p. 38). Belmont, CA: Wadsworth Publishing Co.

Herron, J. D. (1975). Piaget for chemists. *Journal of Chemical Education*, 52(3), 146–150.

Hurd, P. D. (1982). Transformation of science education: Changes and criteria. *Science Education*, 66(2), 281–285.

Hurd, P. D. (1984). *Reforming science education: The search for a new vision*. (Occasional paper No. 33). Washington, DC: Council for Basic Education, p. 3.

Kantowitz, A. (1975, September/October). Controlling technology democratically. *American Scientist*, 63(5), 505.

Landrie're, J. (1977). The challenge presented to cultures by science and technology. Liege, UNESCO, p. 10.

Lawson, A. F. & Renner, J. W. (1975). Piagetian theory and biology teaching. *The American Biology Teacher*, 37(6), 336–343.

Manenschijn, G. (1985). Reasoning in science and ethics. In D. Gosling & B. Musschenga (Eds.). *Science education and ethical values*, (p. 39). Washington, DC: Georgetown University Press.

McCurdy, D. W. (1980). President's report. *The Science Teacher*, 47(6), 56.

McKinnon, J. & Renner, J. W. (1971). Are colleges concerned about intellectual development? *American Journal of Physics*, 39(9), 1047–52.

Mendelsohn, E. (1976). Values and science: A critical reassessment. *The Science Teacher, 43*(1), 22.

National Science Foundation and the Department of Education (1980). *Science & engineering education for the 1980's & beyond* (Report No. NSF 80–78). Washington, DC: U.S. Government Printing Office.

National Science Foundation. (1981). *Only one science: Twelfth annual report of the National Science Board,* NSB 80–1. Washington, DC: U.S. Government Printing Office.

National Science Foundation. (1983). *Educating Americans for the 21st Century: A report to the American people and the National Science Board* (CPCE-NSF–03). Washington, DC: National Science Foundation.

National Science Teachers Association (NSTA). (1982). *An NSTA position statement, science-technology-society: Science education for the* 1980s. Washington, DC: National Science Teachers Association.

Pauling, L. (1983). Throwing the book at elementary chemistry. *The Science Teacher, 50*(6), 25–29.

Rhodes, H. T. (1985, May 22). Reforming higher education will take more than just tinkering with curricula. *Chronicle of Higher Education.* New York: Cornell University, p. 80.

Romey, W. D. (1968). *Inquiry techniques for teaching science.* Englewood Cliffs, NJ: Prentice Hall, Inc.

Seaborg, G. T. (1966). In a guide to science curriculum development. (Bulletin #161), Madison, WI: Wisconsin Department of Public Instruction, p. 3.

Shamos, M. H. (1983, December, 1984, January). You can lead a horse to water. *Educational Leadership, 41*(4), 30–33.

Talley, L. H. (1973). The use of three-dimensional visualization as a moderator in higher cognitive learning of concepts in college level chemistry. *Journal of Research in Science Teaching, 10*(3), 263–269.

Waks, L. J. (1985, Summer). Needed: A theory base for integrated learning in science, technology and society. *SSTS Reporter Science through science technology and society.* University Park, PA: The Pennsylvania State University, Science through Science Technology and Society, p. 3.

Wiesner, J. B. & York, H. E. (1964). The national security and the nuclear test ban. *Scientific American, 211*(4), 35.

Yager, R. E. (1981, September). Science education. In *ASC Curriculum Update.* Washington, DC: Association for Supervision and Curriculum Development.

Yager, R. E. & Penick, J. E. (1985). Taking new goals for school science seriously. *Educational Leadership, 42*(8), 86.

Coping With Math Anxiety

Cleland V. Cook

Introduction

The twentieth century has been called the "Age of Anxiety." Some social historians believe that the anxiety level was higher in the middle of the twentieth century than at any other time since the Middle Ages (Marmor, 1983). The world's awareness of the threat of nuclear war, AIDS, world hunger, terrorism, and political unrest is greater now than ever. The vivid television coverage and the inability to solve these problems may have caused the anxiety level to be higher now than ever.

It is impossible to escape from anxiety, and it would be unwise to do so, even if one could. Anxiety is a normal and natural response that is important to the safety and security of a person. There are no innate differences between men and women, young and old, and different national groups in their capacity to experience anxiety. Many scholars agree that the capacity to experience anxiety depends on the nature of the threatening object or situation and on the individual's sense of inner strength. An individual will be less anxious if the individual feels that he/she can cope with that which is threatening (Manor, 1963).

Although humans have always experienced anxiety, it has only recently become a topic for research. The study of anxiety started in 1895 when Sigmund Freud conceptualized anxiety neurosis, which he believed resulted from the discharge of repressed libido. In 1926, he changed to a more general view in which he attributed anxiety neurosis to conflict between mediation with reality and instinctual drive (Kutash, 1980). Freud's concept of anxiety has three descriptive attributes:

(1) a specific unpleasurable quality, (2) efferent or discharge phenomena, and (3) perception of these (Sarason, Davidson, Lightall, Waite, & Ruebush, 1960). According to Sarason et al., not much has been found from research that would warrant changing Freud's concept.

Before 1950, there was little experimental work done on anxiety using human subjects (Spielberger, 1977). This has drastically changed. Now there are numerous articles and books, or portions thereof, that deal with human anxiety and many of them are of an experimental nature. Computers, statistical packages, and more knowledge of anxiety have enabled researchers to study relationships between anxiety and many other characteristics more thoroughly during the last twenty years.

The concept of anxiety is commonly divided into two categories: anxiety as a state, and anxiety as a trait. Anxiety as a state is the emotional state, and all the various subsequent reactions to it; anxiety as a trait refers to the predisposition to be anxious, and is similar to a personality trait (Sinclair, 1985). A person in a high anxiety state feels threatened. Some researchers classify this as either fear or anxiety, while others differentiate between the two. If differentiated, fear is used when the object or event causing the emotional state is known, while anxiety is used when the specific cause of the emotional state is not known. A person's reactions to fear and to anxiety are similar. Although the cause of anxiety can be an imagined phenomenon, a high anxiety state is real and can be extremely threatening.

Math Anxiety

The term "math anxiety" is relatively new but already widely known. The identification with a particular academic subject is somewhat unique. Studies dealing specifically with mathematics anxiety and its relationship to performance in mathematics, career choices in mathematics-related areas, and other characteristics, originated and have increased dramatically during the last two decades. Until recently, individuals and society did not seem concerned that the proportion of women in mathematics and math-related careers was much smaller than that of men. The public concern for equal opportunities for minorities and women is relatively recent. The thrust for equal opportunities gave great impetus to the study of math anxiety.

Some earlier studies indicated that math anxiety for women was significantly higher than for men. Some people concluded that this was a major reason why women did not select math courses as electives in high school or pursue math-related careers. The attempt to verify, or refute, that math anxiety was a basic cause for this disparity led to numerous studies comparing the effect math anxiety has on math performance.

The lack of women in mathematics is not caused by lack of ability to do mathematics. There is not any basis for believing that males are innately superior in mathematics. Hackett (1985) found that self-efficacy expectations are more important in career choices than measured abilities for college-age men and women. She found that both college men and women still view math-related careers as less appropriate, or even inappropriate, for women. Fennema and Sherman (1977) found that mathematics performances were similar for males and females when the mathematics background was controlled.

The belief that there is a vast difference in the math anxiety level is not supported by research. The conclusion by Dew, Galassi, and Galassi (1983) is typical. They concluded that gender differences in mathematics anxiety may exist, but the differences are much smaller than what had been suggested earlier.

The fact that math anxiety exists among college students is well documented. Betz (1978) found that math anxiety occurs quite frequently among college students. High school preparation strongly influences how college students feel about mathematics. Math anxiety was moderately and inversely related to the ACT math subtest scores and moderately related to trait anxiety and test anxiety.

It is difficult to assess how math anxiety affects performance. Fulkerson, Galassi, and Galassi (1984) found math anxiety was not significantly related to math performance. Cognitions that may occur to college students while solving math problems did not differ as a function of math anxiety or gender.

Students with higher levels of mathematics anxiety tended to receive lower course grades, have less mathematics background from high school, and have lower grade-point averages in college (Frary & Ling, 1983). But Lowe (1982) found that there was no significant relationship between anxiety and final course grade, nor between test anxiety and final course grade, for a group of community college students. However, statistically significant relationships were found between math anxiety and self-reported attitudes toward mathematics, and between test anxiety and attitudes toward tests. Asking students how they feel about math anxiety and test anxiety is a reliable method of identification of the respective anxieties (Lowe, 1982).

In a study of community college students, Giangrasso (1982) found high math anxiety students used significantly fewer quantities and varieties of problem solving heuristics, made more structural errors, and had lower product scores. Giangrasso reported that high mathematics anxiety is related to poor problem solving performance and that anxiety appeared more debilitating among men. The construct of math anxiety did not significantly increase prediction of grades for students in a college algebra course when math aptitude was controlled (Llabre & Suarez, 1985).

The ultimate response of a high math anxious student is a strict avoidance of mathematics. In the past, some college students were able to avoid mathematics by selecting a college or course of study not requiring mathematics. Now most colleges require some mathematics for graduation. This trend is occurring simultaneously with a tendency toward increased high school graduation requirements, higher college entrance requirements, more rigorous freshman math courses at the college level, and a higher proportion of non-traditional students entering college.

Historically, many non-traditional students have had difficulty in mathematics and have had trouble competing with recent high school graduates. The academic preparation of these students in mathematics is often less than that of recent high school graduates. The poorer background and the time span since the last mathematics course was taken make the typical college mathematics courses very difficult for them. This combination of factors increases anxiety for individuals in a group that already has high anxiety levels. These recent trends will tend to magnify the problems of the non-traditional student.

Courses in mathematics are probably the most difficult when compared to other courses for many non-traditional students. Most non-traditional students have not utilized mathematics at the algebra level or above since their last high school mathematics course, and some may not have had even that level of mathematics in high school. They have utilized some of their reading skills, and with their maturity and experiences are perhaps more able to compete in less technical areas. Many non-traditional students have a history of high math anxiety and the anticipation of more difficult mathematics increases their anxiety level significantly.

Reduction of Math Anxiety

Some programs have been developed to respond to people with high math anxiety. Tobias (1978) lists twenty-one programs designed to deal with people who avoid mathematics or who have high math anxiety. Many of them are located on college campuses. The higher number of non-traditional students entering college increases the need for such programs. Studies have shown that these programs can be successful.

One of the better known programs is called "Math Without Fear." The features of her six week workshop: working on building positive attitudes, developing a realistic view of math, setting a reasonable work schedule in a relaxing atmosphere, writing an autobiography, having reasonable goals, and having the help and support of others, contributed the most to the success of the program (Tobias, 1978).

Shodahl and Diers (1984) described a successful course that lowered the students' mean mathematics anxiety level and taught them how to manage their anxiety level so they could further develop their mathematics potential. Group discussion and sharing, practice with diaphragmatic breathing, muscle relaxation, work-guided imagery while music designed for relaxation was played, and having successful professional people share their personal experiences of mathematics anxiety with the students, contributed most to the course.

Support groups and tutorial sessions reduced anxiety and increased confidence in mathematics as measured by the Syracuse Mathematics Scales (McTeer, 1982). The students discussed their problems, fears, and frustrations related to mathematics with the group and instructor, and the instructor helped examine these fears and problems and demonstrated different approaches to possible solutions.

Using math anxiety reduction techniques in addition to the regular class reduced math anxiety as measured by the Mathematics Anxiety Rating Scale (MARS) and increased math competency as measured by the Mathematics Placement Examination (Handler, 1983). The average final course grade was one letter grade above that of the control group. Although this inverse relationship between anxiety and competency in mathematics was not supported statistically, the average student showed a significant decrease in anxiety. Themes (1982) found that the three methods, Ellis' Rational-Emotive Therapy, Meichenbaum's Cognitive Behavior Modification, and Mathematics Skills Intervention, all reduced mathematics anxiety as measured by MARS for a group of college women.

The methods used and the expectations of the mathematics teacher affect the anxiety level. The use of a basic calculator allowed undergraduate students to solve statistics problems more quickly and accurately and with less anxiety about the problem-solving situation, particularly as problem difficulty increased (Lawrence, 1982). High expectations by the instructor reduced math anxiety and facilitated test performance among traditional college students, but caused non-traditional students to have increased anxiety and debilitated test performance (Cross, 1982). Math anxiety scores were lowered by effectively combining the diagnosis of basic mathematics skills deficiencies with remediation techniques in an existing college structure (Frye, 1983).

Not all studies showed successful results. A combined academic-counseling program in mathematics anxiety for black college women did not significantly change their math anxiety, test anxiety, performance, or attitude toward mathematics. But the students did indicate that they felt the program helped in all aspects (Glass, 1982). Students who studied college algebra with a self-paced approach did not differ significantly in performance or in mathematics anxiety, as measured by the Sherman Mathematics Anxiety Scale, from students in the traditional mode of instruction (Smith, 1983). Relaxation-desensitization procedures with practical examples did not reduce math anxiety significantly for students in general education college mathematics courses (Goodall, 1980).

Studies show that there are numerous college students who suffer from math anxiety. Some programs designed to reduce math anxiety or to teach students how to cope with their anxiety are successful for a significant proportion of the students involved.

Implication for the University

The University has two major areas of concern with respect to math anxiety. One is the concern for the current student, and the other is the concern for the education of all teachers who teach mathematics.

The University needs to be able to identify the high math-anxious students who are on campus. This number is increasing due to more non-traditional students and to more core requirements in mathematics for graduation. The University should consider developing special programs or methods for dealing with both traditional and non-traditional students who have high math anxiety. An excellent place to pilot a program would be with students with high math anxiety levels who are enrolled in the non-college credit mathematics course. The University, through its mathematics departments, needs to provide students with good instruction. The selection of texts, homework assignments, and testing are potential factors that can increase math anxiety and these should be given proper consideration.

Even with good instruction, there is still a need for a mathematics laboratory or some other identifiable location where a student can receive immediate additional help. Remediation in mathematics is difficult, and this difficulty increases with the length of the time span in which help is needed. The University admits there are students with poor backgrounds, poor attitudes and poor self-confidence levels with respect to mathematics, and consequently has an obligation to meet their academic needs.

The second concern, and perhaps one of greater importance, is the preprofessional education of elementary teachers and secondary mathematics teachers. The major emphasis should be on prevention of high math anxiety and not upon the treatment of the problem. The teachers of mathematics are the ones who can be the most influential in the prevention or curtailment of math anxiety.

The University is obligated to give teachers a background that will be most beneficial to their teaching. For elementary teachers the background needs to include more appropriate college work in mathematics than most of them currently receive. They need to have a thorough knowledge of the mathematics they are to teach. This knowledge includes understanding much beyond that needed to perform the arithmetic operations efficiently and successfully. They need to have some understanding of how the mathematics they teach is related to mathematics that their students will learn later. Foundations and concepts that are fundamental to algebra, geometry, statistics, and other areas are introduced and developed in the elementary grades.

There is a tremendous number of diverse mathematic topics that a graduating elementary teacher needs to understand and be able to teach. Better knowledge of mathematics would give more assurance that the teachers themselves understand the relationships between concepts and topics in mathematics. A good foundation in mathematics would help teachers develop abilities and skill in asking good questions and good follow-up questions, in reacting well to student questions, in interpreting student answers, in assessing student learning difficulties, in designing remedial work, and in being a better role model. Teachers with good mathematical backgrounds are more apt to have good attitudes toward mathematics and be more confident when teaching mathematics.

The University must insure that their graduating mathematics teachers have knowledge of numerous ideas that have a positive effect on teaching and math anxiety. Teachers at all levels need to realize the value of success. Success is the key to mathematics, as it is the foundation for all of the positive values like self-confidence, self-reliance, persistence, and perseverance. Students possessing these qualities will be able to cope with their math anxiety level and not avoid mathematics or math-related areas.

Elementary teachers, through their classroom actions, can define and control success for each of their students. As the student gets older, success becomes less controlled by the teacher, but the teacher's influence is still strong. The teacher must attempt to have each student experience success. It is often assumed that the nature of mathematics makes it more difficult for the student to experience success. But, due to the nature of mathematics, one could argue the opposite. If the teacher knows the subject matter and the student, and can properly assess where a student is currently at with respect to a mathematical concept, then the teacher should be able to develop an appropriate question or problem that would almost guarantee success. The question or problem could be one of review or drill which the student is capable of answering.

The proper amount of review and drill should develop confidence and understanding. A teacher should be able to make a transition to new material by challenging each student at an appropriate level. That level is one which challenges the student and yet allows him/her to complete the task successfully. The nature of mathematics allows this step to be either very small or very large.

Many high school and junior high mathematics teachers will have a major or minor in mathematics. These teachers are better prepared in subject matter and have been successful in mathematics. Most of them have a relatively high self-confidence level and possess good attitudes toward their own ability to learn mathematics. They often lack an understanding of students who experience considerable difficulty in mathematics. Colleges need to assure that mathematics education majors and minors deal with this problem in their pre-service education. The teachers will have the responsibility of teaching students whose knowledge, abilities, anxiety levels, and confidence levels, as they relate to mathematics, are extremely varied.

College teachers have a situation similar to secondary teachers. They need to be able to deal with students, especially in the lower level courses, who perform very poorly in mathematics. Poor student performances are often due to the students' poor attitudes toward themselves and toward mathematics, which have grown out of their earlier experiences.

Good teaching techniques and good classroom procedures at all levels are the best constraints for preventing math anxiety in students, for helping the already math-anxious students reduce anxiety, or for teaching students how to cope with their anxiety. Teachers need to continually strive to become better teachers and improvements can be made if they are willing to work at it. This may mean changing procedures and methods so students become more involved in the learning process. The student can be involved in establishing classroom procedures and be kept informed of what he/she is expected to do and to learn. Surprises and fear of the unknown lead to higher math-anxiety levels.

The teacher should be able to get students involved by asking interesting and stimulating questions. Teachers need to react to answers from all students in a positive way and especially in situations when incorrect answers are given. The students need to be encouraged to guess, to make decisions and not be afraid to be wrong. They need to know that their mathematics teachers did not always solve mathematics problems correctly when they were students and, as teachers, can still make errors. Students should know that it does not take a mathematical brain to learn mathematics, but it does take self-discipline to do the daily homework. The emphasis needs to be on thinking and on developing logical thought processes throughout mathematics with much less emphasis placed on correctness of answers. Teachers need to help students develop strategies and problem solving techniques to support or reject what they have conjectured.

Mathematics instructors need to be aware of how students learn. Many teachers present a new concept as though it should be digested immediately, which is seldom the case. The students need to deal with it in their own minds. A spiral teaching approach is useful. A student will gain much more insight and understanding of a topic or concept in a certain amount of allocated time if it is spread out in an appropriate manner. Three or four short periods of time spent on some future topic will be extremely beneficial to student understanding and require less total teaching time. This approach is especially worthwhile when a lot of new vocabulary is required, or a lot of new ideas is needed to introduce a concept.

The teacher must be taught to be tolerant, respectful, and open-minded toward problems and concerns of the student. Students learn at different rates; they have different interests, backgrounds, likes, and dislikes. One needs to challenge each of them and yet have each of them experience success.

Teachers need good attitudes toward those students who have difficulties, and they need to foster these good attitudes in their students. Due to the nature of mathematics, it is usually obvious to other students and the teacher when a student is having considerable difficulty. Poor homework and inability to participate effectively in class are daily reminders. Other students, unsure of their understanding of the mathematics being taught, may believe that they will soon be in the same situation. As their anxiety increases, the probability that they will be in the same situation also increases.

The evaluation of student performance is very important. Poor test results affect student attitudes, self-confidence, and other desirable characteristics. Tests need to stress the thinking process and understanding. This emphasis needs to start at the kindergarten level and continue throughout the system. Much of present testing encourages memorization and does not encourage thinking. Students should be allotted a reasonable time to complete tests. Successful test experiences will contribute to better future test results and to other positive characteristics.

By using individual and group incentives, the teacher can build a classroom atmosphere which is supportive and nonthreatening. Teachers must be constantly aware of the slower students in their classes. Teachers' insensitive reactions to quick correct answers from brighter students can have a negative effect on students who are not as quick. Teachers need to allow every student the opportunity and time to think and to arrive at an answer. That process is often more valuable than the answer.

The teacher is most critical in keeping the math anxiety level low and in helping students cope with their higher math anxiety levels. The mathematics textbook also has a crucial role in most mathematics classes. Textbooks often set the sequence of topics, the vocabulary development, the explanation of concepts, the problems assigned, and how topics are interpreted and reviewed. Textbooks need to be carefully selected to fit the students for whom they are chosen. It is very important to select texts that students are able to read.

The teachers of mathematics should also be extremely concerned about their students' ability to read. Teachers need to develop the mathematics vocabulary at all levels and help the student learn to interpret what they read. More emphasis on reading will enable students to learn with less dependence on the teacher. This independence will contribute to some of the positive characteristics found in good mathematics students.

The homework assignments and how they are assessed should be done carefully. Checking homework for correct answers only gives the student a poor impression of what is important. Allowing homework to contribute directly to the course grade can lower the pressure created by tests. The homework needs to contribute to the course goals; which should stress understanding and problem solving with less emphasis on correct answers. The students need to experience success with homework as well as with all the other aspects.

Supplementary materials should be provided for both enrichment and remedial work. The enrichment material should be readable by the student; appropriate library material should be available and the student should be encouraged or perhaps required to read a portion of it.

Nonsexist textbooks, designed to develop the basics while emphasizing problem solving, need to have reasonable and appropriate problems that are related to the student's world as much as possible. Students need work on how to attack problems. They need work on formulating meaningful relationships and equations and not on just solving them. Emphasis needs to be on the thinking processes, guessing, estimating and decision making.

Summary and Conclusions

Math anxiety encompasses an unpleasant emotional state and all the subsequent reactions to it. Numerous college students have high math anxiety. Many of these students avoid taking mathematics and consequently are unable to pursue math-related careers. If they do take mathematics, the high anxiety interferes with learning. Inconsistent results found in different research articles may be caused by the large number of interacting variables involved in the learning process.

Programs have been developed which reduce the anxiety level for a large portion of the high math-anxious students enrolled. These programs work on getting the students to realistically assess their current status with respect to mathematics, and then to begin building good attitudes toward mathematics and toward themselves with the help and support of their peer group and instructors.

The University has students enrolled in mathematics who have extreme difficulty in learning mathematics due to their anxiety levels. The number of students with high math anxieties may increase due to changes in core requirements and to the increasing number of non-traditional students that are enrolling. The University needs to make sure that the quality of mathematics instruction is high, especially for the general student. The University should consider developing assessment procedures and programs to deal with these students more effectively. The non-college mathematics courses should be an appropriate place for a pilot program. There should be some identifiable place on campus where a student can go to receive immediate help. Perhaps, a mathematics laboratory with appropriate material should be developed.

The long term solution should be one of prevention. Good teaching techniques and classroom procedures are essential ingredients. The sequential nature of mathematics allows problem areas to occur at any level and if not remediated immediately can undermine future learning. These difficulties destroy the positive characteristics that are important in learning mathematics and in preventing higher anxiety levels.

There are implications for the University in its pre-service education of elementary and secondary mathematics teachers. Students should be carefully selected for this program. The pre-service education for those teaching mathematics should include sufficient mathematical content to insure that the teachers are competent in mathematics. Teachers need to understand how the mathematics they teach is related to the mathematics that their students will learn later. The teacher is a role model for the student, but it is the University's obligation to make sure that the example set is good.

A good background in both content and methodology will enable a teacher to make wise decisions with regard to all aspects of teaching. Good decisions in selecting textbooks, library material, teaching techniques, classroom procedures and in assessing and remediating learning difficulties, will keep the anxiety level within an acceptable range for most students. The University must attempt to educate teachers so that they have the necessary background and the skills to perform these teaching duties as well as possible.

References

Becker, J.R. (1981). Differential treatment of females and males in mathematics classes. *Journal of Research in Mathematics Education*, *12*(1), 40–53.

Betz, N.E. (1978). Prevalence, distribution, and correlates of math anxiety in college students. *Journal of Counseling Psychology*, *25*(5), 441–448.

Cattell, R.B. (1963). The nature and measurement of anxiety. *Scientific American*, *208*, 96–104.

Clute, P.S. (1982). The effects of anxiety and method of instruction on achievement in a survey course in college mathematics. *Dissertation Abstracts International*, *43*(6), 1866–A.

Crawford, C.H. (1980). *Math without fear*. New York: Franklin Watts.

Cross, J.L. (1982). The effect of instructor expectations on state-anxiety and test performance of traditional and nontraditional age university students. *Dissertation Abstracts International*, *43*(02), 399–A.

Day, H.I. (1985). Motivation. *The international encyclopedia of education*, by T. Husen and T. N. Postlethwaite.

Dew, K.M.H., Galassi, J.P., & Galassi, M.D. (1984). Math anxiety: Relation with situational test anxiety, performance, physiological arousal, and math avoidance behavior. *Journal of Counseling Psychology*, *31*(4), 580–583.

Dew, K.M.H., Galassi, J.P., & Galassi, M.D. (1983). Mathematics anxiety: Some basic issues. *Journal of Counseling Psychology*, *30*(3), 443–446.

Fennema, E. & Ayer, M.J. (Eds.). (1984). *Women and education: Equity or equality*. Berkeley: McCutchan.

Fennema, E., Pedro, J.D., Wolleat, P.L., & Becker, A.D. (1981). Increasing women's participation in mathematics: An intervention study. *Journal for Research in Mathematics Education*, *12*(1), 3–14.

Fennema, E. & Sherman, J. (1977). Sex-related differences in mathematics achievement, spatial visualization, and affective factors. *American Educational Research Journal*, *14*(1), 51–71.

Frary, R.B. & Ling, J.L. (1983). A factor-analytic study of mathematics anxiety. *Educational and Psychological Measurement*, *43*, 985–993.

Frye, E.W. (1983). The effect of knowledge of level of mathematics basic skills on math anxiety. *Dissertation Abstracts International*, *44*(4), 1013–A.

Fulkerson, K.F., Galassi, J.P. & Galassi, M.D. (1984). Relation between mathematics cognitions and performance in math anxious students: A failure of cognitive theory? *Journal of Counseling Psychology*, *31*(3), 376–382.

Giangrasso, A.P. (1982). An exploratory study of the relationship between mathematics anxiety and the processes used by developmental community college freshmen to solve verbal mathematics problems. *Dissertation Abstracts International*, *42*(07), 3048–A.

Glass, G.I. (1982). A study of mathematics anxiety among female college students. *Dissertation Abstracts International*, *43*(06), 1866–A.

Goodall, C.G. (1981). The reduction of mathematics anxiety utilizing relaxation and desensitization and presentation of practical examples. *Dissertation Abstracts International*, *41*(12), 5012–A.

Greenwood, J. (1984). My anxieties about math anxiety. *Mathematics Teacher*, *77*, 662–663.

Hackett, G. (1985). Role of mathematics self-efficacy in the choice of math-related majors of college women and men: A path analysis. *Journal of Counseling Psychology*, *32*(1), 47–56.

Handler, B.H. (1982). Reduction of mathematics anxiety in college remedial algebra students. *Dissertation Abstracts International*, *44*(01), 95–A.

Kutash, I.L. (1980). Anxiety. *Encyclopedia of psychology*, *1*, 78–79.

Lawrence, J. (1982). The effects of calculator usage and task difficulty on state anxiety in solving statistics problems. *Dissertation Abstracts International*, *43*(03), 729–A.

Llabre, M.M. & Suarez, E. (1985). Predicting math anxiety and course performance in college women and men. *Journal of Counseling Psychology*, *32*(2), 283–287.

Lowe, S.S. (1982). Relationships between math anxiety, test anxiety, and math performance. *Dissertation Abstracts International*, *43*(05), 1403–A.

Marmor, J. (1983). Anxiety. *The encyclopedia of mental health*, A. Deutch (Ed.), *1*, 217–226.

McTeer, P.M. (1982). Math anxiety: An intervention strategy to reduce math anxiety. *Dissertation Abstracts International*, *43*(10), 3249–A.

Meissner, W.W. (1977). Anxiety: Psychoanalytic theory. B. B. Wolman (Ed.), *International encyclopedia of psychiatry, psychology, psychoanalysis and neurology*, 79–81.

Partner, B.E. & Weaver, R.A. (1984). Attitudes and strategies for improving mathematics achievement. *Teacher Educator*, *20*, 26–31.

Sarason, S.B., Davidson, K.S., Lighthall, F., Waite, R.R., & Ruebush, B.K. (1960). *Anxiety in elementary school children*. New York: John Wiley & Sons, Inc.

Shodahl, S.A., & Diers, C. (1984). Math anxiety in college students: Sources and solutions. *Community College Review*, *12*, 32–36.

Sinclair, K.E. (1985). Students' affective characteristics and classroom behavior. *The international encyclopedia of education*, 4881–4886.

Smith, T.H. (1983). The effects of a self-paced college algebra program on mathematics achievement and mathematics anxiety. *Dissertation Abstracts International*, *44*(01), 97–A.

Spielberger, C.D. (1977). On the relationship between manifest anxiety and intelligence. *Journal of Consulting Psychology*, *22*, 220–224.

Themes, E.P. (1982). Three methods of reducing math anxiety in women. *Dissertation Abstracts International*, *44*(01), 97–A.

Tobias, S. (1978). *Overcoming math anxiety*. New York: W.W. Norton.

Tobias, S. & Weissbrod, C. (1980). Anxiety and mathematics: An update. *Harvard Educational Review*, *50*(1), 63–70.

Some Positive Values of Sport in American Universities

Mary S. Mock

Emphasis on sport in colleges and universities seems to be increasing every year. Recent events, unfortunately, focus on the negative side of sport. Universities receive publicity for drug scandals, for Title IX disputes, and for other conceived means to deceive and break established rules. The focus of this paper is to be more positive in nature and to place emphasis on some positive values of sport in collegiate communities.

Values, for the purpose of clarification, are defined as the worth, the merit, and the importance of related qualities. Because values are usually intangible in nature, this axiological foundation discussion will be limited to the three major objectives of inquiry as identified by Osterhoudt: morality which is studied by the subdiscipline ethics, beauty which is studied by the subdiscipline aesthetics, and the common good which is studied by the subdiscipline politics (Osterhoudt, 1978).

The Implications of Morality

The ethical status of sport is most generally concerned with the content and form of moral conduct. Specific areas of reference concern the idea of fair play, the criteria of moral conduct, the motivation of moral conduct in sport, and the obligation to provide comparable opportunities for the female athlete.

121

The theory of what is fair and unfair is intuitively established in the minds of people. At times this common sense approach is violated in contemporary sport as pointed out by John Rawls in his *Theory of Justice*. His theory is basically concerned with institutions since education and sport (for example) exist (at least in theory) to serve the public good.

To relate the idea of justice and games, Rawls outlined four examples as they relate to desirable game outcomes: (1) the first is to perform according to the rules; (2) the second is to realize the motives that players expect to achieve by the end of the game; (3) the third is to recognize the unlimited reasons a player may participate in a game; and (4) the fourth is the shared and common denominator of all participants—to play fairly—to perform well (Rawls, 1971).

Francis Keenan, in suggesting parallel thoughts to Rawls, reemphasized the importance of fair play:

No one can guarantee that the best team shall win; all that can be guaranteed on any particular occasion is that the outcome shall not be unjust. In sport, emphasis should be placed upon principles which inhere more fully to guarantee a just outcome (Keenan, 1975).

Rules and playing by the rules place a value on fairness—the guide for all sport participants. Keenan summarized his stand on justice and fair play by stating that "we are all accountable to ourselves and the opposite also holds: those for whom success is fairly earned can revel in the accomplishment and reap the social goods and benefits such as self-respect which accompany success in sport" (Keenan, 1975).

Michael Novak, the religious philosopher who has written a unique book on sport, has also taken a comparable view of justice by stating "sports celebrate honor, fair play, and the rule of law while it dramatizes the myth of the solitary man. . . . The American Way is to be decent, moral, trustworthy, law-abiding, tolerant, just, egalitarian, and so forth" (Novak, 1976).

To encourage fair play in an academic environment is to promote attitudes and ideals that are already a part of the community. The very premise of playing well and playing fairly is expounded by those in administration, those on the faculty, and the student body as a whole. To expect fair play in the university athletic teams is generally understood. In addition, teams must abide by the rules of their governing organizations for violations carry severe penalties.

An absorbing interest of the public and students has created an atmo-sphere not always purest. . . . There has been evident improvement in the rules; what is needed most is to improve in the ethical standards of all persons interested in athletics. Conformity to athletic rules is too much of a technicality and not enough of a principle—athletics, like every other form of amusement or business, must eventually rest on sound ethics. It is unfortunate in the extreme that it becomes indifferent to the ethical conditions surrounding the game—it is a manifest waste of energy to spend time in denouncing athletics; what is needed is efficient leadership by men to whom principle is dearer than anything else. . . . We shall never reform athletics simply by rules, we shall reform it only when we have inspired young men to cling to high ideals and to be governed by sound ethics (President Thompson, The Ohio State University, 1904).

The problem of morality in sport has been defined in numerous ways. Howard Slusher was of the opinion that the intimate nature of the value of achievement is not in man acting in sport the way he thinks he should act. Rather, the real meaning of truth is strictly an individual one. "Real morality cannot be achieved until man is willing to risk his self in the sport experience" (Slusher, 1967).

Moral questions are entertained concerning sport itself. Does sport encourage man to be "good" and "right"? Slusher indicated the absolutes of good and right simply do not exist. The areas are no longer black and white but man must "deal with the 'gray areas'" (Slusher, 1967). Man cannot avoid the decision-making process, and Slusher offered this solution:

The only answer I know is that man must do what he feels is good. Values and ethics, as moral derivatives, need to be unclouded so that man can act with a decisiveness that indicates position and reflection. But this is only the start. For the more immediate and intimate man becomes to sport, the greater will be the effort to reach the zenith (Slusher, 1967).

Rules, and participating in sport and abiding by these rules, was also discussed by Anthony Ralls. "If one is to play a game, one must keep the rules" is an expression that can lead to two possible conclusions: (1) If you are playing a game it is necessary to play by the rules; and (2) If you are playing a game, then you are in trouble if you do not keep the rules (Gerber & Morgan, 1979). Ralls affirmed that persuading people to play the game is synonymous with persuading them to keep the rules. "If everyone is playing the game is to be true, it must be true that everyone must keep the rules" (Gerber & Morgan, 1979).

Slusher has also equated morality with physical fitness. It is this dual selection, when one selects sport he also selects fitness, that leads to confusion and a compromise of ideals. Is fitness a moral quality of sport? Slusher emphatically stated that:

> The "fit" in sport are not those with qualities of concern, love, empathy, care, passion and respect for personhood. To survive in the world of sport man better not have these qualities. To be hard, to be tough, to be strong and to be rough—these are qualities that pay dividends (Slusher, 1967).

Moral conduct in sport is inherent in the concept valuation of winning and losing contests. "The greater the emphasis on winning, the greater also is the proclivity of players to interpret the rules in a strict, legalistic manner, and so to regard them as external sanctions, rather than exhortations to follow the inner convictions of conscience" (Osterhoudt, 1978).

Other writers distinguish between degrees of competition—playful activity is a free and creative activity in which the only goal includes the momentary joy of the activity itself. Athletics, as distinguished from this, is a "physical contest designed to determine human excellence through honorable victory in a contest" (Osterhoudt, 1978). The moral problems usually are common in athletics due to the intense emotional nature of competition and the excessive desire or pressure for victory.

The final moral issue to be addressed in this paper is that of the availability of athletic programs to the female competitor. The most recent influence on assuring equality of competition is Public Law 92–318, more commonly referred to as Title IX. This federally mandated legislation was a part of the Educational Amendment Act of 1972. Essentially the political influence of educators and sports persons have resulted in the encouragement and financial reinforcement to promote programs for the female sport participant. Regardless of the impact of this legislation on the courts, every institution has a moral obligation to provide competitive opportunities for women.

The Implications of Beauty

Sport is viewed, appreciated, and enthusiastically received by participants and spectators all over the nation. Many philosophers and educators have studied the impact of the aesthetic value of sport. Few writers are in agreement as to the relationship between sport and aesthetics and art forms. Paul Ziff, in "A Fine Forehand," examined the problems of defining the aesthetics in sport and concluded that there are no aesthetic features which are novel to sport. He countered that although some sports such as gymnastics and figure skating display aesthetic aspects, most other sports do not. "And those which do, form (as their aesthetic element) in them is itself a grading factor, and so itself ancillary" (Ziff, 1974). This appeal to form is merely a "by product, or epiphenomenon of technical aspects" (Ziff, 1974).

Another essay written by R.K. Elliott reinforced the view of Ziff and attempted to explain the relationship between quality and aesthetic features of sport. Although he likened the beauty of sport more to nature than to art, Elliott wrote that every sporting activity is primarily engaged in for the final outcome of winning. Beauty, if present at all, is only a secondary outcome. In art, however, beauty is of primary importance.

Although Ziff and Elliott held minority opinions regarding aesthetics in sport, most writers take a conservative view of the authenticity of sport as it might relate to art. David Best, in his essay, "The Aesthetic in Sport," divided sport into two subcategories—purposive and aesthetic. The former included sports where achievement is measured and directed toward the external end—winning and losing. The latter, aesthetic sports, contained movements that are pleasing to view or to perform with a high degree of skill. Best concluded, although most sports are superb aesthetically (they contain and present pleasing patterns of movement), they are not art.

The positive value of beauty was described by George Santayana. Although it gives the impression of being external and existing independently, beauty " . . . exists in perceptions, and cannot exist otherwise. A beauty not perceived is a pleasure not felt and a contradiction" (Santayana, 1955). To elaborate further on this theory, Terence J. Roberts has attempted to apply this idea to the beauty of sport. Roberts indicated two elements exist in sporting events that can be understood in aesthetic terms. These include the apperceived ideal (lines, movements, and proportions) and expressions (ideas or emotions, thought or felt in association with the perceived object or event) (Osterhoudt, 1978). To clarify expression, Roberts wrote that:

> . . . expressive images of courageousness, unselfishness, sportsmanship, fortitude and upstanding character are quite significant and certainly legitimate from an aesthetic standpoint . . . it is a beauty of ours which

we objectify into the event and gain a pleasure from it; we believe it to be so because it makes us happy to believe it is so (Roberts, 1975).

Another advocate of this type of philosophical stand was Joseph Kupfer. In addition to citing the grace of the human form as an aesthetic feature of sport, Kupfer believed that aesthetic values in human interaction were important. The tension between opponents, the participant's perspective of himself in relation to his teammates, and the mental as well as emotional contests that are a part of activity are included in this interaction. To summarize this thought, Kupfer, in his essay "Purpose and Beauty in Sport," wrote: "Sport instantiates man's capacity to improvise in the midst of structured stress. It emphasizes and crystallizes the element of venture—that summons to new openings within the world's limits, so often unrecognized or unheeded in our everyday lives" (Kupfer, 1975).

In contrast to the previously mentioned conservative views on the values of sport as it relates to art, a few individuals have definitely given sport a priority in the world of art. Paul Kuntz likened sport to art by listing commonalities of the two: the playful and spontaneous nature of each, the striving to excel in both, the emotional and aesthetic characteristics common to both, the relationship of the audience—spectator to sport and critic to art, the status of both as by products of leisure time, and the influence of sport and art on history and culture (Osterhoudt, 1979).

One of the few writers who has tried to establish a concrete basis for the concept of sport as art was James W. Bell. According to Bell, sport and art are integral parts of life and cannot be easily separated. Daily activities are distinguished in two broad categories: useful art and fine art. Under the former, sport is concerned with the development of a healthy body through exercise. The latter category equated sport with art—as a "work" or a "product." Bell clarified this position when he wrote: "It would seem that just as the artist has molded his mind and body for a finished product, similarly, the athlete has molded his mind and body for the purpose of producing a product" (Bell, 1976).

Bell further explored the topic when he skillfully applied the "work of sport" to other art-related areas of pleasure, play, and expression. He concluded by commenting that "sport is an expression. It is an expression of the personality of the artist-athlete and also, is a reflection of the outlook of the age in which it is produced. As society has changed, so has its art, athletes and athletic events" (Bell, 1976).

The Implications of the Common Good

To clarify the exact relationship of the common good, Osterhoudt made the following observation. "Social and political philosophy examined the moral character of social life and political, or governmental power. It concerns the nature and significance of the socio-political organization or the general principles of the common good" (Osterhoudt, 1978). The socio-political status is specifically concerned with (1) the relation of sport to other forms of socio-political institutions; (2) the general role of law, justice, and political power and organization in sport; and (3) the relationship of sport and the common good or public interest. These areas overlap with the particular forms of existential experience and philosophic investigations related to views of selected people, groups of people, or institutions.

Social justice is primarily concerned with protecting the rights of all people, especially people who are less fortunate than others. John Rawls has developed a theory he called "Justice as Fairness." His theory, however, has many more implications relating to the institution of sport than the sense of fair play mentioned earlier. Rawls developed a general conception of justice and developed two principles which give the general conception its specific form. These specific principles are:

1. Each person is to have an equal right to the most extensive basic liberty compatible with a similar liberty for others.

2. Social and economic inequalities are to be arranged so that they are both: (a) reasonably expected to be to everyone's advantage; and (b) attached to positions and offices open to all (Rawls, 1971).

These principles are to govern social institutions so that the best individual and cultural interests are served. Keenan, in his adaptation of Rawls's "Theory of Justice" to the sport institution was quick to draw the comparison by stating:

> Sport mirrors the corruptions of society generally, and of unjust men more specifically. Any social institution which has captured the attention of the masses as has sport has an opportunity to reverse the mirror image by showing what is possible when men of good will work together. Perhaps the ideal will never be reached, but just men engaged in competitive cooperation can provide a model for other social institutions, a model of the kind of union that is possible not only in sport, but in culture

generally. When institutions have rediscovered and renewed their vitality and formulated a true and just picture of themselves, we shall be able to understand each other better (Keenan, 1975).

A majority of the general works regarding the common good or socio-political status of sport speculate as to the value of competition versus playful activity. James Keating in his essay, "The Ethics of Competition and Its Relation to Some Moral Problems in Athletics," has defined competition as ". . . an attempt, according to agreed-upon rules, to get or to keep any thing either to the exclusion of others or in greater measure than others" (Osterhoudt, 1978). Keating felt this definition automatically excluded criminal activities and the fallacy of people competing against themselves. To apply competition to the common good, Keating wrote:

> Whereas some isolated individuals and primitive societies may be relatively free from the competitive spirit, an over-all view reveals that competition appears to be an ineradicable trait of human nature. It is true that not all men compete with the same intensity. Some even tend to escape it whenever possible. Still it is difficult to see how any active person can escape all forms of competition for a single day. Competition being therefore an indisputable fact of life, the real question is how to keep it within proper bounds. Men should be esteemed not because they abstain from competition, but because they hold in check that fierce desire for supremacy which threatens the observance of the agreed-upon rules which alone distinguish competition from internecine warfare or deceptive and destructive conflict (Osterhoudt, 1978).

Robert Osterhoudt argued the position taken by Keating by citing three ways in which the competitiveness of athletics differs from the competitiveness of playful activity: (1) in playful activity, competition allows a heightened joy and pleasure for all and functions as a means to a more venerated end; while in athletics competition is to function as a means to an end in itself; (2) in playful activity the competitive motif appears altogether accidental although this competition is a necessary condition for athletics; and (3) competition as construed in athletics is not in harmony with the ends sought for playful activity (Osterhoudt, 1978). He disputed the distinction proposed by Keating by stating that playful activity and competitive athletics, although being similar in phenomenal appearance, are vastly different in terms of their goals or the primary intentions of their participants. According to Osterhoudt "What we have here . . . is the germ of two radically discrete manners of conceiving man, the social substance, and the common good—two inclinations which are so clearly and distinctly different as to be incompatible'' (Osterhoudt, 1978).

Another educator who disputed Keating's philosophy was William A. Sadler. Keating viewed competition as an acquisitive stance; it was oriented towards obtaining something. According to Sadler, Keating's conception of competition failed to consider this influence on universal cultures. Sadler showed four types of social order which differ as to dominant values and thus differing with views of competition: (1) a being society is past-oriented, submissive to nature, fatalistic, and having no notion of competition as defined by Keating; (2) a becoming society is present-oriented, cooperative with nature, and having the notion of competition as occurring within a condition of moderation and cooperation; (3) a doing society is future-oriented, controlling of nature, practical, productive, utilitarian, and having a favorable view of competition; and (4) a having society is future-oriented, acquisitive of nature, consumptive, and having such a favorable view of competition as to develop spectator as well as participant interest (Osterhoudt, 1978). Keating's definition, according to Sadler, was limited to the doing and having societies. He also explained that the conceptualization of playful activity as described by Keating was also included in these two societies. The attempt to reduce play to pleasure eliminated the seriousness of the learning activity. Play in a child's world and in a therapeutic environment can represent significant growth, discovery, and rehabilitation. To summarize, Sadler wrote:

> Competitive play can be recognized as constituting an interdependence between opponents whose contest mutually testified to their personal worth. From this perspective, a true sportsman is not a hard worker who is legalistically concerned about his attainment but a good player who cares about our experience of our game. If one views competition and play consistently within the same value orientation of becoming, then apparently both modes of activity may converge to form an intrinsic element of self and social development (Osterhoudt, 1978).

Summary

This article has revealed any number of intangible values that can be associated with university athletic programs. However, philosophers and educators cannot seem to agree upon the impact of these values as they relate to the objects of inquiry. Therefore, it seems important that each individual involved in athletics formulate his own unique ideas and place the emphasis accordingly. One of the nine principles for educational excellence states that learning should occur throughout life. Application of the values of morality, aesthetics, and common good could promote this principle when applied correctly by those who direct athletic programs.

Many writers concentrate on the influence of winning, however, it has been noted that athletics can easily deal with the more intangible values as they relate to everyday life. Michael Novak has taken a more philosophical stand to express perhaps the greatest value of all.

> If I had to give one single reason for my love of sports it would be this: I love the tests of the human spirit. I love to see impossible odds confronted. I love to see impossible dares accepted. I love to see the incredible grace lavished on simple plays—the simple flashing beauty of perfect form—but, even more, I love to see the heart that refuses to give in, refuses to panic, seizes opportunity, slips through defenses, exerts itself far beyond capacity, forges momentarily of its bodily habitat an instrument of almost perfect will. . . . That is the way I believe the human race should live (Novak, 1976).

References

Bell, J. W. (1976, May). Investigation of the concept-sport as art. *Physical Education*, 81–84.

Best, D. (1974). The aesthetic in sport. *British Journal of Aesthetics. 14*, 197–213.

Gerber, E. W. & Morgan, W. J. (Eds.). (1979). *Sport and the body: A philosophical symposium*. Philadelphia: Lea and Febiger.

Keenan, F. W. (1975). Justice and sport. *Journal of the Philosophy of Sport. 2*, 111–123.

Kupfer, J. (1975). Purpose and beauty in sport. *Journal of the Philosophy of Sport. 2*, 83–90.

Novak, M. (1976). *The joy of sports (end zones, bases, baskets, balls) and the consecration of the American spirit*. New York: Basic Books, Inc.

Osterhoudt, R. (1978). *An introduction to the philosophy of physical education and sport*. Champaign, Illinois: Stipes Publishing Co.

Rawls, J. (1971). *A theory of justice*. Cambridge: The Belnap Press of Harvard University Press.

Roberts, T. J. (1975). Sport and the sense of beauty. *Journal of the Philosophy of Sport. 2,* 91–101.

Sabock, R. (1969). *A history of physical education at Ohio State University— men's and women's divisions, 1898–1969.* Unpublished Ph.D. dissertation. The Ohio State University.

Santayana, G. (1955). *The sense of beauty.* New York: Dover Press.

Slusher, H. S. (1967). *Man, sport and existence.* Philadelphia: Lea and Febiger.

Ziff, P. (1974). A fine forehand. *Journal of the Philosophy of Sport. 1,* 92–109.

Part III: Means

Various means by which the goals and objectives of undergraduate education are accomplished are addressed in this section. Teaching strategies and methods are examined. Although lectures are frequently used for teaching in colleges and universities, they have strengths and weaknesses. Alternative devices are available. They, too, have advantages and disadvantages. Recent innovations in college teaching are worthy of further exploration. The "how" of teaching is often related to the "what" of teaching.

Michael R. Hoadley and Philip A. Vik diagnose several major components of effective college teaching. They focus on the purpose and goals of college instruction, the roles and competencies of students and professors, and on a variety of teaching methodologies and strategies. To be effective, college teaching must address the student as a "total person." Teaching must attend to cognitive, affective, and psychomotor needs. Teachers must provide environments that help students to recognize and realize their potentials. Students must be actively involved in the learning process through the employment of effective teaching methodology.

Because of the prominent use of the lecture method in colleges, H. Virginia Monroe and Charles E. Eicher believe that any consideration of alternative ways of teaching must address alternatives to the lecture. They describe a variety of other possible methods including: Personalized System of Instruction (PSI), the discussion method, learning via case studies, field experiences, simulation models, contract learning, and the use of computers for instruction. They believe that there is an interest in moving from teaching methods that rely heavily upon behaviorists' modes of teaching to modes that can accommodate higher levels of learning. Alternative methods of teaching that use newer theories from cognitive science, Eicher and Monroe believe, can bring about revolutionary changes in educational practices.

Although most students in college are able to meet successfully the academic demands of undergraduate education, there are a number of bright students unable to do so. John W. Woodley and Joe N. Crank present learning and teaching strategies that students and professors can use to help students comprehend and use written materials in their classes. They conclude their section by suggesting that a major resource for undergraduate students may be what can be learned and discovered from other students.

Effective College Teaching

Michael R. Hoadley and Philip A. Vik

Effective college teaching can do much to enhance the education of undergraduate students. In order to understand fully and appreciate the impact of college teaching, several major components must be diagnosed. Key concepts focus on the purpose and goals of college instruction, the roles and competencies of the student learner and the teacher, and the variety of teaching methodologies and strategies available in the total learning process.

What is the purpose of college teaching? The primary reason for teaching is the dissemination of knowledge and sharing of experiences so the student can develop some degree of competence in the subject matter. Students need specific content facts, theories, methods, and exposure to experiences of others to use as building blocks in the development of competence. While more facts will not suffice for all future endeavors, the exposure of the student to incorrect information and methods can erode the learning process such that a faulty foundation of knowledge may be established. Such results would obviously be counterproductive to the goals of education, especially at the college level.

What is the goal of teaching? At the college level, students must develop higher expectations of themselves and expect to reach those higher standards. Those expectations and standards are far in advance of the lower level needs of basic growth and development. Therefore, each student must strive to attain the highest level of personal potential possible. According to Maslow (1943), such a level of optimum potential is referred to as self-actualization. Although self-actualization may be considered the ultimate goal of college level teaching, several

135

variables must be considered in the total analysis of the learning situation.

What is the role of the instructor? The college level instructor should be considered a scholar first. That person must be competent in the subject matter in order to properly disseminate information. As a professional, the college level instructor has a vested interest in the field and therefore displays his/her willingness to continue to learn everyday. Such an individual also serves as a role model to students by continually aspiring for personal and professional improvement. No person can be a perfect role model, but the saying "practice what you preach" is very appropriate in the field of education. Failure to follow one's own advice can greatly disrupt credibility.

The competence and professional manner of the college instructor can further be enhanced by organization and evaluation skills. Being well-organized promotes learning by instilling confidence of one's abilities in the learners. An organized approach often lends itself to a similar approach by the students. Evaluation plays an important role because it helps a good instructor establish goals and objectives which serve as markers for assessment. Matching the subject matter with the learning level of the students not only establishes evaluation as a benefit to the learners, but for the instructor as well.

Ultimately the effective college instructor teaches students to become "self-directed learners," *i.e.*, students learn how to learn. Students need to be able to apply knowledge of specific concepts to new situations. Application of insights gained through classes can then be used in making intelligent decisions in the future. Obviously such higher level learning moves beyond the realm of rote memorization and involves consideration of the cognitive, affective, and psychomotor domains. As a mentor of the students, the college professional has a unique opportunity to positively influence the educational actions, attitudes, and beliefs of many individuals. The philosophy should be one that everyone can learn. The effective college instructor arranges conditions so that learning is activated, supported, enhanced, and maintained (Hart, 1981).

The college teacher must be an effective communicator. The college instructor needs to provide a positive classroom environment so learning opportunities are supported and maintained (Gullette, 1984). Studies indicate that a "relaxed classroom atmosphere" is very important to students (Jordan, 1982). Instructors who are able to gain a positive rapport with students find that the learners are more comfortable asking questions and actively joining discussions. The enthusiasm displayed by the instructor can instill excitement in a particular field, even to the point of motivating students to go beyond the normal scope of study. The leadership exercised by the instructor in the processes of modeling, consensus building, and feedback support the concept of a positive classroom climate. In the long run such a climate not only provides for an orderly environment, but also tends to place more emphasis on academics and higher expectations for success.

Another aspect of being a good communicator is to be a good listener. Quite often the college instructor is placed in the position of being a counselor. Counseling about subject matter is foremost, but at times even personal and professionally-related matters must be addressed. Therefore, the instructor must be able to speak on various issues with a certain degree of competency in order to be responsive to the needs and interests of the students. Open lines of communication promote interaction and two-way communication among the students, as well as with the instructor and significant others.

An effective teacher promotes self-awareness in students. The classroom is meant to be a place where students learn as much about themselves and others, as they do about the subject matter. Another important factor to consider is the maintenance of reality in the classroom. Although an instructor needs to go beyond concrete ideas in teaching, the abstract also needs to be based in reality. Students need to be able to take concepts and apply them to the real world. This ability to apply information and realize that specific cases require different approaches when dealing with problems is another facet of the total awareness process.

An instructor at the college level must be personable and humanistic. The teacher should be sensitive to the needs and interests of the students in order to act accordingly. One obvious way is to treat students as individuals. An effective instructor respects the opinions of the learners, as well as their right to freedom of expression. Specific cases will require different approaches when dealing with problems, but the teacher and students can learn much from each other.

What is the role of the student? Students are individuals who enter a classroom with varying backgrounds, ideals, expectations, needs, and skills. Although some instructors might view the varied composition of a class as a negative factor, the truth of the matter is that different perspectives enhance the total learning situation.

One of the more important roles for a student is to be an active participant in the class. A student's willingness to share information and experiences, as well as ask questions and participate in discussions, are often thought to be essential to the learning process (Hart, 1981). In order to begin to comprehend new ideas, a student must internalize the information. Each student should listen selectively and establish his/her own meaning to the material. Active participation in class helps clarify concepts which, in turn, leads to increased memory and internalization.

Students must be responsible for their own work. The attitude fostered should be one in which the student puts forth his/her best effort, knowing there will be times when the answers of others will be more correct and/or more appropriate. Students need to learn from mistakes. Mistakes should be seen as learning opportunities, rather than moments for personal ridicule or even academic defeat. The mature attitude of willingness to learn, rather than passivity to learning, will benefit everyone in the classroom. By acknowledging the problems which have been identified through study, evaluation, and correction of their own work, students are better able to correct misconceptions which later on might cause greater difficulties in learning.

Students must show self-control and positive behavior in the classroom. Cooperation is a key element in learning. Students who are considerate of the teacher and other students will help create a more positive learning environment. Student efforts should be viewed as beneficial to everyone in the process of learning because something can be learned or reinforced from everything that happens in the classroom. Students who demonstrate self-control and consideration for others will find such skills mandatory for survival and acceptance into the real world.

Beyond consideration of the roles of the instructor and students, what instructional methods and strategies can be employed to accomplish the task of learning? Teaching and instructional methodologies are defined as proven means of delivering subject matter to students. Some of the major types of teaching methodologies include lecture, inquiry, contracting, gaming and simulation, small group instruction, and instructional modules (Bailey, 1984). Based upon a particular philosophic foundation, each methodology addresses the multitude of variables which affect student achievement and attitude. The success of a methodology is dependent upon the receptivity of students to the educational techniques of presentation, practice, discovery, and reinforcement (Laska, 1984). The combination of teaching techniques and the transfer from one technique to another aid the instructor in attaining the overall goal of maximizing student learning.

The lecture is the most common teaching technique used at the college level and is thought of as being delivered by the instructor (Schwartz). However, the lecture discussion can be from teacher to student, student to teacher, or student to student and can be a means for achieving two-way communication (Anspaugh, 1987).

Another teaching technique is brainstorming, which is an activity in a group session in which ideas are given by the class members with special procedures employed to avoid any discussion, criticism, or analysis. A list of all ideas is maintained for later use. The buzz session is a small group activity to discuss a specific topic with minimum structure, maximum emphasis upon interaction, and full opportunity to express ideas related to the topic. The demonstration is an activity in which participants observe planned, carefully presented examples of real or simulated behavior illustrating certain techniques, materials, equipment, and procedures as they might realistically be employed. Role-playing is a spontaneous dramatization involving one or more persons assuming designated roles in relation to a specific problem in a given situation.

A teaching methodology is not considered an entity in itself. Each is considered rather complex because a variety of activities are involved, which require careful organization and planning. Each methodology benefits the students in a variety of ways, one of the most important of which is the development of critical skills for application in other learning situations.

Components found within major methodologies or as a separate approach are instructional strategies. Although a complete list would be rather extensive, common examples include case studies, field trips, demonstrations, guest speakers, audiovisual aids, homework and in-class activity worksheets, and use of computers (Anspaugh, Ezell, & Goodman, 1987). As compared to the methodologies, an instructional strategy is not as complex and does not have a strong philosophical base. Due to simplicity in nature and singular purpose, planning time for use of an instructional strategy is considerably less. The most common criticisms are that instructional strategies have limited benefit in the development of critical skills, as well as limited application to other learning activities (Bailey, 1984).

Also found in each major teaching methodology and instructional strategy are instructional techniques. Such techniques include verbal and nonverbal behaviors. Examples of verbal cues include lecturing, questioning, criticizing, reinforcing, direction giving, and the act of giving and accepting emotions. Nonverbal cues include mannerisms, gestures, use of time, use of space, facial expressions, eye contact, silence, touching, and the energy level. Both types of cues can be effective given the right circumstance.

The most effective teacher would appear to be the person who uses a combination of major methodologies, instructional strategies, and teaching techniques in the delivery of subject matter. Whatever combination is selected is actually the decision of the instructor. An important consideration to remember is that the intent of such instruction is to meet the needs, interests, and level of development of the students in relationship to their anticipated profession.

There are several important points which the college instructor must consider when deciding upon implementation of a methodology, strategy, and/or technique. Probably most important is the decision to consider a variety of teaching methods. An effective teacher realizes the value of various methods in different situations and circumstances. Different methodologies may encourage class involvement by different class members. The old adage that "students learn by doing" also supports the idea of more class involvement, so active participation enhances active learning.

An effective instructor should have clearly defined instructional objectives. Objectives defined at the beginning of a course provide direction for the teacher and the students, as well as what is expected in the course. Expectations are then evaluated by checking goals and instructional objectives against student performance. Questions asked frequently during the class also inform the instructor what the students are learning and serve as checkpoints for understanding. Such evaluation aids the students by providing a clearer idea of direction to be taken when studying. Immediate feedback also allows students to correct faulty learnings and move on to more in-depth and higher level cognitive learnings. Teachers also benefit by determining how effectively they have taught and by detecting class strengths, weaknesses, and problem areas. As a result of such information, instructors are able to cope with and correct deficiencies, as well as increase the learning levels of students. During the actual teaching-learning episode, the instructor must be observant to the situation and willing to make corrections as necessary. The moment any instruction begins, the instructor must be able to process and analyze the data in order to effectively alter the teaching plan, corroborate it, impeach it, or make adjustments in action in order to enhance fully the learning process.

The effective instructor uses motivational techniques which arouse interest and curiosity on the part of the students. More active learning will take place if the instructor is able to capture and maintain the attention of the students. The teacher should encourage different points of view and be receptive to new ideas. This supports the idea of creating a classroom climate of trust, support, and acceptance which encourages students to risk raising different points of view. The positive classroom allows students to verbally and mentally question information presented by the instructor. Good instructors take time to answer questions from students before moving on to new or more complex material. This approach can be very influential in enhancing a student's self-esteem because the self-image of the student is a correlate of his/her participation in class. The end result is a better foundation of knowledge and ultimately greater allowance for student growth, both personally and professionally.

The effective instructor should incorporate personal and practical experiences in the classroom which provide a better understanding of concepts taught. According to Carl Rogers and others, "learning is aided perhaps most of all by the quality of personal relationships" (Frederick, 1981). A multitude of opportunities should be available to assist students in connecting concepts to practical and/or personal experiences. Student learning is substantially increased when real and practical experiences transform abstract conceptions into concrete expressions. The instructor must also make every effort to provide students with alternative models, visions, or interpretations. Usually there are several "schools of thought" on different concepts and ideas and it is important that the instructor present each, even those not congruent to the instructor's way of thinking. Consideration of such material helps students to advance from the typical mode of dependent memorizing and to move on to the more desirable professional skills of independent thinking and problem solving.

In summary, effective college teaching should address the "total person" concept of the student. An instructor who merely focuses on the cognitive needs of the student may do an injustice to the learner. Teaching must also be attentive to the affective and psychomotor domains. Furthermore, it is the duty of the college instructor to challenge each and every student to go one step beyond the normal expectations of the classroom. The instructor must provide an environment which is conducive to the idea that each student recognize his/her own potential and be willing to strive for it. By exposing the students to new ideas and experiences, forcing the learners to make intelligent decisions requiring critical thought, and actively involving the students in the learning process through willing and desired participation, a positive exchange of ideas can be expected which benefit both the mentor and the pupil. At that point the most optimal gains have been made in the learning process of the college student because the most effective teaching methodology has been employed.

References

Anspaugh, D., Ezell, G., & Goodman, K.N. (1987). *Teaching today's health.* Columbus, OH: Merrill Publishing Co.

Bailey, G. D. (1984, April). How to improve your presentations by keeping your mouth shut. *Performance and Instruction, 23*(3), 27–28.

Frederick, R. (1981). The dreaded discussion: Ten ways to start. *Improving College and University Teaching, 29*, 109–114.

Gullette, M. M. (1984). The heart of good teaching. *Change, 16*, 8–11, 48.

Hart, L. A. (1981, March). Don't teach them; help them learn. *Learning, 9*, 39–40.

Jordan, J. R. (1982). The professor as communicator. *Improving College and University Teaching, 30*, 120–124.

Laska, J. A. (1984). The four basic methods of instruction. *Educational Technology*, 42–45.

Maslow, A. A. (1943). A theory of motivation. *Psychological Review*, 370–96.

Schwartz, L. L. Criteria for effective university teaching. *Improving College and University Teaching, 28*, 120–124.

The Venerable Lecture: Alternatives and Improvements

H. Virginia Monroe and Charles E. Eicher

Lectures dominate undergraduate education. Going to class in any major university in the country is almost synonymous with attending a lecture. Osterman (1982) estimated that 85 to 90% of all course offerings at the undergraduate level are taught via the traditional lecture method.

The lecture method has been the choice of teachers in higher education for centuries, having been traced back to the pre-Christian academy of Plato (McLeish, 1976). In ancient Greece, the lector was "the reader of lessons" (Erickson, 1984), and lecturing, or giving a public reading, was the primary means of passing on knowledge. Prior to the advent of the printing press, when manuscripts were rare, the lector read from the only copy of the text to which the group had access. What was born in Greece as a necessary means of education has survived, with few mutations, to the present day.

Technological challenges, of which the printing press was but the first, have led to numerous and logical predictions of the lecture's demise. For example, in 1913, Thomas Edison predicted that moving pictures would completely change education within the next ten years since his new invention could be used to teach every branch of human knowledge (Waggoner, 1984). Nonetheless, the lecture survived and went on to demonstrate its immunity, not only to moving pictures, but to talking pictures as well.

Lecturing has also survived the blows of its detractors. "Boring" and "confusing" are two of the barbs frequently hurled by students.

Yet these objections of style are but sticks and stones compared to the powerful weaponry in educators' arsenals. Their shafts go to the heart of the lecture when they state that, by its very nature, the lecture emphasizes the acquisition of facts rather than the gaining of understanding. Furthermore, educators recognize that the passive posture of the student during a lecture should be its Achilles' heel, since passivity is a well-known enemy of intellectual initiative, personal responsibility and long-term memory. Nonetheless, although the objections unleashed have at times momentarily changed the lecture's complexion, succumb it has not.

What Are the Alternatives?

In undergraduate education there are a number of instructional strategies that serve as alternatives to the lecture method. Insight into the longevity of the lecture can be gained by looking at these alternatives—the lecture's competition.

Personalized System of Instruction

First initiated on a college campus twenty years ago, the Personalized System of Instruction (PSI), also known as the Keller Plan, became a major instructional alternative in undergraduate education (Keller & Sherman, 1974). Keller and his colleagues observed that the traditional lecture method failed to apply what was known about the principles of behaviorism to the college learning experience; opportunities to respond and immediate feedback on learning success (reinforcement) were lacking (Schiller & Markle, 1978). Therefore, the PSI was designed to incorporate more opportunities for reinforcement and to provide for more active student participation.

A PSI is characterized by student self-pacing through small units of instruction and by reliance on written material as the primary source of information. Typically students read the required material on their own and take a quiz when they feel they are ready. Although they must pass each quiz before they can move to the next unit of instruction, there is no penalty for failure and maximum credit for success.

To design a course as a PSI, an instructor must carefully analyze what is to be learned, determine appropriate intermediate and terminal objectives, divide course content into a series of sequential units and prepare self-study packets for each unit. Great care must be taken when selecting and preparing written materials, as this represents the most important form of communication between the teacher and the students.

The research on PSI has been largely favorable. Walberg, Schiller and Haertel (1979) reviewed 12 studies that compared PSI with the conventional lecture method at the college level. They reported that most of the studies found the PSI method to be superior, not only on achievement and retention measures, but on measures of attitudes and interest in the subject as well. Comparable findings were reported four years later by Oddi (1983) following a similar review of the literature.

To account for the positive findings associated with PSI, both the material to be processed and the PSI process itself have been highlighted. The type of material being processed by students during a lecture is auditory whereas in PSI it is visual. And as Erickson (1984) notes, "In general, . . . adults can process information faster and better via the eye than the ear" (p. 34). Others accounting for the findings note that higher achievement and retention rates are assured under PSI because without achieving at a prescribed level students cannot proceed through the course. The same is not true in a lecture course; students may continue with the course in spite of misunderstanding or glossing over large segments of the material.

Nonetheless, PSI has not revolutionized undergraduate education, nor is it without its critics. When using this technique, administrative frustrations are frequently encountered. Rosenkoetter (1984) found the PSI he developed for an undergraduate psychology course to be a "clerical nightmare." In addition, he reported that the need for sufficient rooms to administer, score and review quizzes taxed the available facilities. Cost is another debit in the PSI ledger since student proctors are needed for PSI courses and a larger quantity of duplicated materials per student is required. Also, those concerned with grade inflation have been critical of the distribution of unusually high grades that is typically associated with PSI. Finally, a higher non-completion rate has been noted when using PSI, and some researchers have been critical of studies which report only the outcome data on those students who have successfully completed the courses.

The Discussion Method

Another major instructional strategy, one that has been around as long as the lecture, is the discussion method. "Active student involvement" is what the discussion trades on since student involvement is known to enhance retention. Furthermore, when listening to others and mentally preparing to respond or to promote a personally valued idea, students are actively involved in critical thinking (Vygotsky, 1962).

Indeed, studies have shown that the discussion method can be effective in improving problem analysis and critical thinking skills (Kulik & Kulik, 1979). In addition, through discussions students can improve their ability to effectively communicate their ideas—certainly an important life skill.

However, the discussion method will undoubtedly never become the primary means of undergraduate education since five is the optimum number of group members for maximizing interactive communication (Hare, 1962). This ideal number renders it too expensive to be used with much frequency in most institutions of higher education. And as discussion groups increase in size in response to economic exigencies, student gains in critical thinking, problem solving and communication skills diminish.

Inefficiency is another major shortcoming of the discussion technique thereby making the technique of preference dependent upon the instructional objectives. As Bloom (1953) summarized:

> . . . if the objective of education is the development of knowledge about a topic or field, the lecture is a far more efficient method of communicating such knowledge and of securing the attention of students to these ideas than is the discussion. However, if the objective is the development of abilities and skills which are problem solving in nature, the least efficient discussion is superior to most of the lectures. (p. 169)

Finally, research data suggests that discussions are not equally beneficial for all students. Students who score high on measures of anxiety score higher on achievement measures when the instructional method has been the traditional lecture. The reverse is also true: less anxious students do better when class discussions are the primary mode of instruction (Gage & Berliner, 1984). Another finding of interest is that high ability students express a preference for the lecture format; this may reflect that they feel held back by low ability students during large group discussions or that they are frustrated with the slower rate of topic coverage that is inherent in the discussion method.

Other Instructional Options

Other alternative instructional strategies include field experiences, simulation techniques (including laboratory experiences), individualized instruction and computer assisted instruction. For numerous and multiple reasons, economics and availability of appropriate materials being primary among them, none of these constitute a viable challenge to the lecture method as the dominant instructional strategy in undergraduate education.

What Explains the Lecture's Longevity?

Explanations for the lecture's robust and long life have been many and varied. Waggoner (1984) attributes its survival to the system of rewards in higher education. He states that if more attention were given to teaching and class preparation there would be less reliance on the lecture method. But in the higher education system, faculty minimize their attention to teaching because ". . . ways are sought to ransom time for the more professionally lucrative research, publication and consulting. Unfortunately, the lecture method of teaching accommodates this cycle of events" (p. 8).

Waggoner's argument cries for debate or data since instructor time associated with various teaching techniques has not been established and a strong case can be made for discussions being the easy way out. Also, Waggoner's survival-by-default argument overlooks the lecture's unique pedagogical strengths which may be contributing to its tenacious grip on undergraduate education. As Spencer said, "The decrying of the wholesale use of lectures is probably justified. The wholesale decrying of the use of lectures is just as certainly not justified" (in Brown, 1982, p. 93).

The lecture method has positive attributes that have undoubtedly contributed to its survival. Economy is one of the lecture's major assets which requires little explanatory embellishment. Through the use of the lecture, the student-to-faculty ratio can be raised to what some would consider unseemly heights since theoretically class size is only restricted by the available facilities: rooms and public address systems.

The flexibility of the lecture method is also legend. A lecture can be adapted to cover a broad or a narrow aspect of a field; it can be adapted to the age, background or interest level of the audience; modifications can be made easily, in fact midstream; and it requires little in the form of setting or equipment. The lecture's flexibility yields one advantage of particular note: it allows it to be easily updated, thereby reducing the lag time between developments in a field of study and their incorporation into the curriculum. Other sources of information that are costly or time consuming to produce are at a disadvantage in this regard.

Probably the most important characteristic of the lecture that its defenders have articulated is that its economy and flexibility have not required the sacrifice of the social or human element. The human element provides a model and makes possible a personalized perspective on a whole field of study. Topics can be related to real-life situations appropriate to the audience. Affective aspects of knowledge and inquiry are given a forum for expression. The potential strengths of the lecture technique arising from its human element were summarized by Erickson (1984).

> The resiliency and the popularity of the lecture are justified. The teacher can be an inspirational force for students, an examiner of value judgements, and a source of the latest knowledge and a perspective on a topic. Sometimes the lecture is the single most effective method of arousing interest, initiating action, and challenging the attitudes and beliefs held by students (p. 28).

In summary, the lecture's longevity is certainly related to its economy, probably related to its flexibility and humanity and maybe related to faculty apathy. However, for many of the objectives of undergraduate education, namely, the acquisition of facts and concepts that undergird creative and critical thought in any area of specialization, the lecture method is a very defensible instructional strategy considering the available alternatives and constraints. Realistically we should expect this instructional technique to maintain its position for some time. Therefore, those interested in improving the means by which undergraduate education is accomplished would do well to focus at least some attention on the improvement of the lecture.

What Characterizes Effective Lecturing?

Gage (1978) refers to teaching as a practical or useful art and states:

> When teaching goes on in face-to-face interaction with students, the opportunity for artistry expands enormously. No one can ever prescribe successfully all the twists and turns to be taken as the lecturer, the discussion leader, or the classroom teacher uses judgment, sudden insight, sensitivity, and agility to promote learning. (p. 15)

Indeed there is ultimately a quality about good teaching that is ineffable just as there is in good art. Nevertheless, there are aspects of all art forms that are describable, modifiable and potentially measurable and teachable. The same should be true of lecturing.

As any student can tell you, there is great variability among lectures. They differ in their structure, their purpose and in their delivery. Some are strictly a one-way communication system captured by the cartoon in which a teacher is saying to her class, "Now class, it's my job to talk and it's your job to listen. If you finish before I do, please let me know." Others, by contrast, involve considerable interaction between the lecturer and students with the lecturer asking and eliciting questions, correcting misperceptions and delivering reinforcements. Lecture variability has prompted some writers to propose classification systems (Sweeney & Reigeluth, 1984; Woods, 1983) which may prove to be useful in future studies of the lecturing process.

The literature on effective lecturing is rife with accounts of personal experiences and expressions of personal opinions. McLeish (1976) sought the opinions of students in an attempt to identify characteristics associated with good teaching. He asked students to describe the behaviors of effective professors and then asked them to select, from a list of ten qualities, the three they considered to be the most important. The five characteristics most frequently selected were: systematic organization, ability to explain clearly, ability to encourage thought, enthusiastic attitude toward the subject, and expert knowledge. The five characteristics least frequently selected were: fairness, tolerance, sympathetic attitude, speaking ability, and pleasing personality. McLeish summarized his findings by stating that students regarded effective teaching to be the result of knowledge, organization and commitment to the area of specialization.

Research based on outcome data rather than opinion indicates that lecture effectiveness is a function of delivery, structure and content. Regarding delivery, instructor expressiveness and dynamism have been demonstrated to be critical variables. Coats and Smidchens (1966) found a significant relationship between lecturer dynamism and student performance on a multiple choice exam. On the basis of a meta-analysis of the research, Abrami, Leventhal and Perry (1982) concluded that instructor dynamism had a substantial impact on student ratings of instruction and a small but significant impact on achievement.

Lecture structure is also a critical variable. For example, conceiving of a lecture as a presentation of neatly encapsulated principles and facts and structuring the presentation accordingly, does not provide the most effective structure for learning. Rather, student learning is enhanced when a lecture is structured around questions designed to pique student interest (Erickson, 1984).

Using advance organizers is another lecture structuring technique with demonstrated effectiveness. An advance organizer is a brief introduction to the structure of the information to be presented—a mental scaffolding to which the new information can be attached (Gage & Berliner, 1984). Following a meta-analysis of the research, Luiten, Ames and Ackerson (1980) concluded that advance organizers are most effective under two conditions: when instructing high ability students and when the material must be processed aurally rather than visually. Lecturing to college students in most instances meets both of these conditions.

Content has also been demonstrated to be an important variable in effective lecturing. For example, researchers have established the importance of information density, which is defined as the number of separate ideas or facts presented in a given time period. Russell, Hendricson and Herbert (1984) varied information density by varying the blend of new versus elaborating material. They concluded that the amount of information a student can learn in the span of a lecture is limited; exceeding this limit can defeat the instructional purpose.

The picture of an effective lecture begins to emerge. It is one in which the instructor uses advance organizers and structures the content around important or fascinating questions. Variety is used in its delivery and a sense of excitement or obvious commitment to the importance of the material is conveyed. Finally, information density is controlled. This last characteristic does not reduce the amount of material for which the student is responsible; alternate sources of information are simply being used.

Where Should We Begin?

Undergraduates need field experiences, independent work and small discussion groups; they need instruction in which computers and simulations are appropriately used; they need experiences in which they must take greater responsibility for their learning and suffer the natural consequences of their behavior. Such variety is needed for many reasons including the need to guard against boredom. Thus, when alternatives to lecturing are appropriate to the objectives and feasible within the constraints of available facilities and monies, they should be used. However, in most institutions of higher education, the lecture technique will remain as the dominant instructional technique in the undergraduate program.

Therefore, in our efforts to improve undergraduate education, we can no longer continue to overlook the systematic improvement of lectures. Heralding the lecture's weaknesses has not harmed it, however, bearing them in mind may help us improve upon it. For example, noting that intellectual dependency may be encouraged by the lecture method, we can set in motion efforts to counteract dependency. Perhaps professors who attempt to cover all important concepts in their lectures are inadvertently encouraging intellectual dependency; the students learn to rely upon the teacher to read the text for them and to sort the chaff from the grain. Under these circumstances lecture attendance could easily be seen as an alternative to independent reading.

Our current information regarding the improvement of lecturing is sufficient to aid us in our initial systematic efforts. We know, for instance, that the improvement of the skills of teaching assistants through workshops and seminars has been repeatedly demonstrated (Levinson-Rose & Menges, 1981). Yet many universities have instituted no systematic program for working with new teaching personnel. In spite of information to the contrary, we continue to operate as though knowledge of the subject matter is sufficient for good teaching or as though lecturing skills cannot be improved.

Currently student feedback on teaching is the procedure used most frequently with the stated purpose of improving college teaching. We know that whenever employed, student feedback should be paired with consultations since by itself, student feedback has not been demonstrated to be effective (Levinson-Rose & Menges, 1981).

Finally, lecturing is not for everyone. It should be recognized as the mark of a good teacher to be able to judge when lecturing should be abandoned. The development of PSIs should be encouraged for many reasons, one being as an alternative for those instructors who find the lecture method to be a poor fit with their personal style.

In conclusion, there is artistry and "personality" involved in all teaching and certainly in lecturing. Yet acknowledging this should not release us from the responsibility of finding techniques to improve upon the method or to improve upon the skills of individual faculty members. Rather, it should sharpen the sense of challenge, for even in the finest artistry there are improvements to be made to counteract the lecture's inherent weaknesses and thereby enable us to more fully capitalize on its strengths.

References

Abrami, P. C., Leventhal, L. & Perry, R. P. (1982). Educational seduction. *Review of Educational Research, 52*, 446–464.

Bloom, B. S. (1953). Thought processes in lectures and discussions. *Journal of General Education*, 160–169.

Brown, G. A. (1982). Two days on explaining and lecturing. *Studies in Higher Education, 7* (2), 93–103.

Coats, W. D. & Smidchens, U. (1966). Audience recall as a function of speaker dynamism. *Journal of Educational Psychology*, 57, 189–191.

Erickson, S. C. (1984). *The essence of good teaching.* San Francisco: Jossey-Bass Publishers.

Gage, N. L. (1978). *The scientific basis of the art of teaching.* New York: Teachers College Press.

Gage, N. L. & Berliner, D. C. (1984). *Educational psychology* (3rd ed.). Boston: Houghton Mifflin.

Hare, A. P. (1962). *Handbook of small group research.* New York: Free Press.

Keller, F. S. & Sherman, J. G. (1974). *The Keller plan handbook.* Menlo Park, CA: W. A. Benjamin, Inc.

Kulik, J. A. & Kulik, C. C. (1979). College teaching. In P. L. Peterson & H. J. Walberg (Eds.), *Research on teaching: Concepts, findings, and implications* (pp. 70–96). Berkeley, CA: McCutchan.

Levinson-Rose, J. & Menges, R. J. (1981). Improving college teaching: A critical review of research. *Review of Educational Research, 51*, 403–434.

Luiten, J., Ames, W. & Ackerson, G. (1980). A meta-analysis of the effects of advance organizers on learning and retention. *American Educational Research Journal, 17*, 211–218.

McLeish, J. (1976). The lecture method. In N. L. Gage (Ed.), *The psychology of teaching methods* (pp. 252–301). Chicago: University of Chicago Press.

Oddi, L. (1983). The lecture: An update on research. *Adult Education Quarterly, 33*, 222–229.

Osterman, D. M. (1982). Classroom lecture management: Increasing individual involvement and learning in the lecture style. *Journal of College Science Teaching, 12*, 22–23.

Rosenkoetter, J. S. (1984). Teaching psychology to large classes: Videotapes, PSI and lecturing. *Teaching of Psychology*, 11, 85–87.

Russell, I. J., Hendricson, W. D. & Herbert, R. J. (1984). Effects of lecture information density on medical student achievement. *Journal of Medical Education, 59*, 881–889.

Schiller, W. J. & Markle, S. M. (1978). In O. Milton (Ed.), *On college teaching* (pp. 153–183). San Francisco: Jossey-Bass.

Sweeney, J. J. & Reigeluth, C. M. (1984). The lecture and instructional design: A contradiction in terms? *Educational Technology*, 7–12.

Vygotsky, L. S. (1962). *Thought and language*. Cambridge, MA: MIT Press.

Waggoner, M. (1984). The new technologies versus the lecture tradition in higher education: Is change possible? *Educational Technology, 24*, 7–13.

Walberg, H. J., Schiller, D. & Haertel, G. D. (1979). The quiet revolution in educational research. *Phi Delta Kappan, 61*, 179–183.

Woods, J. D. (1983). Lecturing: Linking purpose and organization. *Improving College and University Teaching, 31*, 61–64.

Helping the Student with Learning Problems

John W. Woodley and Joe N. Crank

In many high school settings teachers work to prepare the students for what they are to face in college. Those teachers conscientiously stay in close touch with their students' work and progress from day-to-day, monitor assignments as they are due, follow-up in cases where problems arise and provide support, encouragement and direction as the student progresses. Those are characteristics of an effective teacher at the high school level.

Yet when students enter the university setting, the situation is often quite changed. In many undergraduate classes each student is merely one face in a sea of faces which the teacher meets each class session. These teachers usually see the students only two or three times a week, have no idea of how the students are progressing other than what is recorded in the grade book, are unaware of problems many of the students are having, and have little personal contact with the individual students unless the students themselves seek it. Many introductory level classes in a university have a minimum of sixty to a hundred students per section and sometimes have enrollments much higher.

Indeed the situation has changed drastically from what is often individualized, personal attention of high school. Obviously, the demands of college for students generally exceed those of high school (Stephens & Weaver, 1985). That shift in demands can be quite marked for many students.

It may be concluded that the overwhelming majority of students at the university level successfully meet the academic demands of the undergraduate setting. That is, most students have been able to read materials throughout their school careers in such a way as to successfully comprehend texts and other written materials and to use that comprehension effectively. They have also performed well enough on college admission tests to gain admission to the university.

Academic and Cognitive Skills of Different Groups of Undergraduate Students

In view of the academic skill problems of many undergraduate college students who have learning deficiencies, it appears incumbent upon institutions which desire to maintain students in school to improve those students' skills, so they can be more successful in meeting the academic demands of the undergraduate program. A situation exists in which many students are intellectually competent but have academic needs to improve skills, make better grades and remain in school.

This leads to the question of what must be done in order to allow these students to perform adequately in these classes to allow them success in their college studies. What strategies should these students adopt to enhance their chances of success? What instructional strategies should the teachers of their classes employ to provide greater chances of success? Discussion of possible answers to these two questions form the basis of the balance of this paper. Specifically, we will address two points:

1. strategies for acquiring information from text, storing that information in systematic ways and expressing the information coherently;

2. teaching strategies that college teachers can utilize to increase student learning.

Learning Strategies

Special support services are needed to teach skill deficient students those skills found necessary for achievement in the post-secondary undergraduate setting. Recently, research has focused on the cognitive and learning strategies of skill deficient secondary and post-secondary students. Deshler, Schumaker, Alley, Warner, and Clark (1982), and Sheinker, Sheinker, and Stevens (1984) presented reviews of the literature on the use of cognitive and learning strategies in young adult learners. Alley and Deshler (1979) define learning strategies as,"techniques, principles or rules that will facilitate the acquisition, manipulation, integration, storage, and retrieval of information across situations and settings." As an individual progresses through school, the reading and written language demands change and become more complex. Specific strategies can be learned which may enhance the acquisition of college content material, the storage of newly learned information, and the demonstration of newly learned information.

Acquisition of Information

Acquisition of information from textbooks can be difficult for many learning deficient (LD) college students. Armbruster (1984) drew attention to certain aspects of textbooks which she called "inconsiderate text." For example, Armbruster has emphasized that the overall text structure is important as a guide to understanding. Authors need to establish a "global coherence," an arrangement of ideas in a text which indicates which ideas are related. Different types of structures indicate narration, description, problem solving approaches, comparisons and contrasts, temporal sequences, or cause and effect structure.

In addition, Armbruster identified a lack of "local coherence," that is, cohesiveness from sentence to sentence. For example, texts may lack clarifying transitional words, connecting or subordinating words, or cues which signal importance such as underlining, italics or boldface print. Furthermore, texts may not be written at levels appropriate to the targeted group or may lack introductory and summary statements. Emphasis must be directed to texts which correct such deficiencies in order to promote learning important information. Authors of textbooks need to be aware of the textual features which Armbruster discussed. College instructors can also intervene at several levels to influence textbook choice and use.

Awareness of textbook structure can be useful prior to textbook adoption in an undergraduate course. For example, the organization of a textbook which is "reader friendly" should be a criterion when choosing between different texts.

Textbook Strategy. A first step toward enabling students to benefit from college textbooks, therefore, is for the teacher to identify the book features that may impede student learning. Based on such knowledge, teachers may help students find the basic structure in a chapter as well as key elements that will facilitate comprehension. The University of Kansas Institute for Research in Learning Disabilities has developed a task-specific learning strategy called Multipass to improve reading comprehension through the recognition of textual organization (Schumaker, Deshler, Denton, Alley, Clark, & Warner, 1982). With this strategy, teachers show students how to make several "passes" through a textbook gaining more information each time. The instructor can point out the importance of comprehension of chapter titles, introduction, summaries, overall organizational patterns, pictures and graphs, and table of contents. It must be kept in mind that many reading deficient students have not learned skills which proficient learners take for granted and have learned without instruction. Key information in boldface print or italics, new terms, important people, dates, and study questions should also be emphasized so that students may independently apply the strategy to readings assigned at later times. Teachers and instructors in secondary and post-secondary settings have reported that both they and their students benefited from the strategy.

Self-Questioning Strategy. The Self-Questioning Strategy (Clark, Deshler, Schumaker, Alley & Warner, 1984) involves a series of steps to guide student inquiry. Specifically, students read the title, the subtitle or first sentence in a passage and ask themselves questions about this introductory information. Next, students are to read the text to find the answer to the questions they have posed. Finally, students repeat the answer to solidify their understanding of the material. Students are also taught to mark the text with special symbols indicating the type of question answered: "who," "why," "where," "when," and "how." During discussions with the entire class, instructors can focus on the same questioning techniques to assure that students are reading content material carefully and are extracting important information.

Paraphrasing Strategy. The Paraphrasing Strategy (Schumaker, Denton, & Deshler, 1984) is also designed to help reading deficient college students cope with reading demands and to enhance comprehension. Paraphrasing may be used specifically to develop a student's recall of main ideas and specific facts in a text or hand-out. Research has shown that students' comprehension and retention scores increase in proportion to the quality and quantity of the paraphrased statements they make while reading a passage. However, many students laboriously read lengthy passages rather than divide the material into small units and interact with the author's message. Through the paraphrasing strategy, students are taught to read a short passage of material, ask themselves what has just been read, and rephrase the main idea and specific facts in their own words. As with other reading strategies, the paraphrasing strategy can be used in class discussions to check students' understanding of content materials. In addition, instructors can learn how to paraphrase text material or class discussions, to correct misunderstanding, and to direct student inquiry.

Visual Imagery. Visual imagery is a strategy for improving the reading comprehension of prose material through improved recall. Warner (1978) developed a visual imagery strategy for use with low functioning adolescent students and found many of his students improved test scores on comprehension tests after being taught an imagery strategy. Briefly, in using visual imagery the student is asked to read short passages of materials and to visualize the scene which is described, incorporating actors, action, and details. This process is repeated to incorporate additional information into the scenario as needed.

Interpreting Visual Aids. Another strategy for acquiring information from printed material involves better use and interpretation of visual aids such as maps, graphs, pictures and tables. For college students with limited reading abilities, such attention to visual aids can increase the student's ability to extract needed information from textbooks, or other assigned readings.

Storage of Information

Once information has been acquired, it must be stored, at least temporarily, until expression and demonstration of that information is requested in the form of a test or written product. Storage of information is usually accomplished through the use of memory strategies. Included in storage strategies should also be listening and note-taking devices. Two memory strategies can be easily adapted to college-level demands. *The First-Letter Mnemonic* strategy is designed to aid students in memorizing *lists* of information. Students are taught to use mnemonics, or memorization aids, involving the first letter in each word of the list to be memorized. Either single words, phrases, or sentences using the first letters of each word in the list are formed to aid memorization. *The Paired Associates* strategy is designed to aid students in the memorization of pairs or small groups of related information, such as dates and events, people and accomplishments, or authors and works. Strategy-deficient undergraduates can be taught memorization techniques which utilize visual imagery, associations with familiar things in the students' own lives, and a first syllable memorization technique.

For students who have trouble recording complete lecture notes, a listening and note-taking strategy can be learned. This kind of strategy is designed to train students to focus on a speaker's cues in determining important items. This is particularly important in lecture classes where discussion is limited. A note-taking strategy involves listening to a lecture, identifying the speaker's verbal cues about important information, noting the key words following the cue, and organizing these notes into outline form for future reference or study.

Expression and Demonstration of Competence

Expression of stored knowledge is usually manifested through written exercises or completion of assignments and tests. Writing is perhaps the greatest demand of college undergraduates, thus the ability to express one's self in writing is of paramount importance. Strategies have been developed and can be learned by skill-deficient college students which teach students how to recognize and generate complete sentences in four areas: simple, compound, complex, and compound-complex. Paragraph writing strategies can be learned which teach students how to monitor their work as well as to generate topic, detail, and clincher sentences. Error-monitoring is a strategy designed to teach students to re-read passages they have written to locate errors in four common areas: capitalization, overall editing and appearance, punctuation, and spelling. The use of *idea diagrams* (Armbruster & Anderson, 1982) is incorporated into the first two steps (thinking and organizing) of a theme-writing strategy. Theme-writing strategies teach students how to generate ideas and how to organize these ideas into logical sequence.

Two other strategies which can help the student express or demonstrate knowledge are assignment completion strategies and test-taking strategies. The reader should continue to keep in mind that many skill deficient college students lack basic strategies that more proficient learners have acquired perhaps without instruction and who use strategies automatically. In assignment completion the student is taught to write down, schedule, complete and turn in assignments. The strategy involves using an assignment notebook to record assignments for each class, analyzing whether additional information or help is needed, obtaining that help, scheduling time for assignment completion, planning the materials that are needed and the subtasks that need to be done to complete the assignment, completing the assignment, and handing it in on time. Time management is integral to the effectiveness of this kind of strategy. Test-taking strategies are designed to aid students in the completion of tests. Effective test taking involves deciding on priorities and scheduling time when taking a test, reading and following instructions, reading each question carefully, and strategically deciding on the answer, abandoning hard questions the first time through the test, estimating answers when necessary, and surveying the test to determine whether all questions have been answered and to check work.

Conclusion

In view of the fact that tutorial support for college students produces short-term, however temporarily helpful effects, and that remedial education of reading and writing/spelling skills is extremely time consuming, a strategies approach to helping skill-deficient college students appears to be optimal. Several self-instructional programs are available for learning task-specific strategies. However, instruction via sound teaching practices would produce the best learning effects. A complete learning strategies curriculum would include strategies which are general enough to promote acquisition, storage, and retrieval of information presented in many undergraduate courses.

Teaching Strategies

While teachers at the undergraduate level in college are often experts in their academic areas, they often lack such expertise in teaching skills (Stephens & Weaver, 1985). However, the responsibilities of these subject matter experts is primarily to provide instruction for those students in their classes. When students encounter difficulty in reading and studying at the college level, the blame for such difficulty is often laid on the students and the inadequacy of their previous educational experience. However, consideration should also be given to the nature of reading and studying at the college level and the role of college teachers in the educational program (Stephens & Weaver, 1985). By adopting effective instructional strategies, college teachers can enhance students' learning.

The instructional strategies presented in this section do not place great demands for time on the part of teachers. We know that the demands for time for many college teachers already exceed the time resources they have available. These strategies have been selected because they serve to facilitate learning without requiring special background or training. Yet they do require a commitment on the teacher's part to working with and for the students to increase their learning. Such a commitment is the first step in helping the student who is having difficulty learning in the college classroom.

The most common method of instruction at the college level is lecture. Lectures are economical in that they can present large amounts of information in a relatively short time. Yet lectures can represent a sizeable problem for students with learning problems because they require either an effective note-taking strategy or a considerable capacity for remembering information from an oral presentation. College teachers can utilize a format for lecturing that supports students' efforts to take notes and recall information. Organizing lectures with the following points in mind can support students' note-taking efforts:

1. Arrange lecture material around certain key concepts. Clearly identify those concepts for the students while lecturing and tie specific points into those concepts while progressing through the lecture. This allows students the opportunity to divide lecture notes into readily identifiable sections to facilitate later review and study of the material.

2. Provide an outline of the lecture on the chalkboard before beginning the lecture. This outline need not be detailed, but can merely identify the major concepts to be presented. This can serve as an "organizational map" to aid the students in organizing the lecture material and identifying the major concepts being covered.

3. Pause between key concepts. Use this as a time for students to catch-up on lecture notes, ask questions and provide a break in their notes between concepts. A pause of thirty seconds to a minute would be adequate in most situations if no questions are asked by the students. It helps students if teachers alert them in advance why they will be pausing and how they can take advantage of that time.

4. Use visual aids such as transparencies or the chalkboard to support the lecture whenever appropriate. Such aids provide assistance by reinforcing and extending the points made. They also provide a means for students to organize the materials presented by using the visual aids to indicate points of emphasis in the lecture.

Reading and writing are mutually supportive in aiding students' learning (Stephens & Weaver, 1985). Learning has been described as being composed of three stages: perceiving, ideating and presenting (Smith, Goodman & Meredith, 1976). Writing can be effectively used at all three stages as a means of facilitating learning and enhancing understanding. Most commonly, writing is considered a means of collecting information from students to indicate what they have learned or know for the purpose of grading or evaluating progress. Yet writing can be a personal tool to enhance learning, a tool that is not always formally graded or evaluated.

When students enter college classrooms and prepare to be involved in the class for that day, they bring with them as many thoughts, ideas and concerns as there are individuals in the class. The problem that any teacher faces is to bring together those students so that they all can effectively attend to what is to happen in class. One effective means to accomplish this is to begin class sessions by asking students to write what they know, or need to know, about the topic to be covered that day in class. Such writing is private and personal, allowing students to explore the topic and their knowledge about it by focusing on it and relating it to their personal backgrounds. Even if the students can write nothing about the topic, this can serve to help them pinpoint their own lack of knowledge in that area. This writing activity serves to bridge the mental state of students as the class begins and the serious in depth work which is to occur in class. The common experience of thinking and writing about the same topic serves to bring unity to the class and often yields a more beneficial class for all.

Another use of writing is to conclude a class session or unit of study by having the students take a few minutes and write down what they have learned or come to better understand through the class activities. This is not a test but, instead, a period of self-evaluation. The purposes of this activity can be two-fold. First, it requires the students to tie together their learning well enough to write it down. This thought brings clarity to the students and allows them to actually identify what they are learning in the class. Second, the teacher can collect these statements (this is most beneficial if the students do not place their names on the papers, allowing them to state what they have or have not learned without fear of the teacher using such statements for evaluation). These statements can be used to help the teacher evaluate his or her instructional effectiveness. These statements can provide information about whether the students have learned what the teacher intended and which areas, if any, should be further addressed in class.

While most college teachers provide students the opportunity to ask questions during class periods, many worthwhile questions go unasked because of fear on the part of the students of looking foolish before a group of strangers and friends. Therefore, a further use of writing would be to have the students periodially write and turn in to the teacher questions regarding the course and the material to be covered which they believe deserve further attention in class. By doing this anonymously, students can ask those questions they wouldn't dare ask in class. Yet, also by writing the questions out, the students themselves must come to terms with their own levels of understanding and cognitive clarity. This can serve to enhance student learning as well as provide valuable information to the teacher.

Whenever college students are asked how they determine what they should highlight or underline while reading, the most common response is always "whatever is important." This is clearly a common sense answer, but it really sheds little light on the students' strategies. After all, that response only becomes clear when another question is answered, "How do you know what's important?" The answer to that must relate to knowing what they are seeking or why they are reading. In order to help students set clear purposes for what they are reading, it is important to let students know as early as possible what they are going to be expected to do with what they are learning from their reading. If tests are part of the instructional plan, tell the students what types of tests will be given. When a student reads in preparation for a multiple choice test, the types of things to be underlined or highlighted are quite different than when preparing for an essay exam (Spargo, 1983). The sooner the student knows what type of test to expect, the more efficiently and effectively can the study time be used. If tests are given with more than one type of question on it, let the students know what types of questions will be asked. Providing the opportunity to know what to expect yields clarity of purpose which can lead to more effective studying.

Helping students to set a purpose for their studying and reading is something most college teachers could accomplish without drastically altering their approach to teaching. In addition to providing information about the type and nature of tests, college teachers can provide information about what they would like to see students get from their reading. The more specific the teacher can be in establishing purpose, the more efficiently and effectively the students can read the material.

Many college students attempt to study/read all the material they are asked to read for a class. That is, students attempt to read the material carefully and analytically, learning from the material while reading it. This type of reading is slow and laborious, consuming large periods of time. College teachers frequently give students reading assignments which are to be completed by the time the related material is covered in class. In many cases, thoroughly reading the material before class is ineffective because the students lack the necessary knowledge for understanding the material. In those cases, the thorough reading will be more effective if it is completed after the class presentation has been completed. One option for dealing more effectively with reading is to have the students preview the material prior to class and then study/read the material after the class session. Previewing ". . . gives students some idea of what a text selection is about in advance of reading it" (Vacca, 1981, p. 107). It is the process of systematically examining a passage to determine the main ideas and general thrust of the passage. The benefits of previewing reading material before the class presentation are that it (1) allows students to determine what they do or do not know about the topic, (2) permits students to identify which sections of the text he or she will need to read with great care and which do not need to be read so carefully, and (3) creates a sense of intellectual readiness for the presentation in class. By saving the study reading for after class, the material is likely to be easier because the students will have the additional knowledge and background for making the reading effective. What at first seems like a longer, more complex reading activity can actually save time and make studying generally more effective. Teachers can aid their students by suggesting the strategy to their students and emphasizing it by indicating during the lecture or presentation which sections in the reading material are particularly important or worthy of careful study/reading.

Reading and learning in college classes represent a major undertaking for most students at the undergraduate level. It may well be that the major resource available to undergraduate students is what they can learn and discover by working with other undergraduate students. The teacher can suggest to the students that they form study groups outside of class. The common learning that takes place by students discussing material, asking each other questions and exploring the class material can result in greater understanding of the class content. This process can be facilitated by forming small groups within the classroom and using the class time to complete appropriate small group activities. The benefits of such groups for learning often make them an almost indispensable tool for increasing learning (Estes & Vaughan, 1985). Successful group activities in the class make the formation of outside study groups more likely. The combined teaching strategies of study groups outside of class and small group work within the class can yield strong positive effects in terms of student learning.

The need for such approaches by college teachers was made clear by Stephens and Weaver:

> . . . if needed changes are to be effected in higher education, it will take creative thinking, a commitment to quality teaching by colleges and universities, and a willingness on the part of professors to develop new instructional methodology suited to the learning needs of the great majority of today's students (1985, p. 72).

We have presented specific ideas to allow college students and teachers of those students to enhance learning in college level content classes. We offer these suggestions, not as an endpoint in improving college instruction and learning, but as a starting point in a mission we all need to accept as our own—"meeting the learning needs of the great majority of today's students."

References

Alley, G., & Deshler, D. (1979). *Teaching the learning disabled adolescent: Strategies and methods*. Denver: Love Publishing.

Armbruster, B. B. (1984). The problems of "inconsiderate text." In G. Duffy, L. Roehler, & J. Mason (Eds). *Comprehension instruction: Perspectives and suggestions*. New York: Longman, Inc.

Clark, F. L., Deshler, D. D., Schumaker, J. B., Alley, G. R., & Warner, M. M. (1984). Visual imagery and self-questioning: Strategies to improve comprehension of written material. *Journal of Learning Disabilities, 17*, 145–149.

Crank, J. N. (1984). *The identification of learning disabled students at the University of Kansas*. Unpublished manuscript.

Deshler, D. D., Schumaker, J. B., Alley, G. R., Warner, M. M., & Clark, F. L. (1982). Learning disabilities in adolescent and young adult populations: Research implication. *Focus on Exceptional Children, 15*(1), 1–12.

Estes, T. H. & Vaughn, J. L. (1985). *Reading and learning in the content classroom: Diagnostic and instructional strategies* (2nd ed.). Boston: Allyn and Bacon, Inc.

Schumaker, J. B., Denton, P. H., & Deshler, D. D. (1984). The *paraphrasing strategy*. Lawrence, KS: The University of Kansas.

Schumaker, J. B., Deshler, D. D., Denton, P., Alley, G. R., Clark, F. L., &

Warner, M. M. (1982). Multipass: A learning strategy for improving reading comprehension. *Learning Disability Quarterly, 5*, 295–304.

Sheinker, A., Sheinker, J. M., & Stevens, L. D. (1984). Cognitive strategies for teaching the mildly handicapped. *Focus on Exceptional Children, 17*, 1.

Smith, E. G., Goodman, K. S. & Meredith, R. (1976). *Language and thinking in schools* (2nd ed.). New York: Richard C. Owen Publishers.

Spargo, E. (1983). *The college student*. Providence, RI: Jamestown Publishers.

Stephens, E. C. & Weaver, D. R. (1985). Improving student achievement and instructional effectiveness in higher education. *Forum for Reading*, 69–72.

Vacca, R. T. (1981). *Content area reading*. Boston: Little, Brown and Company.

Warner, M. M. (1978). *Teaching learning disabled students to use visual imagery as a strategy for facilitating recall of reading passages*. Unpublished doctoral dissertation, The University of Kansas.

Part IV: Environment

The environment can affect how much students learn or do not learn. Colleges and universities must examine their practices so they are as effective as possible. With fewer students of college age, institutions of higher education are becoming increasingly aware that they must do as much as possible to keep capable students in school. The environment involves more than merely the classroom. It includes what happens to students outside the formal learning setting as well. Helping students to make the transition from high school to college and helping older students to return to the college environment are important considerations.

The concept of the "broader college community" is important to understanding undergraduate education. Loren M. Carlson and Jack A. Sumner address the meaning of community and its elements. They believe that a broad concept of community is essential for the proper utilization of a significant resource at the undergraduate level. Two dimensions entail an adequate view. One involves the perception of an on-campus and off-campus learning experience. The other perception requires an understanding of the strengths and breadths of both and their contributions to learning. The community, including the nation, is served best by making the state and the nation the college campus.

Working with students, college and university educators have seen cocurricular offerings evolve as a result of their willingness to listen to students and value their partnership. William C. Edwards writes that theoretical models and evaluative devices are now available to achieve even greater advances. Now is the time for administrators, advisors, students and faculty to work together to use these tools to increase student participation. By doing so, the contribution of colleges and universities to the education of the student as a whole person will be enhanced.

The transition from high school to college is difficult for most students. Beginning with examples from several colleges of how they attempt to orientate new students, John F. Bryde and Corinne Milburn summarize much of the research on helping students to adjust to their life as a college student. They report on a study and make recommendations to high schools and colleges on how they can assist students to make the transition more successfully. Students need help in becoming aware of their feelings and reactions, and help in coping with their day-to-day problems.

Critical of the National Institute of Education study group's report, *Involvement in Learning*, William R. Donohue views their recommendation to increase services (front-loading) for first-year and second-year undergraduates as correct, but long overdue. He summarizes the evidence that it is cost-effective to invest resources when students are most vulnerable and motivated—when they are freshmen. Declining enrollments, budget cuts, and rising standards make the prospects for "front-loading" uncertain. Nevertheless, it may be the most advantageous practice for colleges and universities to follow in the years to come.

Don Monroe and Gale Wiedow focus their concerns on the basic principles and procedures of academic advisement. They believe that it should involve more than class selection, remedial intervention, and advisement about university policies and procedures. Properly considered, academic advisement should concern, not only academic matters, but the entire undergraduate experience. Advisement must be well planned, conscientiously implemented, carefully monitored, and continually modified. Monroe and Wiedow provide an historic perspective, a modern definition of the process, anticipated results, a description of the process, and a plan of action. They believe academic advising is an important aspect of the environment in which the undergraduate experience takes place.

O. J. Christensen and A. D. Albertus summarize the developmental and psychosocial factors and needs of traditional and nontraditional undergraduate students. They make suggestions for working with older, nontraditional students that include: the need to understand adult development; the conducting of a needs assessment survey of adult students; the importance of broadening the scope of student services for older students; and the requirement for better advisement of adult students.

The Broader College Community

Loren M. Carlson and Jack A. Sumner

Introduction

As the direction of higher education administration in the United States continues to drift toward a greater interest and attention to an emphasis on the reallocation of resources and change, the need for thoughtful planning and an increased focus on the manner in which resources are distributed is important. Additionally, as the trend continues toward administrative practices that are more in line with management or business like accountability styles, the need for careful consideration of all the resources available to institutions of higher learning becomes more apparent. This paper proposes that a view of the broader college community by those concerned with the future is important to undergraduate education and offers possibilities and promise for improvement in all academic and operational areas.

The readiness of higher education to accept new changes is increasing as national attention has again been directed toward education and the fundamental reexamination of all aspects of education. Higher education has been the specific focus of studies, such as the Newman Report (Chronicle of Higher Education, 1985), while other studies have centered on teacher education and preparation. Some efforts have already begun with a look at different levels of involvement through such efforts as the Temple University Project in Philadelphia. In a thoughtful and far-reaching plan prophetically termed as A New University for a New Century (Niebuhr, 1983), the conceptual base of this project includes a broader college community that is collaborative and within the university infrastructure suggesting that a reinvention

171

of the university is possible. Reinventing for the broader college community has both internal and external dimensions. Dimensions that mean taking on new responsibilities for the education of students within the institution, as well as doing things that help with the education of students outside, or external to the institution. Through the effective use of a broader college community, as conceived in the Temple University Project, the higher education learning environment can become a source of increased educational opportunities and greater diversity, an attribute that has characterized the system of higher education in the United States since its beginning.

Background

The tradition of cooperation between community and college has been established. It can be seen in the history of the first 150 years at Rutgers where the essence of the cooperative spirit that built a sense of community was described this way:

> The citizens of New Brunswick deeply interested in the celebration were enlisted to insure success especially giving their cordial cooperation in opening their homes to visitors, in placing private conveyance at college disposal, in participating in the pageant and in composing the anniversary chorus.

In reviewing the successes that higher education institutions have had in applying the concept of "community," widespread and far-reaching impacts have been made in the work that Land-Grant Institutions have been doing since the Morrill Act of 1862. This landmark effort demonstrated how, with the Cooperative Extension Service situated on the campuses of colleges and universities, higher education could work collaboratively and effectively with rural farming communities to solve community problems. Since that time, the college model, including the community college approach, has spread throughout the world and programs in foreign countries have patterned their systems in a similar way. These replications have been for the most part, however, tied to a government or political subdivision rather than a responsibility of the local university or college in the foreign country. The point is that higher education institutions have demonstrated ways in which institutions can cooperate with communities in a productive and positive way.

It is important to point out, though, that higher education's success record in understanding the concept of "community" has not always been enviable and, in some instances, has been considered to be inappropriate. At times, institutional structures and reward systems prevented or impeded the attempts by colleges to make meaningful contributions to communities. The results of studies reported in a series of papers funded by the Ford Foundation in the '60s and '70s (Pendleton, 1975) showed that higher education's work in the urban communities was ineffective and often judged a failure. The problems were complex and the adjustments among institutions were slow and poorly conceived. Furthermore, academicians didn't understand the unique problems and the circumstances of the poor. Lacking a knowledge of the conditions of this unique population group, they never appropriately responded to the needs of these communities.

The Community

In suggesting that we view the college as an abstraction it is helpful to review some important points. The general understanding of community describes it as the place where we live or the place where members of our family were born. This perception has limitations when applied to the college-community concept. What is proposed here, is that the broader college community is truly broader (and deeper) than the physical boundaries of the campus and/or the community of a college.

As a useful starting point in understanding a broadened perception of the concept of community, Warren (1963) says that a community seems to be the best combination of units and systems providing the major functions for those social units that have meaning for the locality in which they function. The implications here are that a set of proper combinations and meanings are critical to understanding successful programs and what makes them work.

An even more global look at the concept of community as it functions in higher education settings has been proposed by Tollet (1975) with the proposition that a world or national community is possible. Representing more than the physical boundaries of a country, state or area, such a world or national community in its educational context, would include cross-national acceptance of the commonality of knowledge teaching and the curriculum. For some colleges, such as the University of Maryland and its European campuses, this approach has more relevance.

At the present time, education reformers are including this expanded perception in their areas of study and recommendation. For example, The Nation at Risk report (1983) has resurrected the proposition that an important direction for America is to move toward the ideal of a Learning Society. The emphasis on using the community is alluded to as:

> . . . educational opportunities extending far beyond the traditional institutions of learning, our schools and colleges. They extend into homes and workplaces; into libraries, art galleries, museums and science centers; indeed, into every place where the individual can develop and mature in work and life.

Other explorations of the meaning of community have been presented differently. One of these is the concept of the "learning community" described by Boo and Decker (1984), stressing the broader involvement of existing resource areas. This approach suggests that an imaginative reworking, a new look and a widened perspective of the way in which we look at learning experiences can contribute substantially to educational improvements.

Society tends to look toward higher education for answers and creative solutions to making changes that will be best for society and its members. It seems that the colleges are best able to exercise leadership and direction toward making significant changes. This includes changes in how things are taught and what is taught to college students. Ideas that have promise for conceiving that a broader college community is possible have been examined. One suggestion is that we should have been moving toward major institutional initiatives in higher education more than 10 years ago. This had been proposed by Hesburgh, Miller and Wharton (1973) suggesting that the curricula should be redesigned toward fostering the emphasis on self-education and lifelong learning in the undergraduate learner.

By way of being more descriptive in our understanding of the concept of community, the introduction of the term "communitization" has been used to describe how a community can be developed within the framework of the university's physical facilities. Communitization moves closer toward capturing the essence of a broader community in the context of the structure of institutions of higher learning. Sebok (1972) alludes to it in this way:

> . . . communitization is a modus vivendi for the micro-society of higher education. It is an interdependence. A team effort that must be accepted

by communal members as a logical means of realizing common goals. It is an all-encompassing plan by which students, teachers and administrators may come together for a short time and experience the optimum benefits of educating, learning and living within the broader framework of real community. . . . (p. 1)

An understanding of this broader community concept is facilitated by an expanded perception of community in terms of the environment or surroundings of the higher education setting. At the same time, the internal, on campus, dimension of "community," has some explicit descriptors. It is helpful to examine the somewhat specific and operational definitions as described by Pace (1979) used in a survey of nearly a thousand colleges and universities in this country. The community dimension of the College and University Environment Scales or "CUES" is described in the following way:

Community. The items in this scale describe a friendly, cohesive, group oriented campus. The congenial atmosphere gives a feeling of group welfare and group loyalty. The faculty members know the students, are interested in their problems and go out of their way to be helpful. Student life is characterized by sharing and togetherness rather than by privacy and cool detachment. (p. 156)

The emphasis on congeniality and group cohesion provides an important attribute for the community dimension of the college environment.

Yet another approach to education and learning has been developed by Hiemstra (1975) with the concept of an educative community where an emphasis is on mature involvement of all citizens and wherein all individuals accept the task of educating. A significant aspect of this approach is the recognition that the truly educative community will approach the education of individuals with a distinctively different process from the process of just schooling the student. This concept has significant and long reaching implications for education and deserves serious and deliberate consideration by educators seeking to work on developing improvements in the total educational experience. It also works toward gaining greater acceptance of those not directly involved in education. In addition, a truly educative community represents a radical departure from acceptance of the idea that an individual's learning can only take place at a specific time in a specific place. The educative community represents the essential elements of all the concepts of a learning society and related "community" concepts in a way that is positive and practical.

An important question that the practitioner asks when dealing with concepts is "will it work?" The experiences of colleges in our country have demonstrated that given certain circumstances and situations the notion of an educative community, a collaborative community, a perception of the college as a broader community has some important and interesting results.

Successful Examples

In order that undergraduate student study experiences may be enhanced through the use of a community of higher learning experiences, it is important to begin to look at some of the activities that are currently or potentially in the realm of possibility. Boyer has suggested that the importance of other experiences outside of the classroom can be used more effectively. He says:

> As we look at college students it becomes clear that their most powerful influence is felt outside the classroom—a fact well documented by Art Chickering, Sandy Aston and others. Even common sense suggests that if just 16 hours in a week is spent in class, then out-of-class experiences will be enormously consequential. (p. 13)

The external dimensions of community includes acting jointly on collaborative projects outside of the institution with other colleges or communities. Successful collaboration between colleges and communities begins with involvement. Involvement of the community in the affairs of the university has some interesting and far-reaching benefits and implications. An example of how it can work has been demonstrated in the successful efforts of Montgomery College. In its open forum with the "focus on the future" the involvement includes the community, legislators, local and state councils, and organization leaders as a cooperative planning community. Involvement in the long term goals for land and facility use has been addressed by the University of California-Irvine. The institution emphasizes the private-academe-community interface as important to the facilities and land-use planning process of the university.

The traditional view of on-campus experiences means such activities as the classroom and laboratory experience, the use of library and resource center facilities, and planned or casual contact with course instructors and advisors. Other opportunities often overlooked or underutilized are also available. All of these opportunities should focus on the learning aspects of extracurricular activities, the formal and informal student initiated activities and the use of non-campus community resources. Among these resources are the facilities, agencies, organizations and resources that are shared with the general public. In the southwest, the University of Arizona's Centennial Hall is the largest performance center in Southern Arizona offering a broad spectrum of activities that contribute to the coalescence of the University and the community. The University of Minnesota-Duluth with the Tweed Museum of Art and Minnesota Repertory Theater are demonstrated ways in which that college uses buildings and structures to create a cultural community for the area.

Another example, though not a large auditorium, hall or building, has been successful at the University of Wisconsin. Since 1934, the arboretum of the University of Wisconsin has been a source of educational enlightenment, not only for the Madison community and the state, but for nearby states as well, including special restoration and conservation projects of similar facilities such as the Morton Arboretum in Lisle, Illinois.

The expansion and growth of technology has created a rate of change that universities and colleges have difficulty in maintaining. One troublesome aspect of this rapid rate of change is the acquisition of material and capital equipment when it's needed. Cooperative programs have helped to solve these problems. The cooperative efforts of education and industry in Northern California communities created "Silicon Valley" and contributed to the microcomputer revolution. Collaborative ventures have also been conducted in the widespread uses of facilities and equipment in university and community hospitals. Special work has been conducted in libraries with projects in specialized and costly facilities such as the University of California's Scripps Institute, the Bodega Marine Laboratory and Lawrence Berkley Laboratories.

The opportunity to participate in a meaningful way in community betterment, community improvement and community projects are valuable educational experiences. Tulane University, through its Mardi Gras Coalition, provides a unique and valued community service experience for students during the Mardi Gras Festival in New Orleans. Students not only learn from observation and experience but those that are trained in cardiopulmonary resuscitation and basic first aid, as well as child care, participate actively in providing service during the event. William Jewell College uses the community to teach sociology and race relations from the perspective of a Black, Indian, Mexican, Japanese or Jew by spending class time each week in a Kansas City community. The class has also involved the major metropolitan news-papers and the black community.

The University of Massachusetts in Boston provides a career train-ing program through the Gerontology Program and Institute in the University. Labor union meetings, governmental council sessions, fraternal groups and even a return visit to the school that the under-graduate left a few years earlier may be an opportunity for learning. It is at times surprising to recent graduates how much their former teachers have learned in the years that they have been away.

Community events, site visits, or industry tours other than during traditional semester or quarter periods, also provide educational op-portunities for undergraduates. Using that "interim" period for off season learning is a notion borrowed from the European approach to "recurrent education" for graduated students. The benefit of having an educational experience out of step with the existing system is revitalization and change in perspective. This can happen to the undergraduate student as well.

Bringing an institution of higher learning together in a sense of community also provides educational experiences to which the under-graduate student might not otherwise have access during the school year. This also means that consortia or cooperative approaches can help with cost sharing and savings.

The examination and review of societal, community and institutional changes provides innovative and creative challenges for educators if an understanding of the broader college community is fully grasped. This expanded perception of the college community steps beyond the immediate boundaries and confines of the campus. This necessitates a perspective that sees all of the opportunities and promise that is afforded by a comprehensive off-campus program. Such a perception is both stimulating and invigorating in its boundless and boundary-less potential.

In order to better understand what off-campus learning is, it is helpful to address it from the perspective of the accomplishments in the state. In South Dakota, the traditional off-campus experience is perceived to be a class in a remote high school, with limited library facilities, taught by a faculty member teaching an overload with pri-mary emphasis upon graduate study. Or it may conjure up visions of a graduate center with a program of study leading to a degree.

Contrary to both of these notions, off-campus learning through the University of South Dakota involves something much more complex, and it is aimed primarily at undergraduate education. The following table illustrates the point for credit courses.

Statewide Educational Services
Enrollments in Percentage of Credit Hours
1984–85

Services	Enrollment Percentages
Extension	
Undergraduate	52.5%
Graduate	47.5%
Televised Courses	
Undergraduate	54.5%
Graduate	45.6%
Independent Study	
Undergraduate	100%
Air Force Contract	
Undergraduate	100%
Grand Total	
Undergraduate	64%
Graduate	36%

A great many Americans, including educators and policy makers, mistakenly believe that the typical college student is a young person recently graduated from high school attending class on a full-time basis. The reality of our nation's campuses is strikingly different.

Part-time students accounted for 42% in 1982 of all students, compared with 34% in 1972. This is projected to increase to 48% in 1992. In total numbers, there were 5 million part-timers in 1982 and that is expected to increase by ten percent in 1992, while full-time student numbers will decline. Today's college student is older and getting more so. From 1982 to 1992, higher education enrollments will decrease by 616,000 nationally. But there will be a *gain* of 902,000 students 25 years and over and a *loss* of 1,517,000 students 24 and under (Chronicle, 1985).

The off-campus student body is made up almost entirely of older, part-time students. The University of South Dakota experience is that there are more women than men in most off-campus classes, sometimes by a two to one ratio. Off-campus enrollees, most of whom are women, now bear the brunt of national and state policies which discriminate against part-time and older students. *Students attending less than half-time are not eligible to receive Pell Grants, Guaranteed Student Loans or National Direct Student Loans.*

Testifying before a select group, representing the House of Representatives Subcommittee on Education, Dr. Harvey Steadman, President of the National University Continuing Education Association, last July stated that colleges channel almost all discretionary federal aid to full-time students. Further complicating things for the part-time older student, off-campus courses in South Dakota and many states carry higher tuition rates than comparable on-campus classes. Higher tuitions are necessary because off-campus classes often do not qualify under formula for state assistance. This state policy has consistently discriminated against the off-campus student in South Dakota. Some other states, i.e., Kansas, have recognized that the off-campus student is as entitled to receive state support as his/her on-campus counterpart.

There is some evidence to suggest that higher tuitions are the major barriers in pricing students out of the market (Cross, 1981). Barriers in this sense mean circumstances beyond the immediate control of the student. Yet they are occurrences or conditions, that when changed or removed, create or open opportunities. Further, *adults who are potential students are often unaware of the opportunities open to them*, do not want to take advantage of them, or share the belief that college is for the young only. The 1984 report of the Commission on Higher Education and the Adult Learner pointed out that fewer than 4% of the employees eligible for employer-sponsored tuition assistance use those benefits.

State-Wide Educational Delivery Systems—The University of South Dakota Model

Courses for credit are offered through a variety of delivery systems-for off-campus and part-time students. Not all courses offered through the Division of State-Wide Educational Services (SWES, formerly the Extension Division) are truly off-campus in nature. Funding short-falls have forced the institution to rely upon the self-funding system of SWES for some on-campus courses and the operation of the interim. The following is a description of the SWES structure of services:

1. *Independent Study by Correspondence.* This unit includes college level coursework and study through the use of printed materials, audio cassettes and related support from the SWES staff and independent study faculty assigned to the student.

2. *Extension*. In this area the off-campus centers and the graduate centers are included. The interim session is also part of the extension operation, which consists of on-campus classes, and off-campus study tours. A major activity in this area is the internship which provides real world experiences for students in those areas related to their study. A substantial part of the work of this unit is the summer session supplementation program.

The regular on-campus course supplementation activity involves programs in religion, EMT non-credit training, and the remediation non-credit courses. Workshops for credit and the criminal justice consortium are also part of the extension thrust.

3. *Televised Courses*. Through the use of appropriate media, tele-conferencing offerings for credit are provided supplemented by IN-WATS advising support activities by the division.

Off-campus courses are taught by either regular or adjunct faculty who are approved by the credit-granting department for the course being taught. The faculty of the Independent Study Division often includes emeritus professors. All courses offered are approved courses which appear in the university catalog. The same standards are followed for all courses no matter where they are taught.

What is called lifelong learning is here today for about half of the American adult population. About 5 million persons are enrolled in credit-granting programs, another 46 million are being educated by other educational providers—mostly "in-house" by a company's own education staff (Hodginson, 1985). It is significant that business and industry spends an estimated $40–$60 billion annually on their education and training programs (The College Board, 1985).

Demographically, nationally we are approaching an era when youth will be in short supply—social security and other programs need to take heed. We cannot afford the luxury of being a throw-away society which dumps people out on the street if they fail in college the first time around.

Off-campus undergraduate programs, many of which require no formal admission procedures—but feature open admissions—provide one way to permit these persons a second non-threatening chance. The University of South Dakota experience is that many of our enrollees are drop-outs who left college ten or fifteen years earlier and have a desire to go back to school for a host of reasons. A recent survey report, *American Attitudes Toward Higher Education* from Opinion Research Corporation, Princeton, indicated that four of every ten

American adults want to obtain further education, preferably at the college level (Chronicle, 1985). A successful off-campus experience, often is the springboard that a person needs to propel him/herself back into education. Unfortunately, not all people can afford, or are able, due to time and job commitments to return to the campus.

In our efforts to upgrade academic quality, we need to guard against the danger of academic elitism which closes doors for the poor, the minorities, and older students who have had to leave college or who have never had the chance to go in the first place.

The Future

We need to do what we have been doing in continuing education. But, we need to do more and to do it better. New techniques and processes give us that chance. But, these alone will not fulfill all the needs of the broader college community. New degrees need to be developed. We need a general external degree. Old residence requirements need to be adjusted to meet modern technology. Not everyone needs to sit at the feet of the master—because it can now be done electronically.

The electronic university with television, video cassettes, audio cassettes, two-way teleconferencing, and personal computer is now a reality. The new laser video disk may even permit an institution to put an entire library's holdings and documents on just a few small, hard disks, thus supplanting printed materials. In many respects the old tutorial system is coming back full circle where individualized learning can be done economically.

The experiences of off-campus systems can help contribute to the achievement of more traditional goals and objectives. As the *Report of the Commission on Higher Education and the Adult Learner* (1984) concluded:

> . . . The ability of this nation to compete in the world marketplace and to maintain its strength as the bulwark of democracy will increasingly depend upon an educated and trained populace. We cannot afford to have that education and training stop at age eighteen or twenty-two; the future of America demands that the continuing needs of our nation of learners be served.

To use all of the resources available in the college community means that change must take place. This means change in the way in which we use and see institutions of higher education. Obrien (1986) alludes to this suggesting that it's important to change our perception of higher education institutions from just a place of teaching to a place of learning. He says, "we must find ways to make the university a learning community, not simply 12 hours of teaching interspersed with homework, football and fraternities" (p. 144).

References

Boo, M. R. & Decker, L. E. (1985). *The learning community.* Washington, D.C.: National Community Education Association.

Boyer, E. (1986, November–December). College: Raising a new vision. *Change.*

Chasteen, Ed. (1987). Balancing the cognitive and the affective in teaching race relations. *Teaching Sociology,* Vol. 15.

Chronicle of Higher Education. 40 percent of adults want further education, but most say they would need student aid. (1985, October 23). Vol. XXXI, No. 8.

Cross, P. (1981). Why adults participate—and why they do not. *Adults as learners.* San Francisco: Jossey-Bass.

Green, E. (1987, March 11). For lots of students, Mardi Gras makes Lauderdale look like amateur night. *Chronicle of Higher Education.* Vol. XXXIII, No. 26.

Hesburgh, T. M., Miller, P. A., & Wharton, C. R., Jr. (1973). *Patterns of lifelong learning.* San Francisco: Jossey-Bass.

Hiemstra, R. (1972). The educative community: Lincoln, Nebraska. *Professional Educators Publications.*

Hodgenson, H. (1985). All in one system. Washington, D.C.: *Institute for Educational Leadership.*

National Commission on Excellence. (1983). *A nation at risk: The imperative for education reform.* Washington, D.C.: U.S. Government Printing Office.

Niebuhr, R. A. (1983). *A once in a century update of the educational model: A pressing task for lifelong learning, collaboration in lifelong learning.* Washington, D.C.: American Association for Adult and Continuing Education.

Nunley, C. (1987). Focus on the future: Involving institutional constituencies in environmental examination. *Planning for Higher Education.* Vol. 15, No. 1.

Obrien, D. (1986). The university as a place of learning. *Liberal education.* (p. 144). Washington, D.C.: Association of American Colleges.

Pace, R. C. (1979). *Measuring outcomes of college.* (p. 156). San Francisco: Jossey-Bass.

Pendleton, W. C. (1975). *University/city relations revisited.* New York: The Ford Foundation.

Report of The Commission of Higher Education and the Adult Learner. (1984).

Rutgers University. (1917). *Rutgers College: The celebration of the one hundred and fiftieth anniversary of its founding as Queens College, 1766–1916.* New Brunswick, NJ: Rutgers University.

Scully, M. G. (1985). Nation is urged to link college with civic goals. *Chronicle of Higher Education, 3.*

Sebok, R. (1972). A state college communitization scheme. The communitization process in academe. *Proceedings of the 54th Annual Conference of the National Association of Student Personnel Administrators,* p. 1, April 9–11.

The Office of Adult Learning Service. (1985). *Trends in adult student enrollment.* New York: The College Board.

Tollett, K. S. (1975, Winter). Community and higher education. *Daedulus: Journal of the Academy of Arts and Sciences,* Volume II. Cambridge, MA: Academy of Arts and Sciences.

Warren, R. L. (1963). *The community in America.* Chicago: Rand, McNally & Company.

Cocurricular Activities

William C. Edwards

"Whenever you have a collection of activities in which persons invest substantial amounts of time and energy you have potentials for human development" (Arthur W. Chickering, 1977).

Also in 1977, Alexander W. Astin published a report summarizing conclusions reached at the end of a ten-year longitudinal study of factors related to student "persistence" to graduation from college. Among the many statements identifying significant relationships was the following:

> For many undergraduates, extracurricular activities provide some of the most significant consequences of college attendance. In certain respects, these activities offer an opportunity to develop skills that are more relevant to later life than the knowledge and cognitive skills acquired in the classroom. Undergraduate extracurricular activities may be the forerunner of adult achievement in a variety of fields.
>
> As a general operating concept, the administration of a college or university should strive to encourage students to get more involved—to invest more of their time and physical and psychic energy in the educational process.

This chapter will discuss the extracurricular programs and services (particularly those in college unions) designed to provide environments which encourage student involvement. It will be argued that the benefits to student development that certain of these activities provide is ample justification for their elevation to the status of "cocurricular" i.e., an integral part of an institutional commitment to education of the whole person. Concrete evidence will be cited to substantiate claims related to changes in students which come as a consequence of their involvement in out of class activities. Practical applications of developmental theory within college unions will be illustrated.

The Evolution of a Cocurricular Environment

The origin of what we now know as cocurricular activities programs (including union buildings) on the college campus can be traced back to the apparent lack of institutional support for the out of class efforts of the student debating societies at Oxford and Cambridge Universities in the early 1800s. The societies banded together into "unions" so that they could address the issue of survival in the face of university disapproval. (The term union in fact was applied to these activities long before it was used to describe elements of the modern labor movement.) The universities chose not to provide the sort of spaces or services that students wanted so the debating groups took it upon themselves to create environments where they could freely govern their own activities and services. During the forty years that it took for the universities to actually begin building unions, the students had solidly laid the cornerstones of what were to be regarded as standard community centers on campuses all over the world. Their preferences for debate halls, meeting rooms, reference and informal reading libraries, art exhibit areas, hearthside lounges, recreation rooms, and areas serving food and beverages are, by and large, recognizable in contemporary facilities. The physical presence of union buildings on the modern campus as well as the social, intellectual, and recreational opportunities that are provided owe their existence as much to enterprising student consumer advocates as they might to far-sighted institutional planners, administrators, and faculty members.

The building booms which occurred after each of the world wars and during the sixties brought more numerous and larger union buildings to campuses. With the increase in the scope of most union operations (and debt incurred in building of many facilities), came more and more "business oriented" enterprises. In the opinion of the writer, the original intellectual, social, and recreational objectives of unions were often overshadowed by those related to revenue generation. However, it would appear that the hue and cry of the late sixties and early seventies (much of which was planned in and around the union) reversed the trend toward domination of the union by professional service managers and placed it within the grasp of student consumers.

The Value of Cocurricular Programs

During the fifties and early sixties, there was much speculation as to the value of participation in organized activities. In 1957, Minahan showed, in a graduate thesis study published by ACU, that there is a direct, positive relationship between students' union experiences and their post-college citizenship activities.

> Eddy (1959), in delineating the "principal of participation," emphasized that students may gain valuable experience, develop useful skills, and broaden their horizons in activities outside the classroom and in the larger community. To realize such benefits, students must have the opportunity to assume real responsibilities similar to those demanded of citizens in our society. The union provides such opportunities! (Marine, 1985)
> It has been found that student leaders themselves are concerned about the means by which greater involvement of students in programming might be guaranteed as well as the need to delineate the benefits which a volunteer experience might provide. In essence, they also see a need for responding more completely to the cocurricular needs of students and creating a motivational environment. This situation provides us a valuable opportunity to emphasize human development concepts in a practical sense as a potential motivating element. (Donant & Spoden, 1981)

With a firm footing upon such intellectual endeavors as debate and group process, and with budgets supported directly by large numbers of satisfied community users, it would seem that participating union leaders would lose no sleep over questions of legitimacy within the campus scene. But alas, strong student influences over program content and service offerings and a virtual explosion in the number of special interest groups sometimes gave campus decision makers the impression that activities in general were moving farther and farther away from the original "well considered" program envisioned by union pioneers. Most serious practitioners of "educational" programming felt that their events and services were accomplishing important goals but were uneasy about the fact that proof beyond anecdotal evidence was a scarce commodity. Finally the inspired leadership of the Association of College Unions—International began to expose its members to the thinking of educational pioneers such as Sanford, Chickering, Astin, Crookston, and others. Students and staff members alike began to recognize that the formal student development approaches that were being suggested could be done, and done well by working practitioners; best of all the techniques lent themselves well to third party evaluation.

The AT&T Managerial Performance Study

One such third party is AT&T which has used information accumulated from decades of human resource studies in order to guide their recruitment activities for college graduates. In the late twenties, college achievements were related to salary performance for 1,310 personnel who had been out of school for four years and had been with the Bell System for two or more years. Scholarship was the most important with intellectual extracurricular achievements second.

In the early '60s, 17,000 graduates who had matriculated before 1950 and gone to work for Bell within five years after graduation were surveyed. Salary (after adjusting for seniority, location, and department) was used as a measure of success. Scholarship was again the most important factor followed by college quality. Extracurricular achievement involving substantial leadership was the third most significant indicator (Howard, 1984).

Primary data for the most recent study came from two longitudinal studies. One was begun in 1956 and a parallel effort was begun in 1977. In order to confirm the company findings, two additional samples were extracted from ten outside organizations (two government agencies and eight profit making firms). Specific participation information on college activities was requested. The nine categories were athletic, social, scholastic, musical, special interest, student government, school paper, debating, and other. In seven categories, respondents were asked to indicate their leadership responsibilities. An assessment center approach including a variety of tests and exercises was used to gauge the relative managerial performance capabilities of the participants.

The results of the study were similar to those produced by the earlier efforts. College major was the best predictor and involvement in extracurricular activities was the second best predictor of managerial characteristics for graduates. The number of extracurricular activities as well as number of leadership experiences related to later managerial performance, administrative and interpersonal abilities, and the motivation to work and advance. New managers with extracurricular experiences during college were generally more effective and had a higher probability of making middle management. The advantage is a temporary one, however, in as much as later advancement beyond middle ranks was not found to be related to college activities (Howard, 1984).

When examining individual factors, a larger number of activities related to decision making, creative skills, and personal impact; more leadership positions related to forcefulness; and

> . . . both number of activities and number of leadership positions were related to tolerance of uncertainty and resistance to stress. . . .
>
> It was clear from analyses that not all extracurricular activities had equal import. Participating in student government, the school papers, and debating teams was most likely to relate to meaningful performance criteria, while participating in athletic activities showed no such relationships. (Howard, 1984)

AT&T's general conclusion with regard to participation in extracurricular activities was that "[they] still seem to be good indicators of managerial performance and should be retained as selection indicators. Participating in large numbers of activities is a good sign as well as holding several leadership positions" (Howard, 1984). One of Astin's explanations for increased growth among participants in student government activities is that there tend to be more opportunities for interaction with peers, and "this interaction seems to accentuate the changes normally resulting from the college experience" (Astin, 1984). On the other hand, Astin observes that intense athletic involvement much like over-involvement in college studies (to the exclusion of all else) isolates a person from group influences that are instrumental to growth in a few important areas. Involvement in the total mix of activities available is the catalyst which can maximize the value of an undergraduate education.

The Iowa Student Development Study

Another kind of study was conducted at the University of Iowa. Researchers administered assessments to 1,000 entering freshmen during orientation. These students were chosen at random and were asked to complete one of six measures; three cognitive and three psychosocial in nature. Almost four years later as second semester seniors the

60 to 80% of the original individuals willing and able to repeat retook the tests using the same instrument. Students also provided information about their activities and living patterns during the undergraduate years. The scores on the second try were compared to those recorded as freshmen to assess change and detect any relationships that might exist between growth and reported nonacademic experiences. The results indicated that cognitive development increased significantly but could not be tied to any aspect of the undergraduate experience; psychosocial development increased significantly in the area of interpersonal relationships in both the areas of tolerance and quality of relationships (Hood, 1984).

The areas studied were tolerance and acceptance of differences; capacity for mature and intimate relationships; ability to perceive others and listen to them; and the ability to understand different views non-judgementally. Generally, growth trends in these areas were not found to relate to specific college experiences. However, a statistically significant relationship was found between participation in campus organizations and recreational activities on two developmental dimensions; the more involved a student was, the higher the student ranked on the quality of relationships scale; and those who were leaders indicated that they had more positive images of themselves and felt more confident about expressing beliefs and decisions (Hood, 1984).

> The results of this study indicate that participation in various types of extracurricular activities such as those provided by college unions is related to growth in certain psychosocial areas of development. The results offer empirical support for the statements of union professionals emphasizing the value of providing such activities on campus and encouraging participation in them.
>
> The concept of student development involves an increased emphasis on the cultural, recreational, and social development within college unions. This concept also emphasizes developmental programming activities designed to teach students the skills needed for the maximum use of their environment and suggests increased emphasis on intervention strategies that deal with students' psychosocial needs (Hood, 1984).

These formal research efforts validate what the author has observed over two decades: intensely involved students who actively participate as responsible volunteer committee members and leaders as well as above average building service employees are likely to complete their undergraduate degrees, are more confident, rational, and tolerant when confronted with previously unencountered situations, and are highly motivated entrants into the job market. Furthermore, even those who participate as spectators at only a few events are often exposed to sensory images and ideas which can create lasting impressions or point out new alternatives and directions. However, as an administrator held accountable for the total impact of a cocurricular program which is critically dependent upon the level of coordination of physical facilities, human resources, services, and events, I am most concerned about the opportunities for growth that are missed. In general, most would agree that many, if not most people, have not availed themselves of untold opportunities to further their own development. This condition is especially appalling at an institution responsible for advancing skills, knowledge, and intellectual curiosity through a process of higher education.

Setting the Stage for Student Development

A change in campus attention toward support for staff and faculty interventions which improve student retention may help more students to avail themselves of developmental opportunities. The ACT Center for the Advancement of Educational Practices in its book, *Increasing Student Competence and Persistence: The Best Case for General Education* urges "faculty and administrators to view general education from some perspectives they may not have considered important in the past" (Forrest, 1982). ACT can serve as a key source of comparative data as institutional leaders begin to assess and control elements of their own unique campus environments. Their studies support one of the most fundamental assumptions related to the enhancement of educational outcomes for large numbers of students: simply put, an institution must seek to retain students.

ACT encourages colleges and universities to make a conscious unified effort to integrate freshmen into the academic and social life of the campus so that they feel encouraged to return as sophomores. A positive relationship was found between a set of criteria that ACT calls "campus-centeredness" and the likelihood that students will return after the freshman year. The high end of their scale includes institutions where a college sponsored residence program is predominant; *participation* in college-sponsored extracurricular activities is high (curiously the number and variety of activities had no significant effect); most students are full-time; and a low percentage of student employment prevails.

Though the effect of these elements taper off and disappear after the first year and in fact may eventually be counterproductive to achievement of competency score gains and persistence to graduation, ACT encourages the following:

• Develop dormitory, extracurricular, and financial aid programs that will allow freshmen to concentrate on adjusting to college life.
• For commuting freshmen, provide short-term dormitory experiences as well as special workshops, retreats, or trips.

It is interesting that the ACT conclusion on the effects of undergraduate student employment in general seems to be at odds with Astin's contention that employment on the campus is positively related to staying in school since involvement in campus life is enhanced. Astin asserts that a part-time job in the college community will tend to cause an increased number of interactions with peers and with faculty which leads to an increased sense of investment in the campus. Another dimension of the same question is suggested by AT&T research which finds no relationship between earnings during college and eventual managerial success. However, Astin states that "retention suffers . . . if the student works off campus at a full-time job" (Astin, 1984).

Efforts to extend orientation activities and to provide for academic success courses and tutoring are worthwhile priorities employed by institutions who actively assist students with their adjustment to living and studying at a college or university. Student activities personnel and the supervisors of part-time student workers are in the unique position of having frequent opportunities for one to one exchanges with students. This group, as well as academic advisors, can contribute to an atmosphere of caring which seeks to build favorable student trust and personal confidence levels.

The union has much to contribute to the establishment of this "campus-centeredness." The ambiance of its physical facilities and the skills and demeanor of its employees and volunteers can project a warmth and sense of welcome that is a positive influence on the behavior of users and their interest in returning. In surveys, "pride of place" emerges as a common positive attitude. Students acknowledge that they can be proud of comfortable, visually appealing, and clean spaces and tend to use them more heavily and with greater respect and ownership than more impersonal "service stations." Students are more likely to become involved in activities which are complemented by a favorable environment. Union/activities people can and should study behavior patterns and work to accommodate diverse tastes and preferences so that the effectiveness of activities can be maximized. Assessments of "what students want" are not enough. It is the responsibility of administrators to expose student opinion leaders to new and successful approaches in use at other institutions.

"Virtually every institutional policy and practice—affects the way students use their time and the amount of effort they devote to academic pursuits" (Study Group, 1984).

Understanding how and why people use facilities and programs is not a simple process. Quantitative methods do not always tell the full story, particularly if the very nature of their components predetermine or narrow alternative responses. Qualitative approaches can be open-ended and therefore may be more difficult to analyze and interpret. There really can be no substitute for being there. Quality is best felt. Reading about a program or the reactions of participants is no substitute for attending an event or using a service or facility on a regular basis. "It permits the evaluator to understand a program to an extent often not possible using only the insights of others" (Swenson, 1985).

James Hurst of the University of Wyoming and James Banning of Colorado State University are leaders in a campus ecology movement which concerns itself with the interaction of students and the physical and human environment of colleges. Direct observation of the behavior patterns of people who use the union building on a daily basis can give administrators clues as to the messages being given (both intentionally and unintentionally) to users and participants. The focused interview technique is used quite successfully in commercial marketing to accumulate information that can be used to make qualitative improvements. The effective use of this approach on campus might also provide some meaningful interactions that have the potential for positive individual growth. Participation by marketing or psychology students could prove to be very effective.

Once students view the campus with pride and begin to invest themselves in its culture, unions can play an important programmatic role in developing the dimensions that are meaningful to skill levels and readiness of students for life. Astin emphatically encourages practitioners to move from the role of technician to educator by developing a philosophical foundation for their work. What follows are brief descriptions of the activities of individuals and organizations who are dedicating their efforts to extending resources and opportunities to ever widening circles of students and college community members. Each program reflects an underlying philosophy tailor-made for a particular campus situation. Ken Barclay and Randy Donant (1981) suggest that the first step in beginning a student development effort is to do large scale surveys that will suggest the appropriate developmental theory best suited for application within the specific educational environment. Consideration must be given to resources available and external as well as internal priorities.

Developmentally Based Activities

The fun and games of stringing crepe papers for dances and shooting a game of billiards to pass the time has long since faded into the history of student unions. Staff members, student leaders, and volunteers are deeply involved in attempting to adequately meet the ever increasing expressed needs of the student body while at the same time addressing developmental issues. Effective approaches to enhancing student involvement are known but require an enormous amount of commitment and energy to sustain. Specific examples include: traditional workshops and retreats; credit courses related to academic survival; community service programs; mentor programs; developmental transcripts and assessments; comprehensive programs for up to four years; survey generated data based programming; and application of student development theories to the supervision of student employees.

Traditional Workshops and Retreats

The organization and operation of leadership programs and group dynamics activities is a basic component of volunteer committee structures nominally assembled to plan and present program events. Basic training and educational techniques are utilized and developmental impact is dependent upon the patterns of interaction that result rather than the actual experience. The process is more important than the end product. More comprehensive student development workshop approaches are being used at the University of Minnesota—Twin Cities by Ronald Krumm, Director of the West Bank Center.

Credit Courses

There has been in the last decade an assertive tendency by activities/ university union professionals to move into the classroom. This in most cases has not been an easy task to accomplish. Campus politics and academic policy have, in many cases, created effective barriers in achieving this goal. These courses generate anywhere from one to four units of credit. In many cases, they include an intricate internship opportunity for credit, especially for the graduate student. Based on department-approved courses of study, topics include goal setting, motivation, value clarification, interpersonal relationships, and many other elements of group dynamics.

Some institutions are attempting to create entire academic programs. For example, the University of Massachusetts, Amherst, is currently developing a program of courses in "student controlled businesses" as well as student educational research and advocacy. In many cases these programs have originated as a result of projects or events created by student government associations (Barclay & Donant, 1981).

Community Service Programs

Student volunteer programs which are beneficial to participants and the community are active on many campuses. At the University of South Dakota, there are two programs which have been sustained for over ten years. One involves student volunteers who "adopt a grandparent" and agree to visit them weekly in a local nursing home. The other is the "big pal–little pal" program which matches a college student with a middle school child. Participants communicate with one another by telephone and get involved in group social and recreational activities. In each program, a professional social worker or counselor observes the various interchanges and offers feedback to the student chair who in turn evaluates student participants. Professional school students often invest time and energy in outreach projects such as tax preparation and legal aid. With appropriate organization and feedback, volunteer programs can develop interpersonal skills and attitudes as well as academic specialties.

Mentor Programs

Few campuses are found actually implementing its [mentorship] philosophy in any structural fashion. Nonetheless, these programs exist and are growing. The classic mentor model comes out of the University of Nebraska, Lincoln. It is called the Student Development Mentoring/ Transcript Project, which was developed by Robert C. Brown and his staff at the University of Nebraska. . . . Based on the Nebraska model, the purpose of the mentor program is to establish personal development goals through (1) self-assessment and exploration, (2) goal setting, (3) identifying specific experiences and activities that will contribute to personal growth, (4) evaluating the experiences, and (5) documenting the progress of completion of activities through a student development transcript. Student activities departments have been involved with other administrative offices in developing and coordinating many mentor programs (Barclay & Donant, 1981).

Efforts to Develop Critical Thinking Skills

The learning of critical skills can be achieved very effectively through union/activities programs. Colleges and universities have tried various approaches to incorporating critical thinking experiences such as examination of ethical considerations and the clarification of values into an undergraduate education. This area is difficult to approach in the traditional classroom setting. These skills are best learned and practiced by using experiential learning techniques such as role play and focused interaction (Brookfield, 1987).

Union/activities staff members can create and sustain an effective critical thinking laboratory which can have a significant impact on the outcomes of the undergraduate experience. The University of South Dakota is making an effort to establish and maintain a climate conducive to critical questioning in its student activities center. Staff members are developing the requisite skills and making an effort to model critical behavior in all of their dealings with students, staff, and faculty. Initial student training incorporates role play and interaction. Emphasis is given to the transferability of the assumptions and attitudes introduced in the retreat environment to subsequent individual and organizational transactions. In everyday operations, standard procedures such as the use of formal written program proposals in support of verbal presentations provides an opportunity for students to share plans and ideas with their peers. Staff members encourage students to expect and appreciate questions and comments from peers and others who hold different perspectives. It is stressed that constant evaluation at every stage of the process can help to improve current and future programs. Staff and student leaders believe that this kind of experience is uniquely suited to the development of skills critical to the success and happiness of each individual.

Developmental Transcripts and Assessments

It is unusual for a college to invest resources in efforts to provide developmental feedback on any dimension other than academic performance. This is probably due to skepticism about the value and methodology associated with such attempts at assessment. Successful efforts have included the following:

• Roger B. Winston, Jr., Theodore K. Miller, and Judith Prince of the University of Georgia have developed the standardized Student Development Task Inventory.
• University of Nebraska-Lincoln has created the College of Student Development Self-Assessment Inventory.
• Coffman Union at the University of Minnesota-Twin Cities has used various student development assessment approaches.

Assessment inventories are questionnaires which cause students to think about their own personal development, and with the assistance of an advisor, set measurable goals which actualize developmental prescriptions. Once established, the transcript becomes a record of activities or achievements which demonstrate personal growth. The transcripts can be used to supplement resume information. Obviously there is a requirement that both the advisor and the advisee be completely committed to the process because of the time required to select the correct mix of participations and monitor progress. The development of microcomputer software applications for tracking individual progress while providing for group summary information should enhance the chances of widespread use.

Survey Generated Data Based Programming

Marketers of consumer goods, services, and entertainment have invested considerable sums in finding out about the patterns of use (or projected use) of their products. Now college activity programs are beginning to do the same. Jay Boyer at Prince George's Community College in Largo, Maryland, uses questionnaires completed by the entire student body each semester to determine the demographic composition, program interest patterns, desired program delivery methods, and the preferred approaches to publicity and promotion. The survey findings which show indicated preferences by total population and by specific age groupings, are shared with various programming organizations on campus and serve as a planning tool.

A survey conducted at each program event [information is gathered by recording student identification numbers or by using computer linked validation by means of a magnetic strip card] indicates the proportion of full-time and part-time students, average age, racial composition, sex, and day/evening status of students in the audience. Since part-time students tend to be more heterogeneous than the full-time student population, research indicating interests, program times, and delivery systems for a wide range of subgroups of the part-time populations becomes a valuable tool in effective programming (Boyer, 1985).

Supervision of Student Employees

"If you want to apply theory, you have to understand the abstract and move it to the concrete and vice versa" (Allen, 1985).

Kathy Allen, Dean of Student Development at Mt. St. Mary's College, was a union director for ten years. She decided more than a decade ago to attempt to apply the ideas of Chickering to supervision of part-time student employees in the Moorhead State Center. Her approach was to translate the developmental vectors into relevant achievable goals. To make the goals more actionable with reference to everyday duties and obligations, Allen identified appropriate skills that could be taught and measured. "The assumption is that if individuals can achieve these skills, then they will achieve the goals of student development" (Allen, 1985).

Identical sets of skills needed to achieve particular goals appeared on a recurring basis so Allen developed a list of "Life Skills" which would be readily transferable to the many situations that a fully functioning adult would encounter.

> Life skills are the objectives to achieve [those] goals. The advantage of using the life skills as objectives is that their accomplishment can be measured by the actual behavior of the student. This ability to measure results takes the ambiguity out of developing students. It gives you direct feedback which helps you see what helps and what hinders a student's development . . . daily duties become the action plan for achieving these objectives.
>
> For each of the life skills, I have developed a list of interview questions. By comparing a student's answers with the student's performance on the job, the questions' validity and reliability in helping identify skills are tested constantly (Allen, 1985).

John Naisbitt, in his latest book, *The Year Ahead*, states:

> In the eighties, we are moving from the manager who is supposed to have all the answers and tells everyone what to do, to the manager whose role

is to create a nourishing environment for personal growth. We have to increasingly think about the manager as teacher, as mentor, as resource, as developer of human potential.

Comprehensive Programs for Up to Four Years

Some campuses are beginning to establish comprehensive four-year programs which aim to bring together services, programs, faculty, staff, and other resources of the institution in order to effectively meet the developmental needs of students.

Each year is developed, in most cases, around a theme. For example, the freshman year may concentrate on self-assessment, the sophomore year on career exploration and decision making, the junior year on leadership, and the senior year on job-seeking skills. Slippery Rock University has a four-year, comprehensive program much like the one described above called "LEAP." These programs require a great amount of coordination and cooperation among all elements of the student affairs division of a university as well as key departments in the academic sector (Barclay & Donant, 1981).

At Longwood College in Virginia, staff members who have been working with a comprehensive program for the last few years made the following observations.

It is not enough to focus simply on involving students. To encourage comprehensive and meaningful involvements, you need resources beyond yourself; the concept of involvement needs to be broadened to include faculty and staff as well as students.

Generally, a relatively small core of students is quite active in a variety of involvements, with a great mass of students being content to take classes and do little else.

Like the students . . . there is a core of faculty most concerned with and involved in student life; the majority seem relatively uninvolved (Gorski et al., 1985).

Concluding Remarks

The educators who work with students in planning and presenting cocurricular programs and services have seen their offerings evolve over the years as a result of a willingness to listen to those students and value their partnership. The rewards have occurred much like the educational development that had happened: most on a one-to-one basis. Now that formal theoretical structures and evaluative devices are available, it is time for administrators, student activity advisors, students, and faculty to cooperatively use these tools to increase student involvement, and by so doing enhance the contribution of higher education to education of the whole person.

In one of the four statements included in "The Role of the College Union," adopted by the members of the Association of College Unions at its 33rd conference in 1956, it was proclaimed that,

> The union is part of the educational program of the college. As the center of college community life, it serves as a laboratory of citizenship, training students in social responsibility and for leadership in our democracy.
>
> Through its various boards, committees, and staff, it provides a cultural, social, and recreational program, aiming to make free time activity a cooperative factor with study in education.
>
> In all its processes, it encourages self-directed activity, giving maximum opportunity for self-realization and for growth in individual social competency and group effectiveness. Its goal is the development of persons as well as intellects.

References

Allen, K. (1985, April). Student development: Applying theory to student employees. *The Bulletin of the Association of College Unions—International*, 17–22.

Astin, A. (1984, July). Student involvement: A developmental theory for higher education. *Journal of College Student Personnel*, 297–307.

Astin, A. (1977). *Four critical years*. San Francisco: Jossey-Bass, 293 pp.

Barclay, K. & Donant, R. (1981). Educational processes available to students and staff in an activities/university union environment. *The Proceedings of the 61st Annual Conference of the Association of College Unions—International*, 31–35.

Boyer, J. (1985, August). Serving the new majority. *The Bulletin of the Association of College Unions—International*, 4–6.

Brookfield, S. (1987). *Developing critical thinkers*. San Francisco: Jossey-Bass, 293 pp.

Butts, P. (1971). *The college union idea*. Stanford, CA: Association of College Unions—International.

Chickering, A. (1977). Potential contributions of college unions to student development. *Proceedings of the 57th Annual Conference of the Association of College Unions—International*, 23–27.

Donant, R. & Spoden, S. (1981, February). Volunteerism a vehicle . . . human development the force. *The Bulletin*, 10–12.

Forrest, A. (1982). *Increasing student competence and persistence. The best case for general education.* The American College Testing Program, 1982, 51 pp.

Gorski, B. et al. (1985, June). Student development: The Longwood experience. *The Bulletin of the Association of College Unions—International*, 21–25.

Hood, A. (1984, December). Student development: Does participation affect growth? *The Bulletin of the Association of College Unions—International*, 16–19.

Howard, A. (1984). *College experiences and managerial performance.* New York: AT&T, 1–33.

Marine, J. (1985, February). The college union's role in student development. *The Bulletin of the Association of College Unions—International*, 22–23.

Minahan, A. (1957). *The college union and preparation for citizenship.* Ithaca, NY: The Association of College Unions.

Naisbitt, J. (1984). *The year ahead.* Washington, DC: The Naisbitt Group.

Swenson, M. (1985, June). Some simple research can shed light on your problems. *The Bulletin of the Association of College Unions—International*, 16–17.

Helping to Make the Transition from High School to College

John F. Bryde and Corinne M. Milburn

The topic of this article is indeed timely. Proof of this is seen in the flurry of activities which colleges provide for their entering students. An article, entitled, "Colleges strive to keep freshmen happy," written by the Associated Press education writer, Lee Mitgang (1985) suggests that the first four weeks are the most difficult time for incoming freshmen. Mitgang presents various plans of colleges and universities across the country, which aim to keep freshmen happy and in school by devising ways and means to help them overcome the main blocks to adjustment and happiness; namely, homesickness, feeling of alienation from the faculty and from their fellow students, loneliness and anxiety from being separated from their home, parents, and lifelong friends, as well as irritating habits of newly assigned roommates.

While freshman orientation is hardly a new college rite, the activities have taken on added urgency in the last few years. Nationally, statistics have shown that the most crucial time for the students, as to whether they will stay or leave, is during the first four weeks. This is the time during which they decide whether they feel they can eventually become comfortable with this new environment. This is the judgement of Lovly Ulmer, Coordinator at the University of Kansas.

Colleges around the country are updating their freshman orientation program by mixing fun and outdoor activities with intellectual activities, including seminars and workshops on subjects such as alcohol, drugs, roommate problems, and plain old homesickness.

Water seems to hold a certain charm. At Harvard University, the

1,600 freshmen begin their college experiences with a boat ride in Boston Harbor. The students must pretend that they are immigrants. This is to show them that the Harvard experience is larger than the campus. In St. Louis, Missouri, students at Washington University are treated to a four-hour Mississippi River stern wheeler cruise. Spokeswoman of the University, Carol Basking, says, "We have the idea of giving students a picture of St. Louis, helping them to fit into the community and not just the University."

Because the transition from high school to college affects parents as well as students, a number of schools have extended the orientation process to include parents. Vanderbilt University in Nashville, Tennessee, offers parents a talk about the sufferings of separation, directed at dealing with the loneliness parents and students almost universally feel. Carnegie-Mellon University in Pittsburgh and Canisius College, a private Jesuit institution in Buffalo, New York, also invite parents to join students for orientation lectures.

Adjusting to roommates often creates a sense of tenseness and to ease the anxiety, Syracuse University requires freshmen to draft and sign formal agreements with their roommates that set down clear ground rules for study hours, stereo playing, overnight guests, and any other potential sources of friction. In a similar view, Hood College in Frederick, Maryland, has printed a "Roommate Negotiation Workbook" to help new roommates head off living problems.

Orientation activities are not limited to students and parents. To overcome the feeling of the huge gap between students and faculty, the University of Colorado at Boulder, Colorado, offers book discounts to its 3,500 freshmen to get them to mingle with the faculty. This is accomplished at the annual, "Sex, Drugs, Wok, and Roll" seminar for incoming freshmen at which fresh egg rolls are served along with advice. In addition, the university offers $2.00 discounts on student bookstore purchases for every faculty autograph a freshman gathers during orientation. The autographs act as proof that the students have made an effort to meet their future teachers and also serves as the first step to get the students to know the professors personally.

A variety of techniques are used at the different schools, but most commonly orientation includes outdoor fun, especially at those institutions that can boast of beautiful surroundings.

Review of the Relevant Literature

Researchers tend to agree that transition from high school to college is difficult for most students. There is further agreement regarding the need for orientation and student development. There is no agreement, however, on the best method of orientation nor on the content of the program.

Reiss and Fox (1968) suggest that the transition from high school to college is difficult for many students yet seemingly easy for others. They, as most other counselors, agree that all students, however, do face some adjustments in the new environment of college.

Although each student thinks that his or her experiences are unique, transition problems are common to every first year student. The full impact of the college experience is usually disconcerting at times to all students. Even those students who are in complete control have their periods of doubts and despair (Lindgreen, 1969).

Transition problems are not limited to academics or institution adjustments. Many other variables must be considered. To the student from a small rural community simply finding one's way around a university several times larger than the town where he or she grew up can be a traumatic experience. For others who are away from home for the first time, the problem of loneliness can be devastating (Holmes & Rahe, 1967; Tollefson, 1975).

University of Nebraska-Lincoln (UNL) professor of human development John Woodward, has conducted research on loneliness over the past 20 years. His findings show that college students, particularly incoming freshmen, are more lonely than virtually all other social groups except single parents, alcoholics, rural high school students, and female inner city high-schoolers. He attributes the loneliness to the fact that most students have been cut off from their family and life-long friends; their support system has literally been uprooted. Not only are they trying to survive in a strange environment, but they are being forced to make numerous decisions on a regular basis and decision making, he says, is a very lonely process. Woodward states, "that loneliness is very normal, but it becomes a problem when it interferes with someone's ability to function" (Woodward, 1985, p. 1).

Numerous studies of American college freshmen (Astin, 1975; Gardner & Jewler, 1985; Sanford, 1962; Woodward, 1985) have documented that excessive freedom is one of the major transition problems. It is difficult to move from the parental protection of the home to the freedom of the college dormitory.

Gardner and Jewler (1985) argue that the single greatest problem facing college students is the problem of freedom—too much freedom (p. 4).

Erich Fromm (1965), in his book *Escape from Freedom*, alleges that freedom is an enormous problem because it is a burden with which most people do not know how to cope. He contends that freedom, because of its very nature, is something many people cherish while others find it threatening.

Gardner and Jewler (1985) also viewed freedom from another perspective, the freedom of the student to make decisions. They found that students make decisions, which have a definite affect on their academic life, at regular intervals during the first few months on campus.

Much has been written on the effects of Greek organizations on college students (Feldman & Newcomb, 1973; Schmidt, 1971; Scott, 1965; and Wilder et al., 1978).

Becker, Geer and Hughes (1968) concluded that some fraternities did have a positive impact on college grades. Considerable controversy still exists concerning the influence of fraternity and sorority membership on college students. Some observers praise the Greek organizations for their contributions to individual development and training in interpersonal relationships. Others associate Greek membership with superficiality (Marlowe & Auvenshine, 1982).

In surveying students a variety of problems surfaced but probably more important, to most students, than having an individual problem solved with professional efficiency is "the need to be treated as a unique person and to find compatible people on the faculty as well as among students, who recognize and value that unique personality and with whom common interest can be shared" (Tollefson, 1985, p. 57).

Importance of Orientation

Students and faculty both at the high school and college levels need to be more aware of transition problems, the probable reasons and the possible solutions. It is essential to remember that students are different and, therefore, will react to transition problems differently. The maturity, emotional, motivational level, and temperament of the student, however, cannot be ignored.

Another important factor is the environment. The environment of college life is very different from that of high school. In high school someone, either a parent or a teacher, is always there to assist and advise; but in college one is in control of one's own destiny. The protective environment has been removed and the students find that they are on their own and probably for the first time in their life. There is a variety of circumstances that challenge new college students' ability to adjust. The potential impact of these circumstances is evident in the research and development of The Social Readjustment Rating Scale by Holmes and Rahe. The scale contains 43 life events, each of which, may produce a drastic change in a student's life. Twelve have been identified as directly related to college freshmen; several of these life change units are listed below:

- begin and end school
- change in school
- change in social activities
- change in sleeping habits
- change in eating habits.

In addition to the life change units, the following factors have also been identified as sources of stress and pressure:

- larger, more complex environment
- stronger sense of responsibility
- achievement and competition
- loneliness (Holmes and Rahe, 1967).

Almost every college student at some time during the first few months will experience a myriad of emotions ranging from confusion to frustration and even disappointment. Adjusting to a new environment is not the easiest task in the world. It takes time and patience to learn to live with a group of strangers who come from a variety of backgrounds. Students' ideas on studying, sex, religion, politics, drugs, and drinking will reflect many different and sometimes shocking viewpoints. Competition for higher grades may run rampant. Working part-time may become a necessity. Culture shock will inevitably be present.

Summer orientation will have attempted to smooth the way, but orientation should be a continuous process. Freshman orientation is certainly not new. The first known course for credit was established in 1911 at Reed College, Portland, Oregon. But somehow it never really caught on; it never became a required part of the freshman curriculum. According to Gardner and Grites (1984) the contents of such a course should be defined by the needs of the students but all courses should include the following basics:

- to motivate and help students understand their role as a student
- to clarify why they are in college
- to provide information about an academic program

- to understand occupational implications of their choice of major
- to develop or improve study and time management skills
- to know college's procedures, resources and services.

College life is both an intellectual and emotional experience. Students must learn to adapt to the new academic world at the same time that they are maturing socially and emotionally. All aspects are interrelated and can contribute one to another.

Closely aligned to freedom is ineffective time management. Human nature appears to dislike planning even for the day ahead. It's as if predetermining a course of action limits one's freedom. Many college students fall easy prey to the "time tray" unless they learn early to plan, set goals, prioritize, organize, and make decisions. Failure to follow through on any of the strategies may be detrimental (Mackenzie, 1972).

College life has always been different but since the sixties these differences have become more visible to the general public. Numerous studies have been published on the American college student and particularly on the first year student. Astin (1975), Baker and Siryk (1980), Chickering (1972), and Feldman and Newcomb (1969), noted figures in this area, have done much to increase public awareness of the impact of college on students and to point out the need to understand the changes the students encounter as they interact with others in the collegiate environment.

Student Surveys

Research on attrition shows that approximately 40% of first year students do not reach their junior year (Bringman & Jacobs, 1979; Muskat, 1975; and Pantages & Creedon, 1978). How can this drop-out rate be lowered? How can the transition from high school to college be made easier?

In attempting to answer these questions, the writers used the results of a questionnaire. The survey, relating to student experiences before coming to college and after coming to college, was given to 60 students. The students selected to participate in the study were juniors and seniors, because it was felt that since they had survived the trauma of transition, they would probably be more objective in their responses than students still in the process of transition.

The question "What changes would you put in the high school now that would help present high school students find a pleasant transition to college?'' evoked the following responses. For brevity, repetitive responses are avoided.

• Study skills need to be stressed. Lack of proper study skills is one of the biggest problems of adjusting to college.

• When colleges recruit, high school students need to hear from professors, counselors, and college students as well as admissions personnel. Students could benefit from hearing about college life including the difficulties they might encounter.

• More preparation on how to deal with loneliness.

• High schools should allow students the opportunity to experience more freedom, in order to develop better self-discipline.

• More emphasis on academics, particularly English, grammar, literature, and composition. Special emphasis on writing skills and reading should be included.

• High schools should offer a seminar or mini-course (pre-orientation) which would include tips on studying, keeping up with assignments, dorm life, Greek life, financial aid, time management, and interpersonal relations. A few days or a week of ''on campus living'' would be nice if it could be arranged.

• Encourage students to visit colleges and see the environment in which they will be living.

• Have students assume more responsibility for getting their school work done.

• Warn students about the difficulty of college exams as compared to high school; explain that grades often drop during the first semester of college, but usually rise after the transition period.

• Encourage students to seriously question their career goals—not ''just what do you want to be, but why?''

• Loosen up the structure in the high school so first year college students aren't so devastated by the abrupt change when they go to college.

• Emphasize socialization. Some students do not make friends easily or relate well to people. These students need help to overcome their shyness and become more outgoing.

• Provide more information on financial aid and stress the importance of starting early in the senior year.

• Emphasize time management. How does a first year college student with only 16 hours of classes for the entire week manage his or her time? Seminars or workshops on time management should be available for all high school seniors.

The same study asked the students to respond to the following:

1. After coming to college please list: (a) the most pleasant experiences you had, and (b) the hardest experiences you had.

2. This is a serious question: If you had ALL POWER administratively on the campus for one week, and then had to go back into the student ranks, what changes would you make so that the transition from high school to college would be as pleasant as possible and as academically profitable as possible?

In response to the item concerning the most pleasant experiences encountered on making the transfer from high school to college, the most frequent responses were the following:

> their newly found independence; making new friends from such a wide variety of personality types; first parties and social activities; wider variety of sports activities; the stimulating environment of a college campus, totally taken.

In response to the item concerning the hardest things to take, the most frequent responses were the following:

> In spite of the multiplicity of new stimuli, the sheer inner loneliness during the first month was the most frequently listed response. Flowing from this was the painful feeling of alienation, isolation and feeling faceless in huge crowds of people. Feelings of insecurity and anxiety flowing from demands for competition in alien territories were prominent sources of acute discomfort. Homesickness for parents and life-long friends were common and difficult experiences. The loneliness of making important decisions by themselves was painful for many and financial worries were a common burden for many of the students.

In response to the item as to what they would do if they had all power for a week, the following were representative by reason of their frequency:

> A better system of orientation so that new students could be worked into campus activities more quickly, thereby making new friends as soon as possible; also, more effective orientation would more quickly provide answers to questions many felt were not being answered. Administrators and teachers should be closer to the students and more available for help. The most sympathetic and sensitive teachers should be provided for

the freshmen. Smaller classes were opted for frequently. Required courses not pertinent to one's major field would quickly be eliminated by many. A suggestion to use upperclassmen for advisors and counselors on a one to one basis was made by a surprisingly large number of students (and these were upperclassmen making the suggestions). Several wanted pass/fail courses across the board as the best way of eliminating test anxiety. Eliminating noisy students in the dorms was a common goal of many having "all power."

Conclusions

The transition from high school to college is unique and challenging. It's a time of new beginnings and new freedoms. It allows students away from the familiar home environment to determine who they want to be. But in addition to being challenging, new beginnings add stress to an individual's life. Stress is inherent in any transition from the safety of the known to the vagueness of the unknown.

In the transition sometimes too much emphasis is put on "going to" college and not enough on what will insure success after the student arrives. Granted, success may have different meanings for different students, but most would agree that academic achievement, personal and social development is a part of any definition.

Recommendations

Before coming to college:

1. More attention should be given to preparing students for college level courses.
2. Provide more responsibility; allow students then to make choices and decisions.
3. Offer a series of mini-courses on interpersonal relations, time management, study habits and other topics of interest to the students.
4. Provide college type assignments and assist students in developing their writing skills.
5. Help students realistically assess their potential for college.

After coming to college:

1. Provide summer orientation sessions for both students and parents.

2. Offer an orientation course during the first semester. The course should carry at least 1 hour of credit, because attaching credit to a course presumes that it will be evaluated and most students tend to regard more seriously those courses that are for credit. One additional recommendation would be to delete the option and make the course mandatory for all incoming students. All students could benefit from interpersonal relations, problem-solving and communication skills which should be an integral part of the content.

3. Train advisors. Often professors are willing to work with students and would like to help them with scheduling problems, etc., but are lacking in advising skills regarding changes in university requirements. Provide in-service for faculty advisors to keep them up-to-date.

4. Poll students regularly regarding their transition problems and utilize this feedback in modifying and up-dating orientation programs.

5. Encourage faculty to be humanistic in their dealings with first year students. Most of these students, because of one or more or a combination of transition problems, need special attention. In addition, they need to know that the university is not just another cold institution, but a place inhabited by warm and caring people.

There is a need to provide a framework to help students understand the concept of transition and most of all to create a positive and cooperative environment so students can become aware of their feelings, reactions, and adjustments and focus on coping with their day-to-day problems.

> Change and growth take place when people have risked themselves and dare to become involved with experimenting with their own lives.
>
> —Herbert Otto

References

Astin, A. W. (1975). *Preventing students from dropping out*. San Francisco: Jossey-Bass.

Baker, R. W., & Siryk, B. (1980). Alienation and freshman transition into college. *Journal of College Student Personnel. 21*, 437–442.

Becker, H. S., Geer, B., & Hughes, E. D. (1968). *Making the grade: The academic side of college life*. New York: John Wiley & Sons, Inc.

Bringman, S. L., & Jacobs, L. D. (1979). *Persistence/attrition: A longitudinal study of the freshman class of 1974.* Indiana University, Bureau of Educational Studies and Testing.

Chickering, A. (1972). Undergraduate academic experience. *Journal of Educational Psychology. 67,* 134–143.

Feldman, R. A., & Newcomb, T. M. (1969). *The impact of college on students.* Vol. 1. San Francisco: Jossey-Bass.

Fromm, E. (1965). *Escape from freedom.* New York: Avon Books.

Gardner, J. N., & Jewler, A. J. (1985). *College is only the beginning.* Belmont, CA: Wadsworth Publishing Company.

Gardner, V. N., & Grites, T. J. (1984). The freshman seminar course: Helping students succeed. *Journal of College Student Personnel. 25,* 315–320.

Holmes, T. H., & Rahe, R. H. (1967). The social readjustment rating scale. *Journal of Psychological Research. 11,* 213–219.

Katz, O. et al. (1968). *No time for youth: Growth and constraint in college students.* San Francisco: Jossey-Bass.

Lindgreen, H. O. (1968). *The psychology of college success.* New York: John Wiley & Sons, Inc.

Mackenzie, R. A. (1981). *The time trap.* New York: McGraw-Hill Book Company.

Marlowe, A. F., & Auvenshine, C. D. (1982). Greek membership: Its impact on the moral development of college freshmen. *Journal of College Student Personnel. 23,* 58–70.

Muskat, H. (1975). Educational expectations and college attrition. *National Association of Student Personnel Administrators Journal. 17,* 17–22.

National Education Association (NEA). (1984). *The 1984 NEA almanac of higher education.* Washington, DC: NEA Communication Services.

Pantages, T. J., & Creedon, D. F. (1978). Studies of college attrition: 1950–1975. *Review of Educational Research, 48,* 49–101.

Reiss, J., & Fox, M. G. (1968). *Guiding the future college student.* Englewood Cliffs, NJ: Prentice-Hall, Inc.

Sanford, N. (1962). *The American college.* New York: Wiley.

Schmidt, M. R. (1971). Relationship between sorority membership and changes in selective personality variables and attitudes. *Journal of College Student Personnel. 12,* 208–213.

Scott, W. A. (1965). *Values and organization: A study of fraternities and sororities.* Chicago: Rand McNally.

Wilder, D. H., Hoyt, A. E., Doren, D. M., Hauck, W. E., & Zettle, R. D. (1978). The impact of fraternity or sorority membership on values and attitudes. *Journal of College Student Personnel, 18,* 445–449.

Tollefson, A. L. (1975). *New approaches to college students' development*. New York: Behavioral Publications, Inc.

Woodward, J. (1985, September 24). UNL researcher finds college students more lonely than any other social groups. *Volante*, University of South Dakota, Vermillion, S.D.

Front Loading the Freshman Experience

William R. Donohue

Introduction

In a report on the conditions of excellence in American higher education titled "Involvement in Learning: Realizing the Potential of American Higher Education" (1984), the National Institute of Education (NIE) study group underscored in its early recommendations the importance of reallocating faculty and other institutional resources toward increased services for first and second year undergraduates. They call it "front loading." It is long overdue, but it may be a pipe dream. The paper discusses why.

Retention committees and study groups over the past decade have pointed repeatedly to the freshman year exodus. Career counselors, registrars and academic advisors have talked exhaustively about the difficulties entering, and especially first generation, students have with both interpersonal and academic transitions. From learning technologies to activity indicators, the data have been clear and known for decades; students who get involved and who get help early do better. Where has the National Institute of Education been?

Where does the National Institute "get off" at recommending such a dramatic resource reallocation? Haven't they read about the other crises in higher education: federal funding, salaries for faculty, higher admission standards, athletic scandals, decreasing interest rates, and affirmative action? Don't they know that apartheid, nuclear war, and Central America are the issues, not the E. F. Hutton jargon of "front-loading?'' Are students some kind of ''whole-life'' or ''term'' insurance?

Why are the policy makers and study groups of American higher education just now recognizing the importance of greater services to its entering students? How can the college presidents and funding agencies of today justify such radical resource allocations in light of other pressing problems?

In this article, special attention will be focused on these questions. Drawing on longitudinal student services research and the immediate budgeting dilemmas facing today's higher education planners, it may be that the questions have the same answer. This article will focus on the unique challenges of teaching and servicing the college freshman. They are the ''front end'' of this ''loading'' concept and present a beautiful, if not overwhelming, opportunity.

This paper will assert that it is cost effective to invest the time (front load if you will) in young people and nontraditional students alike, when they are at the same time most vulnerable and motivated as freshmen. The resources may be regenerating and the long range payoffs may not be that distant. The risks are considerable; the attitudes entrenched; both will take courage to address.

In spite of the tardy report from Washington, this article will conclude with a firm endorsement of the NIE recommendation and underscore the need to open the institutional throttle on the freshman year experience.

Involvement: What Is It and Why Is It So Important

''College administrators should reallocate faculty and other institutional resources toward increased service to first and second year undergraduate students'' (1984, p. 25). The National Institute of Education begins its energetic series of recommendations with this charge—a strategy to ''front load'' with key levers of institutional involvement. The strategy emphasizes intense intellectual opportunities with freshmen and the finest faculty, selected use of and training for teaching assistants and a full range of services and advising. This first recommendation includes the revising of state funding formulas to support underclass students.

The theme of the NIE report is involvement in learning. For the freshman student, nearly everything is learning; there are so many new experiences. Ironically, however, the classroom experience may be the most familiar form of involvement of all. For the faculty member, involvement suggests a renewal of personal relationships with students, of relearning how to advise, and a new look at curricula and student assessment. Administrators are asked to involve themselves with front loading by maximizing the exposure new students receive to well trained advisors, excellent faculty and quality services. As the NIE report continues, administrators need to document and measure those experiences as well.

Why? The theme of involvement is important for several reasons, but the report focuses primarily on retention. A student who stays longer learns more they say.

Retaining Students

One campus described its retention problem as "institutional dry rot . . . a gradual, barely detectable, irreversible destruction of the ship's structure and fiber" (Western Illinois University). The nautical analogy continued with "financial leaks" and "curricular listing."

What Works in Student Retention (WWISR), published in 1980 by the American College Testing Corporation (ACT), provides a most practical summary of successful strategies in combating institutional attrition. They begin:

> The idea is simple enough: if schools can retain more students once they are admitted, then enrollment will hold steady or decrease at a slower rate. It is no easy task, however, to understand the variables involved in retention; and it is even more difficult to influence retention rates, which may be affected by numerous conditions and circumstances beyond institutional control (1980, p. 1).

Citing references to more than 400 citations for 40 years of research related to retention, they proceed to describe the myriad of complex student and environmental variables. Few clear solutions exist. Nearly all, however, employ "front loading."

Of the six concluding recommendations, three seem to parallel the NIE report: the need for academic stimulation and assistance, the need for future building, and the need for involvement experiences.

Two short years later, ACT published "Increasing Student Competence and Persistence." This research report sheds an even fresher and sharper analysis on student retention. The new message from ACT was that the techniques used by many institutions to retain students may work, but the primary ingredient must be meaningful interaction with the faculty. In the end, if you are not motivating students with quality classroom teaching, all the retention gimmicks and superficial involvement will fall short.

Their study of 44 institutions focuses on the importance of quality-general education as the prime vehicle for helping students persist in college. General education is also said to work best with quality advice and extracurricular support, not just superior classroom instruction. Some 50 features were studied at these institutions while 3,318 students were tested using the College Outcomes Measurement Program (COMP). The authors documented conclusively that institutions who measured the most significant growth in general educational development the freshman year were also the ones measuring the highest student persistence to graduation.

Like its predecessor, the ACT report seemed to pre-empt the NIE report with the conclusions that quality academic advising, extended orientation programs and a sense of "campus centeredness" were the keys which accompany a strong general education program. Additionally, they cited the importance of strong remedial programs and clear curricular objectives.

ACT began its final recommendations: "probably the single most important move an institution can make to increase students' persistence to graduation is to ensure that students receive the guidance they need at the beginning of their journey. . . ."

Who Are The Front Enders?

Other than the U.S. taxpayer, probably few groups reveal as much about themselves each year as the American college freshmen. They are surveyed longitudinally as well as sampled to measure immediate trends.

We know their average college board scores, their parents' mean income, their high school preparedness and their adolescent aspirations. We inquire about their political leanings, their attitudes toward crime and punishment. One-fourth will take remedial classes their first semester (Department of Education), yet nearly half will express a need for assistance with educational and career plans (ACT Service Report, 1984). Thirty-eight percent feel their study skills are lacking and only seven in ten will return to their enrolled school to begin their second year (Astin, 1984).

Less statistical observations and descriptions are offered by others:

You won't want to come into the office today anyway, the freshmen are coming and its a mess over here. . . .

It certainly is a mess. Hundreds of station wagons packed with steaming students, their families and endless belongings seek non-existent parking spots along a few feet of curb while nervous parents bicker about when, where and how to park. Campus police do what they can but they know it's beyond their control; the rules will have to bend a little. *It is* the messiest day of the year . . . also my favorite.

They appear in town like green shoots, sprouting up everywhere, looking for light. Their faces hang out the windows of dorms like tiny new buds on an old, old tree.

Yes, today is the beginning of a new life. One day you're Mama's child, living at home; the next day, you're a freshman and on your own. The end of childhood. Instant adulthood. Or is it? Freshman! I like the word. The very label itself suggests the dilemma. Should it be pronounced with the emphasis on the fresh or the man? It points both ways. It doesn't matter whether you think of adulthood as a journey or as an arrival; today it is clearly a step on a path. Freshman fantasies and freshman fears can be seen on every young face (Gardner, p. 3).

The Hazen Foundation offered a less romantic description of the freshman experience.

The freshman experience is crucial to the college and the student. It is the time when the student's critical attitude toward his studies and college in general is formed, when college must demonstrate the relevancy of liberal learning to a ready-to-believe but not-yet-convinced student audience. Unfortunately, this is just the time when colleges are most likely to present the least concrete courses taught by the least experienced teachers. The body-of-knowledge theory, with its insistence on progress only from general to specific, seems to demand an apprenticeship in generalities before the student can progress to anything of personal interest or relevance. And this is reinforced by a Puritanical notion that if something might appeal to a young person, it cannot be good for him (The Student, p. 12).

This young man or woman may be a shy eighteen-year-old, a young Republican, with some poor study habits but lofty aspirations. They may also be politically apathetic and academically undecided, interested primarily in joining the band or a fraternity. In truth, the widest imaginable mix is the norm on most campuses. The likelihood of a student changing a major two or three times is as great as them never declaring one. The diversions which await them are as extensive as the abilities and interests they bring.

The Hazen Foundation (1967) offers additional typologies.

There are some, perhaps as many as ten percent, who are constricted by serious emotional problems, and there are others, probably even fewer, who are singularly free of such problems. But the majority are at neither extreme, for though they are haunted by self-doubts and insecurity, they can learn their way out of them, only if they meet the right set of circumstances.

A minority will graduate at the age of 21 after four uninterrupted years at the same college; a majority will be dropouts in some sense, taking many years to finish, transferring from college to college or never graduating at all.

All of them, wherever they come from, are reflections of the extraordinarily rich, complicated and nerve-wracking culture that has been built in the United States. If they feel lost in a contemporary university, it is because often they feel lost in contemporary society.

Sanford, in *The American College* (1967), concludes his chapter on the entering student with a more academic analysis:

Assuming that development is progressive and that it may ventuate in such desired states of the person as freedom of impulse, enlightenment of conscience, and differentiation of the ego, he asks what the freshman has accomplished and what major tasks still await him. The main argument is that "freshman" is a stage of development—one that might be called late adolescence. The maximum crisis of adolescence is over, and the controlling mechanisms are again in ascendency. But these mechanisms, uncertain and unseasoned, as they are, tend to operate in a rigid manner, thus forming the main basis for the authoritarianism that is a distinguished characteristic of this stage. The freshman's stage is also distinguished by instability in respect to self-esteem. In his uncertainty, the freshman vascillates between overestimation and underestimation of himself, between over compensatory self-forwarding maneuvers and withdrawal. He is highly susceptible to other people's appraisals, and overeager to commit himself to self-defining social roles (p. 196).

The most graphic description is offered in *Education and Identity*:

During the first few weeks of college a student steps with hesitancy. Soon he changes. He becomes independent; but it is the independence of a hog on ice. He is on slippery new territory and without familiar footholds; he responds with wild thrashing and bewildered and anxious immobility. Free of accustomed restraints or outside pressures, he exhibits random activity or rigid adherence to behaviors appropriate to former situations. The dominant impression is instability. There is a conspicuous lack of coordination and little observable progress in any direction (Chickering, 1969, p. 12).

Whether we are talking about a shy eighteen-year-old, a hog on ice, or a percentile, the previous authors have generally described the traditional population for yesteryear's freshmen. In 1985 the kaleidoscope is far more colorful. Disabled, veteran, older, international, underprepared, and minority populations are present in ever more dramatic numbers. The National Center for Educational Statistics estimates that over 40 percent of the people enrolled on today's campuses are over 25 and that by the early 1990s nearly half will be nontraditional (cited in Palmer, 1985). They are providing tuition revenues where a depleted "traditional" post high school population has diminished and requiring services at a need level never before imagined.

The challenge to teach and service this group of freshmen may never have been greater. The span of anxiety and experience brought by today's nontraditional population is at the same time supportive of the creative instructor and overwhelming for the neophyte.

When the ACT Persistence Study recommended "guiding students at the beginning of their journey" they must include the disabled automobile welder, the Nigerian and the single parent. The richness of their journey has already outdistanced many of their faculty. The federal government has mandated states through the 1973 Rehabilitation Act and several subsequent laws to support the physically disabled and extended 175 million dollars of its own to support the developmentally disabled. Campus diversity has never been greater.

Unfortunately, as Chickering relates, these diverse entrants meet remarkably similar programs, similar patterns of teaching and expectations for study, similar living conditions and for faculty and peer relationships. High attrition and transfer rates are not surprising when such diversity meets such singularity. When significant differences are ignored, some students will be missed entirely and many barely touched.

In concert with the NIE study sixteen years before its release, Chickering remarks about the early attrition studies, "the most complex and creative are the ones who leave. What kinds of changes would occur if these differences were taken seriously, if curriculum, teaching and evaluation were modified or supplemented so that persons . . . could work more effectively?" (1969, p. 285).

If diversity were the only dimension distinguishing this generation of freshmen, it is possible the teaching and servicing of this population would only be monumental. As it happens, there has also been a phenomenal attitudinal switch in the past 15 years. Alexander Astin, in surveying five million college-bound freshmen, has noted that what was an idealistic generation has turned sharply pragmatic. In 1968, 40 percent of the students felt that getting ahead financially was a goal they considered very important. Developing a philosophy of life, on the other hand, was a very important goal for four of five college-bound students. In 1983 these two categories had almost reversed themselves (Astin, 1983).

A professor at the University of South Dakota recently remarked, "I've never found teaching so easy, the students will do anything to get an A . . . somehow I miss the challenge of the argumentative and more inquisitive student."

In short order we have reviewed the diverse, changing, and complex population called the "front" of a loading process. We know that they are impacted more than any class in an undergraduate experience. Yamamoto (1968) states that changes in attitude, values, and critical thinking are more prevalent than at any time during the college experience. What then must we load them with?

Loading the Front End

Institutions wishing to increase the percentage of full-time entering freshmen who return for their sophomore year should promote a campus-centered life for freshmen. This involves strong residence life programs, extracurricular activities and financial aid programs which support student concentration on adjusting to campus life.

Student affairs professionals have maintained this concept for years. As daily practitioners in student living and success patterns, they developed living-learning centers and extended orientation programs, long before they became the catch phrases of every national study group or ACT report. Two of the most noted include Michigan State University's residential life program which mushroomed during the growth spurt in the early '60s and the University of South Carolina's "University 101" program which paved the way for extended orientation programs nationwide in the early '70s.

Although they did not call it "front loading," Michigan State University pioneered the concept of providing freshmen and sophomore living and learning centers which specialized in faculty who liked teaching undergraduates, in providing academic advising in the residential units and "loading" the environment with a cadre of professional staff who lived and ate with the students. In spite of its 40,000 students and high-rise residence halls, students were made to feel "centered" and part of a learning enterprise.

The University of South Carolina has shared for many years what most student affairs professionals feel is the model program on extended orientations. Their's is a semester long, three credit class on adjustment and skill development. This institutional commitment to assist freshmen with their transition to higher education has resulted in grants, textbooks, and a wealth of research on the freshman experience. Most importantly, they were able to retain a significantly high number of their students. Now, they even offer a parallel "course" for new faculty and staff (Adelman, p. 16).

These examples do not stand alone, for many others have contributed to the long standing acceptance of student affairs professionals that this type of program is key to both retention and a quality of life on campus. It is amusing that upon the heels of the national studies have come a rush of "new" creations in the orientation and "front loading" business. This fall, Harvard University brought its freshmen into Boston Harbor on a cruise ship simulating the experience of new immigrants, employing them to experience the richness of their geographic area. Dozens of other tricks, treats and home grown celebrations are receiving similar attention by the media. How ironic it all seems in that it was Harvard who many centuries ago began "front loading" with their Masters in Residence concept.

In a short span of time, these orientations to schools and experiences try to make a new student feel welcome, immersed in the academic spirit, and better prepared for the challenges lying ahead. For some campuses, it is a week of pomp, color and whoopla. Others will have a day or less to attempt the same thing. For most, the brief orientation is the norm because it is all they can invest. The NIE suggests this may be short sighted.

There are other "front end" devices and levers which receive less attention. Student Development Centers have sprung up around the country specializing in academic advising, tutorial programs, early warning systems, peer advising, remedial education and a host of adjustment programs to assist first generation, nontraditional and other student populations. The federal government has more than doubled appropriations in the last ten years to this same end providing special services to minorities, disadvantaged and learning disabled students. Theirs, too, was a front load.

What Are the Realities?

If front loading works and is such a great idea, why isn't everyone doing it as the NIE and other study groups have recommended? It doesn't dress up too well in academic regalia. It looks too much like fluff. It really isn't what higher education is all about. So say many legislators, governing boards and presidents.

What then is higher education about? Drastic budget cuts? True, these are real. Congressional deliberations over a new federal tax code alone may cost higher education 11 billion dollars in gifts if President Reagan's plan is adopted (cited in Jacobson, 1985). Reduced interest rates on shrinking endowments? Higher insurance premiums and longer faculty salary negotiations? Declining enrollments and rising standards? Revised core curricula? Yes, they all are real and omnipresent.

When not struggling with these realities, athletic scandals, divestiture demands, and other local battles more than keep a contemporary administration occupied. Keeping up with national study groups, their criticisms and recommendations, would seem enough for many.

Recently there was a study group on the study groups. Among other assaults on the volumes of studies available to today's undergraduate educators, Howard Bowen estimated that the seven most frequently made recommendations in the various studies could easily add 46 percent to a college's budget (cited in Jacobson, 1985).

Front loading, however, works from a dollars and cents point of view, as well as a developmental one. If you keep more students as a result of better student retention, the tuition dollars, in most instances, pays for the investment. The NIE goes further, they suggest a change in the funding formulas themselves. That works even better.

Take, for instance, the following three examples: foreign languages, biological sciences and psychology. All are commonplace on most campuses and are funded differently by most state and institutional formulas because of laboratory needs. One campus funded their FTE allocations for these departments as follows: foreign language 455, biological sciences 595, and psychology 839 (representing the number of credit hours each fulltime faculty member must justify). This is for upper level (junior-senior) courses.

The same departments were funded as follows for teaching lower level courses (generally freshmen and sophomores): foreign language 699, biological sciences 874 and psychology 1,049.

If 100 freshmen or 10 percent of this institution's freshman class (one third of the normal exiting population) were retained and each took a class in each of the three named departments, 900 credit hours would be generated. If those same students were to persist to graduation, taking only the required number of credits to graduate, 10,000 additional credit hours would be produced or the equivalency of 10 to 15 FTE faculty.

If on the other hand, the funding formula were reversed so that entering students (freshman and sophomore curricula) generated the more rich formula associated with upper level and graduate faculty, the FTE faculty generated would produce nearly double the faculty figure already cited.

Risks

Can the truly excellent faculty become interested in teaching freshman classes? Will faculty submit to being retrained to assist new students through the maze of changing core requirements in an advising relationship? Will administrators negotiate front loading with faculty unions and governing boards? Can orientation programs be "sold" to a public which already thinks higher education is watered down with frills? These are only a few of the risks in front loading.

A great risk lies in not trying. An even greater risk lies in letting the potential evaporate from unsuspecting, underprepared, over-bureaucratized new students through administrative nonchalance or insensitive instruction and advising. Chickering (1969) and the folks at the Hazen Foundation (1967) think that teachers ought to give less information and coordinate more student academic activities. They could generate more student resources and less busy work, converting students into less passive recipients and more active producers. Yes, there are risks with the disciples of front loading. They think it is a professional, ethical responsibility, not a risk at all.

Conclusion

The vulnerability and potential for change in the freshman student have been demonstrated through repeated study. The motivational and attitudinal levels now present in this diverse population may never have been higher. The federal economic support may as well be at its apex in our society. It seems that now is the time to take the risk.

To fully throttle the concept of "front loading" so chided in this author's introduction as hackneyed insurance slang may well be the best insurance for higher education as it looks to the lean and changing years ahead.

References

Adelman, C. (1984). *Starting with students: Promising approaches in American higher education*. National Commission on Excellence in Education, National Institute of Education, Washington, D. C.

Astin, A. (1983). *The American freshman: National norms for fall 1983*. American Council on Education and The University of California at Los Angeles.

Chickering, A. W. (1969). *Education and identity*. San Francisco: Jossey-Bass, Inc.

Gardner, J. (1985). *College is only the beginning: A student guide to higher education*. Belmont, California: Wadsworth Publishing Company.

Jacobson, R. L. (1985, October 9). Leading advocates of reform in undergraduate education find that it is not so easy to move from rhetoric to action. *The Chronicle of Higher Education*, p. 24.

National Center for Educational Statistics (1985, September). Washington, D.C.: Department of Education.

Noel, L. & Beal, P. (1980). *What works in student retention*. Iowa City: American College Testing Corporation.

Palmer, S. E. (1985, July 3). Congress showing more than usual concern about the needs of nontraditional students. *Chronicle of Higher Education*, p. 16.

Palmer, S. E. (1985, June 19). Charities charge gifts would drop 17%. *Chronicle of Higher Education*, p. 21.

Sanford, Nevit (Ed.). (1967). *The American college*. New York: John Wiley and Sons, Inc.

The Hazen Foundation. *The student in higher education*. (1967).

Western Illinois University (1974). Staff report on retention.

Yamamoto, K. (1968). *The college student and his culture: An analysis*. Boston: Houghton Mifflin.

Academic Advising

Don Monroe and Gale Wiedow

Undergraduate education—when that is mentioned the immediate thoughts and images evoked are of the lecture hall which is filled with eager students anxious to be challenged by the seasoned professor. Or perhaps, what is visualized is the process characterized by long nights at the library or deep intensive study by students in their residential hall, shuffling through mounds of materials in quest of knowledge. But is that education? Does education exist exclusively in terms of classes and study? Most faculty and students would suggest that education is much more. It is a diverse and pervasive experience which includes academics, but is not limited to it. Additionally, an important part of the experience which leads to intellectual growth on the part of students is informal interaction between students and faculty outside of the classroom, including academic advisement.

The term academic advising might be too narrow to describe fully the role of faculty in the guidance process. The word "academic" tends to limit the activity to one of class selection, remedial intervention to enhance study skills or test taking, and the advisement of students relative to university policies and appropriate procedures. In reality, the process is much more than that. It includes a number of smaller "steps" which, when properly implemented, enhance not only the academic success of students, but their entire undergraduate experience. Sounds easy? Perhaps, but the advisement process, to be effective in practice for a majority if not all students, must be planned, conscientiously implemented, carefully monitored and continually modified to insure maximum effectiveness (Grites, 1979). The purposes of this article are to give an historical perspective to academic advising,

227

to provide a current definition of the process, to state the anticipated results of a successful advisement program, to describe the process more thoroughly and to outline a plan of action so that effective advisement of students can be implemented. This article is written in the context that knowledge of academic advisement is an important part of understanding the environment within which an undergraduate educational experience takes place, and it is central to establishing a productive climate in which the University can accomplish its stated mission.

Academic Advisement in the Past

First, an historical perspective on academic advising is needed. In the past, the reputation of a college or university was based more on the quality of its faculty, the elegance of the campus and buildings and the intellectual prowess of the students. But this reputation was built over many years in which the "goodness of fit" of students to the institution was made (Grites, 1979). This concern for "fit" starts with recruitment and admission of students. To be effective in attracting prospective students, colleges have developed elaborate strategies. These strategies encompass travel to high schools and junior colleges, inviting students to campus for "Red Rouser Days," developing on-campus activities for high school students such as debate tournaments and music contests, writing to high school counselors, developing and distributing brochures and videotapes, and asking alumni for assistance. This type of recruitment produces a pool of candidates who are measured against the current entrance standards. In the past there were generally open enrollment standards resulting in admission of all students who applied. Today, the standards tend to be more exclusive and restrictive. Finally, the capabilities and the needs of the students are considered vis-à-vis the curriculum of the school. Can students' needs be met? It is at this point that advisement becomes crucial. Furthermore, the needs of students are developmental and dynamic. That is, they change during their school career and as these needs change so should the type of advisement. Grites (1979) noted that the most effective institutions accurately and quickly detected changes in the academic goals of students and readily adjusted their programs of study. The key ingredient in recognizing changing goals has been the interaction between faculty and students during advising. It begins at admissions and ends with placement services.

Still, faculty at most colleges in the past and today, view advising with much skepticism and cynicism. Larsen and Brown (1983) reviewed studies about academic advising and concluded that most faculty members perceive that few external rewards are given for academic advisement and that they will receive little recognition for their efforts. On the other hand, administrators state that advising is crucial to the mission of their university and believe that their advisement system is successful. Students, however, generally indicate that their advisement has been inadequate or non-exsistent (Grites, 1979). Strathe (1985) stated that when the role of advising is given to faculty members, those who are effective feel punished because of the absence of rewards and those who are ineffective are rewarded because of the absence of consequences for ineffectiveness. Such perceptions by faculty quickly destroy the faculty-student advisement system. In an effort to avert this problem, many noted insitutions have begun to move toward centralized advisement centers staffed by professional counselors. Polson and Cashin (1981) concluded that most faculty members in their sample who responded to a questionnaire on advisement believed that a change is needed in the reward system. These conclusions are reinforced when the results of the second National Survey on Academic Advising in 1983 are examined. The survey results indicate that:

1. Most college administrators believe that they meet their goal in the advisement of students;
2. Most professors state that few rewards are given for advisement and no training is provided;
3. The most popular form of academic advisement is by instructors, although centers are increasing in numbers;
4. Many advisors believe their school needs to expand the resources for advisement; and
5. Most respondents stated that advisement is increasingly seen as important in their institution (Winston, Miller, Ender & Grites, 1984).

According to Trombley (1984), the preferred model of academic advising is the one in which the academic faculty does the advising. She notes, however, that many faculty members do not have the requisite skills to advise successfully thereby indicating the importance of a training program for advisors. Additionally, two areas were identified as being most important to the advising process. One dealt with "information giving" such as keeping track of academic progress of the student and scheduling classes. The other dimension was directed toward personal problem counseling. This can be represented by such interactions as helping to resolve feelings of isolation and extending friendship beyond academic advice. While these two dimensions can be identified in theory, in practice there is difficulty in separating the two. Students often initiate contact with their advisor with questions about class scheduling but have other more intimate and personal concerns troubling them. A discussion of one problem often leads to the other.

Another concern related to advisement is the decline in the number of students available to go to college (Noel, 1976). What has happened is that more colleges are vying for fewer students. So, which students get to a particular college must be the "right ones" and more resources have to be allocated toward retention of those who do attend. In other words, most colleges can no longer afford the bad press from those students who quit, fail or drop-out; nor can these schools tolerate the financial consequences. Noel (1976) identified four factors related to student retention which were identified through follow-up interviews with students who had left college:

1. Isolation—This was expressed through feelings of loneliness or depression.

2. Academic boredom—This was blamed on uninspired teaching or that the instruction was too much like high school.

3. Dissonance—The student perceived that the environment was too "different" from their own background and needs.

4. Irrelevance—The student could not perceive any reasons for being at the particular school.

The ways to overcome these four general concerns relate to a variety of situations, factors and interactions. But high on the list and frequently mentioned by those who do not stay, as well as by those who do stay in school, is the relationship the student has with a faculty member who provides help beyond assistance at registration. A second factor is the perception by students that they have met a professor who cares. These are two important reasons why students stay in school and both relate to advisement. Furthermore, a significant difference exists between students who drop out and those who persist in school in their response to such issues as the amount of help given by an advisor and the perception of the availability of professors (Noel, 1976).

To summarize, advising has been viewed in the past as a simplistic, singular process insuring satisfactory academic progress towards a degree. Such a definition has guided scholars, students, and administrators for decades. The emphasis was on the academic being—the body that went to class, studied at the library, took tests, and after four years of diligent study, walked across the stage on commencement day. The role of the faculty advisor in that process was one of course selector, program monitor and "enrollment policeman" (Kramer, 1984). The process involved one single solitary act—signing the registration card. Today the expectations of this process are quite different.

Defining Academic Advisement

Advising as it existed for years was probably sufficient when societal impacts on students were less diverse and universities were under less stress from declining enrollments, increased costs and keener competition (Grites, 1979). Also, professors did not have as much pressure to publish. In reflection, the whole situation seems to have been more pastoral and simplistic. The student just needed to attend classes, to study the material and to graduate. Today, however, there are added and more complex pressures. In the 1960s the movement evolved which emphasized interpersonal communication. Since professors did not all have such needed interpersonal skills as listening, reflecting and paraphrasing, there emerged a new and different kind of advisement. Student services at college were initiated during this period. They provided advisement and counseling to students. These centers were not staffed by advisors in the traditional sense, but were staffed by trained helpers. Thus, as these new people came to the university to provide a more complex variety of services to students, the definition of advisement changed. This has evolved into the following more generally accepted definition of advisement as stated by Grites (1979):

> Academic advising is a decision making process during which students clear up certain confusion and realize their maximum educational potential and benefits, through communication and information exchanges with an advisor; it is ongoing, multifaceted, and the responsibility of both student and advisor. The advisor serves as a facilitator of communication, a coordinator of learning experiences through course and career planning and academic progress review, and an agent of referral to other campus agencies as necessary.

This definition is one that Kramer and Gardner (1977) explicate in their book. This role of the advisor is more general and includes a broader combination of activities and responsibilities than that which was previously accepted. It includes academic matters but much more as outlined by Noel (1976), it contains five developmental steps:

1. Exploration of life goals,
2. Explanation of career goals,
3. Selection of a program,
4. Selection of courses, and
5. Scheduling of courses.

Such a definition emphasizes the need for expansion of the traditional, unilateral role of the advisor and of the recognition of a multitude of related factors which also have the potential to enhance or detract from the collegiate experience. The definition does not require expertise in all areas. However, it does suggest that the role of advisor be one filled with people who have a genuine interest in students and who have access to accurate information on matters of academic importance. They must also have the ability to make appropriate referrals for concerns which arise outside their purview or expertise.

Expected Results of Advisement

What can be the expected results of advising? Some have already been suggested. As Grites (1979) notes, 79% of the process is done by full-time faculty. He concludes in his review of literature that student-faculty relations has a pervasive influence on the student. The student's attitude changes, career choices are made, plans evolve for attending graduate school, and in general the student's intellect is developed. Astin (1977) concluded from his longitudinal study of the effects of the college experience that students change in attitude, beliefs and self concepts. Grites (1977) relates that students' satisfaction with college is more highly correlated with the frequency of their interactions with faculty than any other aspect of college life including such aspects as peer relations, major, grades and ability. And while this is just correlational data, it persists over all types of student demographic data, thus giving weight to the notion that more student-faculty interactions are valuable.

But paradoxes are cited by Grites (1977) when considering the results of advising. One of these is that some faculty surveyed view advising as "nonessential," but perceive themselves as "adequate."

Another seeming contradiction is that instructors of a course are more often sought after for advice than are non-instructors who have been assigned as an advisor. Yet many students avoid contact with instructors even when they are available for advisement. In addition, freshmen and transfer students tend to seek out advisors more than seniors who tend to seek out "no one." Yet upperclassmen seek out a known faculty member before they go to their assigned advisor. Still, most students express dissatisfaction with the advisement they received.

An example of this is cited by Halgin and Halgin (1984). The psychology department with which they were affiliated grew rapidly in the 1960s. At first, advisement in the department was accomplished by all faculty who were assigned advisees on a random basis. As the department grew, the advisement was less coordinated and it became more perfunctory until mandatory advising was dropped. Then, as the years passed, student dissatisfation with advisement grew. Problems appeared such as students taking courses out of sequence and students lacking required courses when approaching graduation. Finally, a center was established which was staffed with knowledgeable, interested and experienced professors. But only 5% of the students sought these advisors. The students were still dissatisfied and the problems already identified persisted. At that point, only a few years ago, mandatory advising was reinstated. Check points were established where each student had to be advised in order to continue in the program. The participation rate grew to 93%. Expressed satisfaction by students grew and the identified problems began to diminish. Other serendipitous events occurred, too. Non-majors heard about the services and requested assistance. Consequently, the coordinator of the center organized seminars to cover topics such as enrolling in graduate school and the content of the core curriculum. Another outcome was that social events were organized by the center so that students and faculty had the opportunity to interact outside of the classroom (Halgin & Halgin, 1984).

Noel (1976) states that positive advisement programs are related to retention of students who initially enroll and is also correlated with many other factors. Some of these are improved attitudes in students, increased academic performance, improved self concepts and, not the least, increased credit generation. Glennon (1976) supported these conclusions when he examined intensive counseling. He found that attrition rates decreased, student achievement increased, the average student class loads increased and the number of students withdrawing from a class decreased. In addition, Grites (1979) notes that positive advisement programs increase the "bondness" between the institution and the students. All of these points are important and positive.

Still, it is a great deal to ask of a faculty member to teach effectively, to publish cogent scholarly works regularly, to be current in their professional area and to confer effectively with advisees who want to know about liberal arts, life goals, course selection, career plans, graduation requirements, advanced studies and so forth. Furthermore, peer advisement is rated as more effective than faculty advisement even though those students who leave as well as those who stay, value their conversation with faculty and deans (Grites, 1979). This is a dilemma.

Process of Academic Advisement

The most popular form of student advisement continues to be by the faculty (Grites, 1979). In this process, the faculty "selected" through some method such as have been outlined by Halgin and Halgin (1984). Hours for "advisement" are established. Oftentimes the advisees are required by mandate "to see" their advisor every semester. While valuable relationships often develop in this process more often than not this process is not monitored and no training is given.

Thus, another type of advisement which has developed is conducted in a center. Here a centralized location is established. This action has more often been taken in response to swollen enrollments and decreased interest by professors to the advisement process than anything else (Grites, 1979). The staff of these centers can be professors, counselors, and even students. There is release time to participating faculty and student information is put into that location. Many times placement bureaus are part of the center so that they serve as a clearinghouse for jobs as well as advisement. It is often the repository for information about graduate school requirements, announcements and other items of interest. Very often such centers serve nontraditional students, new students, minority students or others with special concerns and interests. These centers also serve students with academic and personal concerns.

A third method of managing academic advisement is with a peer serving as the advisor. This can be formally organized, but informally this is certainly the most often used process. The rap session in the dorm room becomes the source of information for many students regarding which major to take and which courses to avoid even though this information is often inaccurate. Still this method, when formalized and the peers receive training, is the second most often formal method of academic advisement used (Grites, 1979). These peer helpers can be located in residential centers or counseling centers. They can be trained and used effectively and cheaply in a variety of situations. One advantage is that they speak a common language and share common concerns with their clients even though there are problems with their use, such as rapid turnover, the need for training and the need for close supervison.

Another method of academic advising is self advisement (Crockett, 1981). In order for this approach to be used effectively a handbook must be prepared that explains the process. Many students use this system now in conjunction with a checklist, calender, registration material or class schedule. And perhaps this should be the goal for all advisement systems for each student to manage their life independently.

A fourth method is computer assisted advisement such as the one described by Bays (1984) and Spencer, Peterson and Kramer (1983). This is often just limited to registration but can also be used to permit access to current registration information, cumulative grade point, and other pertinent information.

A fifth method is group advising (Crockett 1981; Grites, 1979). This occurs when students either attend or are required to attend sessions sponsored by a "peer advisor," a center, or by the academic advisor. This is a timesaver and does avoid the repetition of certain questions. But this can be used to instruct the students in methods of self-advisement as well. Generally, this is a technqiue used with "special" students such as nontraditional or minority students.

Another method of academic advisement which is little used and will be the last discussed is advising contracts as explained by Grites (1979) and Crockett (1981). Here a negotiated agreement is written and agreed to by the advisor and advisee. Roles of each are detailed, outcomes are specified and deadlines are established. Often this process takes place over several months. Kramer and Gardner (1977) describe this approach but note that little research on its effectiveness is available.

As can be seen by the information presented, the process of advisement can take many shapes. Grites (1979) concludes his discussion by stating that the approach to take is the one "that works." Furthermore, he clearly advocates that no one single approach be used but that an integrated approach be established which can accomplish the goals set by each college or institution. This integration of several approaches means that more of the needs of students should be met than if only one type of advisement approach is used.

Grites (1979) summarizes his review by noting that academic advising can not be done in isolation. It has to be considered in relationship to all other facets of an institution. Furthermore, he notes that each college must develop its own advisement plan since no two institutions have the same needs, fiscal resources and geographical location (i.e., all institutions are unique and therefore must have unique advisement programs). However, he advocates that initially a complete understanding of academic advisement is necessary. He further outlines a set of eight recommendations for establishing a comprehensive advisement program. They are:

1. Conduct a thorough assessment study of the program's overall utility, relevance, and effectiveness,

2. Identify one person whose primary responsibility is to coordinate the advising program,

3. Implement an advisor selection process to minimize the percentage of failure the program must endure,

4. Develop an advisor training program to insure confidence that the program will be effective,

5. Develop an evaluation scheme that has a variety of methods, evaluators, and criteria,

6. Implement some type of extrinsic incentive or reward system to avoid the erosion of advising back to a perfunctory, unimportant and burdensome task,

7. Review the total program every five years using similar methodologies developed through the first recommendation, and

8. Conduct more research on the advising process and its outcomes to generate new information about this process.

Plan of Action

In relationship to the foregoing comments and summary, this section has been developed. In reality, it is an action plan for the development of a comprehensive academic advisement plan.

1. Define the purpose, objectives, and mission of advisement. This is the first step in the plan. The definition of advisement, mission statements, the delineation of purposes, and the development of appro-

priate objectives must be undertaken to give direction and substance to the process.

2. Develop a comprehensive resource library on advising, the advisement process, and university resources. This will enhance the advising process. Such materials, appropriately cataloged and accessible to interested parties, would provide an additional source of information or advisement. This information should be located in an advisement center.

3. Maintain a center for walk-ins and appointments. A centralized, accessible location which students are aware of and encouraged to use, is considered to be a positive element in the advisement process. Students are often spontaneous and respond as a matter of convenience, thereby selecting to visit an advisor at their leisure as opposed to planning well in advance and making appropriate appointments. The walk-in concept permits facilitation of impromptu visits as well as meetings by appointment.

4. Upgrade information on self-advisement. To many students, the advising process might be appropriately accomplished through access to required information. Access to such information might serve the needs of many students academically, and access to information on related resources might provide a mechanism for locating other required resources and services.

5. Select advisors in primary academic areas and develop appropriate reward systems for each. This suggests an individualized approach to advisor selection, insuring genuine interest on the part of participating faculty and the identification of appropriate recognition and compensation (i.e., release time, or the results of advising included in performance evaluations). Release time would be given from teaching and research in order to compensate for the added responsibility of advising.

6. Provide advisors with training. To be effective, advisors must have full knowledge of procedures, policies and resources available in the university community. The coordinated advisement program suggests a formal training component to inform or to reinforce information pertinent to a variety of anticipated student needs and faculty advising skills. Such skills as outlined by Crockett (1981) are important and they include the ability to inform, communicate and help.

7. Select peer advisors. In addition to faculty advisors, a core of responsible, personable and interested students could serve as peer advisors. Given appropriate information and a willingness to partici-

pate in the process, such students might serve as a mechanism for advising that many students would prefer.

8. Measure process and outcomes. Evaluation, the process of comparing end results with initial objectives, should be an integral part of the advising process. Successes and failures should be analyzed in order to determine ways of enhancing the process to improve the quality of advising and to facilitate a positive experience for all involved in the process.

9. Coordinate the advisement using one person. Given the number of students, the nature of graduation requirements, the complexity of curriculums and the necessity for consistency, it appears appropriate to have a centralized advisement process. This is not to be interpreted as one person doing all advisement, but rather, the coordination of all advisement to assure accuracy of information and consistency in dissemination.

In summary, the purpose of this article was to demonstrate the importance of academic advisement in a student's total college experience. In the past, advisement was considered less important and more a simplistic interaction between students and professors such as obtaining a signature on registration day; but today much more is expected. The process now includes information sharing and problem solving. Some of the results of a positive advisement plan at a university include higher student retention rates, improved self-concepts of students, increased cumulative grade point averages of students, additional full-time equivalencies generated for the administration, and expanded "bondness" between students and their institution. Many modes of academic advisement exist in which a student may interact with a faculty member, a peer, themselves or a counselor at a center. Group advisement is another approach and so is computer assisted advisement. A major conclusion is that no one best system of advisement exists and each institution must develop its own comprehensive plan to advise students. The plan should include evaluation of the process, establishment of goals, management of personnel, identification of procedures and delineating resources. In conclusion, an example of a plan was outlined for the advisement of students.

References

Astin, A. W. (1977). *Four criticial years*. San Francisco: Jossey-Bass.

Bays, C. (1984, Fall). Computer-aided advisement language at the University of South Carolina. *College and University*, 32–36.

Crockett, D. S. (1981). *Advising skills, techniques, and resources.* Iowa City: The American College Testing Program.

Glennen, R. E. (1976). Instrusive college counseling. *The School Counselor, 24,* 48–50.

Grites, T. J. (1979). *Academic advising: Getting us through the eighties.* Washington, D.C.: American Association for Higher Education.

Halgin, R. D. & Halgin, L. F. (1984). An advising system for a large psychology department. *Teaching of Psychology, 11*(2), 67–70.

Kramer, H. C. (1984). Advising for the advisor. *National Academic Advising Association Journal, 4*(2), 41–51.

Kramer, H. C., & Gardner, R. E. (1977). *Advising by faculty.* Washington, D.C.: National Education Association.

Larsen M., & Brown, B. M. (1983). Rewards for academic advising: An evaluation. *NACADA Journal, 3*(2), 53–60.

Noel, L. (1976). College student retention: A campus-wide responsibility. *Journal of the National Association of College Admissions Counselors, 21*(1), 33–36.

Polson, C. J. & Cashin, W. E. (1981). Research priorities for academic advising: Results of survey of NACADA membership. *NACADA Journal, 1*(1), 34–43.

Spencer, R. W., Peterson, E. D., & Kramer, G. L. (1983, November). Designing and implementing a computer-assisted academic advisement program. *Journal of College Student Personnel,* 513–518.

Strathe, M. (1985). *Personal communication: Interview on September, 1985.* Cedar Falls: University of Northern Iowa.

Student Affairs Committee. (1984). *Student affairs committee report to the University Senate on April, 1984,* Vermillion, South Dakota: University of South Dakota.

Trombley, T. B. (1984). An analysis of the complexity of academic advising tasks. *Journal of College Student Personnel, 26,* 234–239.

Winston, R. B., Miller, T. K., Ender, S. C., & Grites, T. J. (1984). *Developmental academic advising: Addressing student's educational, career, and personal needs.* San Francisco: Jossey-Bass.

Counseling the College Student: Developmental Factors and Counseling Needs of Traditional and Nontraditional Undergraduate College Students

Orla J. Christensen and Alvin D. Albertus

The authors approached the topic of this article from two age-related viewpoints: the psychosocial factors and needs of the traditional undergraduate students and those apparent in the nontraditional college undergraduate population. Traditional undergraduate students were defined as those persons between 17 and 24 years of age. Nontraditional undergraduate students were defined as those persons 25 years of age and older.

Traditional College Undergraduate Students (17 to 24 Years of Age): Psychosocial Factors

Erik Erikson (1963, 1968) defined a central feature of adolescence and young adulthood as the need to achieve intimacy with others. The psychosocial implications in meeting this need were to move away from dependence on the family of origin and to move toward a social network outside of the original family structure. The themes of autonomy and intimacy have also been discussed by Chickering (1969), Gould (1972, 1978), Walsh (1983) and Levinson (1980). Levinson described external and internal changes which accrued from accomplishing the tasks related to gaining autonomy in the early adulthood period. External changes included supporting self, while internal changes included reduction in emotional dependency, recognizing differences between self and parents, gaining independence and increasing the psychological distance from home and parents, and changes necessary in the development of an initial adult life structure. Seven developmental tasks associated with adolescence and early adulthood were outlined by Chickering (1969): Achieving competence, managing emotions, developing autonomy, establishing identity, freeing interpersonal relationships, clarifying purposes, and developing integrity.

> College years are critical years for all aspects of development and whatever experiences (social, work, academic, community) one has during these years affect the choices made for post-college life. (Okun, 1984, p. 126)

A sociological perspective emphasizing attitudes and motivation of undergraduate college students has been the basis for study by several authors. Group typologies which seemed to describe attitudes of the undergraduate population have been identified as: academic, collegiate, vocational, and nonconformist.

Students in the academic group tended to stress the importance of participation in intellectually-oriented college activities. Those in the collegiate group were more interested in social activities on campus. The vocational group was typified by an orientation toward preparing for a specific career and gaining necessary credentials to achieve that goal while the nonconformist group emphasized individuality and were more critical about campus life (Clark & Trow, 1966). Motivational variation among college students was further examined by Herr and Cramer (1979). They identified one group of students who seemed to be primarily motivated by the need to search for personal identity and self-fulfillment. Their expectations of the college environment seemed to focus on a desire for a supportive milieu. The second group of students discussed in their study was described as motivated by a desire for specific career preparation and credentials, similar to the description found in the Clark and Trow study (1966). Students in the third group were characterized as "avoiders" or students without clear-cut goals for either self-fulfillment or career development.

B. Okun (1984) felt that young adults were confused about others' expectations of them and often feel that they have inadequate role models in terms of the unique problems they must learn to face in their lifetime. Okun suggested that individual, group and family counseling be used with young adults to assist them in facing issues and making choices. She cited education and exposure to relevant information as necessary in addition to counseling (1984).

Traditional College Undergraduate Students: Expressed Concerns and Counseling Needs

The literature is replete with studies of undergraduate college students' perceptions of their major problems, concerns and needs. The interrelationship of early adult development and counseling needs seemed to fall into four broad topical areas: (1) interpersonal; (2) personal/psychological; (3) academic/learning-related; and (4) career-related. Ragan and Higgins (1985) reported the results of a needs survey conducted at five types of institutions of higher education: university, liberal arts college, four-year urban college, predominantly black college, and a four-year technical institute. The results showed that personal needs were as strongly indicated by the undergraduate students as were academic and career-oriented needs. They recommended that teaching staffs as well as student development personnel help students overcome their perceived inadequacies in these areas. The top-ranked specific needs cited by the students included developing study skills, seeking work experience in areas of career interest, management of time and money, development of job-seeking skills, writing and math skills and learning to relax when speaking in front of a group. Earlier studies reported the most prevalent problem perceived by students was in the area of vocational choice and career planning (Kramer et al., 1974; Synder, Hill, & Derksen, 1974; Williams et al., 1973). Weissberg et al. (1982) also observed that personal and social concerns received a lower rank by students than academic and career-related concerns.

Evans (1985) surveyed the perceptions of undergraduate women basing her methodology on the theoretical assumptions of Chickering (1969). The expressed needs of this group were greatest in the areas of clarification of purposes and goals for future life style, knowing their abilities, improving their academic and social skills and concerns about personal appearance and self-image.

Several studies have found that the most serious problem perceived by students and professional counseling staff is that of alcohol abuse

(Henggeler et al., 1985; Seay & Beck, 1984; Kazaluna, 1982; Kuder & Madson, 1976; Perkins, Jenkins, & McCullough, 1980). Additional problem areas cited by the undergraduates and student services personnel included anorexia-bulimia, anxiety, depression, and coping with stress (Cook et al., 1984; Kagan & Squires, 1984; Bauer, 1984; Knapp & Mierzwa,1984). Problems related to group membership and attendant stereotypical social attitudes were discussed in several studies as were the needs expressed by specific minority groups and women (LaFramboise, 1984; Marion & Iovacchini, 1983; Schlossberg, Troll & Liebowitz, 1978).

Following the Clark-Trow (1966) model, Sellacek, Walters, and Valente (1985) conducted a study to compare the four sub-cultures: academic, collegiate, vocational, and nonconformist, on the basis of three questions:

1. Did they seek help from the University Counseling Center?
2. What types of counseling services were provided?
3. Number of counseling sessions attended by each group?

Twenty-six percent of the sample group (582 students) across all four groups sought counseling services. Clients were more likely to be academic and less likely to be vocational. In terms of the types of counseling services provided to the four groups, there were no significant differences. The number of counseling sessions was greatest for the nonconformist group (8.37) and fewest for the collegiate group (1.86). The number of sessions for academic and vocational students was approximately the same (4.13 and 4.00, respectively).

College counseling centers in the past few years have shifted from a remedial, problem-oriented focus to a more developmental model which stressed prevention through a programmatic thrust for mental health and personal growth (Henggeler, Heitmann, & Hanson, 1985). This approach necessitates the use of needs assessments with the student population to determine developmental program emphases. The studies cited seemed to suggest the need for problem-centered as well as developmental-preventive approaches to counseling the traditional undergraduate student population.

Nontraditional College Undergraduate Students (Age 25 and Over)

Population Trends—Traditional, Nontraditional Students

Adult students are returning to colleges and universities in ever increasing numbers. Where much has been written concerning declining enrollments of traditional college students (Peterson & Associates, 1979; Reehling, 1980), the current literature pointed to increasing enrollments of nontraditional students (Reehling, 1980; Mardoyan, Alleman, & Cochran, 1983; Altmaier, & McNabb, 1984). Verification of declining college enrollment among traditional college students came from the Bureau of Census (1980–81) when they pointed to a decline which began in 1981 for persons in the 18 to 21 age group. Concurrently, the number of older persons (22–34 years of age) who were eligible for college increased during the 1970–1983 time span. The National Center for Educational Statistics (1985) provided additional data which supported the decline in traditional students and an increase in nontraditional students. The number of 18–24 year-olds enrolled in college was projected to decline throughout the rest of the 1980s and into the 1990s, while the number of students 25 years old and over was expected to continue to rise.

The National Center for Educational Statistics (1985) also pointed out that students enrolled under 25 years of age increased by 20% from 1970–1983, but predicted that during the following decade this enrollment will fall by 20%. During this same time span, persons 25 years of age and older more than doubled. This trend is expected to continue, showing a 13% increase by 1993.

The difference between female and male college enrollments during the same time period is also dramatic. From 1970 to 1983, men in the 25 to 34 year age bracket increased by 54% (National Center for Educational Statistics, 1985), and are expected to increase slightly during the next decade. Women in this same age bracket (25–34 years old) more than tripled between 1970 and 1983, and are expected to remain stable by 1993.

The National Center for Educational Statistics (1985) also pointed out that among 35–year-olds and over and enrolled in college, the male population rose by 48% in 1983. This number is expected to climb another 39% by 1993. The female population 35 years old and over who are enrolled in college, the percentage more than doubled from 1970 to 1983, and is expected to increase by about 34% in 1993. The implications of these figures are clear. While colleges and universities can expect declining enrollments among traditional college age students, those students who are older will be returning in ever increasing numbers.

Adult Development

As a result of this kind of information, the area of adult development needs to be studied by professors who would teach or counsel adults returning to college. While traditional students have been analyzed extensively over the years, the area of adult development has received attention only recently. Most theorists mentioned adults only in passing. Erikson (1963) was one of the first to separate adulthood into categories. On the eight life stages he mentioned specifically, three pertain to adulthood.

Both Sheehy (1976) and Levinson (Levinson, Darrow, Klein, Levinson, & McKee, 1978) spoke to female and male differences through the middle years. Sheehy (1976) wrote concerning adults from age 18–47. She suggested that women enter midlife by age 35 which is earlier than most men by about five years. Levinson et al. (1978) talked about the midlife transition for men and tended to associate it with age 40.

Life Transitions

What was pointed out by various scholars in adult development (Erikson, 1963; Sheehy, 1976; Levinson et al., 1978; Lowenthal, Thurnher & Chiriboga, 1975) and by writers in life-span development (Ambron & Brodzinsky, 1979; Turner & Heems, 1979) are the various transitions we encountered as we live and grow as adults. These transitions have a definite effect on whether we return to school, what happens in our relationships with family members, whether we decide to remain in the same job or to change to something else, etc. Many transitions tend to occur at predictable times throughout our life-span such as marriage, and birth of the first child. However, while these transitions are predictable, many of the transitions in our lives are not.

Schlossberg (1984) has developed a comprehensive model concerning adults in transition and how to work with them from a counseling perspective. She defined a transition as "any event or nonevent that resulted in change in relationships, routines, assumptions, and/or roles within the settings of self, work, family, health, and/or economics." Transitions may be anticipated, unanticipated, chronic hassles, or a nonevent. Anticipated transitions are those we expect to encounter through the normal course of living and include marriage, birth of a child, a new job, or a child leaving home. An unanticipated transition would include those things that are not predictable such as an accident, death of a spouse, divorce or getting a job promotion. A chronic hassle transition would be characterized as being with us constantly such as a weight problem, disharmony in a marriage, financial difficulties or a lingering illness. A nonevent transition is one of those things we expected to happen but did not, such as not getting a promotion that was expected, or having a vacation trip cancelled that we expected to take.

The transition process involved reactions over time which may be for better or for worse. It takes time to assimilate the various phases which may include pervasiveness, disruptions and integration. Once the assimilation is completed an appraisal of the transition and resources results. Was the transition for better or for worse? Will it lead to preoccupation or to life satisfaction?

Special Educational Programs for Adults

A number of special programs that pertained to the education of adults have been in operation in various parts of the United States for some time. Most basic among these was the Adult Basic Education (ABE) program which existed in varying degrees in many parts of the country. A book by Mezirow, Darkenwald and Know (1975) spoke to the difficulties encountered by those persons over sixteen years of age, out of school, who have less than eighth grade literacy.

At the other end of the educational spectrum for adult learners, Heffernan, Macy and Vickers (1976) speak of educational brokering for adult learners. The idea behind educational brokering was to provide adults with a complete range of educational and career alternatives. Many of the brokering services were geared to helping adults plan a two- or four-year college program or to complete a certification program in their particular field.

Another special program Stern and Missal (1960) reported was an experimental degree program for adults. The idea behind this program was to allow adults credit for life experiences, provide a special liberal arts curriculum for adults, assist professors with methods aimed at teaching adult learners, determine if some adults can be accelerated, and determine what academic credit for adults means. This plan was to lead to a college degree for adult learners.

Somewhere between the levels of Adult Basic Education and experimental college degree programs for adults were found programs in lifelong education (Cave, 1976) and program planning for nontraditional students (Cross, Valley & Associates, 1974). These programs may include working toward a college degree or an upgrading of skills for vocational purposes, but it also includes courses that adults may take for personal enhancement.

Educational/Counseling Needs of Adult Students

The current literature in counseling offered a variety of articles concerning older students returning to campus. The problems of older students returning to campus or recruiting nontraditional students and the difficulties of retention associated with older students were the concerns of Bauer (1981) and Reehling (1980).

Dewey, III (1980), Meers and Gilkison (1985), and Hooper and Traupmann (1984) were all interested in persons age 50 or older or of retirement age returning to college. Among this group of students was a number that were interested in pursuing a degree. A large number of retirement age groups took courses to meet personal growth needs (Dewey, III, 1980). Women over 50 took courses for basically three reasons: (1) some kind of career related goal; (2) reasons related to both career and personal fulfillment; and (3) a desire for self-fulfillment (Hooper & Traupmann, 1984).

Ancheta (1980) found there were no significant differences between counseling needs of traditional and nontraditional students. He also found no differences in the counseling needs of part-time students vs. full-time students or between day and evening students. With contrary results, Mardoyan, Alleman and Cochran (1983) found significant differences between the counseling needs of traditional vs. non-traditional students; being employed full-time, family responsibilities and committing time to a campus, were difficulties which kept the nontraditional group from seeking counseling. Altmaier and McNabb (1984) provided a reentry workshop to aid older students in their return to campus. An unexpected finding of this study was that older students had more favorable attitudes toward returning to college than the younger students. A unique study by Dailey and Jeffress (1980) suggested using the telephone for tutoring nontraditional college students. Among reasons suggested that caused the need for this service were: scheduling conflicts because of employment, lack of transportation, baby-sitting cost and scheduling, and lack of crisis tutoring.

A study of younger students' attitudes toward older students (Peabody & Sedlacek, 1982) indicated generally positive attitudes in academic situations, but in social or intimate situations attitudes toward older students were generally negative. Kuh and Sturgis (1980) tended to verify this attitude difference in their study. Many dimensions of a campus environment were seen in similar ways by traditional students and nontraditional students. However, the social-emotional climate was perceived differently by the adult students and the traditional students. Kuh and Thomas used adult development theory with graduate students and found adult developmental processes were generally applicable to graduate students.

Dean and Erickson (1984) conducted a survey of nontraditional students attending a large university as a part of a study. Personal enrichment and satisfaction was listed by 48% of the respondents in answer to the question "Why are you going to college?" Thirty-eight percent said professional advancement and 36% said to change careers. Another 19% were interested in changing jobs. As some respondents gave more than one response, the percentages exceed 100%.

When asked about transitions that caused a change in status during the past year, the following were noted: 16%, marriage; 6%, divorce; 10%, new children; 16%, death of relative; 13%, marital problems; 10%, illness or accident. Career related transitions included: 12%, job loss; 18%, promotion; 21%, new job; 26%, dissatisfaction with employer; and 29%, dissatisfaction with job.

Services nontraditional students needed most from the university included: 56%, information and help with course selection and registration; 50%, cutting through university red tape; 50%, financial aid; 48%, study skills; and 48%, information about job opportunities. Several students also needed help in selecting a major, 34%; help in choosing a career, 28%; information about campus resources, 28%; referrals for child care, 9%; and housing, 6%.

Counseling Adult Students

Counseling adults requires a knowledge of adult development, an understanding of transitions we encounter throughout our lifetime, and a thorough understanding of counseling theory and practice. To complicate the process, place the adult in a university setting where knowledge of university rules and regulations is necessary, knowledge of various services offered to students and how to access those services is required, and perhaps knowing how to help a student through university red tape is a must.

What would we call such a counseling approach? Perhaps Van Hoose and Worth (1982) have an answer with their developmental approach to counseling. Essentially it incorporates the above points and has much to offer people who wish to understand themselves and lead more effective lives. As Van Hoose and Worth (1982) pointed out, by focusing on an age appropriate task the client will discover issues surrounding the task were normal and most people experience them. This was particularly important to adults in a university setting.

The incorporation of the Schlossberg (1984) model on counseling adults in transition would strengthen the developmental approach. As has been pointed out by having knowledge of adult development, taking life transitions into account, and using a developmental age appropriate approach, counselors would be most effective in working with adults.

Summary, Conclusions, and Recommendations

Traditional undergraduate students' needs center around two developmental tasks as they leave home and enter college. They need to separate from family and establish their own identity and they need to establish their own social network separate from family.

As the undergraduates go through college, there are a number of needs that will confront them. The broad categories include: (1) interpersonal, (2) personal/psychological, (3) academic, and (4) career concerns. Some of the specific difficulties encountered by traditional undergraduate students include: alcohol abuse, eating disorders, roommate problems, study habits, coping with stress, and relationship issues. To meet all of these concerns, college counseling centers in the past few years have shifted to a developmental model which stresses prevention.

Counseling needs of traditional and nontraditional students appeared to differ according to some of the studies cited while others indicated no significant differences. Counseling the traditional college student requires knowledge of the developmental stages apparent for the age group 18–24 while counseling the adult student requires knowledge of the transitions which adults encounter as well as adult developmental processes. As this age group includes such a wide age span it is more difficult to speak of specific problems.

A counseling center which meets the needs of traditional and nontraditional students would be developmental in orientation. The Schlossberg (1985) model on counseling adults in transition would fit well with a developmental orientation. Van Hoose and Worth (1982) suggest age appropriate tasks as part of the developmental model for working with traditional and nontraditional students as they face transitions, the older group may have more transitions (age appropriate) to face than the younger group. As a result, trying to provide services for adult students requires more accommodation.

The general transitions that older adult students face include: marriage, birth of a child, a new job, children leaving home, death of a spouse, divorce, getting a job promotion, financial difficulties, disharmony in a marriage and not getting an expected promotion. Some of these transitions are shared by both traditional and nontraditional students but most of these transitions apply to the older adult students.

Recommendations appropriate for college and university counselors and student services professionals would seem to center on gaining a knowledge of student needs based on developmental processes as well as those emanating out of transitions adults may encounter. Since adult development and the study of transitions in adult life is relatively new, it would appear that professional counselors working with the nontraditional population in the university and college counseling services settings must gain an understanding of the many facets of adult development and adult transitions in order to assist the nontraditional students more effectively.

Several studies cited have predicted that the enrollment of 18–24 year olds will continue to decline into the 1990s while the numbers of nontraditional students 25 years of age and older will increase. Other studies have pointed out that the enrollment of women in the 25–34 year old category tripled between 1970 and 1983 and will be expected to remain stable into the 1990s. Therefore, college and university campuses can no longer be viewed as micro-societies of 18–24 year olds. Student services professionals as well as faculty and administration must understand and accept a broader perspective. The authors recommend that counseling centers and student services professionals lead the way in providing in-service activities for campus personnel aimed at gaining knowledge of developmental processes and life transitions affecting all students.

References

Altmeier, E. M., & McNabb, T.F. (1984, January). A reentry workshop for nontraditional students. *Journal of College Student Personnel, 25*(1), 88–90.

Ancheta, B. (1980, November). Counseling needs of traditional and nontraditional community college students. *Journal of College Student Personnel, 21*(6), 564–567.

Bauer, B. G. (1984, May). Bulimia: A review of a group treatment program. *Journal of College Student Personnel, 25*.

Bauer, W. (1981). Strategies for recruiting and retraining the non-traditional students. *College Student Journal*, 234–238.

Chickering, A. D. (1969). *Education and identity*. San Francisco: Jossey-Bass Publishers.

Clark, B. R., & Trow, M. (1966). *The study of college peer groups*. Chicago: Aldine Press.

Cook, E., Park, G., Williams, T., Webb, M., Nicholson, B., Schneider, D. & Bassman, S. (1984, March). Students' perceptions of personal problems: Appropriate help courses and general attitudes about counseling. *Journal of Student Personnel, 25*.

Cross, P., Valley, J. R., & Associates. (1974). *Planning nontraditional programs*. San Francisco: Jossey-Bass Publishers.

Dailey, A. L., & Jeffress, C. A. (1980, November). Telephone tutoring for the nontraditional college student—A homework hotline. *Journal of Student Student Personnel, 21*(6), 574–575.

Dave, R. J. (Ed.) (1976). *Foundations of lifelong education*. New York: Pergamon Press. Published for the UNESCO Institute for Education.

Dean, G. J., & Erickson, J. P. (1984). *Academic counseling for adults in transition to high-tech careers*. (Report No. CE 039 800). Paper presented at the National Adult Education Conference, Louisville, KY, November 6–10, 1984. (ERIC Document Reproduction Service No. ED 249 371).

Dewey, III, D. (1980, November). New kid on the block. *Journal of College Student Personnel, 21*(6), 498–502.

Erikson, E. H. (1963). *Childhood and society* (2nd Ed.). New York: Norton.

Erikson, E. (1968). *Identity, youth and crisis*. New York: Norton.

Evans, N. J. (1985, March). Needs assessment methodology: A comparison of results. *Journal of College Student Personnel, 26*(2).

Gould, R. (1972). A study in developmental psychology. *American Journal of Psychiatry, 129*(5).

Gould, R. (1978). *Transformation: Growth and change in adult life*. New York: Simon and Schuster.

Heffernan, J. M., Macy, F. U., & Vickers, D. F. (1976). *Education brokering: A new service for adult learners*. Syracuse, NY: A publication of the National Center for Educational Brokering.

Henggeler, S. W., Hertzman, D. E., & Hanson, C. L. (1985, Spring). The shift to a student development model: Impact on students' and professionals' perceptions of needs. *College Student Journal, 19*(1).

Herr, E., & Cramer, S. N. (1979). *Career guidance through the life span: Systematic approaches*. Boston: Little, Brown and Company.

Hooper, J. O., & Traupmann, J. (1984, March). Women students over 50: Why do they do it? *Journal of College Student Personnel, 25*(2), 171–172.

Kagan, D. M., & Squires, R. L. (1984, May). Compulsive eating, dieting stress and hostility among college students. *Journal of College Student Personnel, 25.*

Kazaluna, J. R. (1982). Drinking among college students—A problem to bring out of the closet and meet head-on in the 80's. *College Student Journal, 16.*

Knapp, S., & Nierzwa, J. A. (1984, May). Effects of systematic desensitation and self control treatment in test anxiety reduction programs. *Journal of College Student Personnel, 25.*

Kramer, H. C., Berger, F., & Miller, F. (1974, September). Student concerns and sources of assistance. *Journal of College Student Personnel.*

Kuder, J. M., & Madson, D. L. (1976). College student use of alcoholic beverages. *Journal of College Student Personnel, 17.*

Kuh, G. D., & Sturgis, J. R. (1980, November). Looking at the university through different sets of lens: Adult learners and traditional age students' perceptions of the university environments. *Journal of College Student Personnel, 21*(6), 483–490.

Kuh, G. D., & Thomas, M. L. (1983, January). The use of adult development theory with graduate students. *Journal of College Student Personnel, 24*(1), 12–19.

LaFramboise, T. D. (1984, September). Professionalization of American Indian women in post-secondary education. *Journal of College Student Personnel, 25.*

Levinson, D. (1980). Conception of the adult life course. In N. Smelser and E. Erikson (Eds.), *Themes of work and love in adulthood.* Cambridge, MA: Harvard University Press.

Levinson, D. J., Darrow, C., Klein, E., Levinson, M., & McKee, B. (1978). *The seasons of a man's life.* New York: Knopf.

Lowenthal, M. F., Thurnher, M., Chiriboga, D., & Associates (1975). *Four stages of life.* San Francisco: Jossey-Bass Publishers.

Mardoyan, J. L., Alleman, E., & Cochran, J. R. (1983, March). Adapting university counseling centers to meet the needs of an older student body. *Journal of College Student Personnel, 24*(2).

Marion, P. B., & Iovacchini, E. V. (1985, March). Services for handicapped students in higher education: An analysis of national trends. *Journal of College Student Personnel, 24.*

Meers, B. W., & Gilkison, B. (1985, July). Older students on campus. *Journal of College Student Personnel, 26*(4), 369–370.

Mezirow, J., Darkenwald, G. G., & Knox, A. G. *Last gamble on education.*

Dynamics of adult basic education. Washington, DC: Adult Education Association of the U.S.A.

National Center for Educational Statistics (1985). *The condition of education*, 1985 edition. Edited by Valena White Plisko and Joyce D. Stern, Washington, DC.

Okun, B. G. (1984). *Working with adults: Individual, family and career development.* Monterey, CA: Brooks/Cole Publishing Company.

Peabody, S. A., & Sedlacek, W. E. (1982, March). Attitudes of younger university students toward older students. *Journal of College Student Personnel, 23*(2), 140–143.

Perkins, R. A., Jenkins, S. E., & McCullough, M. B. (1980). A look at drinking on a university campus. *College Student Journal, 14.*

Ragan, T. D., & Higgins, E. B. (1985, September). The perceived needs of undergraduate college students from diverse educational institutions. *Journal of College Student Personnel, 26*(5).

Reehling, J. E. (1983, January). They are returning: But, are they staying? *Journal of College Student Personnel, 24*(1), 491–497.

Schlossberg, N. K. (1984). *Counseling adults in transition linking practice with theory.* New York: Springer.

Schlossberg, N. K., Troll, L. E., & Liebowitz, Z. (1978). *Perspectives on counseling adults.* Monterey, CA: Brooks/Cole Publishing Company.

Seay, T. A., & Beck, T. D. (1984, January). Alcoholism among college students. *Journal of College Student Personnel, 25*(1).

Sedlacek, W. E., Walters, P., & Valente, J. (1985, July). Differences between counseling clients and non-clients on Clark-Trow Subcultures. *Journal of College Student Personnel, 26*(4).

Sheehy, G. (1977). *Passages: Predictable crises of adult life*, New York, NY: Bantam Books.

Snyder, J. F., Hill, C. E., & Derksen, T. P. (1974, May). Why some students do not use university counseling services. *Journal of Counseling Psychology.*

Stern, B. H., & Missal, E. (1960). *Adult experience and college degrees.* Cleveland: The Press of Western Reserve University.

U.S. Department of Commerce, Bureau of Census. (1985, July). *School enrollments—Social and economic characteristics of students: October 1981 and 1980.* (Series P20—No. 400). Washington, DC: by Rosiland Bruno.

Van Hoose, W. H., & Worth, M. R. (1982). *Counseling adults: A developmental approach.* Monterey, CA: Brooks/Cole Publishers.

Walsh, P. B. (1983). *Growing through time: An introduction to adult development.* Monterey, CA: Brooks/Cole Publishers.

Weissberg, M., Berentson, M., Cote, A., Cravey, B., & Heath, K. (1982, March). An assessment of the personal career and academic needs of undergraduate students. *Journal of College Student Personnel, 23*(2).

Williams, G. D., Lindsay, C. A., Burns, M. A., Wall, H. W., & Wyckoff, J. H. (1973, November). Urgency and types of adult counseling needs among continuing education students. *Journal of College Student Personnel.*

Part V: Students

In addition to the *mission*, *means*, and *environment* of undergraduate education, an important consideration is the student. To ignore the nature of the learner is to disregard an important aspect of what is involved in education. Information about what students are like and how they learn must be examined. In addition, colleges and universities need to become knowledgeable about special populations including members of minority groups, older students, and students with certain types of handicapping conditions. The effort required is to help assure that as large a portion of capable undergraduate students as possible are academically successful and complete their programs of study.

Joseph D. Huber and Loraine Webster examine the problem of motivating the undergraduate college student. They define "motivation" and review much of the research, dividing the literature into studies focusing on internal motivation and studies on external motivation. Using the findings from the research literature, they report on a study they conducted on student motivation and provide practical suggestions for college teachers. They conclude that professors must know their students and plan varied lessons, interspersed with humor. Professors must be interested in the subject matter they teach.

Asserting that boring lectures are a result of teachers failing to consider their students in the learning process, F. O. Main and E. G. Poling believe that professors must recognize the importance of "respect," "responsibility," "resourcefulness," and "responsiveness" in their teaching. Students must be involved in the entire learning process. Professors must teach their students with dignity and respect and expect equal treatment in return. Successful teachers will excite their students in a desire for new knowledge and experiences that will advance increased levels of understanding, compassion and humanness.

257

Members of minority groups have needs that must be given special consideration in undergraduate education if they are going to be successful in college. Native Americans represent one of these groups and provide an example of the types of accommodations that are required. Dauna B. Browne and Wayne H. Evans give insight on what institutions of higher education should be doing to assist Native Americans in adjusting to college life. They provide evidence of the cultural values of many Native American students that are in conflict with those values often found in colleges and universities. They suggest courses and experiences that institutions of higher education should use in order to meet the special needs of these students.

The composition of the undergraduate student body is undergoing a change. It is becoming older and increasingly female. Barbara A. Yutrzenka and Lois B. Oberlander believe that the influx of nontraditional students has created a challenge for institutions of higher education. In this paper they report the results of a study they conducted on the differences existing between traditional and nontraditional students in respect to perceived sources of stress and support. They found fewer differences than they predicted. Nevertheless, they conclude that attention should be given to reducing the barriers which do exist for both traditional and nontraditional students.

The number of disabled persons going to college is increasing. Yet, Donald R. Potter provides evidence that many colleges and universities are unprepared to provide the physical environment required to accommodate the needs of such students. Furthermore, colleges and universities are continuing to fail to meet their educational and social needs. Although, largely because of governmental pressures, many institutions are attempting to comply to legal requirements, many other institutions have not developed the policies that reveal a commitment to providing equal access for disabled students. There appears to be no compelling reason for many institutions to do so. Under present conditions, it may be years before some colleges and universities are prepared to meet the needs of disabled learners.

Motivating the College Student

Joseph D. Huber and Loraine Webster

Statement of the Problem

Will Rogers is credited with once saying that "the epitome of motivation is the ability to tell someone to go to hell in such a way that he or she will be looking forward to the trip!"

Of course, Will Rogers's sage advice is easier said than done. If he were alive today even Will Rogers would likely agree that motivating college students to take a successful learning trip is often a formidable task. It does take a great deal of understanding of the learner and a great deal of planning.

Educators are often frustrated by a "missing link" in the learning design. Our most carefully developed curricula and our most up-to-date teaching and evaluation methods are often not enough to ensure that learning will occur when students don't feel incentives to learn. That "missing link" is motivation. We must know a great deal more about the kinds of things which motivate students to think, to work, to be excited, to learn. We need to let this knowledge guide our planning and teaching process (Barber, 1982).

Definitions

MOTIVATION is defined by Webster as "something that causes a person to act such as motive, impulse, incentive, inducement or good." Motivation is an abstraction, a concept, something which is difficult to measure. It is conceptualized as something which inter-

259

venes between stimulus and response, an inducement, reason, or motive to act.

COLLEGE STUDENTS, in the not too distant past, were most commonly defined as learners engaged in higher education in the age range of 18 to 22 or 23. With more and more "non-traditional" students appearing on campuses, this definition needs to be broadened from age 18 to death. In other words, the life-long learning concept has begun to impact the campus setting. Consequently, college students—even undergraduate college students—are now those in their late teens, to and including adult learners of any age.

Review of Relevant Research

Researchers investigating the topic of motivation seem to agree that motivation is not one dimensional. It is multi-faceted; and motivation may be classified as internal or external, intrinsic or extrinsic.

Internal Motivation

Many educators believe the best motivation is self-motivation. They feel that needs, desires, interests and drives that come from within a learner trigger far more learning (and retention) than external influences.

Researchers in the area of internal motivation see people as "acting on" their environments and people acting according to their perceptions. Especially important are perceptions that individuals have about their own competence to succeed at a task if they try (Barber, 1982).

Robert Bills (1982) reviewed the conditions necessary for change and for intelligent behavior. Bills tends to concentrate on the question, "under what conditions does a person have the best opportunity to change (learn) or to behave as intelligently as possible?" Other factors may promote learning such as internal affective conditions, which are hard to measure objectively. These are feelings such as happiness, self-actualization, contentment, optimism, readiness, satisfaction, desire and enthusiasm.

The internally motivated college students are the so called "self-starters" and may be scarce, but there are many ways and means through external motivation—stimulation—which can produce internal motivation—a desire to respond (Broadway, 1985; Huber, 1978; Russell et al., 1982; Trice et al., 1984).

External Motivation

Research abounds on the topic of external motivation. Some studies stress the behaviorist definition that externally motivated learning is initiated by another person and usually involves rewards. Others stress the influence of environment on behavior. Most ask, "What conditions will cause a person to respond as desired?" (Barber, 1982; McQueen, 1984; Read, 1982; Sonnier, 1982).

The goal of behavioristic research is to gain greater and more effective control of behavior. Behavior modification, the most frequent application of behaviorism, seeks to control learners so they behave as their teachers desire. Irrelevant behavior is reduced, desired behavior is increased, and learners become more like what someone believes they should be (Barber, 1982; and Hill, 1984).

But this way of teaching can have drawbacks. Children can be motivated more to get a reward than to arrive at a complete understanding of the educational task. Or worse, the external motivation can actually prevent the child from wanting to learn.

Research on the effects of rewards has the same general structure. The student's level of internal motivation for doing a task is measured; intervention is attempted; and the level of motivation is measured again. Edward Deci (1975) found in his research that when he used money as an external reward, internal motivation decreased, and when verbal reinforcement was used, internal motivation increased.

If it is true that an external reward system can drive out internal motivation, teachers must be very careful which kind they use: praise, reward, penalty, or challenge—when, where, and how much? The student who responds to one can be demolished by another.

Consequently, we begin to see that motivation is at the center of education—teaching and learning. From the foregoing discussion of research we see that motivation is both internal and external and that external motivational techniques are studied to stimulate and determine internal motivation.

Obviously, external motivational forces such as (1) climate, (2) expectations, (3) social relationships, (4) acceptance and (5) rewards are critical factors in promoting motivation and achievement. How can college instructors use these motivational forces to maximize opportunities for learners to become better learners, to remain open to better learning and to use the totality of their experience in behaving and creating the best learning experiences?

1. Climate

Much is now being published on the importance of the total school and total classroom climate as it impacts motivation. James Garbarino (1981) believes it is the total or collective social orientation of the classroom which directly affects the classroom negatively or positively. For example, he found that small numbers of students in the classroom provided its own motivating forces. Small class sizes encouraged a sense of responsibility for active, participatory behavior. With small classes, the individual efforts of teachers to motivate students are amplified. His research convinced Garbarino that a small class tended to create a personalized, social climate in which one-to-one influence (modeling, reinforcement, etc.) had a greater chance of success.

Russell et al. (1982) discussed climate in terms of environmental signs. She and her colleagues stressed the importance of creating a comfortable, safe environment in which the learner feels welcome, safe and at ease. This environmental openness was number one in their list of a hierarchy of inviting strategies for best motivation and learning.

Other research articles described the importance of the learning climate in motivation with terms like exciting, captivating, enthusiasm, and therapeutic (Gephart et al., 1981; Huber, 1978; Read, 1982; Sonnier, 1982).

2. Expectations

Often, college students are not at all clear on what their instructors expect. How can a learner be motivated to learn if he/she doesn't know what the instructor's expectations are? "Faculty should constantly strive to communicate clearly to students and to check the effectiveness of their communication" (Attrition/Retention, 1985).

Initial, clear information and motivation should come at the first class meeting when the instructor distributes and discusses the expectations of the course.

Then faculty should develop mechanisms to continually evaluate students' understanding of the course policies, goals and content. One simple strategy is to have students turn in written perceptions and questions about the course at several intervals during the course. If the course is small this could be done orally. Then faculty can assess and address expectation problems before the end of the semester (Attrition/Retention, 1985).

High or great expectations by a college teacher can motivate the college students to set high expectations for himself/herself. Russell et al. (1982) sees expectations as a part of teaching style.

Expectations and teaching style are related and are both part of "holistic" education. Teachers can be artfully inviting in their expectations. An artfully inviting learning environment occurs when the teacher artfully (intentionally) invites (and expects) students to see themselves as able, valuable, successful and self-directing. This type of teacher is one who motivates in such a way that an active learning environment is created in which students begin to recognize the full range of their abilities (Eckensberger et al., 1984; Russell et al., 1982; and Sonnier, 1982).

3. Social Relationships

Broadway (1985), and Russell et al. (1982), felt that social relationships were critical to motivation in the college classroom. Positive body language techniques, often called non-verbal communication, are so important—smiles, nods, winks, eye contact, and other signs of approval. Physical communication techniques—touching which says "hello" or "I am glad you are here," shaking hands, hugs and pats on the back—are motivating. Verbal communication methods such as statements of concern or support, remembering a person's name or birthday or "I like your new sweater," "How can I help you?" or "Thank you" are highly desirable social interactions which can provide positive motivation.

Social relationships in the college classroom imply two way communication between the instructor and the students. In some college classrooms where only lecturing occurs there is no social interaction but just one way communication going out from the instructors to the students. This can be stifling for social interaction and motivation unless the instructor is a very dynamic lecturer.

Two authors have suggested ways and means to allow more social interaction in the classroom. Rosenau (1968) promoted the idea of cutting teacher talk in half which provided more time for purposeful student talk with each other and with the instructor. Huber (1978) suggested that the instructor be tactful, kind, polite, listen carefully and answer questions very thoroughly and honestly, accentuate the positive and watch for non-verbal SOS signals for help and of boredom.

Enthusiasm was often mentioned in the research as essential to the motivation. Collins (1976) and Rosenshine et al. (1970) defined teacher enthusiasm, reviewed the literature, made many observations, sought the opinions of teacher educators and then proposed these eight indicators of high teacher enthusiasm:

a. Rapid, uplifting, varied vocal delivery
b. Dancing, open eyes
c. Frequent, demonstrative gestures
d. Varied, dramatic body movements
e. Varied, emotive facial expressions
f. Selection of varied words, especially adjectives
g. Ready, animated acceptance of ideas and feelings, and
h. Exuberant over-all energy level.

4. Acceptance

Acceptance strategies will promote motivation in the college classroom. Russell et al. (1982) classified these strategies as personally inviting and professionally inviting.

Personally inviting behaviors send out messages which communicate caring, positive regard and acceptance. Professionally inviting behaviors are directed toward increasing the invitee's (the learner's) efficacy, competence and independence; thus, these behaviors encourage high self-esteem.

At the conclusion of their research, Russell et al. (1982) proposed a ten point hierarchy of inviting strategies. Two of those strategies speak directly to producing acceptance. They are: (a) Developing Trust—respecting the other's confidentiality and (b) Minimizing Risk—choosing the right challenges for students.

Fantini (1980) stated that "In therapeutic teaching there is commitment on the part of the teacher to creating and maintaining a high level of acceptance that motivates and nurtures moral as well as intellectual growth."

Read (1982) concluded an article on "Therapeutic Teaching" by stating, "Finally, it should be noted that these 'therapeutic qualities' can be found in the field of psychotherapy, but increasingly they can also be found in the college classrooms of those teachers who are consistently referred to by students as 'concerned,' 'helping,' 'caring,' 'real' and 'accepting.'" Humane acceptance as a motivational force in the classroom was suggested by Huber (1972). He proposed four precepts to make college students feel accepted: (a) Listening, (b) Openness, (c) Empathy and (d) Love.

5. Rewards

Studies indicate (Bills, 1982; Eckensberger et al., 1984 and Gephart et al., (1981) that some students are motivated by promises of success, others by fear of failure, and some do not respond much to either of these possibilities. It has been estimated that about half of any typical group will respond to grades, money and/or praise as motivational devices, for example, and half will not. However, of the half who will respond, about half of those will respond to promises of success, while the remaining half will respond to fear of failure. In practical terms, that means that if a teacher promises good grades, money and/or praise for hard work in school, about 25% will respond positively and 75% will not respond.

Broadway (1985), a practical student of human nature, stressed the importance of praise as a valuable motivator in the classroom and in the community. In her list of ten ways to get along with people, two deal with praise: (a) Never let an opportunity pass to say a kind and encouraging thing to or about someone. Praise good work done, regardless of who did it. If criticism is needed, criticize helpfully, never spitefully and (b) Be interested in students; interested in their pursuits, their welfare, their homes and families. Let everyone you meet, however humble, feel that you regard him/her as one of importance.

Practical Suggestions

In a *Kappan* article, Benjamin Bloom (1982) examined the characteristics of master teachers regarding motivation. He found that in most cases the master teacher had worked out a detailed plan for instruction. Evidence of progress and improvement were used to maintain motivation and to put renewed and enthusiastic effort into the learning process. Although rarely praised, students were continually kept informed of progress. Also, there was usually an ultimate goal in mind (that might include surpassing records set by others in the field or giving public performances).

Dale Davis (1977) interviewed 84 teachers and compiled the following list of most promising teacher approaches or methods to motivate students:

1. Show interest and concern in student work; give personal help when needed.

2. Be clear.

3. Make materials meaningful to students' lives and future goals.

4. Do not rush; work at a reasonable pace.

5. Use a variety of methods and materials, choosing each one carefully.

6. Plan your teaching and be well prepared.

7. Make goals and objectives clear to students.

8. Show interest and enthusiasm.

9. Involve students through the use of discussion, discovery approaches, individual assignments and at times group planning.

10. Use external motivators (i.e., interest, desire for recognition and praise, good grades, avoiding failure, and concern for the future.)

Student Survey of Motivation

After considering definitions and what other writers have had to say about motivating students, we decided to go directly to one hundred twelve of undergraduate students in the School of Education at the University of South Dakota and ask them what specifically creates interest and enthusiasm for their classes.

We made an assumption that students would tell us that a well-prepared, enthusiastic teacher with excellent speaking abilities would provide the greatest motivation for undergraduate students. We found this to be true but we also discovered undergraduates need more than this to be well-motivated.

An appealing subject which students enjoy, was rated very highly and the highest percentage of positive responses was given to that item. Students also wanted good, informed speakers as teachers. They wanted those teachers to show a sincere interest in individual students. A sense of humor on the part of the instructor was highly valued. Least motivating, although still important, were frequent tests and quizzes.

Many thoughtful remarks were made to an open-ended item. Students indicated they liked "small classes," "less formal classes," "freedom to express ideas and ask questions," and a "relaxed and non-threatening atmosphere." Enthusiasm on the part of the teacher was repeatedly mentioned as important. "A comfortable physical environment without distractions" was seen as conducive to enjoying classes. Vagueness and lack of clarity were deplored. "I hate leaving a class not understanding what is expected of me." A concern for fairness on the part of the professor was reiterated frequently. Another concern preference was for the instructor to take the time to get to know his/her students. "I hate being just a number," and " . . . if the teacher really cares about me I want to do my best and not let him down."

Our conclusions closely parallel those of the writers and researchers cited earlier in this article.

Subject matter is very important. If the course material is relevant, interesting and presented clearly students are going to find the class meaningful and self-motivation will follow. Faculty members can work to improve that elusive thing called motivation through careful planning and preparation. Students indicated that well-planned and organized lessons were important to them. Variety in materials and teaching styles was also rated highly. Perhaps the best recommendations that can be offered to college professors is to know their students, and make every effort to plan interesting, varied classes interspersed with humor. Probably the best concluding statement is one from a student respondent who said, "If the instructor is not interested in what he teaches . . . why should I be interested?"

References

Attrition/Retention Committee Report. (1985, Spring). The University of South Dakota/Vermillion.

Barber, L. W. (1982, September). Motivation. *Practical Applications of Research*. Vol. 5, No. 1.1.

Bills, R. E. (1982). *Education for intelligence or failure?* Washington, DC: Acropolis Books Ltd.

Bloom, B. (1982). The master teachers. *Phi Delta Kappan*, Vol. 63, No. 10.

Broadway, O. (1985). *How to get along with people*. Flint, MI: Mott Foundation.

Collins, M. L. (1976). *The effects of training for enthusiasm on the enthusiasm displayed by preservice elementary teachers*. Doctoral Dissertation. Syracuse, NY: Syracuse University.

Davis, D. (1977). *Motivating secondary school students*. (ERIC ED 137 263).

Deci, E. L. (1975). *Intrinsic motivation*. New York: Plenum.

Eckensberger, H. H. & Meacham, J. A. (1984, May/August). Action theory, control and motivation: A symposium, *Human Development*, 27: 163–210.

Fantini, M. (1980, November). Disciplined caring. *Phi Delta Kappan*.

Garbarino, J. (1981). *Successful schools and competent students*. Lexington, MA: Lexington Books.

Gephart, W. J., Strother, D. B., & Duckett, W. R. (1981, June). Teacher enthusiasm. *Practical Applications of Research*, Vol. 3, No. 1.

Huber, J. (1972, September 30). A new society—SPCS: Humanness in education. *Educators' Advocate*, pp. 3–4.

Huber, J. (1978, Spring). *Taking AIM on adult learners: Attracting, interesting and motivating*. Occasional Paper. U.S.D. Media Center.

Hill, S. D. (1984, Spring). Motivational controls: Power, force, influence and authority. *Teacher Education*, 19: 14–20.

McQueen, R. (1984, February). Spurts and plateaus in brain growth: A critique of the claims of Herman Epstein. *Educational Leadership*, Vol. 41, No. 4, pp. 64–65.

Read, D. (1982, March/April). Therapeutic teaching. *Health Education*, pp. 36–39.

Rosenau, F. (1968, October). How to cut teacher talk in half. *Educational Leadership*, pp. 93–95.

Rosenshine, E. & Furst, N. (1970). Enthusiastic teaching: A research review. *School Review*, Vol. 78, No. 4.

Russell, D., Purkey, W. & Siegel, B. L. (1982, Fall). The artfully inviting teacher: A hierarchy of strategies. *Education*, Vol. 103.

Sonnier, I. L. (1982, Fall). Holistic education: Teaching in the affective domain. *Education*, Vol. 103, No. 1, pp. 11–13.

Trice, A. D. & Wood-Shuman, S. (1984). Teacher focus of control and choice between intrinsic or extrinsic motivational techniques. *Educational Research Quarterly*, Vol. 9, No. 1:11–13.

Boredom: What's It All About?

Frank O. Main and E. Gordon Poling

Boredom and the Professor

The worst hobgoblin of the professor is the boring lecture. A true nightmare is looking out into a sea of glazed faces, bowed heads, and sinking eyelids. Unfortunately, we're easy prey for overpartied and understudied sophomores whose major task for the semester is to decide which fraternity or sorority to pledge.

Our visceral reaction to this malaise is defensiveness. "Are we supposed to be entertainers?" "How can we compete with the explosive media presentations young people are deluged with these days?" Wrong questions all. Instead, we need to be asking what emotional purpose boredom serves—yes, purpose. Alfred Adler, the Viennese psychiatrist, asserted that all emotions serve a very special purpose (A. Ansbacher & R. Ansbacher, 1956). If that's the case, what purpose could possibly be served by the strong emotions generated when we, or our students, are bored?

For a moment, think about the last time you were bored with someone's presentation. What is it exactly, that we say to ourselves prior to succumbing to the emotion? "This person isn't speaking to me!" "I don't have a need to know this stuff!" "This speaker is acting as if I'm a receptacle, not a person!" In short, for one or a variety of reasons, we become bored with instruction when we haven't been taken into consideration in the learning process. We're bored when we feel a sense of meaninglessness—when we feel insignificant. The bored undergraduate then is a person, regardless of age, that "feels," or "privately believes," that the teacher has discounted him or her in the learning process.

Some years ago Mortimer Adler supposed that young people were not good candidates for education. He went so far as to maintain that "education" shouldn't begin until a person was thirty years old (M. Adler, 1956). Adler assumed, inaccurately, that the young were therefore protected and incapable of being educated. We agree with his premise but disagree with his conclusions. A person who is bored has been afforded the debilitating luxury of irresponsibility in the learning process. A person who is bored, be he thirty or thirteen, has simply been discounted in the learning process; has simply failed to find, or have offered to him, a "need" to know—the responsibility to know.

What emotional purpose does boredom serve? As with all emotions, feeling bored has survival value. The glazed consciousness that develops serves to preserve a sense of meaningfulness. Our private logic holds that, "I am deserving of more respect." Or, "I have more important things in my life." Bluntly put, a student who is bored is angry; angry and discouraged about his/her lack of responsibility and input in the learning process and about the significance of the information in question—s/he lacks a responsibility or need to know.

Secondly, outward manifestations serve notice to others. "Take note Doc, I'm not included in this process." Indeed, boredom is a powerful emotion which serves to preserve one's dignity while serving notice to others.

Dignity and Respect

As professors, what we hope for, what we try to emulate, are the wonderful learning experiences we had. Too often, however, we misinterpret the experiences we had. We assume that we learned well because of the marvelous delivery of a certain person. But, in all probability, we had a great learning experience because we found, or discovered a tremendously exciting need to know—responsibility. We had fun learning—we became scholars. In the process, a teacher, or circumstances, offered us respect, responsibility, the opportunity to be resourceful and responsive. While the instructor may not have been interested in our "opinions," s/he realized that we were active participants and not receptacles in the learning process.

Active learning, as described by Eric Hoffer, on the other hand, involves adjusting to and creating change. "Learning" schools produce people who have neither the time nor the inclination to exploit or oppress their fellow man. "Learning" schools and professors, then, hope to teach not only what is already known, but to equip each student to go beyond what is known—to go beyond the professor's wisdom. The learning society, then, brings the student abreast of existing knowledge, and then using itself as a springboard, catapults the student into the future. By comparison, to be learned, is to be prepared to live in the past, according to Hoffer.

Another aspect of the "learned" person or society is often reflected in the methods that we employ to educate. A prevalent attitude of "learned" professors is that the mind is a muscle. Their belief is, "If there's no pain, there's no gain." This seems contradictory to scholarship—learning for fun. Academics often cling to the fiction that the learner must suffer in order to master knowledge. We are vaguely aware of the fact that we are intimidated by or even resent the fact that a student may go beyond our level of knowledge. But, we adhere to, maintain, and even enjoy our rank and superiority.

Hoffer has a pungent capacity for highlighting the impact our arrogance has upon our own learning and teaching. He relays his amazement at an illiterate fellow longshoreman's assessment of the Russians of V-J Day in 1945. The Okie held forth as follows, "Now that we knocked out Japan, we will soon mix assholes with the Russians." It seemed to Hoffer the typical statement of an illiterate man. "What possible reason," Hoffer asked, "could we ever have for fighting the Russians?" The Okie smiled tolerantly; "Have you ever watched boys playing on a sandlot? The moment one bully is down, you have to mix with the next one" (Hoffer, 1977, p. 69). It may be, that the ignorant, given opportunity to grow and actively participate in the learning process, make better prophets than those of us who are sanctioned to profess.

During the last decade, we (politicians, educators, parents and students), have expanded the adolescent years to include people ten to thirty years old. The result of course, is that our campuses are filled with twenty-five-year-olds in a state of prolonged adolescence. This current generation hungers for all the material amenities yet is oblivious to its responsibilities. Accordingly, we suggest that there will be no effective learning in undergraduate education until the curriculum is reformed to consider those between the ages of ten and thirty as responsible, active, accountable learners. Failing this, we are doomed to be bored and boring; to be learned "instructors"—not professors.

Professing and Learning

Some years ago, we conducted a mini-survey of the undergraduates enrolled in the educational psychology classes in our division. The questionnaire wasn't empirically sophisticated, perhaps even shoddy, but the information generated makes our point. We asked simply, "Why are you here?" It probably comes as no surprise that of those polled, less than half (40%) cited anything that related to learning, education or even a degree! A full sixty percent cited vague, unexpressible rationales for their presence at the university. We cite our survey to impress you with the fact that we have some data, humble as it is, to support our private logic.

The major point, however, is that the vast majority of undergraduates have an unkindled, to nonexistent "need to know" what we're teaching. To ignore this fact, is to contribute further to a nation of "learned" relics.

Numbers: Fact or Fiction

In the helping professions: teaching, counseling, preaching, law, etc., in order to give ourselves credibility, we have tried to be "sciencelike." We have tried to be objective and empirical. Like most professional educators, our empirical mini-survey cited above identifies us as CWAMA (count, weight and measure addicts) (O'Connell, 1974). But our addiction to counting and weighing has the potential to be very boring, to be very much apart from scholarship—from the joy of learning. Engaging in CWAMA behavior is often boring because we enumerate to make "our" point instead of trying to include others in our learning. We are drawn to CWAMA activities for precisely the wrong reason—it's impersonal. Because counting, weighing and measuring are impersonal, we think it will lend the aura of science—to "our" case. The opposite is usually true; instead of convincing, exciting and including others, we alienate them. Funny thing about CWAMA behavior, the more objective our pretenses, the stronger our subjective commitments.

For example, we probably wouldn't have cited our survey had the data not supported our hypothesis. Had it supported our beliefs half-heartedly, we probably would have cited the results and casually mentioned the limitations. In short, when we engage in CWAMA behavior, typically we are trying to use numbers as if they had a life and reality of their own. Numbers aren't, in themselves, logical—people are.

Therefore, if we teach while acting as if enumerating brings reason to the world, we are likely to be boring; to alienate and disparage the student. Counting isn't evil, it simply can't be sold as a substitute for reason, participation or commitment. If numbering is treated instead like any other form of human experience, like subjective evidence to help determine what we "ought" to do, then counting, like drawing, is a worthwhile activity.

For the most part, those of us in education count in order to find support for our view of the world. When the numbers don't fit, we say we have counted wrong—we cite limitations. Rarely do we allow reality, evidence, or experience to interfere with our view of the world. We cling tenaciously to our perceptions especially when they fly in the face of reason. Engaging in CWAMA behavior, therefore, is boring. On the other hand, if we allow our enumerating to speak to us, to change our view, we may do a little science.

If we enumerate simply to add power to our perspective, and encourage CWAMA behavior as a means of impersonalizing our judgements, we will be boring and bored—we will be learned. On the other hand, if we acknowledge our own need for respect, responsibility and resourcefulness, we may experience, or reexperience a sense of compassion for the bored undergraduate; for the person who society has locked into a fifteen-year no-man's-land called adolescence. If we feel compassionate then we will inspire our students to be animated, concerned and compassionate as well. Gandhi's gravest concern was that the "educated" were the hardest of heart. To feel compassionately toward the undergraduate is to afford him/her the opportunity to overcome adversity as you have; to be encouraged.

In this simple injunction, opportunity to overcome adversity, we propose, along with others, an alternative educational system. A system that not only includes, but demands the active participation of the students. Corsini has dubbed this alternative system the C–4R system (Corsini & Ignas, 1982). The four "Rs" include those already cited; Respect, Reasonability, Resourcefulness, and Responsiveness. While Corsini intended the system for the secondary school, since our colleges are clogged with adolescents, it's reasonable to aspire to these same values within our colleges and universities.

Respect

Specifically, undergraduate education can only be revitalized if the learner is afforded respect as demonstrated by our willingness to include him/her in the process; to demand that s/he plan the curriculum; to demand that the learning activities are in vivo, live demonstrations of our chosen craft. Campuses of the eighties are cozy, womblike places where students rattle around inside their disciplines without ever being called upon to apply their knowledge to the pressing issues of society, or their own lives for that matter. We should respect our students enough to demand that they "act" on their academic knowledge not simply know.

Responsibility

To say that we need to be responsible, as well as teach responsibility, seems almost banal. Yet, over the past decade we have educated a generation of "professionals" who challenge the very concept; lawyers who are felons, counselors who are sexual abusers, physicians who are chemically dependent, and businessmen who are crooks. What's right about an educational process that allows its graduates to be professionals but not citizens? At a very minimum, citizens ought to conduct their lives in a manner that allows them to flourish without detracting from others. Professionals on the other hand, ought to conduct their lives in a manner that goes beyond this minimum standard. They ought to contribute to the lives of others in some specific way.

Today the educated person, the learned person, may not be a citizen or a scholar. Gandhi's fear was that the educated had lost their compassion. We have the same fear. The educated have become "me" centered; have become takers and not givers. They have lost their social interest—the compassion for their fellow man. Curriculums which "train" people in a craft while allowing the student to maintain an egocentric attitude aren't educational. A learning curriculum is one of shared responsibility; one of shared purpose; one of shared commitment to the welfare of others. What is right with educational methods that produce "me-sturbators" instead of professionals? (Main, 1986).

Finally, we need to give up our arrogant assumption of responsibility for what "they" need to know. Not unlike Eric Hoffer's Okie, undergraduates can, given the encouragement, generate responsible thoughts if they're expected or permitted to develop them. In short, undergraduates need to wrestle with what it is they need to know, even if it means articulating what they don't want to know. Then, they must be held accountable for knowing and accountable for the responsibilities that knowing entails. Carol Bly suggests, as an example, that people should be challenged in public to take a stand on small town issues out of respect for themselves as well as their fellow man. She calls these public encounters "enemy evenings" (Bly, 1981). Her assumption is that there is nothing more condescending than an unwillingness to confront your neighbor with your private convictions; nothing more disrespectful. These "enemy evenings" are precisely the grist needed to inspire responsible conduct of students and ourselves.

These "enemy evenings" would pit committed members of the community on both sides of an issue to a public dialogue. Students would join the dialogue after aligning themselves with one group or the other. By way of example, topics might include:

1. Prayer in the public school.
2. The role of the school board in setting district disciplinary policy.
3. School board vs. parental authority regarding acceptable conduct of students/teachers.
4. The school counselor's role as a family counselor: involvement vs. interference.
5. Busing: Imposed quality vs. guaranteed inequity.
6. The public school's role in environmental education: ecology and hazardous wastes.

These topics could be generated by various agencies in the community or by academic disciplines responsible for teaching in these areas. Once students had joined their chosen faction, they could prepare to take their position publicly. Each student would be "required," no matter how briefly, to take a public position and defend it. These "enemy evenings" might stimulate, or actually require the assumption of responsibility necessary to learn.

Resourcefulness

Some years ago a colleague of ours was teaching an honors seminar. He offered this talented group of scholars the option of using him (the professor) as a resource or using other sources. He invited them to class and said earnestly, "I'll be here if you need me; if you have found other means to study so be it." On the next scheduled class three students showed up and on the next, no one came. While the empty classroom was a sobering lesson in humility, it raises interesting issues. How often, in the name of good education, are we actually needed; more poignantly how often have we actually interfered, or impeded someone's learning? Human resourcefulness and creativity are infinite. Why, then, do we insist on "our" formula for learning. Indeed, if we ask students about how they learn, the variety of answers would be staggering, but typically we don't tap this resourcefulness. Of course there are problems attempting to utilize these skills. The professor's capacity to control the outcome is demolished. Secondly, the students are unaccustomed to thinking about how they learn best.

Sometimes the students can be encouraged to think about their own learning if they are challenged to teach others; to generate a novel curriculum and defend its use. Anything which shifts the students' perspective from one of passive recipient of "stuff" to one of responsible participant, is worthwhile.

Responsiveness

The final R in the formula for defusing boredom is responsiveness. This is a very sensitive issue. Whether a person's compassion, social interest or caring "ought" to be a part of his/her education or not is irrelevant. Graduates will be educated about these virtues whether we attend to them or not. Therefore, the issue can no longer be whether we "ought" to be involved or not, but how we will choose to be involved.

Democratic education which fails to attend to, or ignores its responsibility to foster compassion and concern, isn't education for a democracy. It's in this regard that Mortimer Adler's assumption about irresponsible youth may be most difficult to dispel. We can't demand that a twenty-two-year-old be considerate; we can't punish him/her for failing to be. But, we can model what we expect of him/her. This injunction doesn't mean pampering students, it means simply taking them into consideration before we act. By being responsive to students, we give them permission and instructions to do likewise.

We are usually responsive in direct proportion to our capacity to respond to the needs of others. A lawyer who can't be moved by the needs of others is corruptibly selfish; the counselor who is insensitive to his/her own needs holds his/her clients at emotional bay; the physician who is incapable of feeling love is a technician and not a doctor; the businessman without a social conscience is an economics mechanic.

Conclusions

Curricula which recognizes the importance of respect, responsibility, resourcefulness and responsiveness provide education—those that do not provide these elements may be viewed as monotonous training by our students. If we hope to escape the debilitating effects of boredom, we must involve our students in the entire learning process. We must provide dignity and respect for those that we attempt to teach and expect equal treatment in return. Our students must become active learners and not merely learned, inactive repositories of historical knowledge. We must attempt to excite their desire to venture into new knowledge and new experiences which will advance humanity to increased levels of understanding, compassion and humanness.

References

Adler, M. J. (1956). Adult education. In *Great issues in education*. Vol. 2, Chicago: The Great Books Foundation.

Ansbacher, H. L. & Ansbacher, R. R. (1956). *The individual psychology of Alfred Adler*. New York: Harper & Row, Publishers.

Bly, C. (1981). *Letters from the country*. New York: Harper & Row, Publishers.

Hoffer, E. (1977). *In our time*. New York: William Morrow and Company, Inc.

Ignas, E. & Corsini, R. J. (1979). *Alternative educational system*. Itasca, IL: F. E. Peacock Publishers, Inc.

Main, F. O. (1986). *Perfect parenting and other myths*. Minneapolis, MN: CompCare Publishers.

O'Connell, W. E. (1979). *Super natural highs*. Chicago: North American Graphics.

Native Americans in Higher Education

Dauna B. Browne and Wayne H. Evans

State supported colleges and universities have increased their enrollments of Native American students, making the special needs of these students more visible. Colleges and universities, with their professional experts, are in unique positions to deliver very positive impact on the growth of states and a nation by graduating well-educated Native Americans. That potential impact could be considerably enhanced by higher education faculties who expand sensitivity and commitment to the Native American populations and adjust their approaches to curriculum planning. For the most part, colleges and universities recognize Native American educational needs but have not addressed them in curriculum planning. We need to graduate more capable, well-educated Native Americans who will rise to the personal commitment to improving the quality of life for Native American people across the states and the nation. They must broaden their understanding of unique student needs to include the needs of this minority group.

Attrition rates of Native American students at colleges and universities have been far in excess of other students, indicating a failure to meet unique educational needs of Native American students. Federally funded projects have focused more attention on the needs of Native American students than ever before. These projects, designed to train Native American students for a variety of professional positions, obviously made direct impact on college curricula, through the addition of courses designed to meet project objectives. But they also had important indirect influence on both graduate and undergraduate programs in some unplanned ways.

These new Native American related courses were available to Native and non-Native students alike. The courses and the instructors of Native American descent they brought to campuses brought more visibility to Native American concerns and provided both formal and informal learning opportunities to all who were interested in studying issues and concerns of the Native American people. Perhaps more subtle, but equally important, was the effect on the curriculum when Native American students brought their own interests and concerns to class discussions and small group projects. The effect was a broadening of the involvement of staff and students in the educational concerns of Indian people. Also, in a natural, informal way, Native American students became resource people, exposing instructors and students to a multicultural influence. This influence increased sensitivity of many instructors and students to Native American concerns in both graduate and undergraduate classes.

Native American projects influenced education in other ways, too. Federally funded project offices frequently became informal gathering places for Native American students, who soon learned that they could come to such centers to find a support group of peers. These centers provided the opportunity for Native American students to find positive role models. In addition, they could be assured of finding well qualified Native American faculty and other students, including graduate students, who would take time to listen and advise them.

Unique needs and concerns of undergraduate Native American students were to some extent being met as a residual effect of the federally funded programs. Unfortunately, federal funding for Indian programs has steadily decreased over the past years. Most colleges and universities have been unable to continue Indian programs without federal monies. The loss of these has obviously had a direct negative impact on college and universities' ability to attract and retain students. But, also, it has an indirect impact on those students currently enrolled by diminishing one very important source of support and guidance for Native American students.

Now that even the incidental help of the federally funded programs is being withdrawn, the time has come when colleges and universities must address the atypical developmental concerns of Native American students directly. University retention and graduation rates for Native American students apparently have not shown any improvement in the past fifteen years. The Kennedy Report (U.S. Senate Special Subcommittee on Indian Education) of 1969 showed that only 17 of every 100 Indian students entering high school would go on to college and that only about six of those would complete college work. In a recent editorial commentary, Red Horse (1986) reports that those percentages have not changed. Apparently, colleges and universities are not meeting the educational needs of their Indian populations. Institutions must identify the special concerns of this cultural group and integrate comprehensive plans to address those in the curricula.

A review of the literature reveals considerable agreement about what Native American students need from college programs. For the purposes of discussion, we have grouped these needs into three categories: (1) applying unique Indian linguistic and cognitive styles to learning and other related academic tasks; (2) assistance with clarifying their cultural identities; and (3) assistance in learning how to deal with cultural conflict.

College entrance scores suggest that many Native American students would benefit from opportunities to expand fluency with language—both with speed of reading comprehension and expression with written language. The difficulties many Native American students have in these areas have resulted from incongruence between learning and linguistic styles of Native Americans and the Euro-American designed school system. Ornstein (1973), among others, suggests that cultural background may influence the development of differences in learning style. At this time, there appears enough evidence to suggest that a significant number of Native Americans may be operating from a holistic, relational cognitive style rather than the linear, sequential style that is characteristic of the Euro-American style (Browne, 1983; Cattey, 1980; Ross, 1983). Bill Leap (1985), from his study of Native American languages, has suggested that linguistic differences may be operating. Certainly, linguistic and learning style differences that are culture based need to be considered in designing learning opportunities where students can develop effectiveness with standard English. Native American students need opportunities to become aware of these differences and to interpret them in terms of characteristic learning strengths rather than to perceive "different" as being "less than."

A second important consideration for Native American students is assistance in developing awareness of their own cultural identity. Heaps and Morrill (1979) found that ". . . one of the major educational and counseling tasks in working with Navajo students, other Native American students, or students from any minority or disadvantaged groups, is that of improving their self concept or their cultural identities. . . ." (pp. 13–14). Cultural identity is so important to Indian students that it has, in fact, been identified as the primary predictor of college success (Huffman, Sill & Brokenleg, 1986). In order to clarify cultural identity, students need to verbalize and process values. As they become more conscious of their own culture, they become personally integrated with it. With this internalization, they develop a framework from which to evaluate experiences and make conscious choices which set directions for their lives.

The task of coming to terms with cultural orientation is complicated by the fact that Native American youth are exposed to many variations in interpretation of the original Native American cultural values. The problem is further compounded by elements of the Euro-American culture which have been incorporated by some Native American people. Contemporary Native American culture reflects values distortion resulting from the efforts of the majority culture to disrupt and change their culture (Kennedy, 1969). Survival for Native American people has been dependent on adoption of values (competition, for example) that are inconsistent with their traditional cultural values.

In the process of coming to terms with their own culture, Native American students need assistance with the additional task of exploring their present culture and sorting out the conflicts caused by Anglo attempts to force change. This additional task is necessary to reaffirm their cultural values as a solid base from which to make balanced and harmonious choices about personal cultural identification. They must choose whether to align themselves with original Native American values, to blend values from both cultures, to internalize only Anglo values, or to create a new informed variation. It is not surprising, under these circumstances, that many young Native American people are experiencing confusion with cultural orientation. They need assistance in working through this confusion so that they can internalize a cohesive and functional value system.

The task of helping young people clarify cultural identity is best approached with a multi-track concept, allowing the student to pursue one or a combination of three paths: (1) to become a totally integrated part of the mainstream Anglo America; (2) be in a position to function bilaterally (biculturally); or (3) function in harmony with the traditional Native American culture. Education for the Native American student should become a freeing process that affords these options. Native American students should have the choice to develop individual cultural bases from which emerges the capacity to join mainstream America if they so desire.

Thirdly, Native American students need assistance to transcend cultural conflict in order to contribute to society, whether Native American Indian, white, or both. They must build on the culture they bring to college, acquiring the knowledge and skills they need to function effectively in a multicultural environment. When colleges ignore original cultures, and students are forced to adapt in order to acquire college degrees, they may end up degreed Native Americans who have not developed the cultural base to apply that degree towards realizing personal and cultural goals.

Colleges and universities should not ignore the Native American students' culture and demand that they fit into the majority culture. To do so not only communicates lack of respect for the Native American culture, but also fails to educate because, initially, education for Native American students means beginning with the experiential and language background of that student. And, secondly, it means providing him or her with the environment and experiences necessary to explore new ways of looking at the world and interpreting experiences.

The cultural values of many Native American students are different from and are often in direct conflict with those of the Anglo values at the base of the educational system. The Anglo student has been assimilating these values through modeling and enforcement since birth, and understands the behaviors expected by the educational system. Unlike their Native American counterparts, Anglo students experience little conflict between the values of the family and the social system and those of the educational system. Most Native American students, consciously or unconsciously, experience constant conflict between their value system and that of the educational system. Although they have come through the elementary and secondary school years in Anglo-designed school systems, they have not internalized the basic psycho-social system of the Anglo-American culture. For example, school administrators constantly struggle to combat Native American absenteeism, because these students do not internalize the Anglo-psycho-social value placed on regular and dependable school attendance. Rather, they may continue to give precedence to their own cultural psycho-cultural priority of meeting personal and relationship needs. It is true that some Anglo students also come to school with priorities different from those of the school. Such discrepancies create conflicts when the student's behavior does not meet school's expectations. The student's inappropriate behavior may simply be an indication of failure to cope with the complete system in a functional manner. But in time, most of these students come to accept the values and rules of the school, resolving the conflict, because the basic psycho-social and cultural orientation of the student's home and school are basically congruent.

A developmental task for many Native American students is to come to terms with the value system of the parent culture. For the Anglo student, the structure of the university system provides a framework within which that task can be accomplished. Obtaining a university degree is in part a measure of a student's ability to establish a working harmony between individual goals and values and those of the culture as a whole. For Native American students, however, this developmental task is tremendously complicated. If they are to achieve a university degree, they have to learn to function harmoniously within a structure designed from a psycho-social and cultural base different from their own. Also, because the university's cultural base is different, it does not provide a framework within which they can come to terms with the adult values of their own culture.

While the concerns reported are somewhat similar, apparently there is no one effective model for dealing with them. Success of any particular approach tends to depend heavily upon the ability of the individual staff members who are sensitive to Native American students. Most models for Native American students' success tend to be based on the goal of assisting the student to get through college. With these issues in mind, it is suggested that a systematic, but personal, approach is used which addresses both psycho-social and cultural concerns of the Native American students. This proposed model is based on a review of the literature, and personal experiences of the authors who have worked with students over a period of years.

Any plan to intervene in the developmental process, such as the clarification of cultural orientation, must be based on a model which plans for holistic learning. The plan proposed here should start in motion a learning, self-exploration process that will enable Native American students to deal with cultural differences, and at the same time successfully complete university courses of study. The plan offers Native American students guidance in the process of exploring:

1. Traditional to contemporary Native American culture to clarify their personal value base and to take active roles in reorienting self and perhaps their culture, helping to repair the damage done by the domination of the Anglo culture.

2. Contemporary Anglo cultural values so that they can understand and coexist effectively with that Anglo culture.

3. Anglo values as an alternative to Native American values.

After students have established their personal values and cultural bases, they can select life and career goals which should lead to constructive interaction with a multicultural world without a loss of personal and cultural identity.

The courses and experiences described below should help colleges and universities to provide appropriate education to Native American students. Rather than depend totally on federally funded projects as they have in the past, institutions of higher education need to address individual Native American students' needs within the existing academic budget.

Following is a description of a sequence of classes and process experiences to implement the plan for Native American students:

SELF-AWARENESS

A course designed to develop conscious awareness of individual values and culture. Values and culture of Native Americans and Euro-Americans are studied. Students explore individual cultural values within the context of the broader Euro-American and Native American cultures. In addition, students explore self in relation to the college system to (1) set personal meaning, purpose, and direction, (2) formalize a plan and strategy for obtaining a formal education, and (3) establish goals and plans for the application of their education to the total spectrum of Native and Euro-American culture.

SELF-EXPLORATION SEMINAR

A seminar consisting of small groups designed to facilitate students' discussion and integration of information. The groups serve as ongoing support groups in the first semester and continue in the same group throughout the college experience. These groups serve, also, as informal laboratories for processing of the content provided in self-awareness and career exploration courses. In addition, the groups serve as a source of ongoing direction and guidance in college procedures and general support for academic achievement.

CAREER AWARENESS CLASS

A class taken during the sophomore year to assist students in the exploration of both Native American and Euro-American worlds of work and in bridging the two. The course draws on the expertise of professional and business personnel from both Native and Euro-American communities and schools. Students are encouraged to explore the nature of specific occupations including personal factors such as temperament and attitudes as well as the knowledge and skill they require.

PERSONAL READING AND WRITING IMPROVEMENT

A course designed as an individualized, laboratory experience where students increase their control over the use of standard English in reading, writing, listening and speaking. Programs are based on continuous assessment and attention is focused on helping students develop awareness of themselves as language users. Students work toward increased effectiveness with a variety of kinds of texts utilized in a college setting. They are provided with a learning environment which will encourage the kind of risk taking necessary for development of increased control over the use of language.

PROFESSIONAL WRITING

Many colleges have a course in professional writing that may be appropriate. Such courses typically include a study of communication theory as it relates to the preparation of reports, letters, memoranda and other written communications. Such courses are often designed for upper division students in preprofessional programs.

This sequence of activities will assist Native American students to move beyond cultural conflict to clarify individual cultural identity. They should also encourage instructors to focus on the linguistic and learning styles of the Native American. What appears as "weaknesses" in facility with written language may in actuality be linguistic and learning styles differences. Understanding these differences should be a first step in planning to meet learning needs of Native American students. And it can be a first step for the students toward seeing how their own learning strengths can be applied to academic success.

We have considered, also, Native American students' need to understand the conflict between Native American cultural values and those of the Euro-American designed educational system. This understanding is a necessary basis for learning to adapt to the requirements of the college or university system and function in a multicultural society. We have suggested courses that address specific needs. We have also included an ongoing seminar experience which will provide continuous guidance and support during the college years.

If colleges and universities understand and plan for the cultural differences Native American students bring to their campuses, these differences can be a source of expanded cultural awareness for all students. Where cultural differences are understood and respected, Native American students can achieve and profit from the services the educational community has to offer.

References

Browne, D. B. (1984). WISC-R scoring patterns among Native Americans of the Northern Plains. *White Cloud Journal, 3* (2), 3–16.

Cattey, M. (1980). Cultural differences in processing information. *Indian Education*, pp. 2–5.

Evans, W. H. (1972). *Native American student counselor handbook*. Black Hills State College, Center of Indian Studies, Spearfish, South Dakota.

Heaps, R. A. & Stanley, G. M. (1979). Comparing the self-concepts of Navajo and White high school students. *Journal of American Indian Education, 18*, 12–14.

Huffman, T. E., Sill, M. L. & Brokenleg, M. (1986, January). College achievement among Sioux and White South Dakota students. *Journal of American Indian Education*.

Leap, W. (1985). *American Indian English*. Unpublished manuscript.

McDonald, A. L. (1978). Why do Indians drop out of college? In *The Schooling of Native America*, Thomas Thompson, (Ed.), Washington, DC: American Association of Colleges for Teacher Education, p. 73.

Ornstein, R. (Ed.) (1973). *The nature of human consciousness*. San Francisco: Freeman.

Red Horse, J. (1986). Editorial commentary: Educational reform. *Journal of American Indian Education*, pp. 40–44.

Ross, C. A. (1982, May). Brain hemispheric functions and the Native American. *Journal of American Indian Education*. pp. 2–5.

U.S. Senate Special Subcommittee on Indian Education (1969). *Indian education: A national tragedy—a national challenge*. Washington: U.S. Government Printing Office.

Sources of Stress and Support for the Nontraditional Undergraduate Student

Barbara A. Yutrzenka and Lois B. Oberlander

The composition of the traditional undergraduate student population has undergone a change in the past decade. Colleges and universities have witnessed a reduction in the number of "typical" college students (i.e., 18–22-year-old single males) and an increase in the number of female students and of adults (i.e., older than 25 years of age) returning to school (Epstein, 1984; Schmidt, 1983). Recent reports indicate that women now comprise the majority of all college students (Fisher-Thompson, 1980) and that the proportion of adult students is approaching approximately one-third of the national undergraduate enrollment (Kasworm, 1980).

The influx of older, nontraditional students has created a challenge for institutions of higher education. Clearly the change in the composition of the undergraduate student body requires adaptation by the institution. What is known about the traditional age student may be of minimal assistance to instructors, administrators, and advisors/counselors who are attempting to understand, work effectively with and plan for the educational, personal, and social needs of the nontraditional student (DiBona, 1983). Glass and Harshberger (1974) have suggested that higher education needs to be responsive to the basic psychological and social conflicts that may arise in the older, reentry student by creating an awareness at all levels of the educational system of the unique needs of these students. Furthermore, with the national

289

trend toward a highly diverse student body consisting of students of a variety of ages, Jacobowitz and Shanan (1982) have suggested that traditional youth-oriented policies and procedures be evaluated and, if necessary, changed to encourage age integration on college and university campuses.

Failure to recognize and address the potentially unique characteristics and needs of the nontraditional student is likely to create barriers to learning that could result in his/her failure to persist in or complete his/her education and subsequently, in a decline in overall enrollment at the institution. Thus, the need to expand the knowledge base about specific characteristics, needs and concerns of the nontraditional student appears crucial at this time.

General Characteristics of Nontraditional Students

The existing literature on nontraditional students, while prolific, has tended to focus on general trends, issues, and program offerings and only minimally on specific issues. Numerous studies describe the adult student in the context of adult education programs such as continuing education, extension programs, college-without-walls, or lifelong learning institutes (as summarized in Epstein, 1984). While contributing to the description of adult students as motivated and capable learners, these studies are unable to address specific concerns and potential barriers faced by adults enrolled in ongoing undergraduate degree programs. By the same token, a great deal has also been written on specific demographic characteristics and needs of prospective nontraditional students and nontraditional students already enrolled in degree programs (Blanshan, Livingston, Harrison & Oshini, 1984; Lance, Lourie & Mayo, 1979; Smallwood, 1980; Trussler, 1983) and on innovative courses, programs and services developed to meet identified or assumed needs of the nontraditional student (Doman, 1980; Kasworm, 1980; Uncapher, Carnhan, Altenburger & Quinlan, 1983). Once again, these writings tend to address global issues rather than specific concerns.

The literature which describes more specific characteristics of nontraditional students and which addresses their more immediate and practical concerns is somewhat limited. A large portion of the literature has focused on reasons why so many adults are choosing to return to college on a full-time basis. For example, Epstein (1984), in an investigation of factors which influence an adult's decision to return to college, interviewed male and female students, ages 36 or older, and found that affordable tuition, availability of certain major programs of study, and convenient scheduling were factors which had an impact on the decision to return to college. He also found that these students usually placed a high value on learning. In addition, Epstein found that the return to school was often preceded by what he termed a critical life incident, or a crisis in the life of the adult. Conversely, the Wisconsin Assessment Center at Green Bay (1983), in an analysis of ten separate surveys, found that the return to school by the adult student (i.e., a student age 25 or older) was a planned and well thought out event rather than a response to a crisis. Several studies have suggested that nontraditional students are highly motivated and approach their education with at least the same seriousness as traditional students (Epstein, 1984; Jacobowitz & Shanan, 1982). The Wisconsin Assessment Center (1983) found that adult students had both a commitment to and a capacity for learning, approached college with a great degree of determination, and proceeded through college at a regular pace, carrying a full course load each semester. The Wisconsin Assessment Center also reported that 98 percent of returning adults who had graduated said they would return to school again if they had it to do over.

Qualitative differences between reentry and traditional-aged students include the fact that the returning student, who has previously been a part of the work force, often experiences a loss of status when returning to school. The adult student faces a reduction in earnings, less opportunity for community contact and involvement, and may feel that he/she has become less productive. Glass and Harshberger (1974) have speculated that since society in the United States places such a great emphasis on being a producer, the return to college for the adult who has been a part of the work force may be accompanied by feelings of worthlessness. Thus, the data suggest that the older, reentry student might find it difficult to adjust to the college environment.

Sources of Stress For Nontraditional Students

Because higher education as a whole has traditionally been youth-oriented, the adult returning to college often finds that he or she seems out of place (Glass & Harshberger, 1974). Based on 60 in-depth interviews with women students over the age of 30, Levy (1981) found that it is not so much the chronological age as life cycle differences that creates dissimilarities between nontraditional and traditional-aged students. Levy found that the adult women encounter many situations which are unfamiliar and, therefore, difficult for them. These included being in an environment where age influences the ability to make friends with other students, and being a student prevents them from making friends with faculty who might be closer to their age. The nontraditional students also discover that they have less in common with neighborhood and other friends who are not attending college. In addition, Levy reported that these women find that they have little time for the traditionally youth-oriented activities and organizations that their particular campus offers. They also discover that their undefined role on campus is equally as ambiguous and undefined for faculty members who are not used to dealing with older students.

In a study of attitudes that younger university students have toward older students, Peabody and Sedlacek (1982) found that while traditional-aged freshmen have positive attitudes toward older students in academic situations, that they have negative attitudes toward older students when social interaction is involved. The results of this study and Levy's (1981) results concerning the difficulty nontraditional students experience in establishing relationships on campus reflect the apparent loss of an important source of support during matriculation. In a survey of traditional and nontraditional students' perception of their environment, Kuh and Sturgis (1980) found that nontraditional students did not perceive the college environment to be supportive of them or tolerant of individual differences. Levy (1981) found that traditional university networks which bring students together and provide social support are not available to nontraditional women students because of the nature of activities on campus which are organized around the younger students. However, Levy did report that the women in her study who were 30 years or older reported receiving some support from groups of students who shared similar status with them. Kirk and Dorfman (1982) reported that psychological support from friends was positively correlated with satisfaction with school among nontraditional female students.

Several studies have examined specific sources of stress for nontraditional students. Kirk and Dorfman (1983) found that reentry women ages 35 and older indicated that time and multiple role demands are the major stressors for them. Levy (1981) also found that women over 30 who reported multiple responsibilities at home had difficulty adjusting to college. The impact of multiple responsibilities are also reported to affect older male students, who, in one survey, were less successful than women in their adjustment to college when they were required to be employee, family member, and student (Malin, Bray, Dougherty, &

Skinner, 1980). A number of studies have found that the returning, older student has a need for flexibility and finds that adjustment is easier when multiple roles are lessened or eliminated (Ballmer & Cozby, 1981). Additional sources of stress for students include dissatisfaction with outside job, number of years since previous school enrollment, and variability of financial aid availability (Kirk & Dorfman, 1983). Environmental stress factors experienced by both traditional and nontraditional students include academic concerns, interpersonal relationships, sexuality, and to a lesser extent, time management, term papers, career planning, and rate of reading (Beard, Elmore, & Lange, 1982).

Purpose Of This Study

While the aforementioned studies have attempted to describe the nontraditional student and some of the issues and concerns facing his/ her experience as an undergraduate in an institution of higher education, there continues to be a need for more empirically based research. In response to the limited amount of empirical research regarding specific stressors encountered by undergraduates, the current study was designed to examine sources of stress for both traditional and nontraditional students, and to determine whether there are significant differences between the two groups in either degree or type of stress encountered. A second, related focus of this study was to examine the impact of social and university-based support systems on the experience of stress and, again, to determine if significant differences exist between traditional and nontraditional students in both the perceived availability and their utilization of these support systems.

Method

Subjects

Two hundred traditional and 200 nontraditional undergraduates enrolled on a full-time basis at the University of South Dakota were randomly selected from an enrollment list provided through the University's Office of the Registrar. (For the purposes of this study, a nontraditional student was defined as a student who is at least three years older than the traditional age of students in their respective academic class.) Equal numbers of males and females from each of the four classes were selected for each category. Of the students contacted, 154 (40%) returned completed questionnaires. Of these, 75 were traditional (28 male, 47 female) and 83 nontraditional (35 male, 48 female) students chose to participate in this study. Participation was strictly voluntary and no form of remuneration or academic credit was offered.

Materials

Demographic Questionnaire. This questionnaire consisted of 21 items designed to assess general demographic and social information about the subjects (e.g., age, sex, marital status, grade point average, major).

Inventory of Stressors in Undergraduate Education (ISUE). The ISUE was designed specifically for this study to identify areas of potential stress encountered by undergraduates in the college environment. It consisted of 83 items which were subdivided into four categories: (a) institutional stressors (e.g., obtaining admission information, accessibility of support services at convenient times); (b) academic stressors (e.g., fear of getting bad grades, missing class); (c) situational stressors (e.g., time pressures, lack of peer group contact); and (d) attitudinal stressors (e.g., lack of motivation, lack of confidence). A large number of the items in this questionnaire were modeled after similar items in survey instruments employed by the Ohio State University (Blanshan et al., 1983) and the University of Alberta (Trussler, 1983), with permission from the authors to utilize selected portions of their survey instruments having been verbally obtained. Subjects were asked to indicate whether or not they have experienced the potentially stressful situation during the current academic year, and if so, to rate the degree of stress experienced on a six-point scale ranging from "not stressful at all" (1) to "extremely stressful" (6).

College Schedule of Recent Experience (CSRE). Developed by Anderson (1972), this 47 item questionnaire is a modified version of the Holmes and Rahe (1967) Schedule of Recent Events and was designed to measure stressful life events in a college student population. Subjects indicate whether or not they have experienced a particular life event in the past academic year. The cumulative score of those items endorsed is considered to be a measure of stress experienced by the respondent.

Brief Symptom Inventory (BSI). The BSI (Derogatis, 1975) is a 53 item inventory designed to assess a person's general level of psychological distress. Each item on the BSI is rated on a five-point scale ranging from "not at all" (0) to "extremely" (4). The ratings are summed and divided by the number of items answered to result in a General Severity Index (GSI). The GSI is considered to be the BSI's most sensitive global indicator of the respondent's distress level.

DeBoe's Inventory of Social Support (DISS). This 29–item questionnaire was developed by DeBoe, Smith & Quevillon (1984) to assess social support in the areas of receiving emotional and esteem support, initiating conversations about personal problems, and neighborhood network count. Subjects rate how often they are involved in each of the activities listed on a five point scale ranging from "not at all" (1) to "about every day" (5). The final score is a summation of the item scores.

University Services Questionnaire (USQ). This 36-item questionnaire was designed specifically for this study to assess the number and types of services provided by this University that are utilized by the subjects. Subjects were asked to indicate whether or not they have utilized a particular service (e.g., Admissions Office, Campus Ministry Centers, Academic Advisor), and if so, to rate how satisfied they are with that service on a six-point scale ranging from "not satisfied" (1) to "extremely satisfied" (6).

Procedure

Subjects were contacted by mail and asked to complete the packet of questionnaires. Confidentiality and anonymity of individual responses was assured. Since no remuneration or academic credit was offered, appeals were made to their sense of altruism and interest in enhancing the quality of life for undergraduates at this university. Subjects were asked to return the completed survey in an enclosed stamped envelope. A follow-up reminder postcard was mailed to each subject approximately two weeks later encouraging completion and return of the survey packet if not already done.

Results

Background Information

Demographics. Of the 83 nontraditional students sampled, 43 percent were male and 57 percent were female. The average age was 28 years, with a range of 21–50. The predominant ethnic/racial background was Caucasian (89 percent). Forty-six percent of the nontraditional students indicated they were single, 40 percent married, and 14 percent separated or divorced. Forty-five percent of these students indicated that their current residence was a local house/apartment, 27 percent commuted from a distance greater than 20 miles from the university, and 12 percent commuted from a distance less than 20 miles. Only 14 percent lived in university housing. Slightly more than half indicated that they were unemployed while matriculating (51 percent), while 45 percent worked part-time and 4 percent worked full-time.

Of the 75 traditional students sampled, 37 percent were male and 63 percent were female. The average age was 20 years with a range of 18–23. The predominant ethnic/racial background was Caucasian (95 percent). Ninety-one percent were single and 9 percent were married. Fifty-two percent of these students indicated that they lived in university housing, 35 percent in local houses/apartments and 8 percent commuted to the university from locations outside the immediate locale. Slightly more than half of these students reported that they were unemployed while matriculating (52 percent), while 48 percent reported they worked part-time. No traditional students reported full-time employment while enrolled as a student.

Academic Information. The proportion of nontraditional and traditional students from each class, respectively, were as follows: Freshmen 22 percent and 15 percent; Sophomores 18 percent and 29 percent; Juniors 28 percent and 27 percent; and, Seniors 32 percent and 29 percent. A slightly higher proportion of the traditional students sampled (58 percent) reported grade point averages (GPA) of 3.0 or better when compared to nontraditional students (50 percent), and a slightly lower proportion of traditional students (36 percent) had GPAs of 2.0–2.9 when compared to nontraditional students (46 percent). Sixty-nine percent of the traditional students were enrolled in 16 credit hours or more while only 30 percent of the nontraditional students carried this many credits. A higher proportion of nontraditional students (68 percent) were enrolled in 12–15 credit hours.

Sources of Stress and Support

To analyze differences between nontraditional and traditional students on number of potential sources of stress, degree of stress experienced, and sources of support experienced within a specific academic year, three-way analyses of variance were performed on each of the relevant measures across the variables of traditional versus nontraditional status, sex, and class level. Since there were no significant interactions involving the traditional versus nontraditional variable, and since this is the variable of interest in this paper, only main effects involving this variable will be reported.

Results indicate that with regard to number of potential stressors experienced during undergraduate education, there were no significant differences between traditional and nontraditional students in the overall number of items endorsed on the ISUE ($F = 1.74$, $df = 1,142$, $p = .24$). The only ISUE subscale which differentiated between the groups was the Situational subscale in which nontraditional students endorsed significantly more items than did traditional students ($F = 4.01$, $df = 1,142$, $p = .05$). In addition, traditional and nontraditional students did not significantly differ on the CSRE ($F = 1.15$, $df = 1,142$, $p = .29$).

There were no statistically significant differences between nontraditional and traditional students on the stress rating assigned to ISUE items ($F = .83$, $df = 1,141$, $p = .36$), though the data approached significance with both the Attitudinal ($F = 3.70$, $df = 1,143$, $p = .06$) and the Situational ($F = 3.73$, $df = 1,142$ $p = .06$) subscales. With the exception of the Situational subscale in which the trend paralleled the results above, the statistically nonsignificant trend in the stress ratings was for traditional students to rate the ISUE items as more stressful than did nontraditional students. This is consistent with the significant difference obtained on the General Severity Index of the BSI in which traditional students obtained higher overall mean symptom ratings than did nontraditional students ($F = 7.48$, $df = 1,153$ $p = .007$).

Finally, while there were no significant differences between nontraditional and traditional students on the number of University-based support services utilized ($F = 2.75$, $df = 1,142$, $p = .09$), there was a highly significant difference between these two groups on social support as measured by the DISS ($F = 7.67$, $df = 1,152$, $p = .006$). That is, traditional students indicated significantly higher levels of social support than did nontraditional students.

Relationships Between Stress and Support Measures

Several Pearson Product-Moment correlations were computed to determine the relationships between the measures utilized in this study. Separate correlations were computed for nontraditional and traditional students. Significant (p >.05) positive or negative correlations of .4 or greater were considered to reflect sufficient magnitude of relationship between variables. Results indicated that for both groups of students, the GSI of the BSI was positively correlated with the number of stressful life events endorsed on the CSRE (nontraditional rxx = .418; traditional rxx = .677) and with the overall rating given to items endorsed on the ISUE (nontraditional rxx = .559; traditional rxx = .677). All remaining correlations were either significant but of insufficient magnitude (i.e., rxx <|.4|), or nonsignificant.

Discussion

The purpose of this study was to provide an empirically based description of the differences that may exist between traditional and nontraditional students with regard to their identification and experience of stress and support during their undergraduate education. Though results indicated differences between these groups of students in demographic characteristics, level of psychological distress, and perceived social support, numerous similarities were clearly apparent in number and type of stressors experienced, degree of stress associated with stressors, and utilization of university-based support services.

Perhaps some of the more obvious and expected differences between the traditional and nontraditional students sampled in this study were related to demographic data. For example, compared with traditional students, nontraditional students were, by definition, older, more likely to be currently or previously married, and more likely to live farther from campus. These demographic differences were consistent with those that have been previously documented (c.f. Kuh & Sturgis, 1980), with the possible exception of age of nontraditional students. Ninety percent of the nontraditional students in this study were between the ages of 21 and 35, with an average age (28) slightly lower than those reported elsewhere. At the same time, however, in those studies in which only degree-seeking, full-time students were evaluated, the majority of nontraditional students were under 35 years old (Sewell, 1984; Wisconsin Assessment Center, 1983), findings consistent with the current data.

Results also indicated that traditional and nontraditional students differ academically. For example, while both groups carried adequate amounts of credit hours to qualify them as full-time students, nontraditional students tended to carry fewer credit hours when compared with traditional students. This would be consistent with the finding that nontraditional students reported having greater nonacademically related time commitments (e.g., family, commuting), and, thus, may have accommodated their multiple demands by choosing lower credit hour loads. Nontraditional students also had slightly lower grade point averages (though still well within the average and above average range) than traditional students. These findings are inconsistent with Von der Embse and Childs's (1979) study in which older students (over 27) were more likely than younger students (under 27) to have GPAs in the high range. However, both Von der Embse and Childs's study and the current study reflect the relatively high levels of academic achievement of older, nontraditional students.

With regard to the identification of potential sources of stress, experience of stress, and sources of support, more similarities than differences between traditional and nontraditional students emerged. Both the ISUE and the CSRE were utilized to provide an indication of differing amounts of exposure traditional and nontraditional students may have to a variety of potentially stressful situations. Items included on the ISUE were consistent with items identified on various student generated lists of stressful situations related to the college experiences as cited in Archer and Lamin (1985), Johnson (1978), and Zitrow (1984). While there was a trend for nontraditional students to have experienced more of the potentially stressful situations on the ISUE, there were no significant differences between groups in the overall number of situations identified. With regard to the ISUE subscales, nontraditional students identified significantly more items in the Situation subscale than traditional students, but the two groups of students did not differ significantly on any of the other three subscales. Closer examination of Situation subscale items revealed inclusion of several items specifically relevant to nontraditional students (e.g., unavailability of childcare, disruption in family life, commuting to and from school) which probably elevated the number of responses made by nontraditional students in this category. Further examination of the proportion of traditional versus nontraditional students selecting individual items in the other ISUE subscales reflected more similarities than differences between these groups of students in both the number and type of potentially stressful situations they have encountered as undergraduates.

The CSRE was also included in this study as an indicator of exposure to potentially stressful situations/life events. Unlike the ISUE, the

CSRE is a standardized measure designed to address more generic (i.e., not specifically academically-based) sources of stress. Results did not confirm the prediction that nontraditional students would endorse more life events than traditional students due to their age/opportunity for more life experiences. As with the ISUE, only a nonsignificant trend for nontraditional students to endorse more CSRE items was evident. A plausible explanation for this is the time frame imposed on subjects (i.e., during the current academic year) when identifying life events minimized group differences.

The *experience* of stress was assessed by having students rate the intensity of stress they perceived in the situations endorsed on the ISUE and by rating severity of a variety of symptoms related to overall psychological distress on the BSI. There were no statistically significant differences between traditional and nontraditional students on the stress ratings of the ISUE items. Interestingly, with the exception of the Situational subscale, the nonsignificant trend that emerged in the ISUE stress ratings was for traditional students to rate situations as more stressful than nontraditional students. That is, while they tended to endorse fewer situations than nontraditional students, those they did endorse were rated as more stressful. Several individual items given higher stress ratings by traditional students included poor study habits, competition with other students, lack of positive feedback from faculty, and lack of self-confidence. Archer and Lamnin (1985) also report results wherein younger students in their sample identified variables such as grades, competition, studying, and peer pressure as more stressful than did older students.

The statistically nonsignificant trend for traditional students to rate ISUE items as more stressful than nontraditional students paralleled the significant difference obtained between these two groups on their BSI scores. Traditional students obtained a higher overall mean symptom rating when compared to nontraditional students indicating that they were experiencing more overall psychological distress than nontraditional students. Though speculative, one explanation for these results is that, when compared to the nontraditional student, the traditional student has less well developed stress management skills. For many, the undergraduate experience may be their first exposure to stressful life events requiring an independent coping response, while nontraditional students may have been exposed to, and developed coping mechanisms to deal with a variety of stressful events.

With regards to scores on the various stress measures, the ISUE and CSRE total scores were not significantly related. There were significant, moderate correlations between the BSI and both the number of CSRE life events students reported having experienced as well as the overall stress rating given to the ISUE situations. Thus, the greater the number of generic stressful life events experienced, and the higher the rating given to perceived college-related stressors, the greater the likelihood for psychological distress. These results were similar for both traditional and nontraditional students.

To determine if nontraditional students differ from traditional students in their perception and experience of social support, two measures of support were administered. Results indicated that when compared with traditional students, nontraditional students reported significantly less social support on the DISS. Though this measure was not specifically designed to differentiate between school related support and other sources of support, there appears to be potential for some overlap when dealing with undergraduates. For example, given that traditional students are more likely to live on or near campus, the availability of a more expansive and interrelated social network and of readily available "confidants" is expanded. Upon examination of DISS items, this indeed appeared to be a contributing factor to the higher scores obtained by traditional students. When considering a measure of support specifically designed to address university based support, traditional and nontraditional students did not differ on the number of services utilized. They tended to utilize and underutilize similar services with only few exceptions. More than 70 percent of both groups indicated use of core services such as Admissions, Registrar, Student Health, Academic Advisors, Financial Aids, and Student Center. For most other services listed, fewer than 40 percent of all students sampled reported utilization. Most noticeable included in these "underutilized" services were personal counseling services, placement offices, special services, and campus ministry. This study did not address factors involved in service utilization. However, identification of these factors would provide valuable information to university service providers and administration concerned with evaluation of services.

The relationship between the DISS and the USQ was not significant for either group of students indicating that each instrument was measuring independent sources of support. Contrary to predictions, these measures did not appear to significantly moderate or "buffer" the experience of stress by either traditional or nontraditional students. That is, correlations between the DISS or USQ and the ISUE ratings, CSRE, or BSI were either not significant or of insufficient magnitude to support the expected inverse relationships. These findings are consistent with those reported by Ganellan and Blaney (1984) in which social support did not buffer effects of life stress. While it is possible the measurement tools utilized in this study account for the lack of significant correlations, the possibility also exists that the phenomena of stress and social support are not related to each other but instead are related to a third, unidentified variable such as personality or life satisfaction.

Conclusions

The results of this study indicated that though differences exist between traditional and nontraditional students in specific aspects of perceived sources of stress and support, fewer differences emerged than would have been predicted based on the bulk of the literature. In fact, similarities between these groups in the number, type, and rating of stressors and life events and in the utilization of university support systems were quite apparent. One possible explanation for the number of similarities may be related to what Kasworm (1982) described as the greater similarities in psychological, socioemotional, and behavioral characteristics of younger (traditional) students and closely age-related older, nontraditional students. She reported greater differences between younger (26–29) and older (30–36) nontraditional students and, consequently cautioned against treating nontraditional students as a homogeneous group. Since the traditional and nontraditional students in this study were relatively close in age, the differences between them may have been reduced. However, it is also possible that in this sample, the designation of traditional versus nontraditional based on age is not the key factor that would differentiate the groups. Perhaps marital status, sex, or minority status would be more salient factors when attempting to differentiate between or identify unique needs of "nontraditional" undergraduates.

Finally, it is possible that the differences between the traditional and nontraditional students in this study have been moderated by this University's concerted efforts in the past few years to attend to the perceived needs of both groups of students. Particular emphasis has been placed on integrating the nontraditional student into campus life by supporting an organization for nontraditional students, developing a handbook for nontraditional students, and increasing awareness of administration, faculty, and students with regards to characteristics, needs, and contributions of older students. Continued attention should be paid to reducing barriers that may exist for both traditional and nontraditional students by examining current institutional services and policies, increasing awareness of the types of services that exist and encouraging their utilization when appropriate, and by encouraging continued research and evaluation of the needs of the entire undergraduate population.

References

Anderson, G. E. (1972). *College Schedule of Recent Experience.* Masters Thesis, North Dakota State University, unpublished.

Archer, J., & Lamnin, A. (1985). An investigation of personal and academic stressors on college campuses. *Journal of College Student Personnel, 26,* 210–215.

Ballmer, H., & Cozby, P.C. (1981). Family environments of women who return to college. *Sex Roles, 7,* 1019–1026.

Beard, S. S., Elmore, R. T., & Lange, S. (1982). Assessment of student needs: Areas of stress in the campus environment. *Journal of College Student Personnel, 23,* 348–350.

Blanshan, S. A., Livingston, M. D., Harrison, R. & Ashini, J. (1984). *Re-entry study survey: Office of women's services, The Ohio State University, preliminary report, Association for the Study of Higher Education.* Paper presented at the Annual Meeting of The Association for the Study of Higher Education, Chicago, IL. (ERIC Document Reproduction Service No. ED 245 613).

Derogatis, L. R. (1975). *The Brief Symptom Inventory (BSI).* Baltimore: Clinical Psychometric Research.

DeBoe, J. B., Smith, J. C., & Quevillon, R. P. (1984, May). *Development of an inventory of social support.* Paper presented at the Midwestern Psychological Association, Chicago, Illinois.

DiBona, N., & Golter, B. (1983). Adult re-entry program. *Journal of College Student Personnel, 24,* 271–272.

Doman, E. F. (1980). Re-entry seminar. *Journal of College Student Personnel, 21,* 470.

Epstein, H. V. (1984, April). *The older college student—A changing tradition.* Paper presented at the Annual Meeting of the American Educational Research Association, New Orleans, LA. (ERIC Document Reproduction Service No. ED 243 361).

Fisher-Thompson, J. (1980). *Barriers to re-entry women: College transfer polices, residency, and graduation requirements*. Project on the Status and Education of Women, Washington, D.C. (ERIC Document Reproduction Service No. ED 205 138).

Ganellan, R. J. & Blaney, H. (1984). Hardiness and social support as moderators of the effects of life stress. *Journal of Personality and Social Psychology*, *47*, 156–163.

Glass, J. C., & Harsberger, R. F. (1974). The full-time, middle-aged adult student in higher education. *The Journal of Higher Education*, *3*, 211–218.

Holmes, T. H. & Rahe, R. H. (1967). The social readjustment rating scale. *Journal of Psychosomatic Research*, *11*, 213–218.

Jacobowitz, J., & Shanan, J. (1982). Higher education for the second half of life: The state of the art and future perspectives. *Educational Gerontology*, *8*, 545–564.

Johnson, E. E. (1978, August). *Student-identified stresses that relate to college life*. Paper presented at the Annual Convention of the American Psychological Association, Toronto, Canada. (ERIC Document Reproduction Service No. ED 170 630).

Kasworm, C. (1980). Student services for the older undergraduate students. *Journal of College Student Personnel*, *21*, 163–169.

Kasworm, C. (1982). Lifespan differences between student groups. *Journal of College Student Personnel*, *23*, 424–429.

Kirk, C. F., & Dorfman, L. T. (1983). Satisfaction and role strain among middle-age and older reentry women students. *Educational Gerontology*, *9*, 15.

Kuh, G. D., & Sturgis, J. T. (1980). Looking at the university through different sets of lens: Adult learners and traditional age students' perceptions of the university environments. *Journal of College Student Personnel*, *21*, 483–490.

Lance, L. M., Lourie, J., & Mayo, C. (1979). Needs of re-entry university students. *Journal of College Student Personnel*, *20*, 479–485.

Levy, J. A. (1981). Friendship dilemmas and the intersection of social worlds: Reentry women on the college campus. *Research in the Interweave of Social Roles: Friendship*, *2*, 143–170.

Malin, J. T., Bray, J. H., Dougherty, T. W., & Skinner, W. K. (1980). Factors affecting the performance and satisfaction of adult men and women attending college. *Research in Higher Education*, *13*, 2, 115–130.

Peabody, S. A., & Sedlacek, W. E. (1982). Attitudes of younger university students toward older students. *Journal of College Student Personnel*, *23*, 140–143.

Schmidt, S. (1983). *Understanding the culture of adults returning to higher education: Barriers to learning and preferred learning styles.* Department of Agriculture, Washington, D.C. (ERIC Document Reproduction Service No. ED 242 248).

Sewell, T. J. (1984). A study of adult undergraduates: What causes them to seek a degree? *Journal of College Student Personnel, 25,* 309–314.

Smallwood, K. B. (1980). What do adult college students really need? *Journal of College Student Personnel, 21,* 65–73.

Trussler, M. J. (1983). *Report of the task force on mature students.* Alberta, University of Edmonton. (ERIC Document Reproduction Service No. ED 240 892).

Uncapher, B. W., Carnhan, R. E., Altenburger, J., Regner, J., & Quinlan, K. (1983). *Meeting the needs of adult students: A model designed by adult students.* Pennsylvania State University. (ERIC Document Reproduction Service No. ED 235 735).

Von der Embse, T. J., & Childs, J. M. (1979). Adults in transition: A profile of the older college student. *Journal of College Student Personnel, 20,* 475–479.

Wisconsin Assessment Center. (1983). *The adult student: Research findings; Vol. 1.* (ERIC Document Reproduction Service No. ED 241 733).

Zitrow, D. (1984). The college adjustment rating scale. *Journal of College Student Personnel, 25,* 160–164.

This research project was funded by a Bush Foundation grant awarded to the first author.

Meeting the Problems of the Handicapped

Donald R. Potter

Education beyond high school in the United States is optional but has become a necessary investment in future employment and life satisfaction for many people. Many high school graduates with disabilities want to share in the experiences and benefits of college and university life but for various reasons have often been denied the opportunity. Disabled students have not always been warmly welcomed at college and university admissions offices. Colleges and universities that were established in times when society had little knowledge about or confidence in its disabled citizens, constructed campuses which were architecturally inaccessible. However, disabled persons are entering colleges and universities in increasing numbers (McBee, 1982; Milner, 1981). Several factors have contributed to this growing influx of students with disabilities into two-year and four-year colleges and universities. Advances in medical technology and rehabilitative engineering have made it possible for a variety of disabled persons to enroll in post-secondary programs. The elimination of architectural barriers, long a deterrent for many, has literally opened the doors to higher education for many. Greater public acceptance in recent years has encouraged disabled persons to seek out those institutions that have removed architectural barriers (Perry, 1981). Furthermore, the expansion of vocational rehabilitation services at the state level, the continued pressures of modern society in the direction of college enrollment, and recent trends in post-secondary education to maintain enrollments by tapping nontraditional student markets, are certain to encourage an ever-increasing proportion of disabled students to enroll in post-secondary education programs (Burgdorf, 1980).

The growth of a disabled student population will have a significant impact on the future role and direction of higher education in the United States (U.S. Department of Health, Education and Welfare, 1980). As colleges and universities move into the 1990s, the issue of providing expanded services for disabled students will continue to be an important factor in academic goal setting and campus planning (Milner, 1980; Ridenour & Johnson, 1981). How colleges and universities deal with this and other related issues is of concern to the general public, the academic work place and most certainly to handicapped students. In pursuing higher educational goals, students with disabilities meet many policy, social and architectural barriers. It may be appropriate then to examine some of the barriers which still confront disabled students wishing to enter college and which prevent completion of their programs.

Policy Barriers

In 1977, the U. S. Department of Health, Education and Welfare issued the final regulations implementing the Rehabilitation Act of 1973. Institutions of higher education and other agencies receiving federal funds were required by Section 504 of this act to make their programs and services accessible to handicapped individuals. Policy changes by institutions of higher education often take place very slowly. Institutional policies which had been in place since the formation of that institution perhaps may require the consideration of numerous committees and agencies before any change is initiated. Even following such policy change, institutions may be slow to put in place the necessary personnel or assistance necessary to actually implement the change in policy. One could assume that colleges and universities have been busy since 1977 addressing the issues contained in Section 504 regulations. A review of the literature, however, revealed few reports of national trends on how institutions of higher education have arranged their organizational structures to respond to the needs of disabled students by providing special services and programs for them. Marion and Iovacchini (1983) investigated the efforts made by colleges and universities to provide special services for students with hearing impairments, visual impairments, and diagnosed learning disabilities as well as for those with mobility impairments and other handicaps. It was the author's conclusion that colleges and universities across the country have made a serious effort to carry out the regulations implementing Section 504.

Stilwell and Schulker (1973) collected data in 1971 that suggested that 61.5 percent of the institutions of higher education in Kentucky had developed flexible admission policies for students with handicaps, but often failed to develop the services to support those students. A similar study (Stilwell, Stilwell & Perritt) in 1983 revealed that the majority of the schools (86.7 percent) reported use of flexible admission policies, although progress had been uneven across those institutions in provision of specific services to the disabled student.

The starting point for most students wishing to pursue a college education is the completion of pre-admission tests. Nearly a million persons take the ACT Assessment each year as part of their college planning (Laing & Farmer, 1984). Presumably, even though the examinees' educational and cultual backgrounds differ, this "common task" lets each one compare his or her level of educational development with that of other ACT-tested college-bound examinees. There are times, however, when one of the most difficult parts of a disabled student's admissions process is the taking of standardized tests required for college admission. Some examinees with disabilities are unable to take the examination under standardized testing conditions. Under standard conditions, examinees use regular-print test booklets and take the four subject-area tests in a timed test session of approximately three hours. While ACT provides special test forms and special testing arrangements for students with disabilities, ACT cautions that use of nonstandard materials or nonstandard conditions may mean that test results cannot be interpreted in the same way as those of examinees tested under standard conditions. Does this affect their admission success? What should be the policy for disabled students? Section 504 of the Rehabilitation Act of 1973 (Public Law 93–112) regulations state that admission tests must fairly reflect the applicant's aptitude or achievement rather than reflecting the applicant's impaired sensory or manual skills. Laing and Farmer (1984) examined data collected over five testing years, beginning with 1978–79 and ending with 1982–83. They found that the ACT general prediction equations work equally well for examinees without disabilities and for examinees with disabilities, when both groups take the ACT Assessment under regular testing conditions. Although predicted grades are lower for the latter group, so are their high school grades, ACT Assessment scores, and earned college grades. The correlation between predicted and earned grades is .59 for both of the regularly-tested groups. The specially-tested examinees presented a more mixed picture. Prediction was best for specially-tested examinees with visual disabilities (.52), whereas the correlation of .39 between predicted and earned grades for examinees with motor (physical and learning) disabilities indicates that, for this group, predicted grades are less accurate. As the authors point out, their research seemed to raise more questions than it answered. How comparable are the educational backgrounds of students with differing disabilities (or without disabilities)? Are the procedures for special testing adequate for students with varying disabilities? Is self-selection for special testing the most appropriate means of insuring fairness? More research is necessary to find answers to these and other questions regarding admission procedures for students with disabilities.

Results of a 1981 follow-up survey of a 1978 disabled freshmen group appear to provide us with some reassurance that whatever barriers lie in the path of disabled students in securing admission, once access to college is gained, they will succeed (Lawrence, Kent, Henson, 1982). Each fall, the Student Information Form (SIF) is administered to the entire freshman class at each institution participating in the Cooperative Institutional Research Program (CIRP). A total of 6,259 disabled 1978 CIRP participants were identified as potential respondents. The analyses presented by Lawrence et al. are based on weighted responses to a follow-up survey conducted in 1981 and completed by 760 disabled participants. The majority of respondents had persisted in college, earned good grades, retained high degree aspirations, were satisfied with college, manifested high self-esteem, and look forward to being married, having children, and to pursuing full-time careers. The major policy implication from this study as seen by the authors is: "Give the disabled access to colleges and universities, and they will match the nondisabled in their performance, progress and promise" (Lawrence et al., 1978, p. 1).

While the conclusion of Lawrence et al. (1978) is encouraging, there is too little evidence to justify such optimism. As Laing and Farmer (1984) point out, their investigation of the performance of disabled students on the ACT Assessment raised more questions than it answered. Since the admissions tests scores are one of the major factors to be considered by colleges and universities in the selection of students, it is evident that further research is necessary to assure that disabled students are not unfairly rejected. Perhaps more states will follow Massachusetts's example and determine admission by other relevant factors excluding standardized achievement testing (National Information Center for Handicapped Children and Youth, 1985). Admission to a college or university is, however, only the first step. While it appears that Section 504 has had an effect upon the admission policies, there is no evidence to suggest that even the majority of colleges and universities have developed flexible admission policies for disabled students. But even where flexible admission policies had been adopted, there is little evidence that the nation's colleges and universities have implemented plans and procedures to accommodate disabled students. Policies precede action, and in light of what is known, many institutions are still in the position of determining what their policies will be.

Social Barriers

Once admission to the college or university is assured, housing arranged, and registration completed, the social life for most students begins. The myriad of activities on every campus each fall, from fraternity and sorority rush to dances for new students, all beckon the newcomer to get acquainted and join in the fun; but, what if the student is disabled? As physically disabled students have entered postsecondary programs, emphasis has been placed on the physical accessibility of classrooms, residence halls, lavatories and other facilities. Physical impediments, however, are not the only possible obstacles for these students. To be a part of the college scene one needs friends and social activities. This requires that other students and faculty understand and accept the disability.

Many visibly disabled students as well as nonvisibly disabled students arriving on the college campus express the desire to be considered students first and only when necessary as students with disabilities. As products of our culture, however, professional and nonprofessional members of the college community cannot avoid having many of the prevailing feelings and thoughts about disability and about disabled persons. They may feel discomfort, fear, pity, guilt, frustration and sorrow. They may think of disabled people as courageous, weak, helpless or inadequate. Or, they may not even think of them.

The attitudes of professional and nonprofessional employees as well as students toward students who are disabled have the potential to affect positively students' achievement and behavior. Or their attitudes can pose a formidable barrier which, in a very real sense, can be a greater obstacle than the more commonly considered architectural barriers.

Nathanson (1982) reported that, typically, members of the college community adopt a level, usually based on the student's deficiencies rather than on his or her assets, and encourage the student to conform to what are perceived as the limitations and potentials of that label. There is little regard for the individuality of the student: students who are blind all have the same needs; all paraplegics have the same interests and abilities. People who use wheelchairs on campus are referred to as wheelchair students; people having any kind of physical impairment are the handicapped or crippled; and they all become cases. As Ragosta (1980) pointed out "one pervasive handicap, however, was common with students across many disabilities; the attitude of the public toward the handicapped."

Fonasch's study (cited in Kelly, 1984) surveyed the attitudes of faculty members on several classroom management issues regarding the enrollment of disabled students. Faculty members who had previous contact with disabled students, female professors and faculty members in social sciences and education had more positive attitudes toward the integration of disabled students into the academic community than did their colleagues in other departments. A more positive attitude was also found among collegiate coordinators for disabled students (Kelly, 1984). Having a service program on campus seems to make a difference in the attitudes of nondisabled students toward disabled students (Genskow & Maglione, 1965). What the service program did to positively affect the student attitudes is unknown.

Research has consistently shown that living on campus (e.g., in residence halls, fraternities and sororities) has favorable effects on undergraduate progress and performance (Astin, 1975). However, living in college housing had a strong negative relationship with the outcome for disabled students (Lawrence et al., 1982). It may be that adjusting to life in a college dormitory imposes hardships and pressures on disabled students that the non-disabled do not experience. In addition, college grade point average was negatively associated with having a disabled roommate but positively associated with having a nondisabled roommate, though these relationships were much weaker. While institutional type (e.g., two-year, four-year, etc.) was only weakly associated with college grades, Lawrence et al. (1982) found the environmental variable most strongly related to satisfaction in private universities. Disabled students entering this type of institution as freshmen tended to be dissatisfied with their college experience. Of the various college support services and accommodations, the one having the greatest positive effect on the outcome was participation in disabled student organizations and clubs. The explanation for this may lie in the psychological support provided by such clubs.

It is reasonable to assume that there will be variance among the disabled student population with regard to their personal, social, educational, and physical needs. One of the implications drawn from the study of the 1981 sample of disabled college students was that individuals differ and that some individuals will require more accommodation on the part of their college environment than others (Lawrence et al., 1982). Just as individuals differ in their needs, colleges and universities differ in the degree to which they have elected to meet the challenges of providing post-secondary programs for disabled students. Although there is a paucity of research from which to draw conclusions, especially about social barriers, it seems evident there remains great variance from institution to institution with respect to removal of those social barriers which prevent or impede the progress of disabled students. There is limited evidence to suggest that some campuses have helpful counselors, service programs of some kind, a number of faculty members who apparently hold positive, or at least neutral attitudes toward the disabled student, in general. However, substantial positive evidence is lacking.

Architectural Barriers

The final regulations of the Architectural and Transportation Barriers Compliance Board (ATBCB) were published in Vol. 47, No. 150, August 4, 1982, of the *Federal Register*. ATBCB was charged with prescribing standards to insure that federally assisted buildings are accessible to and usable by disabled persons. The regulations thoroughly cover sidewalks, parking, stairs, elevators, handrails, floors, ramps, entrances, toilet rooms, drinking fountains, controls and operating mechanisms, alarms, tactile warnings, telephones, seating, tables, assembly and conference rooms, and storage areas. "Program accessibility" is the key word in Section 504 of the Rehabilitation Act of 1973. Programs and activities must be accessible if discrimination is to be eliminated and disabled persons are to be afforded equal opportunities for full participation. Section 504 requires that all programs and activities operated by the institution be readily accessible to handicapped persons. Therefore, every facility (or every part of every facility) need not be accessible to and useable by handicapped persons, but all programs and activities are to be easily accessible.

There are between 18 and 20 million people in the United States with a physical handicap requiring specially constructed architecture of some kind for a daily living routine (Cotler & DeGraff, 1976). The employment picture is gloomy at best for many of these people. As a consequence of the handicap, more and more of these individuals are turning to the offerings of higher education to expand their marketability. Have college and university campuses become accessible as the law requires?

Unfortunately, there is only limited data upon which to judge the progress toward accessibility on college and university campuses. Stilwell et al. (1983) examined the degree to which the institutions of higher education in Kentucky had become more accessible than they were ten years earlier. The authors reported that progress had occurred in the reduction of architectural barriers. It should be noted, however, that "progress" (though statistically significant) was indicated when, for example, 66 percent of the schools reported that a ramp was available to the library entrance as opposed to only 38 percent in 1971.The degree of adaptation in Kentucky has apparently been uneven between and within institutions.

Marion and Iovacchini (1983) examined the efforts of colleges and universities in the United States to assure program accessibility for disabled students. The authors sent a survey instrument to 504 compliance officers and coordinators of services for handicapped students at 408 institutions of higher education from all sections of the country. Completed surveys were returned by 155 institutions or 38 percent of those surveyed. Public institutions constituted 70 percent (N = 108), and private institutions made up 30 percent (N = 47) of the responding institutions. The average number of disabled students at the 155 responding institutions during the fall of 1981 was: mobility impairment –52, hearing impairment –8, visual impairments –12, diagnosed learning disability –29, and other handicaps –40. The following services were offered by one or more of the responding institutions: specialized van for transportation, wheelchair loan and repair service, accessibility maps, tactile signs and maps, and special parking places. All of the responding institutions had a compliance officer; 75 percent had other staff members with 504 related responsibilities; and 65 percent had formed a committee to deal with 504 issues. Larger institutions and public institutions had more staff support to serve disabled students. The authors stated that "the results of this survey imply that basic services are being provided by most institutions of higher education to assure program accessibility for handicapped students" (Marion & Iovacchini, 1983, p. 135). This would suggest that there has been a marked improvement over the past decade. Mahan (1974) observed that even when schools stated that they would not reject disabled students, very often the schools were not equipped to make their admission possible. As an example, of the 944 questionnaires returned, Mahan reported that while wheelchair students would not be rejected by 28 percent of the schools, only 9 percent had the necessary ramps to accommodate wheelchair users.

It appears that, with rather few exceptions, the colleges and universities of this nation are not rejecting disabled students as frequently as in the past, but in general they are not barrier free nor adequately prepared for the enrollment of larger numbers of disabled students. There are exceptions. Southern Illinois University at Carbondale has a long history of successful service to and accommodation of students with disabilities. The elimination of physical barriers was the primary goal when the program was begun in 1956, and all buildings constructed since that time are fully modified. The rehabilitation program at the University of Illinois was started in 1947 with the purpose of making it possible for individuals with severe permanent physical disabilities to attend the university and benefit from all experiences that are part of university life and common to all students. Disabled students have lived in 10 regular residence halls, participated in all extramural and intramural social and cultural activities, as well as taking part in a full-scale program of athletics and recreaton. The University of Illinois has graduated 900 disabled students from all colleges and curriculums at the baccalaureate, master's and doctoral levels, and over the years has placed 100 percent of the graduates (Nugent, 1978). St. Mary's Junior College is a co-educational institution in Minneapolis, MN, which prepares allied health and human service technicians. Through its Program for Visually Impaired and Hearing Impaired students abilities are identified, coping strategies are devised and instruction is adopted. Since 1980, sixteen disabled students have graduated as physical thěrapy assistants, occupational therapy assistants, and medical records technicians. These programs have demonstrated success by removing physical, educational and social barriers for the disabled student. The Regional Education Program, funded by the U. S. Department of Education, Office for Special Education and Rehabilitative Services, supported 14 post-secondary model programs between 1975–80 (Anderson, Hartman, Redden, 1981). These models allowed other institutions to pick and choose, modify and alter, ideas which have worked and practices which had been improved through trial and error. The majority of these programs focused on provision of services where none had existed and increasing the degree of participation by disabled students in campus activities.

For various reasons, the number of disabled persons enrolling in post-secondary programs is growing. This appears to be the trend in spite of the fact that many colleges and universities are as yet unprepared to provide the physical environment much less respond appropriately to the educational and social needs of these students. Although fewer colleges report they will reject certain disabled students than a decade ago, many are inadequately prepared to handle them. Most colleges and universities appear to be meeting 504 requirements in the naming of compliance officers, committees and designated counselors. Beyond this, it appears from the limited data, that many colleges and universities are striving to respond to as yet small numbers of disabled students on a personal basis. The picture is not clear as to how well organized our nation's colleges are to handle adequately an increasing number of disabled enrollees. There are a number of institutions that have made a commitment to the disabled student, provide accessible programs, and eagerly recruit students with special needs. There are apparently also those institutions whose policies have yet to reveal their commitment to provision of equal access for disabled students. Perhaps, as some have suggested, there is no compelling reason that all colleges and all programs must be accessible to all disabled students. Instead, it may be appropriate within a region to have one school provide accessibility to certain programs and another school other programs. While this idea may be fiscally, as well as physically attractive, it might take years to decide which program will be accessible where. In the meantime, disabled students will be rejected from admission, forced to look beyond their region or put aside their desire to achieve post-secondary training. Disabled students have demonstrated that they can succeed in college (Lawrence, Kent & Henson, 1982). A number of colleges have been very successful in accommodating disabled students, but there remains a large number of colleges and universities that have yet to make a commitment to the disabled student and prepare the necessary support system.

References

Anderson, W. R., Hartman, R. D. & Redden, M. R. (1981). *Federally funded programs for disabled students: A model for post-secondary campuses.*

Washington, DC: HEATH/Closer Look Resource Center, American Council on Education.

Astin, A. W. (1975). *Preventing students from dropping out*. San Francisco: Jossey-Bass.

Burgdorf, R. L. (1980). *The legal rights of handicapped persons*. Baltimore: Paul H. Brookes.

Cotler, S. R. & DeGraff, A. H. (1976). *Architectural accessibility for the disabled of college campuses*. Albany, NY: State University Construction Fund.

Genskow, J. K., & Maglione, F. D. (1965). Familiarity, dogmatism and reported student attitudes toward the disabled. *Journal of Social Psychology*, 67, 329–341.

Kelly, B. A. (1984). Attitudes toward disabled persons of selected collegiate coordinators for disabled students. *Journal of College Student Personnel*, 25(3), 255–260.

Laing, J. & Farmer, M. (1984). *Use of the ACT Assessment by examiners with disabilities (Report No. 84)*, Iowa City, IA: ACT Publications.

Lawrence, J. K., Kent, L., & Jenson, J. W. (1982). *The handicapped student in America's colleges: A longitudinal analysis. Part 3: Disabled 1978 college freshmen three years later*. Los Angeles, CA: Higher Education Research Inst., Inc.

Mahan, G. H. (1974). Special provisions for handicapped students in college. *Exceptional Children*, 41, 51–53.

Marion, P. B., & Iovacchini, E. V. (1983). Services for handicapped students in higher education: An analysis of national trends. *Journal of College Student Personnel*, 24(2), 131–138.

McBee, M. L. (1982). Helping handicapped students succeed in college. *Journal of the National Association for Women Deans, Administrators, and Counselors*, 45, 1–8.

Milner, M. (1980). *Adapting historic campus structures for accessibility*. Washington, DC: Association of Physical Plant Administrators of Universities and Colleges.

Nathanson, R. B. (1980). Campus interactions: Attitudes and behaviors. In J. P. Hourihan (Ed.), *Disability: The college's challenge* (pp. 17–30), New York, NY: Columbia University.

National Information Center for Handicapped Children and Youth. (1985). *News Digest* (NICHCY Publication No. 1985 0–476–239). Washington, DC: U. S. Government Printing Office.

Nugent, T. J. (1978). More than ramps and braille, *American Education*, 14(7), 11–18.

Perry, D. C. (1981). The disabled student and college counseling centers. *Journal of College Student Personnel, 22*, 533–538.

Ragosta, M. (1980). *Handicapped students and the administration of the S.A.T.* Princeton: Educational Testing Service, p. 1.

Ridenour, D. & Johnson, J. (1981). *A guide to post-secondary educational opportunities for the learning disabled.* Oak Park, IL: Time Out to Enjoy.

Stilwell, W. E., & Schulker, S. (1973). Facilities available to disabled higher education students. *Journal of College Student Personnel, 14*, 419–424.

Stilwell, D. N., Stilwell, W. E., & Perritt, L. C. (1983). *Barriers in higher education for persons with handicaps: A follow-up. 24*(4), 337–394.

U. S. Department of Health, Education and Welfare (1980). *College enrollment patterns differ for handicapped students.* Washington, DC: National Center for Education.

Part VI: Evaluation

How shall it be determined that a college or university has accomplished its missions? What programs should be designed and implemented to evaluate undergraduate education? Important considerations include the evaluation of students, programs, environment, and faculty. Who should do the evaluating, how the evaluation should take place, and when, are examined in this section.

Assessment of undergraduate students has been a concern of the public and academicians for more than three decades. Central to this concern has been the problems involving the measuring of learning versus the giving of grades. Marilyn Hadley and Patrick Vitale describe how standardized tests have come to be used increasingly as a means for evaluating the performance of students and how state officials have become increasingly involved in the evaluation process. The focus has shifted from measuring the entry level abilities of students to the measuring of the learning of students upon graduation. In light of these trends, the authors offer several recommendations on the issues of grade inflation, the use of standardized tests, and the involvement of state agencies.

Much interest has been expressed in the concept of "value added," defined as "a college or university's ability to make a positive, measurable difference in each student's intellectual and personal development." William R. Donohue and David L. Struckman-Johnson examine this concept. They admit to feelings of anxiety as a result of their investigation, cautioning the reader about the inflexible application of the "value added" concept and its psychometric limitations. They conclude that states considering its use should progress with special scrutiny. States that are considering using "value added" should develop a mutuality of commitment, purpose, direction, and design; and should be aware of its limitations.

Arlen R. Gullickson argues that the evaluation of faculty in higher education is ineffective, that is not practical, in most colleges and universities. Advocating that faculty evaluation should be separated into components, he suggests that steps be taken to initiate faculty development for all faculty members and that the objectives and procedures for faculty development be separated from summative evaluation. This, he believes, will result in more appropriate data gathering and analyses. As a result, faculty evaluation will serve faculty improvements in more meaningful ways.

Assessment of Student Achievement

Marilyn Hadley and Patrick Vitale

The focus of the public examination of education has shifted from elementary and secondary schools to institutions of higher learning with the release of a report entitled "Involvement in Learning: Realizing the Potential of American Higher Education" by the National Institute of Education (NIE) study group on the conditions of excellence in American higher education (Mortimer et al., 1984). The purpose of the study group was to make recommendations for improvement in undergraduate education in postsecondary institutions. The report focuses on student learning and makes recommendations for its accomplishment by demonstrating improvements in student outcomes, e.g., in their knowledge, capacities, skills, and attitudes before entering the institution and before graduation. The group contends that the quality of student learning can be significantly improved if postsecondary institutions of higher learning would meet three conditions of excellence: student involvement, high expectations, and assessment and feedback.

It is not surprising that assessment and feedback were identified by the NIE study group, since assessment of student achievement in education serves many functions. It is an integral part of teaching and learning and the questioning and answering process in class and through observation of students (Scriven, 1967). When formative assessment provides feedback to instructor and student about the latter's progress early enough, needed changes in the instructional efforts can be made. On the other hand, summative assessment determines the degree of achievement of major outcomes of a student's course of study (Bloom, Hastings & Madaus, 1971).

Historically, assessment of student achievement has been a concern of both the public and academicians. In the early 1950s, a movement began to improve college and university teaching. A study of teaching practices at that time indicated that faculty skills and efforts to construct reliable tests were limited, thus raising concerns about the use of grades (Umstattd, 1954). Umstattd voiced a concern about measuring learning versus giving grades, and recommended careful study of this problem by institutions.

Becker, Geer and Hughes (1968) echoed the concern of the conflict between learning and grades in their study of college students. As a result of a two-year ethnographic study of undergraduates at the University of Kansas, they found that grades were the major institutional "valuable." Personal intellectual growth and scholarship were important to some students but were not viewed as universally valuable as grades. They also found that students were able to get good grades without necessarily learning. In the students' opinion, success was measured by a good grade point average. Becker et al. (1968) concluded that the anti-intellectualism of grading results in a dilemma of how to reward true achievement rather than grade-getting skills.

According to Oldenquist (1983), attitudes about testing as evil and grading as a way of labeling individuals as successes or failures were a result of the social turmoil of the 1960s and 1970s, an era when the rights of women, blacks, disadvantaged, and handicapped were promoted. It is during this time that scores on the Scholastic Aptitude Test began an 18–year decline and that grade inflation at all educational levels began, which contributed to the public lack of confidence in the traditional evaluation system. Oldenquist attributes the "decline in education" to a reluctance of educators to apply strict standards because they could not see the difference between the elitism implied by standards and the elitism of social class or privileged group.

Current Concerns

In view of the previously cited literature, it is apparent that dissatisfaction with grading and evaluating students has been an issue for more than three decades. What is new in the 1980s is a change in the focus of concern: (1) standardized tests are being used increasingly as a way of evaluating students, (2) the level of intervention has shifted from the local institution to state officials and groups, and (3) the focus of standardized testing is shifting from measuring entry level ability to measuring student achievement.

An important matter in the appraisal of student achievement is deciding what "achievement" means. That is, when we operationally define student achievement, are we speaking of basic skills, knowledge of a particular subject area (e.g., history, chemistry, etc.), general education, higher level thinking skills, or a combination of any of them? Before we evaluate student achievement we need to make a decision about which we are interested.

Current Practices

In order to meet the condition of excellence for assessment and feedback, the Study Group (Mortimer et al., 1984) calls for the establishment and maintenance of high standards of institutional and student performance. It calls for entry standards to be identified and publicly stated in terms of student knowledge and skills, as opposed to the accumulation of a given number of credits because credits are "measures of time and performance, and they do not indicate the academic worth of course content" (p. 13). The purpose of this paper is to describe current evaluation practices used in undergraduate education at entry, during a student's program, and at graduation. The authors will then recommend what can be done to assist institutions in responding to the concerns about evaluation.

Entry level evaluation. Admission criteria for undergraduate programs generally include some combination of college entrance examination scores, high school grade point average or rank in class, and specific type and number of high school courses. A review of admission requirements for sixteen public and four private institutions in five Upper Great Plains states was conducted by the authors using *The College Handbook 1984–85* (The College Board, 1984). Most institutions require high school class rank or standardized test scores (ACT is preferred, SAT is accepted). Three private institutions consider both class rank and test scores along with the high school record. Four of the institutions, all public, still maintain open admission for resident students.

As mentioned previously, the use of college entrance exam scores is generally accepted as one criterion for admission. The mean SAT and ACT scores have declined from the mid 1960s to the mid 1980s. However, this trend seems to have been reversed recently.

Institutions have also used standardized tests for counseling and placement purposes. These efforts have been strengthened by new initiatives taken by legislatures during the past few years (Mingle,

1985). For example, the Florida legislature has mandated that entry tests of basic computation and communication skills be used as screening devices, and students who require remediation enroll in community college "college prep" courses. In New Jersey, all entering freshmen and transfers take a basic skills test of reading comprehension, sentence sense, computation and elementary algebra. Test data are used for course placement and counseling. In Ohio, high school juniors are tested in writing, science readiness, and math skills. Students receive feedback from the college of their choice in time to take corrective action in their senior year.

In summary, requirements and standards used for admission generally include high school grade point average or rank in class, successful completion of certain high school courses, and/or college entrance exam scores. The trend has recently been to increase the requirements and standards. Tests are also increasingly used to counsel and place students in courses.

Formative evaluation of student progression. Once a student is admitted into an undergraduate program, s/he is generally evaluated by professors as part of an individual course as well as in terms of progression in an academic program. Within courses, professors collect information about student behavior in order to assign grades. In addition, professional programs generally set standards for admission into their upper level program, which is usually the last two years of undergraduate work.

The formal evaluation of the student is generally recorded using a five-point scale, ranging from 4 = A to 0 = F (Millman, Slovacek, Kulik, & Mitchell, 1983). A student's performance can be measured in a variety of ways, including tests, papers, classroom discussion, lab work, and attendance. The emphasis on tests and classroom contribution in the 1950s (Umstattd, 1954) has changed somewhat over time to include an emphasis on papers (Barnes, 1984). Assessment is continuous, often with weekly assignments and several tests prior to the final exam.

Becker et al. (1968) describe the teaching/learning situation "as actually an exchange of reward for performance, rather than as some kind of an educational process" (p. 63). They propose that a classroom contract exists on an informal basis, the terms of which are discovered by the student via the course syllabus, the professor's actions and words, and information from students who have had the course previously. Expanding on this idea of a contract, Barnes (1984) suggests that students actively engage faculty in the process of grading and that the final grade is a consequence of negotiations between the student and professor.

In an Educational Testing Service study of graduates during the 1960s and 1970s, it was found that colleges and universities initiated changes in their grading policies to include pass/fail and credit/no credit options (Suslow, 1976). Incompletes were increasingly given in place of Ds and Fs, and grading systems were adopted that included the assignment of greater than four points for A+ (e.g., 4.3 or 4.5).

Grade inflation is described as a progressive rise in undergraduate grade point averages accompanied by a continuous decrease in SAT and ACT scores, which are measures of student ability (Bejar & Bleu, 1981). Since 1974, grade point averages have tended to level out and seem to have remained fairly consistent, indicating that grade inflation has been arrested. However, it does not mean that grade inflation has ended. In contrast to 1964, we are still in a period of grade inflation.

Institutions are aware that grade inflation has occurred, and are beginning to monitor grade distributions (Mingle, 1985). Hambleton and Murray (1977) surveyed faculty and student views concerning the uses of grades in different instructional settings and the appropriateness of grading systems in common use for accomplishing the intended uses of grades. The major conclusion of the faculty and students was that a criterion referenced grading system was more desirable for evaluating course outcome than a norm referenced grading system. The term "criterion referenced test" was coined by Glasser (1963) to describe instruments which would best apportion students to mastery or nonmastery status. Black (1986) indicates how assessment might be developed to be of direct value to both instructor and student via formative assessment with particular emphasis placed on criterion referenced procedures.

Despite the concern about grade inflation, grades continue to be the traditional measure of student achievement in courses and student progression from general coursework to professional schools. A recent development is the requirement of standardized test scores to advance to upper level courses (Mingle, 1985). In Mississippi, the ACT-COMP must be taken in order to enter the teacher education program. Florida requires students to pass a minimum competency exam in order to advance to the last two years of coursework. In Georgia, students may begin taking the Regents tests as sophomores and may retake it as many times as necessary. It must be passed in order to graduate.

Thus, grades continue to be used by faculty to measure student achievement in their courses. Their use is being questioned today, and is increasingly being replaced by standardized tests taken by the students at the end of their sophomore and senior years. This seems to imply a lack of confidence on the part of the public, corporations and college administrators in faculty grading of their students.

Summative evaluation. Until recently, little attention has been given to measuring student performance at graduation. A 1978 survey of institutions involved in accreditation-related self-studies found that only one in three had generated or examined data on student growth and learning (Mortimer et al., 1984). Another finding was that only 23% had measured students' knowledge in their major field.

This situation is changing rapidly, as states increasingly mandate the use of standardized tests for judging student achievement at graduation in an effort to tighten exit standards. Five states have currently implemented the value added approach. Other states (e.g., Georgia) have identified licensing exams as exit measures, especially in the teaching and nursing areas (Mingle, 1985). The Tennessee legislature is requiring institutions of higher education to quantify evidence of improvement in student standardized scores at graduation (Mingle, 1985).

Studies of student performance on subject-area tests of the GRE and other standardized tests have been conducted recently. From 1964 to 1982, student performance on 11 of 15 major subject area tests of the Graduate Record Exam declined (Mortimer et al., 1984). A follow-up study of student performance on 23 different standardized tests during the same time found declines in 65% of the tests (Mingle, 1985).

Thus, exit evaluation is becoming an important aspect of judging student achievement in an undergraduate program. At the same time that states are moving in this direction, however, the NIE Study Group cautions that we must keep our sights on student learning, not just on student test scores.

Summary and Recommendations

The concern about measuring what a student has actually learned versus assigning grades is an historical one. The concern was voiced in the late 1940s and early 1950s at a time when enrollments expanded and a national movement to improve college and university teaching developed. This same concern was also expressed in the 1960s and in the 1970s. Today concern is also expressed about learning versus earning credit hours (Mortimer et al., 1984).

From 1964 to 1974, grade inflation was experienced nationwide. For the past decade, the average GPA has remained fairly stable, indicating that we continue to have an inflated grading system. Mingle (1985) identified the loss of confidence in grading practices of faculty as one reason for state bodies to become involved in higher education. The NIE Study Group (Mortimer et al., 1984) writes that colleges and universities "should establish and maintain high standards of student and institutional performance" (p. 3), implying that these standards do not exist universally now.

State initiatives into areas traditionally reserved for university faculty have increased dramatically in the 1980s and will continue to do so for several years. Involvement by state legislatures and boards of regents has probably also resulted from lack of confidence in higher education institutions' ability to maintain standards (Mingle, 1985). Certainly this involvement is an extension of earlier involvement for reforms in the K–12 grades.

One major result of state level involvement has been an increase in the use of standardized tests. While standardized tests were often required for college admission in the past, current practices are often at three data points: entry into college, progression into upper level undergraduate courses or programs, and graduation. The use of standardized tests allows for norm comparison of large numbers of students across colleges and universities nationally.

The trend toward standardized testing is not receiving unconditional endorsement. A caution has been expressed by the NIE Study Group (Mortimer et al., 1984) that test scores do not become the substitute for measuring learning. It recommends that a comprehensive approach to evaluating student learning be developed, with attention to graduation standards.

In light of these trends, the authors offer several recommendations. These are focused on the issues of grading and grade inflation, the use of standardized tests and the involvement of state agencies.

1. State agencies should involve university and college faculty in studying and adopting changes. Faculty morale is a key factor in maintaining and increasing student learning (Mortimer et al., 1984). Faculty and administrators should set output goals, such as students should be able to think critically, recognize cultural diversity or develop creatively. Data are already available about students at entry which should be used for counseling and placement in courses. As more data become available at exit, faculty and administrators should be involved in assessing to what extent students are meeting the goals of the institution.

2. Standardized tests should be developed at the state or local level if economically feasible. Since the United States does not have a national curriculum, the use of a series of national tests raises questions of validity. A study should be conducted on the influence of standardized tests on local curricula.

3. An instructional model which if based on systematic evaluations, such as that described by Gronlund (1985), should be used in identifying learning outcomes expected of students, preassessing students at entry, providing assessment feedback during the undergraduate program, and measuring for intended outcomes at graduation.

4. Colleges and universities should consider changing to a thirteen-point grading scale if the five-point grading scale (A to F) is currently in use. The thirteen-point grading scale includes plus and minus grades in addition to the letter grades used in the five-point scale, and maintains the numerical values of the five-point scale. Its advantage is realized when grade inflation exists, as it currently does in most colleges and universities throughout the country. With increased grade inflation, there are fewer grade categories and therefore a decrease in discrimination, which affects the reliability (and its validity) of the grade point averages. With the use of the thirteen-point scale, discrimination is increased by increasing the number of categories. As a result, the reliability and validity of the grade point average is also increased.

5. Colleges and universities should consider the use of criterion reference grading (CRG) rather than norm reference grading (NRG). CRG uses the same letter grades as NRG with the exception that the grades are assigned to students to reflect their level of performance. Thus, students are judged upon their own merit with respect to some standards set by the instructor. This could be a way to begin to measure knowledge and skills as opposed to test-taking skills.

6. Colleges and universities should continue to monitor grade inflation at the course, discipline, department, school and college levels to identify and determine the possible causes for increases in grade point averages.

None of these recommendations can be easily implemented. However, each responds to a trend or concern that has developed over the past three decades. Reforms will continue while public concern is focused on higher education. Change should result from a cooperative approach to improving the credibility of grades and measuring learning.

References

Barnes, L. R. (1984). The negotiation of grades as a central feature of an educational exchange program. *College and University*, 59(2), 136–149.

Becker, H. S., Geer, B., & Hughes, E. (1968). *Making the grade*. New York: John Wiley and Sons, Inc.

Bejar, I. I., & Bleu, E. O. (1981). Grade inflation and the validity of the Scholastic Aptitude Test. *American Educational Research Journal*, 18(2), 143–156.

Bloom, G. S., Hastings, J. J., & Madaus, G. F. (1971). *Handbook on formative and summative evaluations of student learning*. New York: McGraw-Hill.

College Handbook—1984–85. (1984). New York: College Entrance Examination Board.

Donohue, W. R., & Struckman-Johnson, D. (1985, October). The value added of a college education. *Understanding Undergraduate Education*. Symposium conducted by The School of Education, The University of South Dakota, Vermillion, South Dakota.

Gronlund, N. E. (1981). *Measurement and evaluation in teaching*. New York: Macmillan.

Hambleton, R. K., & Murray, J. (1977, November). A comparative study and student attitudes toward a variety of college grading purposes and practices. *Research in Education*.

Millman, J., Slovacek, S., Kulick, E., & Mitchell, K. (1983). Does grade inflation affect the reliability of grades? *Research in Higher Education*, 19, 423–429.

Mingle, J. R. (1985). *Measuring the educational achievement of under-graduates: State and national developments*. Denver, CO: State Higher Education Executive Officers Association. (ERIC Document Reproduction Service No. ED 254 139.)

Mortimer, K. P., Astin, A. W., Blake, J. H., Bowen, H. R., Gamson, Z. T., Hodgkinson, H. L., & Lee, B. (1984). *Involvement in learning: Realizing the potential of American higher education*. Washington, DC: National Institute of Education.

Nuttall, D. L. (1986). *Assessing educational achievement*. PA: The Falmer Press.

Oldenquist, A. (1983, May). The decline of American education in the 60's and 70's. *American Education*, 12–18.

Scriven, M. (1967). The methodology of evaluation. *AERA Monograph Services on Curriculum Evaluation*, 1, 39–83.

Suslow, S. (1976). *A report on an interinstitutional survey of undergraduate scholastic grading, 1960's to 1970's*. Berkeley, CA: University of California, Office of Institutional Research. (ERIC Document Reproduction Service No. ED 129 187.)

Umstattd. (1954). *Teaching procedures*. Austin, TX: University Cooperative Society, Inc.

A Closer Look at Value Added

*William R. Donohue and David L.
Struckman-Johnson*

Introduction

Presently sweeping the country from convention to conference are the disciples from Northeast Missouri State University (NEMSU) at Kirksville. Their topic is "value added." On the heels of their publication with the American Association of State Colleges and Universities titled *Degrees With Integrity* (1984), the authors are in great demand. Their work deserves a closer examination.

The subtitle of their publication is "A Value-Added Approach To Undergraduate Assessment." The focus is on a massive amount of testing and measurement to document change and anticipated learning from the collegiate experience. The program has been developed over the last twelve years with careful institutional scrutiny and much legislative attention. We think it deserves closer scrutiny.

It appears that this publication has "piggy backed" on other 1984 studies calling for more involvement and assessment in undergraduate education. These publications have administrators and governing boards searching for new solutions to old problems in the face of declining enrollments and resources with rising needs for accountability. Clearly, these publications are timely and important contributions to today's higher education, but we feel their relation to "value added" needs closer inspection.

A closer look? If someone is improving the blueprint, validating the commitment, and answering the queries for quality education, what is there to examine? The authors will explore three concerns: (1) the credibility of the concept versus the application to date, (2) the measurement design itself, and (3) the application for statewide systems. Throughout, this paper will also examine motivation, testing mechanisms, data use, and impact on teaching. It will be especially concerned with the system-wide use and "top down" approach for South Dakota, the nation's first state to adopt valued added. It will conclude with a strong warning to all managers and "quick fix accountability seekers."

The Missouri Connection

There has been a remarkable pioneering effort in Kirksville. Fraught with risk, much like a heart patient, this former teacher preparatory school saw the potential for a new or stronger life. The risks of rejection by students, faculty, and alumni were great. Even greater was a potential rejection by prospective students wanting a more traditional route, an assault by jealous sister institutions, or misunderstanding by legislators and funding agencies. At this writing, funding, applications, and internal support are all healthy.

This new vibrancy is not without detractors and critics as this paper attests, but such reactions were anticipated from the beginning. And, that may be the most remarkable part of its success; a strong, far looking, patient institutional approach. At each step in the journey, NEMSU welcomed questions and challenges.

The Goals of Value Added

Value added is asserted to be one means toward the end of increased student learning. It is defined as "a college or university's ability to make a positive, measurable difference in each student's intellectual and personal development" (Northeast Missouri State University, 1984). The learning-added goals for the institution are three part: cognitive, affective and psychomotor. In practice the learning goals are measured through a massive commitment to testing and assessment.

The primary commitment is to classroom learning and constitutes the major focus to date. Test-retest usage of the several American College Testing (ACT) instruments attempts to measure underclass general educational development, while nationalized graduate tests assess academic field development.

There are other goals unabashedly identified by the value-added designers. And, they are as tightly measured. College placement success and retention to graduation are vital targets. While the psycho-motor and affective domains of value added were late in development, the exhaustive sampling of student attitudes and satisfaction are becoming as regularized as Graduate Record Examination (GRE) tests.

Finally there are key, but secondary goals. Is anybody taking notice? Has the legislature rewarded this specific and measurable offering of accountability? Have the state's employers recognized the value added to this school's graduates? Are these graduates more sought after and better paid because they have presumably learned more than their predecessors? Are the alumni feeling better about the value now being added to their degrees as measured by annual giving?

How Does It Work

Value added is both a management construct and a teaching-learning process. The *management* of several of testing strategies and 17,000 tests is no small task. Coordinating, and assessing learning patterns is equally diverse in scope. Freshmen are divided into two groups for the purpose of measuring general education. One group takes the ACT COMP (College Outcomes Measurement Program) test at the beginning of their first year and, again, at the end of their second year. The other group repeats, at the end of their sophomore year, the ACT assessment test that all matriculants take before entering NEMSU. The two groups are compared and the results are shared with students and advisors.

Seniors are required to take a nationalized test in their field before graduation. These range from the Graduate Record Examination (GRE) and the National Teacher's Examination (NTE) to tests developed and refined locally. It is these tests which are most scrutinized and which become the focus for "adding value." From a curriculum management point of view the questions become how can we improve learning, scores, and efficiency?

All measurements are then evaluated in terms of overall institutional learning, but not before student input is received through the Student Opinion Survey, the Enrolling Student Survey, and an alumni survey, all offered by ACT. Along with even more specific feedback instruments in various service units, these measurements are included in the total management focus on learning. Can residence hall libraries and computer labs increase classroom performance? Can different financial aid packaging or delivery systems reduce stress on the NEMSU learner?

Management also includes getting the word out. Helping all constituents, internal and external, know the importance of this mission for everyone remotely tied to Missouri or NEMSU is as key to successful test taking as it is to funding, awareness and recruiting. Dean of Student Affairs Terry Smith has a political science Ph.D. and is keenly aware of the constituent impact. In his consultant's report to the State of South Dakota, Smith said, "testing, its uses, and its potential for impacting the quality of higher education are anything but trivial, and the Regents and chief executive officers should expressly reaffirm their commitment to and prioritization of the concept" (1984, p. 7).

The *teaching-learning concept* is two-fold. One portion is the introduction of assessment as a positive learning mode. The non-graded use of general education assessment is used to expose the freshman and sophomore to his or her relative functioning level both nationally and on campus. These tests claim to "pinpoint" student weakness for future study and advising.

The second portion is an institutional commitment to compete, department by department, for higher scores on nationally normed instruments. In some departments, where no nationally normed instrument exists, NEMSU has designed its own. All departments monitor changes in scores, evaluate curriculum design, and encourage students in their preparation for the examination.

The learning is done, theoretically, by both teacher and student. NEMSU has used 12 years of testing to refine its curriculum. The design is for students and faculty to share a focus on learning and the testing process that improves and enhances it.

That's the design. Much is in place and working well. There are problems, some acknowledged, some less discussed. The problems not yet well addressed will be the central focus of our examination. Clearly the former has received ample attention by both NEMSU and its disciples.

Concerns

Concept Versus Application

Of initial concern to the authors is the credibility of the concept versus its application to date. In twelve years, the academic testing has received almost exclusive attention. Only in the last two years has the affective domain been addressed. The psychomotor domain has received even less attention. Are they really "value afterthoughts" to dress up an otherwise enormous testing program?

Secondly, is the relationship of these cognitive elements to the intellectual integrated in a basic developmental philosophical grounding? It appears not, and raises questions of learning for score sake, a not so uncommon theme heard in secondary education.

A third concern directed at the integrated concept of value added is the use of comparisons. The cognitive measures of seniors' levels of achievement have been compared with the national norms for years. Yet the affective component of development has not been as aggressively compared. Two reasons are offered: the high attrition of freshmen and, the absence of counseling services on campus. Are these "values" of higher education, or just fallout from a larger commitment to scores and learning? It may be a premature criticism given the lateness of affective measurement on campus and the absence of psychomotor norming data, but it underlines the notion of testing versus a full commitment to NEMSU's definition of value added. Our primary focus of concern, however, deals with the actual psychometric underpinnings of value added—the cognitive measurements. There are serious flaws which bear scrutiny and exploration.

The Measurement Plan

Alexander Astin (1968), credited with borrowing the value-added expression for higher education, alerted researchers nearly two decades ago about the difficulty in this type of research methodology. The "added inputs" to higher education are very illusive and their interaction is difficult to measure. The designs are not so simple as to allow direct or clear measurement.

One of the classic dilemmas that Astin (1970) points out is whether or not the school itself is an input of added dimension. Or is a particular cognitive skill learned because of courses, people, or individual maturation? He concludes that "Merely collecting data does not assure true college efforts will be identified and spurious efforts will not." We believe that this concern may be of great relevance.

As we explained previously, a major component of the testing program may be the sophomore ACT retest, the ACT COMP freshman-sophomore test-retest and senior exit testing. Although we believe that all three of these measurement plans are problematic and could result in misleading information, space limitations prevent a thorough discussion of all three plans. The ACT COMP test-retest may be the most appropriate of the three components in that the test is reliable and valid for its purpose which is basically the assessment of progress in college. It is flexible (5 different instruments) and can utilize a variety of scoring and measurement options. For these reasons, we think it is most appropriate to focus our attention on the ACT retest and exit testing components of the program.

ACT Assessment Retest Group. The primary criticism of ACT Assessment test-retesting is by ACT itself. In the *only* analysis we are aware of done on the use of the ACT test in this fashion, Lenning, Munday, and Maxey (1969) cited a number of concerns. We will discuss them along with some of our own concerns in the following section of this paper.

The ACT retesting plan can be categorized as a fairly traditional pretest/post-test experimental paradigm but with the obvious absence of a control or comparison group. That is, there is only a treated or manipulated group, not an untreated, unmanipulated group against which to compare changes which occur in the treatment group. Various researchers (Campbell & Stanley, 1963; Cook & Campbell, 1979) have categorized this kind of research design as pre-experimental or non-experimental in the sense that the requirements of a good scientific experiment are far from being met. There are a number of problems associated with this kind of research design which make interpretation of results difficult if not impossible. A few of the most serious are discussed in the following paragraphs.

One problem common to research conducted without a comparison group is the inability to control or adjust for events other than the intended manipulation which could result in a change. An excellent example of this kind of problem is found in the case of the student who takes the ACT Assessment test as a high school junior. The student taking the test as a high school junior or early in the senior year of high school is obviously without the benefit of senior level courses in math and English. At the same time, many college bound high school students will have taken a senior level math and English course by the time they reach college. We now have a group of students who have been exposed to both relevant high school courses and freshman/sophomore level college courses between ACT Assessment testings. How then can any change in scores be attributed to the college courses rather than the senior level high school courses? In fact, without a non-college comparison group, it cannot.

Another problem in no-comparison-group designs is related to the psychometric characteristics of high scores. Specifically, the phenomena of regression to the mean and ceiling effects can make interpretation of pre-post-test scores extremely difficult. When we speak of regression to the mean we are referring to the tendency of persons scoring high on pretests to score closer to the mean on post-tests independent of any manipulation or outside influences and the reverse effect for persons scoring low on the pretest. This phenomenon has no impact on interpretation of scores when groups are not selected on the basis of extreme scores. It can be controlled even when extreme groups are selected if a comparison group is available. Unfortunately, groups may be selected on the basis of extreme scores in that some institutions require higher ACT scores for admission than others. Again, there is no comparison group in the value-added design. One could actually argue that the ACT Assessment scores at the institutions with higher entrance requirements would drop at retest, and the ACT Assessment scores at the institutions with lower entrance requirements would increase at retest — independent of any "value" added to the student. These increases or decreases would be confounded with any other changes that took place and result in change scores with at least some unknown component.

Another sort of problem that exists with high scores is typically referred to as ceiling effect. This simply refers to the fact that there is an upper limit to how well people can perform on exams. If one group has an average pretest score of 50 percent, it clearly has more room for improvement than another group with an average pretest score of 90. Ceiling effects, like effects due to regression to the mean do not exist unless high scoring groups are selected and they can be controlled by use of a comparison group.

A number of additional problems exist within the ACT Assessment retest research design which are not related to the absence of a comparison group, but which nonetheless make interpretation of changes in scores a nearly impossible task. One of these problems has to do with the motivation level of the test takers at the two test administrations. At the time of the pretest, motivation is undoubtedly high for most students in that minimum score cutoffs for admission are specified by virtually all institutes of higher education. At the time of the post-test, the motivation to do well is a function of factors which are almost certainly less relevant to the student. There may be some intrinsic motivation to "meet the challenge" of the exam, and there may be some motivation to do well because it is "important to improving education" at a particular institution. There may well also be, however, resentment as a function of giving up a Saturday morning to take a required exam which results in a score that has no impact either positive or negative on a student. In any case, it would be hard to argue that the motivation at the post-test was as high as the motivation at the pretest.

Another problem unrelated to absent comparison groups but potentially important to the interpretation of change scores is the nature of the ACT Assessment test. The test is by design a selection tool for colleges which is a measure of general ability and knowledge generally appropriate for high school level coursework. ACT itself (Lenning et al., 1969) cites an example of this kind of problem.

> [T]he ACT English test, with its emphasis on grammar and detecting bad writing, would be appropriate for average and below average sections. But the upper sections may study literature. Literature is not covered in the ACT tests. On retest the students who were initially low and average would be expected to show gain because they had just been studying this material. In contrast, the initially high students would show little or no gain and perhaps even regress. Since they had not been studying the material in college, the test for them would be more one of memory than of English grammar and writing. (p. 146–147)

The data provided by ACT in the same article support this logic in that English majors (those most likely to be in literature or advanced sections) show less gain on the ACT English subtest than do math and science majors.

Exit Testing. When we consider the component of the testing program designed to measure knowledge in the major area, the concept of "value added" can no longer be applied. There is no baseline measure of value and hence no way of determining what part of the end product is added and what existed initially. Indeed, the NEMSU disciples will explain when confronted with this paradox that the concept of "value added" is really only relevant to the testing of sophomores. The testing of seniors, they explain, is "norm-based." That is, we compare the scores of our seniors to those of seniors at other universities to determine where we fit in the overall scheme of things.

The use of "norm-based" tests assumes a number of things. Two of the most important are that there are appropriate norm-based tests available for a particular subject area and that the norming group is comparable to the test group of interest—in our case, the entire senior class of a state university. We believe that both of these critical assumptions are problematic.

Appropriate examinations. We believe there are many collegiate majors for which appropriate exit examinations do not exist. The general assumption is that the GRE Subject Test is an appropriate norm-based exam for senior testing. They have qualified this general assumption in some cases, notably for education majors, where the National Teacher Examination (NTE) is the examination of choice. In the case of education majors, one could argue that indeed the NTE is an appropriate examination to assess the success of education majors. At the very least, the NTE is designed for that purpose. We question, however, the blanket assumption that the GRE Subject Exam is appropriate for all those majors for which it exists and further suggest that a multitude of problems exist for those majors without a standardized examination. These concerns are explained in more detail in the following section of this paper.

The GRE Subject Exams are not *by design* measures of a student's progress in a particular major, but rather a selection device for graduate schools. Using the exams as measures of progress can be problematic. The computer science major serves as an example. Within the field of computer science, there is a core curriculum suggested by the Association for Computing Machinery, the major national professional organization of computer scientists. Most universities with computer science majors require this set of core courses in addition to a number of computer science elective courses. Although all students will experience the same set of core computer science courses, the selection of electives is guided by a student's future interests. Those students who intend to seek employment at the end of their baccalaureate education will typically select a set of electives with an applied orientation. Those students whose objectives include graduate school will typically choose a set of electives with a more theoretical orientation so that they will be better prepared for the sorts of experiences typical of graduate education in computer science. The GRE Subject Test in computer science is designed to tap both the knowledge acquired in core courses and in a set of theoretically oriented electives. In other words, the material relevant to success in graduate school. Currently, at some universities, less than ten percent of the computer science graduates attend graduate school. This means that for more than ninety percent of the computer science majors, significant parts of the GRE Subject Test in computer science are based on material they have not been exposed to — not because there is anything missing from their major but because they chose a track directed toward employment rather than a track directed toward graduate school. Although we used the computer science major to illustrate our point, a large number of majors have very similar test content/curriculum discrepancies.

If we are to assume that the exit exam scores are not to be considered trivial then we also must assume that there will be some desire (pressure?) to increase the scores on exit exams. We believe this will cause major problems when the exams are less than totally appropriate for a discipline. Clearly, the easiest way to increase examination scores is to focus teaching on the material most relevant to the exams. In those cases where the designated exit exam does not mirror the department's curriculum, a problem does exist. Does a department modify its course offerings to better match the content of an exit exam or suffer the consequences of not generating increased exam scores on a yearly basis? Does the psychology department change the History of Psychology course from an elective to a major requirement because they know that the GRE Subject Exam in psychology emphasizes the history of psychology? If so, who now determines the requirements of a psychology major—the Educational Testing Service who developed the exam, a supervisory board who mandated the exam, or the faculty?

Let us now turn to the second part of the exit test problem—the absence of a standardized, norm-based exam for some majors. NEMSU developed their own examinations at the local level to address this problem. When an entire system is involved in testing and a major is offered on more than one campus within the system, there is the expectation that intercampus cooperation will result in a single system wide test. Assuming that such tests can and will be developed, let us consider what the results will mean.

The test results from the first year will consist of a set of numbers that will necessarily be viewed in isolation. There will be no norms since these are locally developed exams and there will be no data from previous years. The designers of the test will be obligated to interpret the scores in terms of their subjective opinions of how difficult the exams were relative to the scores of their students. One of the reasons that exams are curved is that examiners can not always predict the difficulty of an exam prior to its administration. It seems unlikely that the designers of local exit exams will be able to do better designing an exit exam the first time than they do in designing a normal course exam the first time.

When the locally constructed exams are given the second year, scores need no longer be viewed in isolation. At least scores need not be viewed in isolation if the exams given the second year are the same as the first year. If changes are made in the exam, then we would again appear to have an exam without a basis for comparison. If changes are not made in the exam, then one could compare the second year's scores to the first to determine if an improvement or decline had taken place. Any differences would, however, have to be considered in light of prior knowledge of the exam topics or questions that filtered down from one year's senior class to the next and any differences in relevant demographic characteristics of the two classes.

Appropriate norms. The second major concern we have with the use of norm-based exit exams is the norming groups associated with the mandated exams. In the case of the NTE, the norm group consists primarily of senior education majors who are assumed representative of the general population of senior education majors. To the extent that this assumption is true, this group of individuals represents what most would consider a reasonable norm group against which to compare senior education majors at a particular university. In the case of those majors designated for GRE Subject Exam testing, the composition of the norm groups is not in the least representative of the senior class in any given major. The GRE Subject Exams are designed as selection tools for graduate schools. Those students who most of us would identify as the best and the brightest make up the majority of the norm groups for the GRE Subject Exams. While this situation is exactly as it should be for graduate school selection committees, it makes interpretation of scores for an entire senior class somewhat problematic. What does it mean, for example, when the average score for seniors in a particular major is at the 30th percentile? In a technical sense it means that the average of the entire senior class of a particular major is at the 30th percentile of that subset of students in the rest of the country who are planning to go to graduate school in that major. In a more practical sense, we submit that there is no way of knowing whether the 30th percentile is good or bad because the norms for the GRE Subject Exam are not applicable to senior classes in general, only to students planning on attending graduate school. Because norms are so convenient, however, we see a danger in the potential misinterpretation of the numbers supplied so easily as a result of exit testing. Dr. Terry Smith in his consultancy report to the State of South Dakota stated the following:

> It would be a mistake for a decision-maker to say "your average GRE is 35th percentile; you must have a weak program." It would not be a

mistake to say "your average GRE is 35th percentile. I know the national competition is stiff. What can we do to raise it to the 50th percentile within three years?" (1984, p. 5)

What Dr. Smith is really saying is that our entire senior class should be as good, on average, as the average student planning to attend graduate school from the rest of the universities in the country. Our concern is that if a high level administrator at an institution with 12 years experience in value added and exit testing can so grossly misinterpret the meaning of norms, it seems unreasonable that regents with no background in testing and measurement will be able to do much better.

A closely related issue is the motivation of seniors as compared to the motivation level of the typical student taking the GRE Subject Test. For most persons taking a GRE Subject Test, the outcome is critical to future career plans and motivation to do well clearly exists. For a senior taking the GRE Subject Test because it is required for graduation, the motivation to do well may or may not exist. One could argue that appropriate "marketing" of the exam could result in motivation to do well. Indeed, "marketing" of exit testing is recommended by NEMSU. One could also argue that no marketing program could generate the motivation level intrinsic in the "normal" GRE Subject Test norm group. We suggest that motivation level is simply another factor confounding any interpretation of student scores in relation to GRE Subject Test national norms.

Conclusion

Who gets the results? How will the data be used? What are the targets? Will a minimum score be required to graduate? Will tenure and promotion for faculty members, or department funding be tied to scores? These questions don't have answers and create a sharp source of apprehension.

Whether or not the scores and comparisons are an opiate for managers, they are clearly a cause for concern. These concerns were expressed by the State Higher Education Executive Officers in the 1985 release of *The modern concept* (Glenny). They state:

Boards should recognize the continuing worth and understanding of democratic process . . . and . . . the most successful [Board] coordination involves widespread participation by faculty and administrators of the coordinated institutions. (p. 14, 21)

Similar concerns were echoed at a national conference in October of 1985 when Kenneth Mortimer (Chairman of the study panel which published *Involvement in Learning: Realizing the Potential of American High School Education*) said, "Academic administrators have only a few years to decide what to do about assessment before the states tell us what to do" (cited in Jacobson, 1985). At the same conference Charles Muscatine followed with, "Whether we like it or not, it is coming under auspices which may be worse than anyone here might organize" (cited in Jacobson).

The authors share an anxiety-added feeling about value added. It emerges first from its swift and inflexible application and second from its psychometric limitations. Nevertheless, NEMSU can be proud of its pioneering effort at the illusive measure of learning in higher education. NEMSU has earned its national recognition. The students, faculty and staff have struggled and grown from their mutual effort.

References

Astin, A. W. (1968). Undergraduate achievement and institutional "excellence." *Science, 161,* 661–667.

Astin, A. W. (1970). The methodology of research on college impact, part one. *Sociology of Education, 43,* 223–254.

Campbell, D. T. & Stanley, J. C. (1963). *Experimental and quasi-experimental designs.* Chicago: Rand McNally.

Cook, T. D. & Campbell, D. T. (1979). *Quasi-experimentation: Design and analysis issues for field settings.* Chicago: Rand McNally.

Jacobson, R. L. (1985, October 9). Leading advocates of reform in undergraduate education find that it's not so easy to move from rhetoric to action. *Chronicle of Higher Education,* p. 24.

Glenny, L. A. (1985). *The modern concept.* Denver: State Higher Education Executive Officers.

Lenning, O. T., Munday, L. A., & Maxey, E. J. (1969, Winter). Student educational growth during the first two years of college. *College and University* . 145–153.

Northeast Missouri State University. (1984). *Degrees with integrity: A value added approach to undergraduate assessment.* Washington, DC: American Association of State Colleges and Universities.

Smith, T. B. (1984). *Value added consultancy report for the State of South Dakota.* Kirksville, MO: Northeast Missouri State University, Office of the Dean of Students.

Faculty Evaluation in Higher Education: Is It Taking Us in the Direction We Want to Go?

Arlen R. Gullickson

The evaluation of faculty is one of the most contentious areas in higher education. There is a continual questioning of the process and what is accomplished through it, and both faculty and administrators express dissatisfaction with it (Newell & Price, 1983; McCabe, 1982). Despite this apparent dislike and the conflict which surrounds it, faculty evaluation remains an integral part of higher education. In fact, by 1977 it was already a *mandatory* process in nine-out-of-ten higher education institutions (Meyer & Smith, 1977).

Davey (1979) in a review of evaluation in higher education states,

> First, most writers agree that the primary purposes of evaluation are twofold: to diagnose the instructor's weaknesses in order to assist in the improvement of his or her professional development (formative evaluation) and to collect data which will be used in the decision-making process relative to promotion, salary increases and tenure (summative evaluation). (p. 66)

He goes on to say that virtually all writers agree on the primacy of the formative evaluation function. His findings, however, suggest that summative evaluation holds sway, and because of that he states "the evaluation process has not effectively stimulated faculty development."

I began this effort with the intention of describing how the evaluation process serves the two purposes. I reviewed recent literature and found numerous instances, surveys, research, and essays, speaking to summative issues. However, I found only a few articles directly related to evaluation for faculty development. Those dealt with programs and strategies conducted outside the realm of faculty evaluation.

As a result, this search led me to the same tentative conclusion (hypothesis) which Davey had reached some years earlier. That is that faculty evaluation, as it occurs in most higher education institutions, does not serve faculty development purposes. This paper explores that hypothesis. Through a review of the faculty evaluation process, (a) a basis for that position is established, and (b) some suggestions are made for modifying the structure of faculty evaluation to enhance its usefulness to faculty development.

Characteristics of the Evaluation Process

Faculty evaluation is moving from being a fairly informal process to one which is tightly structured (Seldin, 1979). Formerly, faculty evaluation may have involved little more than a person-to-person conversation between the faculty member and that individual's supervisor. Recent litigation has challenged the faculty review process, forcing changes in some institutions and stimulating changes in others (cf. Flygare, 1981). Today faculty evaluation is bound together by formal policy, involving a well defined core of data, and a common procedure for decision making.

Policy. Written policy specifies the purposes for evaluation and dictates major characteristics of the process including:

- Who will be evaluated and for what specific purposes,
- Timelines for data collection and notification of decisions,
- Who is to have input into the evaluative process (from whom will the basic data be gathered and who will review, judge, and make recommendations regarding the merit of the individual's work),
- Who is to have access to the evaluative information gathered about an individual faculty member (as well as the limitations of such access),
- Who will make the final decision(s) regarding individual faculty members, and
- Due process provisions which spell out the steps to be followed in the evaluation as well as the steps to be followed by a faculty member

who chooses to formally challenge the decisions resulting from the evaluation.

These policies dictate review of collected data by administrators and peer review committees at several levels of the institution. However, as Donald (1984) notes, the onus of evaluation is most often placed at the departmental level. In fact, in matters of salary and annual review, unless the faculty member chooses to challenge formally the local assessment, no information is likely to be forwarded beyond the departmental level. Therefore, data collected at the departmental level forms the cornerstone of the evaluation process. As such the quality of the evaluation process is dependent upon department level data and the way in which that data is handled.

Data. For purposes of explanation, Stufflebeam (1969) divides evaluation data into four categories:

1. Context. This datum depicts the antecedent conditions surrounding the activities. It could include the qualifications of the faculty member, the policies of the institution, resources available, and a variety of contextual information.

2. Input. This datum focuses on the planning process. It includes such things as objectives, and the strategies set forward to achieve those objectives.

3. Process. This datum describes the activities themselves. Here attention is focused upon improving the procedures to ensure both productivity and high quality in productivity.

4. Product. This datum focuses on the outcomes attained. Here the emphasis is on determining the merit or worth of the products achieved.

Most evaluators combine context, input, and process data under the single heading of formative evaluation. They are listed separately above to clarify the nature of information which would typically be collected for faculty improvement purposes. The fourth category of data, product, is used for summative purposes. Thus the nature of data collected in the evaluation process gives insight into the type of evaluative purpose served.

Generally the faculty evaluation process focuses on three faculty tasks: instruction, research/scholarship, and service. These three do not receive equal weight in the evaluation process. Instruction and research clearly are viewed as more important than service (Donald,

1984), and in the larger institutions (particularly those which grant doctorates) research is viewed as being more important than instruction. Besides being weighted differently, the nature of data collected varies for the three.

Evaluation of instruction focuses primarily on the activity itself (process). Here data are typically obtained either through observation of classes or by student rating of instruction (Donald, 1984). For example, department chairs are frequently called upon to observe classes prior to making an evaluative judgment of a faculty member. But such observations typically occur only once or twice a year, and then the observations are likely to be made without use of any special instruments or protocol to enhance the reliability, credibility, validity, or the diagnostic capability of the observation.

In the past, faculty peers were relied upon to provide an assessment of the colleague's instructional abilities. But, faculty members are reluctant to rate the instructional expertise of their peers, and some research has shown faculty to be lenient, biased and unreliable, in their ratings (Donald, 1984; Marsh, 1984). Perhaps those concerns coupled with the problems encountered by department chairmen in trying to observe and rate faculty instruction have caused the movement toward student evaluation of instruction. Whatever the cause, there has been an increase in the number of institutions using student evaluations; survey research (Cohen & McKeachie, 1980) indicates that by the mid 1970s a majority of institutions were using the technique—an increase of over 25% in less than ten years.

These student evaluations are typically obtained from students near the end of a semester or quarter, and focus on the student's perceptions (ratings) of the teacher's performance during the semester. Usually substantial care is taken to ensure the integrity of this process because the results are routinely summarized and used directly for *summative* purposes.

The use of process data for summative purposes has been extensively argued. A review by Marsh (1984) cites numerous research studies of the practice which have shown that class-average student ratings are quite reliable. Also, he cites research which has been conducted to establish the construct validity of the evaluations. Some have shown a relationship between student ratings of instruction and average student achievement. Others have produced factor structures which appear to be related to student learning.

Limited amounts of input and product data supplement the process information for evaluation of instruction. Here the professor's course syllabi typically constitutes the input data, with information such as the number of students advised, thesis committees served, and the number of courses developed or revised constituting the product data. Rarely is student achievement data used in the assessment of instruction.

Evaluation of research and service depends upon product information. Although the methods used to collect this datum vary across institutions, the data collected by Bowling Green State University appears to be representative. Faculty members there undergo an annual evaluation for salary purposes. This evaluation process requires individual faculty members to complete an activity reporting form (Partin, 1984). In order to assess research and service, each faculty member is asked to list accomplishments such as the number of publications, grants received, papers presented, materials developed, workshops attended, institutional committee service, and amount of community service. In a "nod" toward self-improvement data, individuals are asked to state the number of conferences and workshops attended. As the list of topics suggests, the research and service portions of the form focus on products and in particular on quantity. In those two sections there is no assessment of such issues as the importance of the products to institution, the processes involved in completing the tasks, or the nature (quality) of the products.

If Bowling Green's process is unusual, its uniqueness lies in the fact that it has determined a priori a weighted scoring scheme to award points for each item listed. For example, a journal article published in a refereed journal is awarded 20 points while one published in an unrefereed journal is awarded 10 points. Although the weighting of individual items provides a perspective of perceived worth, the Bowling Green evaluation process does not attempt to assess more directly the quality of individual efforts. That failure to address quality was not an oversight. Regarding research, the author stated that assessment of quality was not included because of the "inherent complexity and subjectivity of value ratings on quality" (p. 53). The faculty in that institution consciously decided that the cost in collection of such data was not commensurate with the payoff in merit monies.

Other institutions gather slightly different information and use different mechanisms for judging the merit of the faculty members' efforts. For example, in assessment of research efforts, often faculty members are asked to list the actual titles of publications as well as where the articles were published. The merit of such publications then is likely to be determined by a review committee's or administrator's judgment of the perceived quality of the journal in which the article was published (Donald, 1984). In cases of promotion or tenure, the more prestigious institutions may additionally seek external review of the article(s) by persons outside the institution.

In matters of primary summative evaluation importance, such as tenure, the specific instruction, research/scholarship, and service data are likely to be supplemented with letters of recommendation. These letters are likely to be solicited by the individual being evaluated. Here again, in the more prestigious institutions, a review committee may solicit evaluative judgment from professionals in the field, rather than relying upon the letters solicited by the individual being evaluated.

The Decision Process. The total set of materials, a document recounting faculty productivity together with student ratings and perhaps letters of support generated by the faculty member being evaluated, is routinely compiled into an evaluation portfolio and sent forward for review. The review process may be quite limited; the department chairman may simply review the material—alone or in consultation with the individual faculty member, render a decision, and inform the faculty member of that decision. That nature of review is most likely to occur in the context of an annual review. If the review is for comprehensive purposes such as tenure or promotion, the portfolio is likely to be sent forward through a series of review committees starting with a local departmental peer review group and ending with a final review and determination at the presidential level. Each review committee and administrator is likely to review the contents of the portfolio, make a recommendation based upon an analysis of the portfolio, add that recommendation to the contents of the portfolio, and forward it to the next person/group involved in the review process.

The Relationship Between Evaluation Process and Purpose

In virtually every respect the evaluation process focuses on summative evaluation. This focus is apparent in the policy, the data and the decision process. Policy dictated timelines invariably coincide with summative decision points, and the persons in charge of the evaluations routinely make summative decisions. Though the data may be a blend of formative and summative information, most of it focuses on products, and what can be termed formative data is analyzed (i.e., counted) to serve a summative purpose. The transformation of data to "countable" form facilitates objective review across committees and administrators. In short within the evaluation process, there is little in-depth (diagnostic) analysis of a faculty member's efforts in relation to goals established.

Feedback from the process includes the administrative decision made, and may include some information of "gross" diagnostic value. This diagnostic information is typically provided in the context of a negative administrative decision, as would be the case where a promotion request has been denied. Because the feedback information is drawn from product type data, it is of limited diagnostic value. Most likely it will stipulate that the work was not of sufficient quantity or not of sufficient quality. Such statements may be coupled with recommendations which are quite general in nature (e.g., improve student ratings, publish more, or publish in more prestigious journals).

The above factors suggest evaluation serves summative purposes, but not formative purposes. That strong focus on summative concerns tends, I think, to interact with two other factors to curtail any focus on formative evaluation. One is a matter of faculty ego, the other is, I think, a matter of practical reality.

First, professionals who hold a terminal degree (Ph.D, Ed.D, and the like) like to view themselves as "developed." That is, they perceive themselves as having attained the requisite skills for their position. This perception is sufficiently pervasive so that, for example, individuals locally have questioned the propriety of establishing programs to help individuals write better research proposals. This attitude results in a resistance to the specification of faculty improvement objectives. Without such objectives it is unlikely that data collection will focus on faculty development activities.

Second, when "faculty development" statements are included in evaluations, they often serve due process concerns. That is, they are included in the evaluative statements to justify the summative recommendations just made, or summative decisions which are contemplated in the future (e.g., the dismissal of a faculty member). Even when they are meant to serve formative purposes they are likely to be viewed negatively and have negative consequences for the individual faculty member. This creates a dilemma for many administrators.

Consider the following. Data which serve formative purposes, and recommendations stemming from those data, will most likely be generated at the lowest (departmental) level. The recommendations are then likely to be forwarded as a part of the larger review. Therefore these evaluative comments will quite likely be read and assessed by others in the decision recommendation chain. In that context, when two faculty members are being compared, if both are rated equally (e.g., as excellent) but for one there is a statement suggesting activities for faculty development while no such statement is provided for the other, the one "not requiring faculty development" is likely to be ranked the higher of the two. Such considerations make it unlikely that a supervisor who wants to support his/her faculty will risk including a formal statement of faculty development needs in any material which will be forwarded. In short, faculty who receive faculty development statements in feedback or recommendations know they are in trouble.

Potential Modifications to Better Serve Formative Purposes

If evaluation of faculty is to serve formative purposes, ways must be found to either overcome or circumvent the problems which stem from the present focus on summative evaluation concerns. I suggest three actions:

1. Require all faculty to engage in individual skill development and evaluate such development.
2. Require the use of formative information in the evaluation process.
3. Physically separate formative and summative evaluation activities.

Faculty Development Requirement. Mandating that all faculty engage in self-improvement activities is an easy step, and perhaps the most important as well. Faculty egos and fears are not likely to be changed by any evaluative action. However, by requiring all faculty to engage in faculty development, the fears certainly will be reduced. If everyone is engaged in some form of self-improvement, then evaluation information related to that activity will be viewed as ordinary rather than extra-ordinary. Thus, requiring all faculty to engage in self improvement would make such activities "respectable," thereby raising the stature of such activities. This, I think, would do a great deal to enhance the willingness of faculty to engage in such activities.

Although the edict to engage in self-improvement may appear cost free, a commitment to such a requirement necessarily incurs several costs. If faculty development activities are to return substantial benefits, then individual diagnosis of faculty skills in the respective areas of instruction, research, and service must occur. Faculty members must be given the opportunity to engage in productive learning activities, and the individuals must be provided regular feedback in their learning attempts. Substantial efforts in this regard cannot occur without allocation of resources to support the efforts.

The allocation of resources and the monitoring of their use necessarily imposes administrative involvement in the faculty improvement process. This involvement has direct implications for evaluation. Experts in evaluation (e.g., Scriven, 1967) argue that to be effective, the person conducting the summative evaluation should not be directly involved in the formative evaluation. There are numerous reasons for this; but two important ones here entail the expertise of the summative evaluator, and probable resultant bias of the summative evaluator toward the product involved.

I suggest the involvement of the supervisor in targeting an area for development. This targeted area can be quite broad (e.g., this year the focus will be on instruction). Together the supervisor and the faculty member can determine the necessary resources; and resource allocation can take place. Such resource allocation will undoubtedly place constraints upon the amount of faculty development activity which can occur. Beyond that point the individual faculty member can be freed to engage in the development activity and document the nature of activity which occurred.

This strategy has three advantages. First, accountability is achieved by including the supervisor in designating the area to be developed. Second, by limiting the involvement of the supervisor, the faculty member can engage in the development activity without fear that either the diagnostic information or the feedback provided as a part of the learning process will ultimately be used against him/her. Third, this frees the administrator to conduct the summative evaluation—a task routinely dictated by institutional policy.

If the supervisor is not involved directly in the development activity, then others must assist. Some institutions have developed resource centers which provide direct developmental assistance in instruction and research (Boice, 1984). Such centers provide diagnostic guidance as well as direct instruction for faculty improvement, and evaluative feedback during the development process. While such centers appear desirable, they are not the only option. Some studies (Doyle & Webber 1979; Marsh, 1979) suggest that faculty are able to self-diagnose their problems. As such, individuals may self-determine areas to develop and may prescribe their own development activities. (Certainly, however, that strategy is prone to the same problems which a medical doctor incurs in self-diagnosis and prescription.) Some may choose to work in tandem with other faculty members. Some may enroll in courses which provide the instruction and evaluation as part of the course. Some may even choose to seek diagnostic and feedback assistance from peers in the field who are known to possess special skills in the area to be developed. Those options would likely result in less institutional cost than the creation of faculty development centers. Which options are chosen and used depends upon the faculty member's needs, the institution's commitment to faculty development, and the resources available for faculty development.

Formative Evaluation Requirement. Explicit incorporation of formative evaluation can do three things; (a) stimulate faculty development, (b) make resource allocation a clear part of the faculty development process, and (c) set the stage for both faculty and administrative accountability. As such it not only plays a major role in planning and development, but it changes the basis for summative evaluation. How it can function to do all of these things can be seen from the role it plays in the decision process.

In the ideal context, decisions are based upon a clear set of standards. Then in a summative context, the merit or worth of an individual is determined by whether the individual's accomplishments meet the designated standards. However, higher education is a complex business in which clear-cut standards of performance are not likely to exist. Without specific performance standards two options remain. The first involves formative evaluation. Here objectives and plans are specified and ultimately subsequent outcomes are compared with those original plans. The remaining option is a normative comparison. That is a comparison of an individual's productivity against either productivity of other individuals or of some hypothetical model.

If there is no formal planning process (i.e., no formal document which stipulates such things as the individual's objectives, the strategy for achieving the objectives, and the resources necessary to achieve the objectives) the necessary data will not exist to make the necessary comparisons. When that occurs, the only option remaining is the "normative" comparison of faculty members. Presently, virtually all faculty evaluations appear to operate from the "normative" basis.

The "formative" and "normative" decision models lead naturally in different directions. The contrast of objectives with outcomes, leads to questions regarding the process (e.g., how the work can be improved). Such questions stimulate diagnostic assessment and lead to changes in practice—formative concerns. Normative comparisons, on the other hand, compare accomplishments across individuals and enable a relative determination of merit. As such the normative model would appear more appropriate for decisions such as tenure, salary, and promotion—summative concerns.

Several strategies for the inclusion of formative planning have been suggested. A popular one is termed "management by objectives" (MBO) (see for example Wooten, 1980). Stake (1967) in an early article on educational evaluation presented a model which contains the essential ingredients of MBO, but which preserves the identity of formative and summative evaluation. In his paper, he set forward a data matrix to facilitate data collection, and most importantly for the arguments made here, he set forward two strategies for evaluative use of data, contingency analysis and congruence analysis.

Contingency analysis is a logical analysis of plans made and actions taken. As such it determines such things as whether the plans appear to lead toward the desired objectives (i.e., whether the plan or action has a logical consistency) and whether the necessary resources are available to enable successful accomplishment of the desired objectives.

Congruence analysis in turn focuses on accomplishments—completed activities and products. This analysis attempts to determine if the desired objectives have been met, and if not, why not. As such it compares the initial plans resulting from contingency analysis with the activities actually conducted and the products achieved. Where the desired outcomes were not achieved either in terms of quantity or quality, a diagnostic assessment is made to determine why the objectives were not attained. These contingency and congruence analyses are intended to be cyclical in that the results of each congruence analysis then feeds into the next planning stage and facilitates the next contingency analysis.

Contingency analysis ensures two important ingredients: (a) formal documented planning, and (b) explicit allocation of resources. Without the contingency analysis, neither the plan (a combined commitment of the faculty member and the administration) nor the allocation of resources (a commitment of the administration) becomes a part of the evaluation portfolio. As a result, the congruence analysis, which requires comparison of results with plans, cannot be effectively completed.

Without the congruence analysis a strong basis for diagnosis in matters such as faculty development is lost. Also, without congruence analysis cost benefit analysis cannot be completed—it is one part of congruence analysis. Thus, without such analysis, accountability is denied for both faculty development and resource allocation. Both are important measures of administrative accountability and substantial tools for administrative development.

Separation of Formative and Summative Evaluation. Because formative and summative evaluation have different goals, one seeking to ensure planning and development while the other seeking to determine relative merit or worth, there is a necessary tension between the two. They compete for the same evaluation resource dollars, but they typically seek different information and serve different audiences. Thus one or the other is bound to be de-emphasized when the two are conducted simultaneously. Routinely formative evaluation loses out.

The separation of formative and summative evaluation would, I think, function effectively to preserve formative evaluation and it would simultaneously help to better focus summative evaluation. My preference is to separate the two in terms of the times when they are completed, and, if possible, in terms of who conducts the evaluations. Formative evaluation is a planning tool; therefore to be effective it must be initiated at the beginning of the program or development cycle and continue during the program or development process. Summative evaluation, because it focuses on relative worth of accomplishments, must occur near the end of the cycle.

Formative evaluation should begin at the point of initial employment, that is when the individual is first hired by the institution. Here, context, input and process data are clearly pertinent to formative evaluation concerns. Educational experience, professional organization membership, assessment of papers and proposals which were not acceptable to external reviewers, and assessment of instructional processes, are quite important for development purposes. Not only does such information assist the improvement of individuals by providing direction and motivation, but it facilitates institutional planning and the allocation of resources.

Summative evaluations naturally occur at distinct points such as tenure and promotion. At such points summative evaluation should appropriately focus on the products attained by the faculty member, and the "institutional fit" between the faculty member and the college or university. Here attention is focused squarely on accomplishments. The achievement of students, publications completed and the quality of the publications, and the amount and quality of service provided by the faculty member, are all pertinent data.

Formative data such as professional organization membership, course syllabi, grant proposals or manuscripts prepared but not successful, and course instructional ratings are not directly appropriate to the needs of summative evaluation. Such data do not answer the essential questions of merit, in essence "pad" the summative evaluation portfolio, and as such are likely to distract attention from the substantive product data. When the input and process data draws attention away from the issue of productivity, the quality of the summative decision is likely to be subverted.

If an annual summative evaluation is not required for salary purposes, it seems natural and appropriate to reserve summative evaluation for those major decision points such as tenure and promotion. Then formative evaluation with its focus on diagnostics and planning may take precedence for a period of several years. Where annual salary evaluations are required, perhaps the best solution is to set forward two separate evaluation periods, one at the beginning of the academic year to focus on formative concerns, and a second one at the end which focuses on summative concerns. This necessarily requires the conduct of at least two formal evaluations each year.

The increased frequency of evaluation, regardless of whether it focuses on summative or formative evaluation is likely to yield additional benefits. Other research in testing and human motivation suggests that an increase in frequency of formal assessments will improve faculty motivation, faculty accomplishments, and faculty attitudes toward evaluation (Green, Beatty, & Arkin, 1984). All three are desirable outcomes.

Side Effects. If my three recommendations are effected, I think a fourth substantial benefit will emerge. Those changes more clearly direct the focus of the data collection toward a specific evaluation objective. In turn, that will limit the nature and range of data collected. When less data are collected, I think people will look more closely at the data which are collected . . . in that context, the quality of data collected will emerge as a more serious concern, and steps will be taken to improve the quality of data.

Presently, as this review suggests, the data tend to be superficial, measures are used because they are easy to obtain and objective in nature; not because they have substantial diagnostic value. Too often administrators, faculty, and students, provide input, and make recommendations and judgments in areas where they lack requisite skills. Students who are untrained in methods or content frequently judge faculty performance on both issues. Faculty most often are asked to evaluate other professors' research and publications. Yet, research by

Blunt (1976) and others shows that, despite the emphasis on research and publications, only a small percentage do publish (an indicator that faculty are not skilled diagnosticians in this area). Administrators in turn tend to be skilled in a discipline area but may have poor pedagogical skills in others, particularly, instructional methodology.

When evaluations are conducted by persons unskilled in evaluation, or without expertise in the necessary areas, the decision and recommendations are apt to suffer. For example, Wood (1978) notes that the physical distance separating two faculty members' offices is associated with the evaluative ratings. Similarly, Meaney and Ruetz (1972, p. 306) note that "a large percentage of administrative decisions are based on the administrator's personal need for survival." Those are not findings indicative of high quality evaluation data bases.

A Concluding Thought. As yet, the higher education community has not separated faculty evaluation into meaningful components. Instead, when a faculty member is to be evaluated, a curious mixture of data for all concerns is collected. This data is then compiled and reviewed with the hope and expectation that the individuals will be improved as a result of that exercise. There is little evidence to suggest such hopes are being realized.

What I have suggested here is that such evaluation does not properly serve us. Once we actively initiate faculty development steps and separate those objectives from summative ones, evaluation will be more able to directly address issues pertinent to each. In that context I think their individual needs for valid information will become more apparent. This I think will lead to different and more appropriate data sources, data collection methods, and analyses. Administrators will not need to be "jacks of all trades" in order to assist faculty in their development efforts. And faculty evaluation may begin to serve faculty improvement in a meaningful way.

References

Blunt, P. (1976). Publish or perish or neither: What is happening in academia. *Vestes*, 19(1), 62–64.

Boice, R. (1984). Reexamination of traditional emphases in faculty development. *Research in Higher Education*, 21(2), 195–209.

Cohen, P., & McKeachie, W.J. (1980). The role of colleagues in the evaluation of college teaching. *Improving College and University Teaching*, 28(4), 147–154.

Davey, E. (1979). Select bibliography of evaluation of instruction in higher education. *Canadian Journal of Higher Education*, 9(1), 65–72.

Donald, J.G. (1984). Quality indices for faculty evaluation. *Assessment and Evaluation in Higher Education*, 9(1), 41–52.

Doyle, K. O., & Webber, P. L. (1979). Self ratings of college instruction. *American Educational Research Journal*, 15(3), 467–475.

Flygare, T. J. (1981). Board of trustees of Keene State College v. Sweeney. Implications for the future of peer review in faculty personnel decisions. *Journal of College and University Law*, 7(1–2), 100–110.

Green, R., Beatty, W., & Arkin, R. (1984). *Human motivation physiological, behavioral, and social approaches*. Boston: Allyn and Bacon.

Marsh, H. W. (1984). Students' evaluation of university teaching: Dimensionality, reliability, validity, potential biases, and utility. *Journal of Educational Psychology*, 76(5), 707–754.

Marsh, H. (1979). Validity of student evaluations of instructional effectiveness: A comparison of faculty self-evaluations and evaluations by their students. *Journal of Educational Psychology*, 71(2), 149–160.

McCabe, M. (1982). Faculty attitudes toward evaluation at southern universities. *Phi Delta Kappan*, 63(6), 4, 19.

Meany, J. O., & Ruetz, F. J. (1972). A probe into faculty evaluation. *Educational Record*, 53(4), 300–307, 372.

Meyer, D. & Smith, C. (1977). A nationwide survey of teacher education faculty evaluation practices. *College Student Journal Monograph*, (Part 2), 11(1), 1–16.

Newell, S., & Price, J. (1983). Promotion, merit and tenure decisions for college health education faculty. *Health Education*, 14(3), 12–15.

Partin, R. (1984). A case study: Evaluating faculty at Bowling Green State University. *Change*, 16(3), 31, 51–53.

Seldin, P. (1979). How colleges evaluate teaching. *Educational Horizons*, 58(2), 113–117.

Stake, R. E. (1967, April). The countenance of educational evaluation. *Teachers College Record*, 68(7).

Scriven, M. (1967). The methodology of evaluation. *AERA Monograph Series on Curriculum Evaluation Perspectives of Curriculum Evaluation*, 1, 39–93.

Wooten, B. (1980). Faculty appraisal—an MBO approach. *Journal of Business Education*, 55(5), 208–210.

Part VII:
The Future of Undergraduate Education:
Dreams and Realities

Introduction

In this final section, the future of undergraduate education is explored. William E. Gardner, the Dean of the College of Education at the University of Minnesota, and Virgil G. Lagomarcino, Dean of the College of Education at Iowa State University were given this assignment. The topic of William E. Gardner's paper is "The Future of Undergraduate Education: Realities." In it, Gardner identifies major elements making up the social and economic contexts of higher education. He argues there are certain facts that influence what colleges and universities can and should do; and he presents a "reform agenda" for undergraduate education. Following the recommendations, he believes, will allow colleges and universities to accomplish better their mission of educating students. Virgil S. Lagomarcino examines several "strands of disparate potentials" in his paper on dreams for the futures of undergraduate education. He addresses four areas of concern: curriculum, students, faculty, and the institutional ethos. Noting that undergraduate education is becoming more career oriented, electives more limited, and general education more inadequate, he proposes five elements of a dream for the future. He suggests ways by which institutions can enhance the role of the professor as a scholar-teacher, how colleges may have greater impact on their students, and what may be done to create a challenging environment alive with facets of life

361

inherent in a democratic society. Finally, Lagomarcino concludes his paper with a proposal that institutions should have the "opportunity to petition its accrediting agency to . . . demonstrate that it seeks recognition that its people and its programs function at a level beyond minimum standards of quality."

The Future of Undergraduate Education: Realities

William E. Gardner

The topic of this article is "The Future of Undergraduate Education: Realities," a topic which seems to suggest that its author will make predictions. I approach this title with some foreboding, remembering the comment by Garrison Keillor in his most recent book, *Lake Wobegon Days*.

> . . . in 1955, a man from the University came and gave us "The World of 1980" with slides of bubble-top houses, picture-phones, autogyro copter cars, and floating factories harvesting tasty plankton from the sea. We sat and listened and clapped, but when the chairlady called for questions from the audience, what most of us wanted to know, we didn't dare ask: "How much are you getting paid for this?" (Keillor, 1985, p. 7).

As Keillor suggests, many predictions are likely to wind up off the mark and make people sorry they asked for your comments in the first place. So to avoid that, I will not make predictions. Rather, I will try to identify the major elements which make up the social and economic contexts of higher education, an approach which rests on the assumption that certain relevant facts bear heavily upon what higher education can and should do. Along the way I will try to point out some of the implications of these events for colleges and universities. Last, I will list my agenda for undergraduate education.

Some Relevant Trends and Facts

The future of undergraduate education will be greatly impacted by the contexts in which it exists. Not that these determine what will happen necessarily, but a realistic look at our future demands that we identify key factors and the implications these hold for higher education.

Demographic Changes

Powerful demographic changes are taking place in the United States which have enormous consequences for the nation's future. An American Council on Education Forum (Demographic Imperatives, 1984) recently summarized the most significant changes:

• The new baby boom is reversing the decline in birth rates and beginning to reverse the decline in school enrollment.
• The over–65 population now outnumbers teenagers.
• The average age of the white population is growing older; that of the minority population is much younger.
• Minorities constitute the majority of school enrollments in 23 of 25 of the nation's largest cities.
• By the year 2000, 53 major cities will have a majority minority population.
• The United States is seeking to integrate into North American culture the second largest wave of immigrants in history—a total of 13.9 million—many of them from Asia and the Pacific Islands.
• Population and education enrollments are continuing to shift from the Frost Belt to the Sun Belt.
• Hispanic population growth has been and continues to be the highest of all groups.
• Asian population growth (103 percent) was actually the highest of all groups during the 1970–80 decade, but this extraordinary growth resulted primarily from immigration and is considered a one-time phenomenon.
• Sixty percent of all Hispanics live in three states (California, Texas, and New York), 85 percent in nine states.
• Hispanics are the most urbanized group, with 88 percent living in cities, but more blacks live in inner cities than any other population group (71 percent).
• Black and Hispanic participation in education diminishes drastically at higher levels.
• The majority of blacks and Hispanics in higher education are enrolled in community colleges or predominantly black and Hispanic institutions.

• Serious erosion has occurred in the rates of black and Hispanic high school graduates who go on to college.
• Eighty percent of all black Ph.D.s and 75 percent of Hispanic Ph.D.s are in education and the social sciences (*Demographic Imperatives*, 1983, p. 4).

The issues generated out of these changes are far too complex for complete analysis here. Moreover, observers differ substantially on how rapidly they will take place. There is no controversy, however, over the direction of the changes, that is, over what will happen. Nor are there differences of opinion over the implications for educational institutions, which will face significant problems as well as policy opportunities because of these facts.

Those implications can be summarized as follows: the nation is becoming more diverse, not less. Minority populations are growing proportionally larger in the total population; the largest minority groups—blacks and Chicanos—are the least well-served by educational institutions presently. The best educated minority people have jobs in social services which are traditionally lower paying than jobs emphasizing backgrounds in science and technology. The majority population is aging far more rapidly than are minority groups. As a larger percentage of this group retires from the workforce, it will depend for support increasingly upon the general economic health of the nation which, in turn, will depend increasingly upon the productivity of young minority workers who are currently in elementary and secondary schools. Thus, it is in the self-interest of the majority Anglo population to attend the education needs of minorities now (*Demographic Imperatives*, 1983).

Changes in the Economy

The national picture is made even more complex by significant changes in the economy. While the nation remains outwardly peaceful and prosperous, basic forces are at work which cause some observers to see hard problems ahead. Marc Tucker, Executive Director of the Carnegie Forum on Education and the Economy, sees the United States this way:

Twenty years ago, the nation was in the middle of the longest sustained period of economic growth in its history. Many economists thought at the time that they had finally tamed the business cycle. Confident of our ability to sustain high rates of growth, we turned our attention to the needs of those among us who had been left out. The nation was motivated in the main by a sense of fairness and decency toward those whose opportunities for advancement had been stunted by circumstances not of their own making. The life-long commitments of many of us were forged in that context.

Today's context, however, is very different. Economic growth is stalled at an annual rate of 1.3 percent. Inflation, now at more than 4 percent per year, stood at only 1.5 percent in the early 60's. A wage earner who took home $20,000 in 1965 must take home about $65,000 in 1985 to enjoy the same standard of living he had 20 years ago. Whereas some 3 million people who wanted work could not find it in the mid-sixties, the figure now stands at around 9 million. The country has shifted from net exporter to net importer, from a creditor nation to a debtor nation (Tucker, 1985, p. 8).

Much of this change Tucker (1985) attributes to factors such as increased levels of education in developing nations and to the march of technology, which has lowered shipping costs and allowed virtually any low-priced labor country to compete with any other anywhere in the world. These facts, coupled with changes in the ways we distribute goods and services, create a bleak future for low skill jobs and, hence, for workers who have only low skill levels.

This situation is interpreted in two contrasting ways. Some observers forecast widespread and chronic unemployment due to technological change. This view holds that we are moving into a situation where we will need only a relatively few highly skilled workers with millions of others working in dull and repetitive jobs demanding little skill and having no future. Tucker (1985) represents what is perhaps a majority of economists who believe otherwise. Citing empirical data, he rejects the notion that job structure and income distribution are being polarized—that is, that higher paying jobs are being replaced by minimum wage opportunities and that higher skilled workers command higher wages—in other words, it is not pre-ordained that the rich will get richer while the poor get poorer. Tucker (1985) and others maintain that the demand for skilled workers will actually increase and that the United States can support a robust economy with virtually full employment, if only the demand for rising skill levels can be met.

Whoever proves to be right ultimately, the implications of the economic changes currently going on for all levels of education are enormous. The requirements for all jobs are rising while the public perception is that academic accomplishments are declining. "Basic" skills, however, and at whatever level acquired, will simply be inadequate for any kind of a job. The same solutions which apply to the woes of American industry, i.e., to increase both the quality of the product and our productivity in making it, apply as well to higher education. We simply must find ways to help students know more and do so at the same time we lower the "unit" cost of having them learn it.

The Universality of the Higher Education System

The single unique and most striking feature of the educational system in the United States is the extent to which people participate in it. Elementary education enrolls virtually all without regard to race, creed, color, or condition of handicapping, but that fact does not provide a basic distinction between us and other nations. The situation at other levels does. Secondary schools engage virtually all adolescents and manage to hold about 75 percent to graduation. While great anguish is expressed over the 25 percent who get away, the record is substantially better than that of other nations. In Western Europe, i.e., school systems managed to keep no more than 36 percent to the end of secondary school (Clark, 1985).

This substantial accomplishment, plus a generous dose of American optimism about the value of higher education, has created enormous upward enrollment pressure. A higher education enterprise of wide scope and great diversity has emerged in this country. Enrollments in higher education have increased by almost 400 percent and the number of institutions by almost 60 percent since 1950. Altogether, two- and four-year colleges and universities this year will enroll more than 12 million students, and total expenditures on higher education will exceed 100 billion dollars, about 3 percent of the GNP. Well over one-half of high school graduates enroll in college and, despite a high percentage of stop and drop-outs, a high proportion earn degrees. Over half of all students are women, one of six is a minority, 40 percent are over 25, and more than 40 percent attend part-time (Study Group on the Conditions of Excellence in American Higher Education, 1984). In a very real sense, higher education has become the ticket to an even larger number of occupations, including but not limited to the professions. Increasingly, the American public views higher education as significant to a person's future; when asked in a recent poll how important a college education is, 64 percent said "very" in 1985, compared to 36 percent in 1978 (Jacobson, 1985).

The size and tremendous recent growth of higher education has had significant effects on colleges and universities, some of which are readily apparent. Relationships have changed between students and institutions and between faculties and institutions. The dependent status that so long characterized students has changed; only a few private, sectarian colleges still act *in loco parentis*. Faculties have organized to bargain with their employers and have maintained as well a solid interest and voice in institutional affairs.

There are implications which are less easily perceived, as well. Burgeoning enrollments in higher education meant building a large teaching force, a group which is now threatened to some extent by the fact that it may not be able to cope with the dynamism of the very institutions it has helped to build. These faculties are critical elements in the reshaping to be done, yet little attention and virtually no money has been devoted generally to their continued development. Of major importance, too, is the fact that higher education's success in attracting larger and larger enrollments precludes the possibility of restraining enrollments as a means of solving a major problem or two. American society has demanded a system of higher education which serves the masses and now that that goal has been achieved, there's no turning back.

A further implication of its sheer size for higher education's future is a more realistic look at its financial ledger. Faculty salaries have lost purchasing power and need improvement. Capital investments and equipment amortization schedules have been all too often ignored. Generally, higher education has probably captured all the efficiencies possible due to large enrollments. The College Board estimates tuition and fees will rise by 9 percent this year over last at four-year public institutions, a figure more than twice the inflation level (Jacobson, 1985). In all likelihood, costs will continue to go up. Students (in the short run at least) will receive less help from their national government in meeting these expenses. Rising costs, of course, have their deepest impact on those least able to pay them.

Emergence of the Information Society

For some time, we have been aware that what is called the "information age" is far more than an academic abstraction or a "high status" educational metaphor. Studies have demonstrated that the information age is, in fact, an economic reality. Information has always been an important economic tool, but now it has become *the* key element in developed countries. More than half of the GNP in the United States, for example, is earned and well over half of its total work force engaged in the production of information. Almost 90 percent of all new jobs created in this economy during the 1970s were in information, knowledge, or service jobs. Clearly, we have become a nation of information workers.

This information age changes the way in which we view resources. It used to be that the location of the world's resources was of central importance and that resources were divided into those which could be renewed and those which could not. We now realize that information is also a resource, and a most unusual one at that, primarily because it cannot be used up.

Other resources are affected by the mechanical processes in thermodynamics; they need repair and ultimately wear out. But information does not. Instead, it expands with use. We frequently talk about an "exchange" of information even though it is basically inaccurate to do so. If you have information and manage to give it to me, you will, of course, still have it and so will I. We have not exchanged it as much as we have shared in its expansion (Cleveland, 1985).

So, the information age is real. But what are its effects on our lives? What is its meaning for higher education?

One implication is contained in the technology of the information age itself. Communication satellites and fast computers have erased distance; every place can be the center of things. One consequence of this is places or areas which used to be regarded as "remote" need be no longer; they exist in the periphery of world events no more or less than all other places in the world. Increasingly, sophisticated in-depth news analysis is available around the clock; the one edition of *USA Today* is "printed" in several locations through satellite transmission. Computers now call on the phone to remind us to pay our bills and to offer us goods and services. The new information technologies linked with improved production technologies have fundamentally reorganized things on a global scale. Clearly, it no longer makes sense, if it ever did, to educate people with the idea in mind that they would actually live their lives in a single state, region, or nation. Among other things, an information age admonishes us to put a high premium on the ability to see the biggest of all possible pictures.

A Reform Agenda

The above analysis describes three aspects of American life and presents an imposing list of issues and problems with which higher education institutions must deal in the years just ahead. Despite the complexity of the issues, I think an action agenda can be developed to respond to these social and economic trends, and toward that end, I will present a four point agenda which would constitute part of a realistic effort to reform undergraduate education.

First, it is imperative that students be educated toward an international and intercultural perspective. This is a goal which has long been with us. Writers like Harold Taylor of Sarah Lawrence College, for example, have developed the basic theme, the idea that in order to be truly educated, people must have a full sense of the world they live in.

> To enjoy any longer the luxury of defining one's nation, one's society or oneself in terms of pride of ancestry, social superiority, or power of destruction is not only supremely dangerous to the survival of the race, but intellectually and socially obsolete (Taylor, 1969, p. 3).

There has been considerable progress toward the development of international perspectives during the past decade, at least in several areas of American life. Business leaders recognize that their enterprise plays out its destiny on an international stage. Indeed, this has become the era of the big multinational corporation operating across national boundaries with much less difficulty at times than national governments have in performing similar functions. Both free trade and protectionist advocates today recognize the need for an international view, and the American farmers have for a long time realized that their livelihood is intimately linked with events elsewhere on the international scene.

Unfortunately, the domain of American education remains largely untouched by international perspectives. Here it can be truly said that we are goal rich but action poor. Superficially, our educational institutions have adopted the trappings of internationalism. At high school and college levels, institutions involve both foreign students and exchange faculty from other countries. Goal statements at both levels, in clear and ringing terms, announce the desirability of international education. But as the spate of recent reports on secondary education made abundantly clear, when people sit down to think about improvements in education, they become as xenophobic as the worst nineteenth century jingoist. In the minds of reformers at the K–12 level, the purpose of secondary schooling is apparently a national one. It is after all a "nation" which was at risk, according to the President's Commission on Excellence in Education. It seems to me significant that the Commission did not mention the world or the globe except in the context of competition. And when we ask what was at risk, the answer, of course, is our competitive edge in the trading world over our major rivals. We could have expected just a little more than what we got from this group.

Slightly higher performance is visible where colleges and universities are concerned. A recently published report sponsored by the Carnegie Foundation (1985) proclaims the significance of an interconnected world. The report adopts a clear-cut global orientation, noting the need to develop in all students an understanding of the international nature of the world, to encourage future leaders from abroad to study at American colleges and universities, and so on. But the report is still laced with competitive language, leaving the impression that we should be interested in things international because they are key elements in a new kind of cultural imperialism.

We show little propensity to support and encourage our students to study internationally. Federal funding for international education programs has been declining across the last two decades. The budget for USIA, for example, declined by more than 40 percent between 1965 and 1983. Interest in foreign languages and the study of international topics at universities and colleges has declined substantially. It is even worse at the high school level where the percentage of seniors who had at least some instruction in foreign language declined from about one-third in 1940 to one-sixth just a few years ago. Foreign language study was required by only 14 percent of our colleges and universities in 1982 as compared with 34 percent in 1966 (Carnegie Commission, 1985). While there are active study abroad programs in many of our universities, the immersion experience, (that is, students living abroad for lengthy periods of time) is pretty much confined to the upper middle class elite institutions.

This situation cries out for attention, and I submit that a fundamental part of a reform agenda must be to orient far more of our concern toward the development of international perspectives.

How do we do that? One way to start is to build more requirements into the curriculum. Language study should be required, as should courses in a variety of disciplines which treat non-western societies and deal with the cross-cutting global issues of our time—population, food, ecology, and the like. But new course requirements will not alone be adequate because they are at the low end of the vividness or intensity scale in truly understanding another culture. Far more effort should be made to facilitate student contact with other peoples, through short-term experiences with foreign students here or by spending part of their educational careers abroad. Thousands of students do have such experiences, but they constitute only a small proportion of the total.

Second, it is imperative that, in particular, public institutions of higher education use learning technologies to become more efficient and effective.

As noted earlier, the new information technologies are working enormous changes in all areas of modern life. It remains to be seen whether this revolution will have the significance or the staying power of the "print" revolution which followed Gutenberg's invention, but by all odds, the changes it has brought to this point have already affected us profoundly.

The new technologies have brought exciting possibilities to those who are in the teaching/learning business. The remarkable adaptability and low cost of microcomputers make these machines potentially powerful devices for learning. Coupled with the emerging video disc technology, such machines promise to facilitate learning in ways that previously were only dreams.

To this point in time, much of this promise is rhetorical only. Computers, video discs and similar high potential learning technologies have little presence on university or college campuses. To be sure, microcomputer laboratories abound and computer departments and programs have mushroomed in recent years. But nowhere in this country has a college really assigned to technology the responsibility for carrying a significant part of the instructional load. Computer labs are used primarily to teach people about computers, not about other college subjects. Computer curricula most often teach the use of computers in a variety of tasks, but not teaching and learning.

There are levels of technology which have more immediate pay-off but which also are basically unused. Here I am thinking of the teaching power of the videotape, for example. It is actually possible to put on tape in an inexpensive way a rich array of educational material and package this in an attractive fashion. Linked with satellite dishes and VCRs, the television set becomes an important educational tool.

We have ignored both complex and simple educational instructional technology for several reasons. Schools of all sorts have traditionally been scandalously undercapitalized, and higher education remains an especially graphic example of a labor intensive industry. Usually the most sophisticated learning tool in the classroom is the ballpoint pen. This undercapitalization has meant that we simply do not think of technologies as a way of solving some of our instructional problems. Also, we have not been very clear about learning outcomes, about what it is that we really expect people to know when they finish one of our courses. The effect of this is that we have not been able to test for the results of learning done independently.

There is much in our current situation which supports the use of technology to put at least some of the learning we expect from students on an independent basis. Costs are rising and will continue to do so. Increasingly, governing boards cry for "cost containment" in education as well as in health care. There is still the crying need to provide access to higher education to the broadest possible range of students. Students from the higher economic groups will continue to be able to afford higher education, but unless we enlist the aid of learning technologies to help us to do our work, students who rely on their own resources will increasingly fall by the wayside.

My recommendation stops well short of replacing professors with learning machines or turning universities into gigantic correspondence schools. It is based on the following assumptions: That the typical university student is intelligent enough to assume the responsibility of demonstrating competence in an area of study without the presence of a human being nearby; that a portion of many of the subject matters we teach in universities can be organized in a self-study way and made available to independent learners; and that a combination of text materials, videotape lectures, review exercises, and wherever feasible, microcomputers, plus periodic discussion sessions with a group facilitator would provide an appropriate independent learning experience for most students.

I think we need to require students to earn some substantial portion of their bachelor's work through independent study, and it would seem appropriate to shoot for one-fourth of the total amount of work ultimately. To implement this idea, we need to take a regular credited course and convert it to an independent study mode using readily available media, including text, study guides, and audiovisual. We need to provide a moderate level of tutoring and an exit exam which reveals the level to which students have achieved.

There are literally dozens of examples of courses which could be taught this way. Most of the so-called remedial math courses taught in college could be put on this basis. Modern foreign language courses are available through independent study in the private sector; most universities, I think, could "out-Berlitz Berlitz," if they were challenged to do so. Also, study abroad courses could conveniently be designed in independent study formats.

There are remarkably successful illustrations of ways to package low cost independent learning. The Open University in Great Britain, for example, combines television lectures with carefully developed test materials and succeeds with the help of short-term summer institutes in providing most of the work required for an undergraduate degree. The British put an enormous amount of money into course design and television production, but frequent offerings of the same courses has lowered the per student cost to a decent level. Other illustrations exist in developing nations, where cash is short but the need for higher education is long. Thailand, for example, has an open university which utilizes the notion of distance education to deliver basic college courses to a staggeringly large number of students. Each course offered in that university uses four or five simple learning technologies (television and audiotapes, text and review materials, small group tutors, micros where appropriate and available), and each is developed according to simple, basic design principles.

To date, Americans have acted as though independent learning was unAmerican, as though they had a divine right to have a conventional four-year public institution available within easy driving distance of their homes. In the more limited future I anticipate, it would seem wise to throw off that notion and declare that students can and should learn independently.

Third, it is imperative that colleges and universities develop closer linkages with high schools. Higher and lower education in the United States developed along substantially different lines. Hence, they have different goals, value different outcomes for the educational process, are governed differently, and have had difficulties in building close relationships. Yet, as noted earlier, both are part of a comprehensive enterprise which keeps an exceptionally large percentage of an age cohort in school for a very long time. Despite their differences, they do share some of the aspects of a universal system.

The current reform movement in education has centered largely on the high schools, with the result that this once proud institution is struggling to maintain a semblance of purpose and equilibrium. Basically what seems to be going on are two movements—one to raise academic accomplishments and one to re-structure the high schools to force more flexibility, to allow students to leave earlier.

One of the high schools' problems is that relationships between higher and lower systems of education have changed substantially in recent years. Some would claim that the relationship between the two has eroded during the last 10 years, citing the fact that universities no longer provide the same kind or level of service that they once did. The problem we face at present, however, does not seem to be a lack of significant contact between universities and the K–12 system. Rather, that this shift has decreased the need for some kinds of ties and at the same time raised the need for new ones. The key issues are linked to concerns over quality, primarily the need to clarify and perhaps raise entrance standards to higher education and the corollary to this, the issue of what requirements should be for high school graduation. In addition, there are new problems of determining the content of high school courses, a topic which universities should address.

Thus, increased collaboration between universities and the K–12 system is not only highly desirable from a political standpoint but necessary if substantial improvement in the educational system is to take place. Such collaboration should take the shape of "partnerships" rather than the one-way foreign aid concept which is so frequently seen as condescending by school people. One clear goal of these efforts should be to change the university and its programs to some degree, as well as to change the K–12 system.

There are many different ways of establishing new or strengthening existing relationships. Certainly, one preferred way to proceed would be to develop a mechanism for liaison (usually involving advisory or policy groups from both sides). Such a mechanism would address major problems of both institutions. One university, for example, has organized its efforts around two major themes: setting academic standards and enriching classrooms for teachers. Under the first theme, the university in collaboration with local school groups considers questions like these: should common floor requirements be established for all; how can incentives be increased for high school students to earn college credit toward graduation for work completed in high school? Under the second theme, the university involved professors and teachers in a variety of collaborative efforts, including short term workshops, designed to update teachers in new subject matter and the rethinking and updating of high school courses.

Finally, and very briefly, it is imperative that colleges and universities take care of their "seed corn" problem; that is, that they provide for the continued development of their faculty resources in ways they have not typically done in the past.

The professional and personal growth of faculty members have been virtually taboo subjects at colleges and universities until quite recently. While business and industry spend considerable time and money to update key staff, higher education has rather blithely assumed that expertise resided in its faculties and that no effort aside from the occasional sabbatical or research leave was needed to keep faculty updated. There was no need to provide structured programs to its faculty to teach them something of the major movements in American society.

Today there is increasing recognition that the vitality of the faculty needs to be a major concern primarily because of the perceived decline in the quality of academic life. Faculty salaries have declined 20 percent in real income over the past decade, and a variety of studies have indicated that anxiety, stress, and alienation are problems of the academic community. Faculty are far less mobile than they have been in the past; on the average, as Bowen (1982) and others have noted, faculty are aging rapidly with about one-half of the professorial staff eligible to retire during the next 10–15 years. Bowen and others have identified this point as part of the problem and call our attention to the need to rebuild both the numbers enrolled in and the quality of our graduate programs.

That would solve only half the problem, however. The faculty who will stay behind while others retire also need attention. They are the ones who must exert leadership so that the necessary adjustments to social change are accommodated. Colleges and universities need to invest a higher proportion of resources in faculty development designed to keep the faculty alive.

In summary, I have argued here that the future of undergraduate education will be deeply affected by societal trends and developments. These will continue to have serious implications for higher education which, in my judgment, demand some basic changes on the part of institutions. I have suggested some structural and procedural changes which will effect the necessary adjustments. This analysis clearly ignores many important aspects of social and academic concerns, to be sure. But I think that the recommendations, albeit incomplete, do provide realistic possibilities of positioning higher education to do a better job in its undergraduate programs, at least in the near range future.

References

Bowen, H. R. (1982). *The state of the nation and the agenda for higher education*. San Francisco: Jossey-Bass.

Clark, B. R. (1985). The high school and the university: What went wrong in America, Part 1. *Phi Delta Kappan*, *66*, 291–297.

Cleveland, H. (1985). *The knowledge executive: Leadership in an information society*. New York: E. P. Dutton.

Demographic imperatives: Implications for educational policy. (1983).

Report of the June 8, 1983 Forum on The Demographics of Changing Ethnic Populations and Their Implications for Elementary-Secondary and Post-secondary Educational Policy. Washington, D.C.: American Council on Education.

Jacobson, R. L. (1985, September 4). The new academic year: Signs of uneasiness amid calm and stability on many campuses. *Chronicle of Higher Education*, pp. 1–3.

Keillor, G. (1985). *Lake Wobegon days*. New York: Viking Penguin, Inc.

Newman, F. (1985, September). Higher education and the American resurgence. Draft Report of the Carnegie Foundation for the Advancement of Teaching.

Study Group on the Conditions of Excellence in American Higher Education. (1984). *Involvement in learning: Realizing the potential of American higher education* (Final Report). Washington, D.C.: National Institute of Education.

Taylor, H. (1969). *The world as teacher*. New York: Doubleday and Company, Inc.

Tucker, M. (1985, Summer). Between a rock and a hard place. *The Wingspread Journal*. Racine, WI: The Johnson Foundation.

The Future of Undergraduate Education: Dreams

Virgil S. Lagomarcino

This afternoon I am supposed to present some dreams; to be creative, in other words, about the future of undergraduate education. This attempt at being a futurist is both a challenge and an opportunity. It could be said that a futurist is one who attempts to sketch alternative happenings yet to come that challenge the imagination and stimulate the mind. Edward Cornish, President of the World Future Society, has noted, "It makes sense for us to think about what might happen in the future so that we can make better choices about what we want to make happen" (cited in Daniel, 1985, p. 17).

While dreams may have a reality base insomuch as they must spring from the conscious experience background of the dreamer, they also contain unexpected flights of fancy, unconnected sequences and yes, even occasional interesting, if not valuable, insights. I will let you judge the effects this afternoon of our dreaming together.

In beginning, I am reminded of a story that illustrates my position. This summer a young friend of mine crossing the street in Campus Town was almost run over by a woman driver who was driving a station wagon with about 7 or 8 children all lumped together in the back. She screeched to a halt and as my young friend jumped safely back, he turned to her and asked, "Lady, don't you know when to stop?" The woman driver fixed him with a cold icy stare and after looking at her young passengers in the back turned to my friend and said, "Sir, I'll have you know that these are not all mine."

Let me be quick to add that not all contained herein will be the exclusive thoughts of the speaker. Even though I have attempted to present my own dreams, I have extracted widely from the current literature. The literature is rich with studies, reports and analyses of undergraduate education, its problems and its future.

At the outset, too, it is worthwhile to note that the type of assignment given to me causes me to differentiate in J. R. Guilford's analysis, between convergent thinking and divergent thinking. In "convergent thinking" one follows the process which goes to an answer that is best, most acceptable or the most conventional or logical. "Divergent thinking" is quite different both in process and substance. It is that type of thought process which causes one to think in several directions as one seeks alternatives rather than to proceed sequentially toward a single or so-called "correct" solution. In divergent thinking no particular specific solution is anticipated.

I prefer to approach my assignment as a divergent thinker would and explore several avenues, several possibilities and would hope to embrace several strands of disparate potentials. So that my comments will not be a loose compendium of unrelated thoughts, however, I would propose to present a skeletal structure or outline of the areas to be encompassed.

It is my intention to address four areas of concern as a part of the dreaming process related to the future of undergraduate education. These four areas are curriculum, students, faculty and the institutional ethos. In each area I will attempt a partial synthesis of the status or the background inherent in each and then I shall project a dream. Stated another way, I shall attempt a brief description of "what is" and then attempt a projection of "what might be."

I would like to conclude with several questions, and a final proposal.

Johann Heinrich Pestalozzi has noted, "Thinking leads men to knowledge. One may see and hear and read and learn as much as he pleases; he will never know any of it except that which he has thought over, that which by thinking he has made the property of his mind." It will be my goal to stimulate thoughts as a prelude to establishing some "properties of the mind."

By way of background, let me point out that the path we have come in almost two thousand five hundred years of development has led us in American undergraduate education to still another period of thoughtful examination of our goals and objectives. Our beginnings can be traced back to the philosopher Pythagoras c. 500 B.C. The Sophists, including Pythogoras, specialized in preparing students in ethics and rhetoric. They were severely criticized by both Socrates and Plato. Institutions of higher learning, their programs and professors have been under periodic scrutiny in many of the periods that have intervened.

A journey that began so long ago in fifth century B.C. Athens has been fraught with philosophical insights, creative discussions and many opinions. Even the term, "liberal studies," which still is considered to be an essential part of an undergraduate education, was known to the ancients.

Listen to Seneca, the younger c. 4 B.C.–65 A.D.:

> Why liberal studies are so called is obvious: It is because they are the only ones considered worthy of free men. But there is really only one liberal study that deserves the name—because it makes a person free— and that is the pursuit of wisdom (from his writings called Epistalae Morales cited in Seldes, 1985).

The pursuit of wisdom itself stresses a journey, a traveling, a search, as opposed to a destination. All of us engaged in that journey need to pause and assess what is and what might be. Today I am primarily concerned with the what might be.

The Curriculum

Let us examine first the matter of the curriculum. Today's curriculum, like ancient Gaul, is divided into three parts. The academic major, the electives, and the general education component. It should be noted that the major is becoming more and more career oriented, the electives more and more limited as the major expands and the general education component more and more inadequate as the general knowledge base grows.

When one examines the undergraduate programs, it is apparent that a number of changes are occurring. More and more undergraduates, for example, are majoring in narrow specialties. The proportion of bachelor's degrees in arts and science, when compared to professional and vocational degrees, has declined. It has been noted, as well, that accreditation standards for professional programs for undergraduates tend to limit the academic work in those areas related to the liberal arts. "The result is that the college curriculum has become excessively vocational in its orientation, and the bachelor's degree has lost its potential to foster the shared values and knowledge that bind us together as a society" (National Institute of Education, 1984, p. 10).

With this as background, let us examine what might be the elements of a dream of the future.

1. The first of these elements would be a clear statement describing what a student should know. The statement, developed by faculty with student input, should delineate what can logically be expected of students. Certainly it would contain a definitive outline of what could best be described as learning outcomes. It would be conceivably possible to develop two types of statements. One could be a general statement that would describe institutional curricular experiences and expectations for all students. The other potential type could be an individual "game plan" that recognizes the larger institutional goals but that would personalize the expected learning outcome for the particular student involved.

This would challenge the student to develop with proper guidance an academic plan that could go beyond merely listing courses. It could include books to be read and discussed; projects to be explored and developed; activities to be undertaken; field experience to be incorporated. The plan instituted no later than the sophomore year could be updated annually or as frequently as changing conditions might warrant.

2. A junior year general examination should be developed to evaluate, in flight, a student's academic progress in terms of the stated objectives. The assessment would be diagnostic in nature and would provide a basis for continued academic planning and study during the senior year. Together the student and his/her advisor/mentor could design continuing experiences to bolster those areas in which progress might be less than what had been desired. Adjustments, to incorporate into the undergraduate experience additional or advanced courses in other areas in which the student demonstrated a greater development or progress than at first contemplated, would be possible as well.

3. A comprehensive final evaluation, perhaps computer driven, that could not only be culminating experience for the undergraduate years, but could be designed to make important recommendations for the student's continued growth and development, would be another important element. The culminating assessment could stress the application of knowledge in problem-solving scenarios utilizing sophisticated adaptation of the video disk and an interactive computer to develop and present the problem. The student's response could be evaluated against a prepackaged analysis by a "jury of experts." The results could be given the student in a printout by the computer and would

serve not only as an assessment (academic diagnosis) but as a recommendation (academic prescription) for continuing development.

4. Students should be given opportunities to broaden and intensify the curricular experience by requiring as a part of the undergraduate program extensive participation in the rigor of research. This could be either guided individual research or the experience could be gained as a part of a team effort or it could be accomplished under the direct tutelage of a professor. The opportunity to participate in systematic research oriented activities would help develop important learning skills and attitudes which could have enduring value.

5. To enhance the written communication skills of *all* students systematic procedures should be developed and implemented. Learning to write effectively is a life long task and all students need to be challenged to perform at a level beyond mere competency. While there is a very real need to provide remedial and/or developmental opportunities for the student with marginal skills, to fail to extend the opportunity to enhance the writing ability of all is to neglect an important function of the academic enterprise.

The Faculty

There appears to be some evidence that there has been over the years a change in the nature, role and function of the professor. This shift from teacher to scholar-researcher has been characterized by an increased emphasis and loyalty to one's discipline at the expense of a commitment to instruction or to the institution itself.

The report of the Association of American Colleges' Project on Redefining the Meaning and Purpose of Baccalaureate Degrees notes:

> As appropriate as research is as the focus of energies and resources in the research university, the exclusive concern with research in the training of recipients of the Ph.D. degree—to the neglect of any concern with teaching or with any professional responsibility other than to scholarship—has encouraged college faculties to abandon the sense of corporate responsibility that characterized professors of the pre-professional era (Association of American Colleges, 1985, p. 14).

The language of académe portrays its values—we refer to teaching *loads* and to research *opportunities* (Association of American Colleges, 1985). Neither research nor teaching can be eliminated from the professional life of those who have the responsibility of "professing."

However, the thrust of undergraduate instruction revolves around the teaching act. Ideally a professor is both a researcher and a scholar-teacher. The skills of scientific inquiry and the development of the knowledge base make teaching most effective, but it is teaching that must be the focal point of the undergraduate program.

The question now becomes what might we do to enhance the role of the professor as a scholar-teacher. I would propose that institutions which nurture the development and support of scholar-teachers would have the following:

1. A strong support system to give substance to the classroom teaching aspect of the professor's life should be created. This support system would include opportunities for faculty renewal through frequent periodic improvement leaves that would serve to provide challenging learning experiences that would be valuable in the professor's classroom. Other elements of a support system could include funding for special developmental projects designed to improve the teaching-learning environment, staff assistance to design effective instructional materials, consultative personnel to conduct teaching seminars to provide analysis of how students learn and a stable of available resource people who are experts in their fields and whose presence in the classroom from time to time would enrich the learning environment.

2. Faculty should be encouraged to appraise their own teaching effectiveness and should be provided with appropriate evaluative instruments and techniques to accomplish this important task. This would not be a function of any evaluation system for promotion, tenure or merit salary. It would be a process that a professional would utilize to augment his/her effectiveness as a teacher.

Faculty should be encouraged and assisted in conducting some follow-up studies of students in an effort to ascertain the students' appraisal of the learning experience and its impact on their own growth and development. The information gleaned could be a basis for a part of the continuing revision and upgrading that must accompany the constant search for improvement of classroom teaching.

3. Outstanding teachers should be assigned to first year students. This assignment can be defended and encouraged for many reasons. Often the courses for beginning students whether they be survey courses, introduction courses, foundation courses or just first courses are the most difficult to teach. They are sometimes difficult, not because of the complexity of material to be presented, but rather

because of the selection of the most relevant aspects of what should be taught from the broad options available. In order to teach this well, the professor must understand and appreciate the whole range of the discipline—an understanding that is possible only if one is highly knowledgeable.

4. Faculty should be provided opportunities to learn to teach more effectively. The development of the "art of teaching" is a continuing process. While each practitioner breathes into the art his/her own particular flavor, there are things to learn about the process. Growth as a teacher may stem from several sources that relate to both process and substance. Too often when we think of process, that is to say the "how" of teaching, we assume that all we need is a "bag of tricks," an overhead projector, and a few illustrative anecdotes.

If teaching is an art, and I believe it is, it is an art based on some scientific principles of the ways in which learning is accomplished. Three factors pertain and can be phrased as questions. How can we maximize our own particular artistry? What do we need to know about the *process* of how students learn? How can we continue to add to the substance of the knowledge base in our discipline and in related disciplines that impinge on our effectiveness as professors? Books are written on each of the foregoing and to attempt a synthesis is to reduce complexity to absurdity. Let me say, however, that discussion seminars of interested faculty who would agree to begin to address the three questions just presented would be a significant beginning!

5. Private monies to be provided for faculty growth opportuntities should be sought. Growth and development would be stimulated by travel, concentrated study, contact with resource consultants, exploring team teaching within and across disciplines, expanding both the real and the vicarious experiences of students as a part of the search for innovative ways to improve instruction.

In these days when state budgets are under stress, there is limited funding for creative, innovative ways for faculty to expand their performance level. Certainly one would not want to infer that all change costs money, but certainly some level of support undergirds many of the exploratory thrusts for faculty development. A concerted effort to add to a support base and to create a Fund for Excellence in Teaching would be a possibility that might result in significant faculty growth.

The Students

As a third part of our presentation, let me reflect on our "reason for being"—the student. We know several things about today's student and we can make some judgments about what students may be like in the decade ahead. We know that the average age of college students is becoming older. We are aware, as well, that: "A rapid jump in the number of women over thirty-five (attending college) accounts for much of the change" ("Tomorrow," 1985, p. 14).

It is well known from survey data (ACE/UCLA Survey) that there has been a solid swing toward a materialistic and career oriented attitude on the part of incoming students (Astin et al., 1980). This thrust toward vocational careerism is what Levine (1980) calls "vocomania."

He characterizes college generations in an insightful fashion portraying—"students of the 1920s as wet, wild and wicked; students of the 1930s as somber and radical; students of the 1940s as mature and 'in a hurry'; students of the 1950s as silent; and students of the 1960s as angry and activist" (p.4).

While the caricatures of the past outlined by Levine may be more myth than reality, we can add to the analysis of the student cohort by noting that the students of the '70s might be classified as sometimes serious and sporadically sedate. At mid point in the '80s it may be too early in this decade to attempt a caricature other than to point out a seeming trend toward a growing materialism and a disturbing tilt toward a "me centered" philosophy.

The impact of the coming wave of students who are described by Winn (1985) as "Precocious and uninhibited, right and self-assertive, but without the foundation of structural learning necessary to take best advantage of traditional higher education . . ." (p. 14) is not yet fully known. These are those who grew up in America's period of "social turbulence of the late 1960s and early 1970s."

Survey data from the ACE/UCLA Freshmen Survey and the analysis by Levine as well as Hodgkinson (1985) would indicate that changes in attitudes, in socioeconomic background, accompanied by changing cultural and family conditions effect today's student and will shape the student who will attend the nation's colleges and universities in the years ahead. The evidence just cited underscores and illumines an attitude of materialistic career oriented values accompanied by a changing family, and social life styles that tend to cause us to build a negative attitude when considering the future.

There is, however, another scenario, reflective of a broader society, that needs to be put along side the data just presented. Voltaire once defined truth as a "statement of facts as they are." Let's examine another set of "facts" in our search for the truth about the future and the students who will populate that future.

In a study designed to analyze the consumer buying trends as a rationale for effective advertising (Meyers, 1984), it has been predicted that a growing segment of our population is "the societally conscious achievers." This group constitutes "the members of the World War II baby boom generation who care more about inner peace and environmental safety than about financial success and elegant surroundings" (p. 19). This is said to be the nation's fastest growing group. While today's college student demonstrates a materialistic orientation, these researchers anticipate a societal swing to a philosophy that embraces an expanding commitment to a value system and life style that is distinctly nonmaterialistic.

The questions one must ask are: What will be the resultant impact on tomorrow's student? Will we have a significant clash of values and life styles? What philosophy will prevail?

As one considers the future and as one attempts to present some dreams of "what might be," the crystal ball can be clouded by the conflicting analysis of differing sets of data. Nonetheless, in anticipating what might happen in the future so that we will be able to make better choices of what we want to make happen, I would submit that the following would constitute some desirable possibilities:

1. students be caused to write extensively and that the writing be critically reviewed.

2. students be encouraged to participate in the research efforts of the faculty.

3. students be afforded greater opportunities for broader participation in individual learning experiences and they be challenged to design, complete and evaluate significant independent study projects.

4. students, particularly first year students, be afforded more intensive guidance and counseling services.

5. students be challenged to be pro-active contributors to the total academic life of the campus; to be partners in significant policy recommendations and to assume responsibility for enhancing the campus ethos.

6. students be strongly urged and aided in becoming acquainted with a broad spectrum of faculty; and to seek out individual faculty as "mentors."

7. students be challenged and guided in a process that would cause them to assume increased responsibility for their own educational growth and development.

8. students be expected to articulate their own goals and objectives consistent with sound principles of the higher education experience.

9. students demonstrate their ability to make an evaluation and assessment of their own growth and development.

10. students begin to develop an attitude that stresses a continuing desire to continue a lifetime of learning.

The Institutional Ethos

The idea of an institutional "Gestalt" would hold that the whole is, indeed, greater than the sum of its parts. The character of the campus may be difficult to define. It is composed of many things, it reflects society at a specific time, it emerges from its local history, it is conditioned by the attitudes and ideas of a dynamic faculty, it varies with the aspirations of its students, it grows with an expanding knowledge base, and is influenced by the economy of the moment.

It is changed by existing conditions and in turn its influence changes conditions. It is an atmosphere that seeks to create knowledge and consequently is often the center of controversy. It can be a climate that is often in the eye of the storm. On the other hand, institutional character can often be classified as a sleepy bulwark serving to perpetuate the "status quo." The campus ethos can reflect a "world apart" an isolated bastion for reflection and study that is almost isolated from reality. It can be a dynamic life or a stagnant existence.

Ideally a campus ethos will reflect a challenging environment that is alive with the cross currents of the many facets of life inherent in a democratic society. Ideally, too, the campus ethos ought to be conducive to the open discussion of differing ideas and ideals. In the words of John Milton; "Where there is much desire to learn, there, of necessity, will be much arguing, much writing, many opinions; for opinion in good men (and women) is but knowledge in the making."

I would dream of an institution that:

1. had a faculty who would be outstanding role models for students.

2. provided opportunities and encouraged social service activities designed to enrich the liberating aspects of the liberal arts.

3. sought to develop "learning communities" from across several disciplines to broaden the intellectual tone of the campus.

4. sought to support the concept of community in establishing a "we-ness," a "one-ness," a "together-ness" that is descriptive of the term "community" itself.

5. demonstrated a commitment to the concept of moving beyond mere competency as a standard for achievement.

6. developed a clear, and relevant statement of a philosophy that would undergird not only the institution's thoughts, but its actions as well.

7. was cognizant of the important relationships beyond the campus that must be a part of its existence—with business and industry, with government and with other segments of the education enterprise.

8. sought to recognize and reward the significant accomplishments of its faculty, to encourage their participation in the larger society and would strive to create an atmosphere of true collegiality in the work place.

9. cause consideration be given in thought and deed to the social, political, and economic conditions of our times (poverty, disease, crime, minority considerations, peace, human rights).

10. provide an environment that would exemplify to students in particular that rational discourse among knowledgeable people holds promise for the resolution of the nation's problems, and that the process of learning is necessary in a continuing quest for improvement in the life of a person or a state, or a nation and the world.

Some Questions

When one considers such a broad issue as examining the future of undergraduate education in America and seeks to project a dream of "what might be," it soon becomes apparent that any analysis must come in answer to some insightful questions. While an attempt has been made to sketch some elements of a patterned response organized around curriculum, faculty, students and an institutional ethos, it is clear that any substantive movement toward realizing a dream will emerge from contemplative discussion and follow-up action.

The questions which follow are designed to stimulate discussion. They are not designed to be all inclusive nor do they represent in interrogatory form the statements made in the body of this article. They are, it is to be hoped, some questions that will cause all of us to examine "what might happen in the future so that we can make better choices about what we want to make happen." Here then are the questions.

1. Are we in higher education so deeply committed to the professional specialities that we have lost sight of the other purposes of

undergraduate education that pertain to the development of the individual and society?

2. How can a cohesive interdisciplinary experience be provided as a necessary ingredient in an undergraduate education?

3. Is there a *hubris* that exists in American higher education that is destructive to its role in society?

4. To what extent should students be responsible for their own educational development?

5. How can we help students to evaluate their own progress?

6. Do our programs reflect the realities of learning in the so called "information age"?

7. Do our "publics" understand what we are about?

8. Have we really accomplished an evaluation of ourselves as professors?

9. Have we made changes as a result of an evaluation?

10. What knowledge do we need to participate effectively as citizens in a democratic society?

11. What should distinguish a baccalaureate degree holder?

12. What should be the relationship or balance between liberal education and technical education in professional majors?

13. What should faculty know about principles of learning, stages of intellectual development and learning styles?

14. How may faculty be rewarded for excellence in undergraduate education?

15. Should the baccalaureate be extended beyond 4 years? Should students enter college earlier? Is the senior year of high school a waste?

16. Does the curriculum square with the institution's expectations for students?

17. Have we solved our problems of articulation with the secondary schools?

18. What should be the philosophy concerning remedial courses?

19. Does the institution exemplify in its demonstrated behavior and responses the ideals it espouses—freedom, justice, equality, integrity, respect?

20. Does the total institutional environment reflect a striving for excellence that extends beyond mere competence? Does the environment reflect an attitude that is conducive to the growth of knowledge, an appreciation of culture, etc.?

A Proposal

In the organization of this article I have attempted to present four areas of the dreaming process related to the future of undergraduate education (curriculum, faculty, students and the institutional ethos). In addition, some 20 questions have been posed to sharpen a basis for discussion. Now in conclusion I would like to present a proposal. A proposal which if it were to become reality would embrace the four areas presented in the narrative section of this paper and could incorporate in its development at least some of the answers to certain of the questions delineated.

First a statement of background is in order. Most institutions either are accredited or are contemplating seeking an accredited status from one of the regional accrediting agencies. Many programs within institutions have been subjected to careful scrutiny by national professional accrediting groups. The vitality of an institution or a program is in part discernible by the outcome of an accrediting visit. If any institution or program achieves a certain minimum level of quality as judged by an institutional report and the visiting team, a seal of approval is awarded. At best, while the visiting team in its analysis may pronounce the institution (or program) to be fit and even include some accolades in its report, it is still affirming that it (the institution) has met only minimum standards. It is, in effect, merely competent.

If we desire to live and function beyond mere competency, we must do something else. In the words of Lewis Carroll in "Through the Looking Glass," "This is a strange sort of country," said the Queen. "Here it takes all the running you can do just to stay in the same place. If you want to get anywhere you must run at least twice as fast as that."

As a part of the process of running on a fast track, I would propose that an institution (program) should have an opportunity to petition its accrediting agency to allow it (the institution) to "show cause," or to demonstrate that it seeks recognition that its people and its programs function at a level beyond minimum standards of quality. I would anticipate that the burden of proof be placed on the institution and that the criteria for the evaluation be the sole responsibility of the institution.

The evaluation would be a judgment of the relevance of the criteria and the extent to which they were met! The successful completion of an evaluation which demonstrates that an institution or program exceeds the level of competency required for accreditation could be made known throughout the whole national academic community and to all interested publics.

The experience to develop criteria and then to establish a program that exceeded minimum accrediting standards would be professionally exhilarating. More important it could extend the value of the accrediting process itself and could result in a higher level of achievement for all institutions so recognized. In conclusion, I would hasten to add, before you brand me as too impractical, that not all efforts to move beyond competency require cash, but they do require commitment!

I have today attempted to posit a dream, or perhaps a collection of dreams. Some, as I first indicated, might contain unexpected flights of fancy, unconnected sequences, and I hope occasionally some interesting, if not potentially, valuable insights.

I would be pleased if there would be a portion of the article that could be classified as "not so wild a dream." Only you can judge.

References

Association of American Colleges. (1985, February 13). Integrity in the college curriculum: Text of the report of the project on redefining the meaning and purpose of the baccalaureate degree. *The Chronicle of Higher Education*, pp. 12–16, 18–22, 24, 26–30.

Astin, A. W. and others. (1980). *The American freshmen: National norms for Fall 1979*. Los Angeles: Cooperative Institutional Research Program, Laboratory for Research in Higher Education. Graduate School of Education, University of California.

Daniel, L. (1985, September 1). Futurists see more jobs, less work. *Chicago Tribune*, p. 17.

Hodgkinson, H. L. (1985). The changing face of tomorrow's student. *Change*, *17* (3), 38–39.

Levine, A. (1980). *When dreams and heroes died: A portrait of today's college student*. San Francisco: Jossey-Bass Publishers.

Meyers, W. (1984). *The image makers*. New York: The New York Times Book Co., Inc.

National Institute of Education. (1984). *Involvement in learning: Realizing the potential of American higher education*. (Publication No. 065–000–00213–2). Washington, D.C.: U.S. Government Printing Office.

Seldes, G. (Ed.). (1985). *The great thoughts*. New York: Ballantine Books.

Tomorrow. (1985, August 26). *U.S. News and World Report*, pp. 13–14.

Winn, M. (1985). The plug-in generation. *Change*, *17* (3), 14–20.

Index

A

ACT (American College Testing)
assessment test, 309–310,323,
332, 336, 337
Problem with, 337
ACT assessment retest
Criticism by ACT, 336–337
ACT COMP (College Outcomes
Measurement Program), 218,
333, 335
Activities, cocurricular
And ACT, 191–192
And AT&T Managerial Perform-
ance Study, 188–189, 192
Definition of, 185
And Iowa Student Development
Study, 189–91
Value of, 187–887
Activities, developmental
"Adopt a grandparent" program,
195
"Big pal/little pal" program, 195
College of Student Development
Self-Assessment Inventory,
197
Community service programs,
193, 195
Comprehensive programs, 193,
199
Credit courses, 194–195
Mentor programs, 193, 195–196
Student Development Mentor-
ing/Transcript Project, 195–196

Student Development Task
Inventory, 197
Student employment, supervision
of, 194, 198–199
Survey generated data based
programming, 193, 197–198
Transcripts, 194, 196–197
Workshops and retreats, 194
Adult Basic Education (ABE), 247
Advising, academic, 170, 218, 223
Contracts, 235
Definition of, 227, 231–232
Dissatisfaction with, 232–233
Evaluation of, 238
History of, 228–231
Mandatory, 233
Perceptions of, 228–229
And retention, 230, 233, 238
Satisfaction with, 233
Training for, 229–230, 237
Advising, academic, centralized,
223, 229, 234, 237
Advising, academic, comprehensive
Development of, 236–238
Recommendations for, 236
Advising, academic, computer
assisted, 235, 238
Advising, academic, faculty, 234,
238
Advising, academic, group, 234,
238

Advising, academic, peer, 234–35, 237–238
Advising, academic, self, 235, 237, 238
Aesthetic education
American, history of, 34–35
Definition of, 31
Mission of, 36–40, 43–44
"Age of Anxiety", 107
Albertus, Alvin D., 170, 241–255
Anxiety
As a state, 108
Study of, 108
As a trait, 108
Architectural and Transportation Barriers Compliance Board (ATBCB), 313
Artists, professional
Preparation of, 44
Arts, in undergraduate education
Importance of, 34
Integration into curriculum, 40–42
Mission of, 36
Association for Computing Machinery, 339
Association of College Unions - International, 187, 200
Athletics
Definition of, 124

B
Baby boom generation, 387
Baccalaureate degrees
Impact of, 63–64
"Back-to-basics" movement, 5, 80, 88, 89
Bacon, Roger, 24
Behavior modification, 261
Bodega Marine Laboratory, 177
Boredom
Purpose of, 269–270
Bowling Green State University, 349

Brainstorming, 139
Brief Symptom Inventory (BSI), 294–295, 297, 298, 301–302
Browne, Dauna B., 258. 279–287
Bryde, John F., 170, 203–214
Buzz session, 139

C
C–4R System
Resourcefulness, 273, 275–276
Respect, 273, 273–274, 276
Responsibility, 273, 274–275, 276
Responsiveness, 273, 276
Campus centeredness, 192, 218, 222–223
Canisius College, Buffalo, New York, 204
Carlson, Loren M., 169, 171–184
Carnegie-Mellon University, Pittsburgh, 204
Christensen, Orla J., 170, 241–255
Civic responsibility
In curriculum, 23, 26, 70
And students, 70
Cognitive Behavior Modification, 111
College and University Environment Scales (CUES), 175
College Schedule of Recent Experience (CSRE), 294, 297, 298, 299–301
Comenius, John Amos, 17–18
Community, college, 169, 171–172
External dimensions of, 176–178
History of, 172–173
Internal dimensions of, 175
Successful examples of, 176–178
Community, learning, 174, 175, 183, 388
Community, national, 173
Community, world, 173
Computer science core curriculum, 339–340

Congruence analysis
And formative evaluation, 355–356
Contingency analysis
And formative evaluation, 355
Cook, Cleland V., 78, 107–120
Cooperative Extension Service, 172
Cooperative Institutional Research Program (CIRP), 310
Core curriculum, 9
Return of, 89
Counseling
Developmental approach to, 250–251
Courses, correspondence, 180
Courses, electronic, 181, 182
Courses, extension, 181
Courses, Native American related, 280
Crank, Joe N., 134, 155–167
Credit/no credit option, 325
Criterion reference grading (CRG), 328
Criterion referenced test, 325
Critical thinking, 101–102
Applications, 86
Component parts of, 83–86
In curriculum, 79, 80–81
Decline in, 80, 88
Definition of, 80
Development of, 196
In historical writing, 86–87
History develops, 82
Impediments to teaching, 87–88
Teachers of, 81
Crouse, Gale K., 13, 47–60
Curriculum, ix, 2, 77–78, 380, 381–383, 389, 391
Arts in, 40–42
Civic responsibility in, 22–23, 26, 70
Critical thinking in, 79–80, 81
Foreign languages in, 48
Geography in, 49
History in, 79
Research in, 383
Service in, 72–73
Types of, 8–9, 20, 26
Writing skills in, 383, 387
CWAMA (count, weight and measure addicts), 272–273

D
Day, John A., 13, 31–45
DeBoe's Inventory of Social Support (DISS), 295, 297, 301
Demonstration, 139
Discussion Method, 133, 145–46
Donohue, William R., 170, 215–226, 319, 331–344

E
Edison, Thomas, 143
Educational Amendment Act of 1972. See Title IX
Educational Testing Service, 325, 340
Edwards, William C., 169, 185–201
Eicher, Charles E., 133, 143–153
Emans, Robert L., ix–x, 1–11, 13–14, 77–78, 133–134, 169–170, 257–258, 319–320, 361–362
England, Joan T., 14, 61–67
Evans, Wayne H., 258, 279–287
Exam, final comprehensive, 382
Exam, junior year, 382
Exchange programs, international
Faculty, 56, 370
Students, 57, 71–72, 370–371
Exit testing, 326, 338–341, 373

F
Faculty, 380, 390
And collective bargaining, 368
As mentors, 387

As role models, 388
As scholars, 383–384
As teachers, 383–384
Faculty development, 375–376,
    383–385
    Administrative involvement in,
        352–353
Faculty development statements
    And due process concerns, 351–
        352
Faculty evaluation, 319–320
    By administrators, 348, 358
    Characteristics of, 346–350
    Of instruction, 348
    Letters of recommendation, 350
    By peers, 346, 348, 353–354, 357
    Purposes of, 345
    Of research and service, 349–350
    By self, 384
    By students, 348, 357, 384
First-Letter Mnemonic strategy,
    159
Foreign languages, 371–372
    In curriculum, 48
Formative evaluation, 352, 354,
    356–357
    Definition of, 345
Freud, Sigmund, 107
Front loading, 170
    Definition of, 215
    Risks of, 225
Future Problem-Solving Program,
    81

G
Gandhi, Mahatma, 273
Gardner, William E., x, 361, 363–
    377
Geography
    In curriculum, 49
    Ignorance of, 48
German University, 4
GNP (Gross National Product), 369

Grade inflation, 322, 325, 326–327,
    328
    Definition of, 325
Grades vs. learning, 323
Grading
    Dissatisfaction with, 322–323,
        327
Grading scale, thirteen-point, 328
GRE (Graduate Record Examina-
    tion), 326, 333
GRE Subject Test, 339–340, 341,
    342
Gullickson, Arlen R., 320, 345–359

H
Hadley, Marilyn, 319, 321–330
Handicapped students, 258
    Architectural barriers to, 313–315
    Attitudes toward, 311–312
    Increased enrollment of, 307
    Model programs for, 315–316
    Policy barriers to, 308–311
    Social barriers to, 311–313
Harvard University, 203, 223
Higher education. See also Under-
    graduate education
    Economic contexts of, 363, 365–
        367
    Environment, x, 62, 136, 141–
        142, 169–170, 206–207
    And union buildings, 186–187,
        192–193
    Environment, cocurricular
    Evolution of, 186–187
    Evaluation, x, 136, 140
    Historical perspective, 4–5
    Increased enrollments in, 367–
        368
    And information age, 368–369
    And K–12, 374–375
    Loss of confidence in, 2–3
    Problems with, 3, 369–371
    Social contexts of, 363–365

And technology, 372–374
  Value of, 367
Higher education, off-campus, 178–179
  Types of, 180–181
  University of South Dakota model, 180–181
Historical writing
  Critical thinking in, 86–87
Historiography, 82
History
  And critical thinking, 79, 81–82
  In curriculum, 79–80
  Definition of, 82
  As patriotic device, 87
Hoadley, Michael R., 133, 135–142
Hood College, Frederick, Maryland, 204
Huber, Joseph D., 257, 259–268

I

Idea diagrams, 160
"Information age", 368–369
Institutional ethos, 361–362, 388–389
  Definition of, 388
Institutions
  Evaluation of, 391–392
  And the future, 388–389
International education
  In curriculum, 50, 52–53, 54–55
  Definition of, 50
  Model program for, 54–57
  Need for, 50–51, 370–371
  Policies for, 53–54
Inventory of Stressors in Undergraduate Education (ISUE), 294, 297, 298, 299–300, 301

J

Jefferson, Thomas, 4
"Justice as Fairness" theory, 127

K

Keller Plan, *See* Personalized System of Instruction

L

Lagomarcino, Virgil S., x, 361, 379–392
Lawrence Berkley Laboratories, 177
Learning, affective, 62–63
Learning, cognitive, 62
Learning, independent, 373–374
Learning, practical, 63
Learning deficient students
  Acquisition of information by, 157–159
  Expression of information by, 160–161
  Learning strategies for, 156–157
  Storage of information by, 159–160
  Teaching strategies for, 161–166
  And writing, 162–163
Lecture, 139
  History of, 143
  Improvement of, 150–152
  For learning deficient students, 162
  Reasons for survival, 147–148
Lecture, effective
  Characteristics of, 148–150
Licensing exams, 326
Longwood College, Virginia, 199

M

Main, Frank O., 257, 269–277
Math anxiety
  Affects on performance, 109
  Gender differences in, 108–109
  And non-traditional students, 110
  Origin of term, 108
  Reduction of, 110–112

Math-anxious students
Need for identification, 112
Math Without Fear Program, 111
Mathematics
Remediation in, 112, 117–118
Mathematics Anxiety Rating Scale (MARS), 111
Mathematics Placement Examination, 111
Mathematics Skills Intervention, 111
MBO (Management by objectives)
And formative evaluation, 355
"Me generation", 70, 386
Methodologies, 23–25, 26–27, 138
Instructional strategies within, 139, 146–147
Instructional techniques in, 139–140
In teaching science, 99–103
Michigan State University, 222
Milburn, Corinne M., 170, 203–214
Milne, Bruce G., 13, 15–29
Minnesota Repertory Theater, 177
Mission, ix, 13–14, 28, 34, 166
Mock, Mary S., 78, 121–131
Monroe, Don, 170, 227–239
Monroe, H. Virginia, 133, 143–153
Morrill (Land Grant) Act, 4, 172
Morton Arboretum, 177
Motivation
Definition of, 259–260
Methods of, 265–266
Student survey of, 266–267
Motivation, external, 257, 261
And acceptance, 261, 264
And environment, 262
And faculty expectations, 261, 262–263
And rewards, 261, 265
And social relationships, 261, 263–264
Motivation, internal, 257, 260
Multipass strategy, 158

N
National History Day, 81–82
National Science Fair, 81
National Teacher's Examination (NTE), 333, 339
Native American students, 258
Attrition of, 279–280
Concerns of, 280
Cultural clarification, plan for, 284–286
Cultural conflicts of, 283–284, 286
Cultural identity of, 281–282, 286
Learning style of, 281
And professional writing, 286
Role models for, 280
A New University for a New Century, 171
Nontraditional students, 234, 241, 258, 260
Attitudes of traditional students toward, 292
Attitudes toward, 248–249
Characteristics of, 290–291, 295–296
Comparison with traditional students, 298–302
Counseling needs of, 248–249
Definition of, 241
Description of, 221
Increased enrollment of, 244–245
Life transitions of, 246–247, 249
And math anxiety, 110
Needs of, 289
Social support for, 296–297
Special educational programs for, 247
Stressors of, 291–293, 296–297
Support services for, 297
Norm-based tests, 338, 340
Definition of, 338
Norm reference grading (NRG), 328
Normative evaluation, 354–355

O

Oberlander, Lois B., 258, 289–305
Oleson, Quentin, 14, 61–67
Olympics of the Mind Program, 81
Orientation
  Extended, 218, 223
  Freshmen, 203–204, 207, 211
  Importance of, 206–208
  Parents, 204, 211
Otto, Paul B., 77, 91–105

P

The paired associates strategy, 159
Paraphrasing strategy, 158
Pass/fail option, 325
Personalized System of Instruction
    (PSI), 133, 144–145, 151
Plato, 381
Poling, E. Gordon, 257, 269–277
Potter, Donald R., 258, 307–318
President's Commission on Excel-
    lence in Education, 370
Public Law 92–318. *See* Title IX
Pythagoras, 380

R

Rational-Emotive Therapy, 111
Reading
  For learning deficient students,
    164–165
Reed College, Portland, Oregon,
    207
Regional Education Program, 315
Rehabilitation Act of 1973, *See*
    Section 504
Remedial programs, 218
Roche, Michael P., 14, 69–76
Role-playing, 139
Rutgers University, 172

S

St. Mary's Junior College, Minne-
    apolis, Minnesota, 315

SAT (Scholastic Aptitude Test),
    322, 323
Science
  Social implications of, 93–94
Science, in undergraduate educa-
    tion
  Crisis in, 93
  Departmentalization of, 95–96,
    98
  Integration of, 98–99
  Purpose of, 95–96
  Relevance of, 102
  Value of, 92–93
Section 504 (of the Rehabilitation
    Act of 1973), 221, 308, 311,
    313, 316
Self-actualization, 135
Self-Questioning strategy, 158
Seneca the Younger, 381
Sherman Mathematics Anxiety
    Scale, 112
Slippery Rock University, 199
Social Readjustment Rating Scale,
    207
Socrates, 380
Sophists, 380
Southern Illinois University at
    Carbondale, 315
Sport
  Aesthetics in, 121, 124–126, 130
  Common good in, 121, 127–129
  Competition vs. play in, 127–129
  Equal opportunity in, 121, 124
  Fair play in, 122
  Moral conduct in, 121, 123–124,
    128–129
Sport, values of, 128
  Definitions of, 122
Struckman-Johnson, David L., 319,
    331–344
Student achievement, evaluation of,
    319
  Entry level, 323–324
  Formative level, 324–325

History of, 322
Summative level, 326
Student Information Form (SIF), 310
Students, x, 257–258, 380, 390, 391
  And civic responsibility, 69
  Description of, 385–386
  Enculturation of, 16
  Evaluation of, 116
  And the future, 387–388
  And Greek organizations, 206
  Motivation of, 259–260
  And need for service, 70–71
  Off-campus, 179
  Privileged few, 17–19
  Roles of, 137–138
  As "self-directed learners", 136
  Sub-cultures of, 242, 244
  "Total person" concept, 141
  Typical, 179, 289
Students, adjustment problems of, 203–208
  Environment, 206–207
  Excessive freedom, 205
  Loneliness, 203, 205, 210, 230
  Roommates, 203, 204
  Survey recommendations, 209–211
  Time management, 208
Students, attrition of
  Factors in, 230
Students, freshmen
  Description of, 218–221
  Orientation of, 203–204, 207, 211
Students, retention of, 217–218, 224, 230
Summative evaluation, 326, 352, 354, 356–357
  Definition of, 345
Sumner, Jack A., 169, 171–184
Syracuse Mathematics Scales, 111

T
Taxonomy
  Use in critical thinking, 83, 89

Teachers
  As advisors, 212
  Desirable characteristics of, 19–20, 26
  As mentors, 74–75, 136
  As role models, 118, 136
  Roles of, 136
Teachers, of critical thinking, 81
Teachers, of mathematics
  Preparation of, 113–116, 118
Teachers, of the arts
  Preparation of, 43–44
Teaching
  Purpose of, 135–136
Temple University Project, 171
Tests, standardized, 328
Textbook strategy, 157–158
Thinking
  Formal operational level of, 101–102
Thinking, convergent
  Definition of, 380
Thinking, divergent
  Definition of, 380
Time management, 160–161, 208, 243
Title IX, 121, 124
"Top down" approach
  And South Dakota, 332
Traditional students, 241, 258
  Characteristics of, 295–296
  Counseling needs of, 243–244
  Declining enrollment of, 244–245
  Definition of, 241
  Life transitions of, 246–247
  Social support for, 296–297
  Stressors of, 296–297
  Support services for, 297
Tweed Museum of Art, 177

U
Undergraduate education. *See also*
  Higher education

Challenges to, 8, 9–10
Contribution to democracy, 2
Definition of, 5–6
Erosion of, 21–22
Evaluation of, 319–320
History of, 380–381
Mission of, ix, 13–14, 28, 34, 166
    Means to accomplish, ix, 133–
    134
Outcomes of, 7
Purposes of, 5–7, 15–16, 25–26,
    27, 28, 62–63, 61, 91–92
Relevance in, 20–21
University of Arizona's Centennial
    Hall, 177
University of California's Scripps
    Institute, 177
University of Colorado, Boulder,
    204
University of Kansas Institute for
    Research in Learning Disabili-
    ties, 157
University of Massachusetts,
    Amherst, 195
University of Massachusetts,
    Boston, 178
University of Minnesota, Duluth,
    177
University of South Carolina, 223
University of South Dakota, 180–
    181, 222, 293
University of Virginia, 4
University of Wisconsin, 177
University Services Questionnaire
    (USQ), 295, 301

V
Value added, 319, 326
    Concerns, 334–335, 342–343

Definition of, 332–333
Evaluation of, 333
Goals of, 332–333
Measurement of, 335–342
And Northeast Missouri State
    University (NEMSU), 331,
    332, 334, 338, 340, 342, 343
Vanderbilt University, Nashville,
    204
Vik, Philip A., 133, 135–142
Visual aids interpretation strategy,
    159
Visual imagery strategy, 159
Vitale, Patrick, 319, 321–330

W
Ward, Stephen R., 77, 79–89
Washington University, St. Louis,
    204
Webster, Loraine, 257, 259–268
Wiedow, Gale, 170, 227–239
Wood, Robert W., 13, 47–60
Woodley, John W., 134, 155–167
Work
    Meaning of, 64–65
Writing
    For learning deficient students,
    162–163
Writing, professional
    For Native American students,
    286

Y
Yutrzenka, Barbara A., 258, 289–
    305